YOUR STARS ARE NUMBERED

YOUR STARS ARE NUMBERED

Your Birthday Secrets Revealed
Through Astronumerology

LLOYD COPE

ELEMENT
Boston, Massachusetts • Shaftesbury, Dorset
Melbourne, Victoria

© Element Books, Inc. 1999

Text © Lloyd Cope 1999

Published in the USA in 1999 by
Element Books, Inc.
160 North Washington Street,
Boston, Massachusetts 02114

Published in Great Britain in 1999 by
Element Books Limited
Shaftesbury, Dorset SP7 8BP

Published in Australia in 1999 by
Element Books Limited for
Penguin Books Australia Limited
487 Maroondah Highway, Ringwood, Victoria 3134

First published in 1971

Library of Congress Cataloging-in-Publication data available

British Library Cataloguing in Publication data available

Book design by Jill Winitzer
Printed and bound in the United States by Edwards Brothers

ISBN 1-86204-363-9

CONTENTS

DEDICATION

A life-changing experience that magically opens doors to unfamiliar knowledge and wisdom is to be treasured. I was extremely fortunate, when I first began to seriously explore and then to study occult subjects in the late 1950s, to encounter astrologer Hugh MacCraig, astrologer Isabel Hickey, palmist Diana Elliot and psychic Reverend Glen Argoe, all of whom were extraordinarily gifted in their respective fields of expertise. I regularly consulted these four outstanding professionals, as well as many others less frequently, and I have attended hundreds of lectures during the past forty years. In my opinion, these four, as well as Florence and Grant Lewi, are members of a select group who stand head and shoulders above their contemporaries as master occultists. To all of them, this book is respectfully dedicated.

ACKNOWLEDGMENTS

I would like to express my special gratitude to Julia Wagner and Kris Brandt Riske. I am deeply grateful to Julia, former Editor-in-chief of *Horoscope Magazine*, for her superlative skills in helping me to revise, update, expand and edit the text of this new edition. A treasured friend, her warmth, generosity, support and expertise have contributed greatly to my writing endeavors. I am equally indebted to Kris, Publications Manager of the American Federation of Astrologers, for her outstanding work in preparing the original edition of this book for this new edition. Without her extraordinary skills, unstinting effort and support as a friend and colleague, the work on this new edition would have been a much more laborious, time-consuming task.

Additionally, this project has benefited immeasurably by the encouragement, contributions, and many years of friendship with Dr. George Speck and

Karen Cini, both very generous with their help and occult expertise. I consider myself indeed fortunate, as an author, to have profited from the steadfast efforts and enthusiasm of all these aforementioned friends in preparing this book for press.

Last but not least, I must thank Patricia Collins, my agent, and Roberta Scimone, Vice President/Editorial Director, Element Books, Inc., for their faith in this project, suggestions, persistence and infinite patience on behalf of getting this book published.

INTRODUCTION

One night, rather late, a number of years ago, Lloyd Cope received an unexpected phone call.

"Hello."

"Hello. Is this Lloyd Cope, the astrologer?"

"Yes, this is Lloyd Cope. Who did you think it would be?"

"Great! I got the right one! I found your name in the Yellow Pages under 'Astrology.'"

"Oh, you did? Well, I'm thinking of taking it out."

"You are? Why on earth would you want to do that?"

"To protect myself from phone calls like this, when I'm trying to get some sleep. Do you realize it's four minutes 'til midnight?"

"No. Is it really? I hadn't noticed. Listen, I've been teaching myself astrology, and I'm very good at it. I don't really need any help, but . . ."

"Then why did you wake me up at this ungodly hour, if I'm not being too inquisitive?"

"Well, actually, you see, I do need a *little* help. Not much. It's about progressions. I'm not sure I'm doing my math right on progressions."

"I see. Look, why don't you phone me at a reasonable hour tomorrow morning, say about 11:15 or 11:20, and we'll set up a convenient time for a series of lessons."

"I just told you. I don't need any lessons. Just a small bit of help with progressions, and . . ."

"All right, all right, whatever you say. A lot of help. A little help. This is not the hour to play with semantics, Miss . . ."

"Mrs. It's Mrs. I'm married. To a Taurus."

"Yes, well, that figures."

"It does? Why?"

"Patience. Taurus is very patient. Now, see here, Mrs. . . . Mrs. . . ."

"Goodman. Linda Goodman."

"Yes, well, Mrs. Goodman, like I said, why don't you call me in the morning?"

"Yes, Mr. Cope, and I'm terribly sorry I disturbed you."

"That's quite all right."

CLICK   CLICK

Two receivers banged into the cradle.

He thought, "Pushy, aggressive female. Who does she think she is?"

I thought, "Cranky, picky man. Who could learn anything from him?"

Final result: I did. I learned a lot.

So will you, when you read this fine book he's just written.

At my suggestion, of course. (Yes, Lloyd, you remember I told you to write a book showing people how astrology and numerology work together, and . . . O.K., I'll be quiet.)

Lloyd Cope's Sun sign is Virgo. Mine is Aries. Which means we sometimes— well, gently disagree. Like cats and dogs. Or Virgins and Rams. Our Sun signs are quincunx. But Lloyd has a Gemini Ascendant, trined by my Moon, and my Mars is conjunct his Moon in Gemini. These links mean that we have a strong mental empathy—a *simpático*, as it were, springing from a dozen or so lives together back in Atlantis or Ireland or Afghanistan—or wherever. Somewhere in this contradictory confusion of our natal planetary positions, we've found grounds for a solid friendship. It balances rather nicely. I push him when he's being all stuffy and stodgy and irritatingly critical—and he stops me when I'm being typically impulsive, rash and headstrong. So far, it's worked out beautifully.

Down through the centuries, there have been a fair number of competent, intuitive, ethical astrologers. Not as many as we've needed, but a fair number. Unfortunately, however, very few astrologers have been—or are— also experienced writers. Consequently, the textbooks—or any kind of books written about the ancient art and science of astrology—although full of wisdom and truth, don't have much zip or zap. Most of them put you to sleep by the end of the first page—and only Edgar Cayce could learn anything while sound asleep.

When astrologers themselves get together, there's usually a unanimous agreement that the best astrologer-writer our metaphysical science has ever produced was Grant Lewi, who was a professional writer for years before he became an astrologer. He was a Gemini. EXAMPLE: In his book *Heaven Knows What*, under the aspect Uranus conjunction Neptune, he writes: "This hasn't occurred since 1819, and will not occur again till 1993. Skip it!" Who else but a Gemini would write that? His books are still best-sellers.

I believe that Lloyd Cope is—or will be—an Aquarian Age Grant Lewi. (We can use all we can get.) He is also a professional writer turned astrologer, and he has Lewi's powerful combination of technical astrological knowledge—colorful expression—quick, clever wit—and razor-sharp observations. Like Lewi, he "tells it like it is." But with all his knack for satirical phrasing and witty invective, which you'll find liberally scattered among the sound astrological truths in this book, Lloyd Cope still manages to convey what one might call "compassionate understanding." There you have it—the bright intelligence of Gemini (his Ascendant)—tempered by the gentleness and desire—no, the *need* to help others—of Virgo (his Sun sign).

I've read this book in the galley proofs. It made me laugh a lot—think a lot—and learn a lot. You'll have the same reactions, whether you're a layman or a professional. It's an important book to read. I truly consider it as helpful to people wanting to know more about the Universal Law of Planetary Influence (and therefore more about themselves and their fellow men) as—well, as "Sun Signs." Could an Aries admit more?

Lloyd was deeply happy and proud when my first book was published. I feel the same way about this first book of his. I'm sure Grant Lewi, in whatever incarnation he dwells at present, would be proud of it too. I'm very sure of that.

The Aquarian Age has a new communicator, and what's more important—a critical, searching, honest and entertaining one. I wish Lloyd Cope a thousand rainbows—and at least a dozen more books as good as this one.

Linda Goodman

AUTHOR'S NOTE

If you were born on the beginning or end date of any Sun-Sign period, you must have your individual horoscope cast for the month, day, year, time and place of birth in order to ascertain which Sun-Sign is yours. This is because the Sun doesn't enter a sign on the exact same date every year. For instance, if you were born on August 23 of any year, your Sun-Sign could be Virgo, but unless you have your horoscope cast, you can't be certain. For example, if you were born before 7:00 P.M. on August 23, 1935, in New York, the Sun would not have entered the sign Virgo. The Sun didn't enter the sign of Virgo in 1935 until the early hours of August 24, Greenwich Mean Time. If you were born on August 23 a year later, however, at approximately 12:20 A.M. Greenwich Mean Time, your Sun-Sign is Virgo. When you hear the phrase "you were born on the cusp," it means that you have a birthdate at the beginning or end of a Sun-Sign period.

Furthermore, if you were born on April 20 in a year that the Sun has moved into Taurus, read the description for May 20 instead. The appropriate interpretation for your Sun-Sign and number will be found by reading that description even though it isn't your actual birthday.

The primary vibratory power of a number (or numbers) combined with your Sun-Sign is revealed (except for master numbers 11 and 22) by the root digit of your birthday. If you were born on the 5th of any month, for example, that description is all that you have to read for your birthday interpretation; if you were born on the 16th of any month, however, you should read the description for 7 (1 + 6 = 7) first and then the "special" supplementary information for the 16th.

If a description in a "special" section contradicts information in the "root" digit (root number) analysis, the "special" interpretation applies more specifically to you. The master numbers, 11 and 22 (birthdays), are not reduced and are interpreted separately at the end of each chapter.

The system of numerology in this book is historically authentic and stems from the Greek mathematician Pythagoras (582 B.C.). In forty years of experience, I have found it to be extraordinarily accurate. According to peerless numerologist Florence Campbell, the connection between letters of the alphabet and numbers was first discovered by Arabic scholars, and it was in Arabia that "final digitting" was brought to the Hebrews by Moses and to the Greeks by Pythagoras. The exceptions are the master numbers 11 and 22, which are extremely important. They are included in this book, but they are frequently reduced to root digits 2 and 4 and are simply omitted as master numbers in numerological systems found in other astronumerology books.

A word of caution: Don't be misled by hyperbole or the infallibility of this or that system. The best test is your own experience; only then can you discover which system works best for you. Just as there are different religions, all with their own tenets, so are there different alphabet number correlations. Despite claims to the contrary, no one has a direct pipeline to God. A Hebrew, living in a country where the Hebrew Number-Kabbala is used, should be charted by that alphabet; a Greek by his own. In the West, the correct alphabet-number correlation table is the one in the Preface (Stars and Numbers) of this book.

As an example of the remarkable accuracy of the Pythagorean number system, Western alphabet correlations, and the power of 22, consider this 1995 headline from the *New York Times*: "AN ODD AIRCRAFT'S TENACITY SHOWS DIFFICULTY OF CUTTING ARMS BUDGET." The article opened with this sentence: "For years the Defense Department has denounced the V-22 Osprey, an aircraft that takes off like a helicopter but flies like a plane, as impractical and unaffordable." Note the word "ODD" in the headline. Is it just a coincidence that this odd, hybrid contraption is named the V-22 Osprey? That the number 22 correlates to the letter "V" (the 22nd letter) of the alphabet? That 22 correlates to Uranus, the planet of oddity, genius, invention and eccentricity? Or that V and 22 combined designate a strange aircraft? Or that Uranus rules Aquarius, the sign of air travel, aerospace technology, innovative breakthroughs and so forth?

Your Sun-Sign description at the beginning of each chapter tells you about yourself from the standpoint of your season of birth. If you're familiar with the popular Sun-Sign descriptions of yourself, you probably get all puffed up when you note that if a Scorpio, you are irresistibly magnetic and sexy; if an Aries, a natural born leader; if a Gemini, the embodiment of wit, versatility and glittering intelligence. Cancerians are great cooks, wonderful parents and remarkably understanding, while Librans ooze charm twenty-four hours a day.

The foregoing traits are all traditional and certainly within the realm of possibility, but no one is perfect, as any Virgo will be happy to tell you. The Sun-Sign descriptions at the beginning of Chapters 1 through 12 delve beneath the patina of admirable qualities we never tire of hearing about ourselves and provide a more rounded picture. Do try to be objective—and keep your sense of humor.

STARS AND NUMBERS

(Astronumerology)

ASTROLOGY

What do you want most out of life? Most of you would no doubt answer, "To be happy," or words to that effect that imply deliverance from life's aggravations and frustrations. By investigating a little further, you'll find that "happiness" has a different connotation for different people—more specifically, for people born under different signs of the zodiac. The Pisces-born, for instance, will likely give you a dreamy, faraway look and an imprecise answer, such as precious things like ideals cannot be expressed quickly by a few cold words. The Capricorn-born, on the other hand, will give you a well-organized response—an admixture of aims and purposes along with some sardonic comments about people and conditions that must be endured in climbing the ladder of success. Capricorns, you see, don't object to cold words—be they few or many—because they feel most secure when contemplating or responding to the realities of life's challenges. To them, warm realities are about as numerous as the whooping crane.

These examples of Sun-Sign types are just doing what comes naturally; they are responding in a manner typical and predictable for anyone born at their time of the year, or yours, whatever it happens to be. Your outlook on life, and your reactions to its necessities, will relate to your "season" of birth.

Geniuses, exceptional business executives, Hall of Fame candidates, criminals and other variants of humanity are more apt to be born at particular times of the year. According to statistical research, a disproportionate number of the greatest artists are born under the Sun-Signs Cancer and Pisces. Pisces is by far the predominant Sun-Sign of great names in music. Since Taurus rules the throat, it will come as no surprise to learn that many of the legendary singers are born under that Sun-Sign. Lawyers love to talk, so again, it's no great surprise that more of them are born under Gemini (communication) than any other sign.

A similar idea, the theory of "synchronicity" by Dr. Carl Jung, offers a companion hypothesis: "A thing born of a moment has all the qualities of that moment." Astrology is, in essence, the study of time spans and their qualities, from "moments" all the way to "epochs." For our present purposes, however, we can confine ourselves to the twelve Sun-Sign types that are, symbolically, the twelve successive stages of soul experience. This is also a good place to make clear the difference between the *signs of the zodiac* and the *Sun-Signs*. There are *no bad traits in the zodiacal signs*, the twelve stages and states of perfection attainable by humankind. When the Sun is in a particular sign, however, human shortcomings enter the picture and can distort the values of the sign. Thus, Virgo is not fault-finding, but unevolved Virgo *Sun-Sign* individuals can be very critical—a distortion of Virgo's analytical skill and quest for perfection when warped ego needs (the Sun) subvert the distinctive attributes of Virgo. Similarly, Aries is not pushy, but Aries individuals can be very pushy.

NUMEROLOGY

Numerology is concerned with the vibrations of numbers and, along with astrology, is a viable interpretation of universal laws as they apply to your makeup and life plan. Numerology—or numbers (number mysticism, of which Plato, 427–347 B.C., a follower of Pythagoras, was a prime exponent)—is the shorthand of the cosmic plan. Numerological wisdom, known to have been highly developed in ancient Egypt prior to 1250 B.C.; is exceptionally accurate, insightful and helpful when integrated with astrological factors. The combination of these two ancient systems is termed *astronumerology*.

When you combine a knowledge of astrological principles with those of numerology, you gain an obvious advantage: The differences between the Sun-Sign types are further refined into distinctions between the destinies of people born on particular dates in the sign. A Pisces born on March 5 can have a life quite different from that of one born on March 17, although both still exemplify the basic traits unique to the sign of the Fishes.

Astrology combined with numerology can tell us when we are scheduled to meet particular types of experience (oftentimes crucial or pivotal in the development of our destiny) and what our characteristic reaction will be. The worst jolt most of us ever experience is when we are forced to fall back on our own resources and face the "moment of truth," when you find out exactly what your assets are. It is usually triggered by the arrival of the planet Saturn—the celestial paymaster—at some sensitive place in your horoscope or by a 4 or 9 year in our personal number pattern. Thankfully, few of us are so unfortunate as to begin figuring things out at a time when there is virtually nothing left to add. The reverse is true when the good luck planet, Jupiter, arrives at a propitious place in our horoscope and when our personal year number is 1, 3, 5, 6 (especially) or 8.

Capricorn will meet good fortune differently than Cancer or Sagittarius. Similarly, Aries will handle a crisis differently than a Gemini or Pisces. The valuable foreknowledge thus provided by these time-tested techniques can guide us to using the most constructive employment of our abilities and help us to ameliorate the consequences of our faults or to cushion the effect of a difficult event.

Just as astrology is based on the wisdom of the zodiac, numerology derives from the power inherent in the vibrations of numbers. Number values have the same origins as astrology; historically, the origins of number theory are lost in those of numerology. The alphabet, to which the numbers correlate, came from ancient Phoenicia. In Babylon of antiquity, a number was a different thing from a figure, or the digit of today. Just as in ancient times— and, above all, in Egypt—names had magic powers, the numbers were symbols, possessing an active force, and their properties were sacred attributes. Numerology actually antedates astrology, since the movements of the planets could not be calculated without mathematics.

Numbers themselves are believed to have been invented or thought out by man primarily as concepts of quantities. The most elementary quality about an object is whether it be one or many. Numbers are a prime factor in bringing order into the chaos of appearances. In life, the numbers 1 to 4 occur with the greatest frequency and have the widest incidence. In certain areas of numerological interpretation, the same numbers appear with greater frequency in the patterns. The majority of people are learning the same lessons by being commonly exposed to the same experiences. In any case, numbers may well be the most primitive element of order in the human mind.

In the occult sciences, we subordinate the personal ego, in the primitive sense, and accept the intelligence that any one of us is only a part of the universe and not the center. "Occult," incidentally, is just another way of saying "invisible." During an eclipse of the Moon, it is said to be "occulted."

This means that its light is temporarily extinguished and all that the Moon customarily illuminates is temporarily made invisible. Everything is still there, even though we can't actually see things the same. Unfortunately, the word "occult" suffuses astrology and numerology with an unnecessary aura of mystery. Actually, there is nothing mysterious about the working of either doctrine. The planets, signs, aspects, numbers and so on simply function as *measuring determinants* of effects compiled from centuries of observation and experience.

The words *month, man* and *measure* apparently go back to a root denoting the Moon. Men measured time by the Moon (and still do in Asia) long before they counted it by years. Man, the measurer, is himself the measure of all things. Just as at any given time we are individually the product of previous choices, man is the sum of the values he has stressed in the collective evolutionary process.

ASTRONUMEROLOGY

Astrology is based on the correlation between celestial phenomena and terrestrial events. Numerology is less complex, but no less profound, and is the shorthand of the cosmic plan—the base without which astrology could not exist. Its origins are more beclouded than those of astrology and are as old as recorded history. The ancient Egyptians, Greeks, Hebrews, Chinese and Hindus made reference to number meanings, extending back to more than 11,000 years ago. More recently, there are many references to astrology in the Dead Sea Scrolls discovered in 1947 in Cave Four in Kirbet Qumram, Jordan. These historic documents date from around A.D. 70 and denote that during that period in history, astrology flourished along with Judaism and early Christianity—news that today's religious fundamentalists don't want you to know.

The truths of universal laws symbolized by astronumerology are immune to passing whims; they do not recognize good or evil. They simply deal with qualities of matter and states of consciousness. For this reason, astrology and numerology are especially useful because they haven't anything to do with the outer trappings of an era. People are happy, confused, successful, generous, braggarts, hurt, selfish, insecure or wise, and it doesn't matter whether you are applying the principles to Julius Caesar, a corporate CEO, a coal miner, a lawyer or a computer programmer.

The essential principles of astrology and numerology are the same in any era. The specifics may be different, but Mars in square (adverse) aspect to Jupiter in a horoscope means the same to an Iowa farmer, a Maine fisherman or a New York policeman as it meant to a Roman soldier of antiquity on the brink of a campaign: an unfavorable risk-reward ratio. To the farmer, it may mean the loss of a crop; to the Roman soldier, the loss of life.

The study of astrology and numerology is an investment in understanding the liaison between what life is and what the possibilities are. Stars and numbers do not indicate fame or obscurity, but they do reveal the possibilities. They deal with the inner order, the structuring of the individual's unconscious potentialities pitted against the larger framework of collective experience. The interwoven patterns of harmony and conflict reveal the trend of the psychological bias of the individual toward his environment. People tend to expect things of life, which is a poor assimilation of the facts. Try that at your local bank, without first having put something into it. Life works on the same principle. Talents are loaned to us and must be paid for. That's why concert violinists must practice thousands of hours to master their instrument. That's their contribution while their inborn flair for music is a cosmic gift. If talents aren't honed and refined, they deteriorate or just coast along on the superficialities.

We live on two planes: the inner and the outer. The inner plane, or consciousness, is the person in the body. Your physical body is the delicately tuned mechanism through which your individual consciousness contacts outer experience. All physical matter is the bridge, or means of communication, between your mind and soul and your unfolding destiny. Considered esoterically, the world outside you is the plane (or cross) of matter and is under the dominion of Saturn, planet of discipline and karma. Your ability to guide and control your inner person determines the effect you make on the outer world, beginning with your actual body, the first limitation your consciousness must deal with. Astrology and numerology reveal to us the potential of this cosmic plan; we are provided the key to our strengths and weaknesses. The inner world is the most important; controlling it has enabled man to master his environment enough technologically to take him to the Moon.

One important thing that we learn from the stars and numbers is that we can't rely on appearances. The mask that people present to the outer world may conceal a far different nature than one would deduce from physical evidence. The attractive physical appearance of individuals who commit heinous crimes is ample evidence of that.

We often find the natives of the various signs overdoing their otherwise commendable traits. *Freedom* for Aquarians doesn't mean that they are *free* to do whatever they want to do, whenever they want to do it, regardless of others' rights or the laws of the land. Radically misguided Aquarians would achieve more by *freeing* themselves from the bondage of their own bad habits. (All of us, even Aquarians, have a few.) Will Scorpios allow their wonderful gifts to be subverted into serving the dark side of the consciousness? The acid of resentment boiling over into revenge burns deep within their souls. Will clever Geminis try to get by in life solely on badinage and humor? And so it goes. The natives of each and every Sun-Sign should be alert to and, if necessary, tone down the negative vulnerabilities of that sign's basic principle. Nor should we ever envy the other signs. Aries bravado can mask an interior beset with frustrations; Scorpio sexual prowess can mask emotional poverty; and Sagittarius luck can finally run out and lead the hapless Archer to a homeless shelter.

Individuals live out their star and number pattern whether they are aware of it or not. There are Leo Sun-Sign Kansas farmers, for instance, as well as sophisticated Leo Sun-Sign New Yorkers, so obviously there are tillers of the soil and city dwellers with an ego challenge. Texans are born under Capricorn—as are New Englanders, where austerity and caution would seem to be more at home—but then there's all that entrepreneurial spirit and money in Texas. What you have is more cautious Texans and even more conservative New Englanders. Regional exterior traits might add insights to the interpretation, but they never alter the basic meanings.

In art, it has been said that to state a problem well is to solve it. The same may be profitably applied to the art of living. To find out through astrology and numerology the strengths and weaknesses in our makeup is a significant step toward solving life's problems. Remember, every difficulty is a potential step on the path of personal evolution; character and fate will meet somewhere in the future at the inevitable crossroads. Each day that we live we plant something to be cultivated, or reaped, or answered for in the future. So whether your life is going to be relatively smooth or difficult will depend to a lesser or greater extent on your actions and reactions.

We may be pursuing glamour when our pattern is for service. We may seek the trivial when we should be serious. We may be too iron-willed and oppressive when a lighter approach would actually smooth the way toward serious goals. There is no virtue or reward in pursuing misguided aims or in tolerating boredom, resentment or inaction in our affairs, which are mostly a reflection of inner misconceptions that bring unhappiness.

Did you choose your vocation, or did it just happen out of economic necessity? Have you avoided the sterility of living life by accepting objectives set by others? Is the banker's son expected to be a banker? Astrology and numerology can tell you when you don't have enough ego or have too much, if you are too pushy or not enough, if you are too talkative or too quiet. They may tell you when you will have to smile, even though you may not feel like it.

We are never in a situation longer than it takes to learn the lesson; until then, we are bound by purposeful limitation. Like an unseen hand, a force directs, impels, uses and tests us as a vehicle. Cosmic intelligence is that force. It always expects the best that is within us, which is sometimes buried beneath layers of confusion, ignorance, anxiety or fear. The various flaws in our individual characters leave us vulnerable to the irrevocable cyclic challenges of the divine plan. Nothing is designed to deliberately hurt us unless we interpret it as such. The intention is to show us the damage that can accrue from the erroneous use of energies. Cosmic intelligence is impartial. It is on both sides of closed doors. Whether it be the halls of state, the office, the home or the heart, it is ready to illuminate in times of need. Sometimes the way is difficult, but the rewards can be beautiful. We need never succumb to pressures when the inner braces are strong.

Of course, insisting on following a path that is not in accord with the cosmic plan is an exercise in futility, as many disappointed travelers on the road of life have learned. It usually ends in a breakdown of the nervous system—the result of the body having become the end-terminal for the discord troubling to the psyche. Awareness of these unseen truths helps us to tune in to eternal values. They enable us to develop a refined and more useful sense of what is appropriate and allow ordinary things to assume the right proportions. How often do we fly into a rage over something trivial, all the while blithely ignoring the larger issues in our lives? If we are willing to be observant, life is always telling us things about ourselves, sometimes things that we may or may not want to know.

Some individuals are endowed with God-given talents but lack the faith, stability, stamina, application or forbearance to develop them. Whatever is lacked must be learned if we are to realize our growth potential. We can even learn from failure. We are always two people: the person we are now and the person we can become. Charles F. Kettering, the inventor of the self-starter and other epoch-making devices for cars, once remarked that he had failed time and time again but that he had always "failed forward." He knew that true seekers can expect failures along the way but that from each one knowledge could be gained and that each failure brings us nearer to success.

Socrates said, "The unexamined life is the wasted life." Those who have the inclination and gift for objective self-analysis are lucky. The study of occult symbolism is an aid in finding the *still, small voice within* that is the real you. It can help you to obtain what you want. Much more important, it will reveal to you why you want it in the first place and, if your reason is legitimate, the motivation behind the cause, as it were. Henry David Thoreau observed that most of us "lead lives of quiet desperation." We might observe that some (or much) of it is self-induced and remediable. Perhaps after you discover some unexpected things about your hidden nature and latent possibilities, your desires will change and life will take on new meanings.

Are you happy with your job? Are you trying to be a furniture salesperson when you would be more content as a librarian? Or in the space program? Are you running an art gallery because the glamour associated with it appealed to you, when you could really find more fulfillment as a paralegal? Are you trying to lead the life of a driven, single business executive when the real you is better suited to marriage and children? (Or are you capable of combining the two?) Or are you an airline flight attendant when your innermost talent lies in the direction of a career in advertising?

Such extremes do exist. I am sure that you know people who have made miserable choices and in desperation invariably blame their unhappiness on ill-chosen professions or vocations. People rarely place responsibility where it really belongs—squarely on themselves. It is common to confuse bad management with "destiny." It is more convenient to project our problems outside, thus absolving ourselves of the responsibility for making adjustments where they really matter: within ourselves. With this submissive approach, all we need do is find the strength to adjust to what we mislabel as *misfortune*, or *the breaks*.

The psychology of stars and numbers is one of the most self-determinative of any of the disciplines illuminating human behavior, and certainly one of the oldest. Even heredity isn't as important a factor as some schools of psychology would have us believe. Brothers and sisters can have few traits in common. Yet, we meet people of totally different parentage and diverse upbringing who are almost identical in characteristics. We have black sheep from illustrious families and great men rising from the ranks of obscurity and poverty who are not explained by environment or heredity. The study of astrology combined with numerology can provide the answers to many such intriguing speculations for those with open minds willing to investigate. In the field of criminology, for instance, where convicted criminals and successful businessmen are shown to have common characteristics, such as excessive individualism (which is easily revealed by astrology and numerology), the possibilities are obvious.

Buried in the subconscious, deep inside all of us, are the answers to life. The soul knows everything, but the channels are blocked by the trappings and pressures of day-to-day living. In Goethe's words: "Everything has been thought of before, but the difficulty is in thinking of it again." *Educate* does not mean "to put in"; it means "to draw out." We are frequently at the mercy of ego pressures, but the occult wisdom of astrology and numerology can help penetrate the veil of appearances to discover both the real motives and antipathies behind important choices. For most of us, the values we adhere to derive from a lifetime's exposure to the veneer of conformist living.

In today's rapidly changing world, people in their mid-forties or fifties can suddenly be adrift and are advised to make radical changes into a new field or direction in life. Many are skeptical or apprehensive, to say the least. To ease doubts and resistance to change and growth, I always point out that Grandma Moses, the American Primitive artist, didn't begin to paint until she was seventy-five years old. Most individuals assume that life, especially in the career realm, is pretty much over by then. The unfortunate truth is that many people are spiritually and creatively atrophied after age forty or fifty, even though the physical body may go on living for many years.

Our initial motivations and attitudes are conditioned by our heredity and early environment, but our destiny is not sealed by them. If we find our lot incompatible, all we need do is break the mold. Many people with strong instincts and a zest for action do just that, prodded by what is known as the "midlife crisis," a standard astrological turning point around age forty to forty-four. Others find it more difficult and need the rationale of faith in other possibilities before doing anything drastic or disruptive with their lives. When you read the chapters on the descriptions of the zodiacal signs, combined with the meanings of the birthdate numbers, you will find out which birth types are apt to take decisive action and which are likely to become hesitant or apprehensive when confronted by frustrations and the necessity to make critical choices and/or changes.

Universal laws are the basis of cosmic wisdom. Combining astrology with numerology, astronumerology is a modern technique for decoding profound insights. It enables us to tap into the ancient secrets of human nature; it then reveals to us how they interrelate and are applicable to mankind in any era and to the evolutionary spiral.

All we need do is listen. Existence itself is the ultimate mystery, the great "Why?" The core of existence is energy in its diverse forms, expressed as experience—used, misused or abused—as it unfolds in space and time. The choice is always ours, to capitalize on or to squander our cosmic birthright. Within each pattern are abundant possibilities for variation. However, you will find that each sign and number has certain basic, recognizable characteristics that are unique and applicable to no other symbol or function in experience.

NAMES AND NUMBERS

(The Power of Your Name)

By this time, you're likely wondering what does all this specifically mean to you? It means that the basic potentials and probabilities of your life are hidden in your combined astrological Sun-Sign and the number or numbers in your birthdate, a technique known as astronumerology. Numbers are everywhere in our lives, and they have meaning at every level of activity and experience. *Nomen est omen*, the Romans used to say: In name is destiny. From the numbers hidden in your name (through the alphabetical equivalents) to the number on your front door, you are under the influence of numerology whether you are aware of it or not. Public examples of celebrities who have won fame and fortune with adopted names are well known, but all of us know, too, of people who have also had "luckier" experiences at one address than at another.

The meaning of numbers follows a logical progression: Once they are assimilated they can be applied to any situation from your whole life plan to the implications of a particular cycle, year, month or day. Number values can also be applied to your name. Each letter in the alphabet has a numerical equivalent, with the result that the individual vibration of your name attracts particular conditions into your life. Perhaps you have the name of a poet, but you are aiming for success in the business world. The name vibration may be too "soft" or reticent for the hurly-burly of commerce, so, obviously, such a name isn't going to make the way any easier.

Often your name is the first awareness that others have of you, your invisible *calling card* in the subconscious of other people. Commentators frequently allude to the subtle attraction that names like Placido Domingo or

Luciano Pavarotti have for the public. It can only help to further a career if people take delight in merely saying the name of a celebrity. Of course, the sound of the name should suggest the idiomatic cultural flavor of the career, and the number should relate to the basic principle. Toscanini sounds artistic, and its letters add up to the spirited and restless 5. Coupled with Arturo, which adds up to the expressive 3, the sum of the name Arturo Toscanini is 8. The broadly authoritative and financially successful career of the legendary conductor fulfilled the *powerful* requirements of the number 8.

Even television and movie critics have made comments in their columns concerning the liability of certain performers' names. They are cited as drawbacks to the career fulfillment of performers who are worthier of success than others who achieve it with less talent but better names. Sound unfair? There is a larger plan to things than what meets the eye in everyday affairs.

Suppose you are visiting friends, and during the course of the evening they announce that Diana Hathaway is dropping by. You will have a different subliminal impression of what to expect than if your hosts say that Sophie Glutz is due to arrive. We aren't aware of the merits of either hypothetical lady, but the psychic reaction to the vibrations of the sound of one name is distinctly different from that of the other. We may learn later that Diana Hathaway is a paroled ax-murderess and that Sophie Glutz is an angel of sterling traits, beloved by all. One thing she'll never be, however, is a glamorous Hollywood star. That's why you know Doris Kappelhoff as Doris Day, Archie Leach as Cary Grant, Frances Gumm as Judy Garland, Ruby Stevens as Barbara Stanwyck and so on. In his book *The Rise and Fall of the Third Reich*, William L. Shirer comments on the significance of Hitler's name change. "Heil Schicklgruber!" is an unwieldy mouthful, in addition to sounding comic—a deadly liability in politics.

So that you may analyze the final number value of your own name, the following diagram will give you the number value of each letter:

1	2	3	4	5	6	7	8	9
A	B	C	D	E	F	G	H	I
J	(K)	L	M	N	O	P	Q	R
S	T	U	(V)	W	X	Y	Z	

The letters in parentheses, K, the 11th letter, and V, the 22nd letter, have the master number value of the 11 and the 22, respectively, and are not reduced. Here's how it works with the name of Abraham Lincoln.

```
A   B   R   A   H   A   M      L   I   N   C   O   L   N
1   2   9   1   8   1   4      3   9   5   3   6   3   5
```

added together = 26   added together = 34

26 reduces to 8   34 reduces to 7

$$8 \quad + \quad 7 \quad = \quad 15$$

15 reduces to 6

The final expression number for the name Abraham Lincoln is 6. Actually, more is involved in a complete numerological analysis of a name, but that is beyond the scope of this book.

However, if you have a nickname, such as Freddy, Shorty, Liz, Pat, or whatever, by which you have been commonly known or addressed most of your life, its expression number may have more impact on the outcome of your life than your birth certificate name. In a similar context, the nom de plume Mark Twain changed the course of destiny, particularly from the standpoint of fame, for Samuel Langhorne Clemens. Adding the middle initial S. to Harry Truman provided the extra power of the number 1 vibration for Harry Truman who, as Harry S. Truman, became 33rd president of the United States.

There is nothing complicated to do—just simple addition. An interpretation of each number's values follows so that you may incorporate the interpretations later in your investigations and findings.

The number 1: INDIVIDUALITY

Number 1 is first, so naturally it stands for an ambitious outlook on life, empowerment and achievement. It is not a good follower and should remember that leadership implies responsibility.

The essential meaning of the first digit is *individuality*. It denotes leadership, honor, dominance, self-assurance, strength, self-esteem, independence and singularity of purpose.

Positively, it signifies spirit, endurance, dignity, initiative, poise, determination, integrity, sustainment, authority, creative ideals, willpower, self-reliance, prestige and fame.

Misused, it indicates false pride, pomposity, egotism, won't-power, monomania, arrogance, conceit and self-satisfaction.

It correlates to the Sun in astrology and the Sun-Sign Leo.

It has an affinity with Leo, Aries and Sagittarius. It is an inner-motivated number.

The number 2: ADAPTABILITY

The essential meaning of the second digit is *adaptability*. Number 2 consists of two 1's, but it is not the simple addition and sum of two 1's. The second 1 symbolizes "the other" and the necessity to blend and conciliate. Number 2 is creative and very receptive to public and mass interests, with the ability to sense trends well in advance of the times. If 2 happens to find itself in a leadership role, its best strategy is to lead by indirection. The 2 denotes sensitivity, caution, absorption, instinct, caring, reaction, sympathy, fluctuation, emotion and fecundity.

Positively, it signifies cooperation, protection, impressions, adjustment, peace, tact, comfort, nurturing, domesticity and psychic potential.

Misused, it indicates touchiness, moodiness, apathy, crabbiness, petulance, withdrawal and pettiness.

It correlates to the Moon in astrology and the Sun-Sign Cancer.

It has an affinity with Taurus and Cancer. It is an outer-motivated number.

The number 3: EXPRESSION

Artistic abilities, beauty, joy, prosperity, pleasures, charm and love are attributes of 3. It is most productive when exemplifying the lighter and brighter side of life, tempered by common sense. The essential meaning of the third digit is harmonious *expression*. It denotes pleasure, luxury, gifts, articulateness, adornment and charm.

Positively, it signifies harmony, mediation, happiness, beauty, congeniality, creativity, romance, decorum, taste, affectional ties and refinement.

Misused, it indicates trivialities, dilettantism, vanity, extravagance, indecision, laziness and greed.

It correlates to the planet Venus in astrology and the Sun-Signs Taurus and Libra.

It has an affinity with Pisces and Capricorn and all the air signs. It is an inner-motivated number.

The number 4: RESPONSIBILITY

Number 4 is the taskmaster and builder; as such, it implies the need for dependability, patience and concentration. Opportunities will be the kind that require slow-but-sure methods for success, and they will probably lack variety. The essential meaning of the fourth digit is *responsibility*. It denotes practicality, depth, perseverance, duty, fundamentals, reliability, discipline, utter reality and rock-solid values.

Positively, it signifies tireless effort, application, details, economy, conscientious endeavor, credibility, serious goals, industry and well-deserved achievement.

Misused, it indicates narrowness, restriction, hardness, monotony, bitterness, dejection, deprivation, limitation and karmic debt.

It correlates to the planet Saturn in astrology and the Sun-Signs Capricorn and Aquarius (co-ruler).

It has an affinity with all the earth and air signs. It is an outer-motivated number.

The number 5: EXPERIENCE

The essential meaning of the fifth digit is *experience*. It denotes change, vitality, audacity, courage, adventure, enterprise, variety, action, flexibility and discord. Remember, 5 means finishing everything that is started so as not to leave a trail of loose ends as a result of impulsiveness or impatience. This number will attract success by a willingness to go wherever opportunity beckons. It is episodic, which is not the same as incomplete.

Positively, it signifies initiative, ingenuity, pioneering, progress, energy, courage and enterprise.

Misused, it indicates restlessness, irresponsibility, haste, scattering, hazards, belligerence, sensuality and thoughtlessness.

It correlates to the planet Mars in astrology and the Sun-Signs Aries and Scorpio (co-ruler).

It has an affinity for Aries, Leo, Sagittarius and Capricorn. It is an inner-motivated number.

The number 6: OPTIMISM

The number of luck and protection, the essential meaning of the sixth digit is *optimism*. It denotes responsibility, expansion, protection, environment, ethics, learning, exploration, congeniality, burdens, affirmation, interdependency and enthusiasm. Along with general good fortune, however, there may be strings attached—"Where much is given, much is expected." Number 6 should cultivate understanding of typical human foibles, acknowledge its own shortcomings and be an anchor of protection, faith and encouragement for the common good.

Positively, it signifies justice, hope, largesse, truth, wisdom, aspiration, integrity, philosophy, fruitfulness, optimism, love, fame, discovery, travel and family values.

Misused, it indicates scattering, gambling, hazards, carelessness, improvidence, extravagance, overexpansiveness, exaggeration, meddling, excess and self-righteousness.

It correlates to the planet Jupiter in astrology and the Sun-Sign Sagittarius.

It has an affinity for Cancer, Sagittarius, Aries and Leo. It is an outer-motivated number.

The number 7: THOUGHT

The essential meaning of the seventh digit is *thought*. It denotes perception, mind, information, intellect, efficiency, exactitude, communication, knowledge, introspection and silence. Very mental in nature, it may unintentionally project aloofness, but it nevertheless appreciates interest and affection. Articulate and communicative, the evolved and productive 7 knows the difference between *aloneness* and *loneliness* and that it is better to be alone than to wish you were. By developing his or her technical, analytical and theoretical gifts, the individual will achieve personal poise and serenity.

Positively, it signifies reason, intelligence, stoicism, research, wit, duty, solitude, concentration and exactitude.

Misused, it indicates verbosity, aloofness, gossip, swindlers, melancholy, nagging, suspicion, nervousness, malice, fussiness and depression.

It correlates to the planet Mercury in astrology and the Sun-Signs Gemini and Virgo.

It has an affinity for all the air and earth signs. It is an inner-motivated number.

The number 8: POWER

The essential meaning of the eighth digit is *power*. It denotes management skills, self-reliance, executive ability, thoroughness, vision, entrepreneurial spirit and practicality. This is a large order; whatever is done though 8 implies considerable influence or links with sources or enterprises that function on a large scale. Number 8 is the number of big business, mass distribution, applied science and far-flung organizations such as corporations in global markets. It is also identified with individual efforts that service big business in smaller capacities and that help keep the vast machinery humming efficiently and productively. Number 8 attracts good fortune by thinking big, but it should avoid going overboard and thinking *too big*, the penalty for which is winding up behind the *eight ball*.

Positively, it signifies promotion, recognition, material freedom, publicity, leadership, investments, administration, production and success.

Misused, it indicates improvidence, strain, impatience, waste, lack, failure, carelessness, excessive money-consciousness and loss.

It correlates to the planets Saturn and Uranus combined in astrology and the Sun-Signs Capricorn and Aquarius.

It has an affinity with Aquarius, Gemini, Virgo, Libra and Capricorn, but is unlimited in its possibilities. It is an outer-motivated number.

The number 9: UNIVERSALITY

Number 9—the final digit—contains all the numbers; appropriately, the essential meaning of the ninth digit is *universality*. It denotes service, penetrating insight, selflessness, completion, healing, intensity, metaphysics, transformation, power of suggestion, the collective unconscious and disclosures. As can readily be seen, the higher the number, the more complex its ramifications. Number 9 will profit most from an impersonal approach to experience. The world is its fireside. It should cultivate tolerance and a broad-based outlook.

Positively, it signifies artistic creativity, genius, attainment, elimination, intellect, government and regeneration.

Misused, it indicates ulterior motives, introversion, extremes, disorganization, personal loss, disruption, expulsion and upheaval.

It correlates to the planet Pluto in astrology and the Sun-Sign Scorpio.

It has an affinity with Scorpio, Pisces and Cancer but is unlimited in its possibilities. It is an inner-motivated number.

The number 11: ILLUMINATION

The essential meaning of 11 is *illumination*. It denotes fantasy, esoteric principles, mysticism, intangibles, illusion, elation, genius, sacrifice, subjectivity, obligation, psychic receptivity and the inner planes. Fragile, nebulous or evanescent forms of truth or beauty are associated with 11, such as music, poetry, film, photography, ESP and so on. If the life path or birthday number is 11, opportunities are less likely to be of the ordinary variety. Personal fulfillment is frequently attained by accepting sacrifices or being a source of spiritual encouragement, guidance or support for others.

Positively, it signifies revelation, creativity, imagination, specialization, sublime inspiration, empathy, compassion, ideals, the supernatural, reverence, hidden resources, occult insight, reincarnation and spiritual vision.

Misused, it indicates deception, disillusion, confusion, debauchery, escapism, duplicity, impracticality, delusion and uselessness.

It correlates to the planet Neptune in astrology, and the Sun-Sign Pisces.

It has an affinity with Pisces, Cancer, Scorpio and Leo but is unlimited in its possibilities. It is a dual inner-motivated number.

The number 22: MATERIAL MASTERY

The essential meaning of 22 is *material mastery*. It denotes intuition, detachment, abstractions, genius, distribution, power, independence, global enterprise, invention, unlimited possibilities and the future. Whereas 11 identifies with psychic channels, 22 identifies with intuition—two distinctly different cosmic sources of extraordinary information or knowledge. Intuition (22) is the instant distillation of diverse known (and perhaps previously unrelated) facts into a fresh original synthesis. It is a remarkable short-circuiting of ordinary mental processes, producing highly innovative results in a flash of inspiration that is elevated to a higher level of perception. Astonishing prophetic insights, often unsought, may also stem from a *blend* of psychic and intuitive promptings or stimuli.

Positively, 22 signifies altruism, originality, reformation, practical magnificence, progressiveness, innovation, utilitarian mission, broad vision, objectivity, occult wisdom and fame.

Misused, it indicates fanaticism, won't-power, perversity, tactlessness and rebellion.

It correlates to the planet Uranus in astrology and the Sun-Sign Aquarius.

It has an affinity with Aquarius, Gemini, Capricorn, Scorpio, Virgo and Libra but is unlimited in its possibilities. It is an outer-motivated number.

There is a tendency to lump together the meanings of 11 and 22, as though their sources and effects were interchangeable. However, their meanings are distinctly different: 11 conveys information through psychic channels, while 22 conveys information through the neuromental system, as though it were a lightning rod. Number 11 is concerned with intangibles and psychic insights, whereas 22 is more concerned with intuition and the concrete manifestation of broad concepts.

The highest function of both, each in its own distinctive way, is to enhance life for humanity. For example, number 11 (and the planet Neptune) is the inspiration behind poetry, social service, healing, music, the dance and so forth. Number 22 (and the planet Uranus) is the cosmic force behind invention, groundbreaking design, vast distribution of computer technology, the Internet and the information superhighway, but it also shelters the many in housing projects.

In the cabalistic tradition, there are 22 letters in the Hebrew alphabet. The X-ray unit is an innovative product of 22 ingenuity and is utilized by 11, represented by doctors, nurses and institutions in ministering to the sick. Biotechnology, the medical wave of the future, is principally the product of the interrelated influence of numbers 9, 11 and 22, and the planets Pluto (9), Neptune (11) and Uranus (22).

DETERMINE YOUR DESTINY

The most important numerological indicators in your cosmic plan are your birthday number and your life-path number. Your life-path number is found by adding *all* the digits of your birthdate together: month, day, year. The sum is then reduced to one digit (except for master numbers 11 and 22), and that is your life-path number.

> For example, the birthdate of Richard M. Nixon is:
> January 9, 1913
> January is the 1 month; added together, the result is:
> 1 + 9 = 10, + 1913 = 1923

All numbers in numerology are reduced to a final digit except 11 and 22. Reducing 1923, you have: 1 + 9 = 10, + 2 = 12, + 3 = 15. The digits of 15 are reduced by adding them together, and the final number, the life-path number of Richard M. Nixon, is 6.

The 11 and 22 are master numbers and are not reduced, since they have a special meaning. The 22 is a cuspal number and applies to individuals whose birthdays occur around the time the Sun is moving from one sign to another. Everyone can't live up to the high frequencies of the master numbers; therefore, if you have them in your pattern, you may have to read the meaning of the root digit (2 for 11 or 4 for 22) to decide how you are responding.

The life-path number indicates the kinds of opportunities that will enable you to achieve fulfillment in your life; it is the cornerstone number of your cosmic plan. Your birthday is the thrust number. If you have lessons to learn in this incarnation, it's not always easy to get into the swing of your individual rhythm, especially if you have been operating counter to your cosmic plan for any length of time. We are all familiar with expressions such as "at sixes and sevens," "the seven-year itch" and "behind the eight ball" when conditions are exasperating.

Conversely, "seventh heaven" and "cloud nine" are expressions of joy and oneness with the universe.

If you have 11 or 22, or the outer planets prominent (or both), you have been put on earth to carry out special work. Just as the outer planets, Pluto, Neptune and Uranus, are the planets of the collective unconscious, so are the numbers that correlate with those planets: the 9, 11 and 22. Their energies are the inner qualities and outer potentialities of the New Age types, the avatars of the Aquarian Age. Fate deals with what we can and cannot change and the wisdom in knowing the difference. Astronumerology (stars and numbers combined) tell us the kinds of experiences we are destined to meet, when we are scheduled to meet them and what we will have to work with to see them through. Just as there is help or difficulty inherent in every planet, the same applies to each number: Whether we choose the positive or negative manifestation to work with is our choice. The ultimate value of any experience, over which we have reasonable control, is never fated. Furthermore, no experience is ever wasted, unless we fail to see the reason for it and neglect to profit from it.

There are few pure types. Some will seem only remotely like their Sun-Sign, yet over time they will exemplify the basic principles in their outlook, if not in their everyday traits. There is a valid reason for this. If you have the Sun in Aries, but six planets (out of ten) in your chart are in the water sign Pisces, you may seem like a bomb with a wet fuse when you're angry. Or Mars in your horoscope may be in a sign *not* conducive to audacity and assertiveness, typical Aries traits. The influence of milder energy principles can moderate the forceful initiative of Mars or Aries. You may have the Sun in Pisces and surprise people who may think you won't talk back. In that case, you might have six planets (out of ten) in Aries, giving the impression of a furious mouse when you're crossed. A woman with the Sun in Sagittarius, a sign not ordinarily domestic, might have a Cancer ascendant. That can alter the emphasis in her chart; she may do well with dishes and diapers, but she can still be the sporty, active, outgoing mother.

• • •

The usefulness of this book will be increased if you have your fully calculated natal, or birth, chart. The readings for the Sun-Signs can then be applied to the sign on your ascendant, your Moon sign, your ruling planet or a stellium (a group of three or more planets in one sign), as long as you differentiate between the emphases implied. For instance, if your Moon is in Capricorn, the reading for Capricorn will describe your involuntary emotional reaction to life, your subconscious response to life's practicalities without thinking about them too much or at all. If your ascendant is Capricorn, your public persona and your customary interaction with people will exemplify your awareness and respect for life's nitty-gritty necessities that establish credibility.

The Capricorn description will reveal your immediate impact on others and the pragmatic impression you make in day-to-day dealings. If your ascendant is Libra, you will gain similar insights by reading that description; remember, it may *not* be your Sun-Sign, but a different facet of yourself. (In some charts, the ascendant and the Sun-Sign are the same, strongly emphasizing the traits of the particular sign.)

Astrologers sometimes hear a client say, "Don't tell me about myself, just tell me when something good is going to happen." To realize our greatest potential is the challenge for each of us, and our stars and numbers are the blueprints of our possibilities. They describe our potential for both positive and negative realization and have the special advantage of telling us *when* developments are likely to occur. To know when an important juncture is imminent in our life plan, and additionally its essential character, allows us to prepare for it. We may then meet it with a maximum of readiness and a minimum of uncertainty or fear. The frequent cause of difficulty is not lack of ability but poor timing in the demonstration of it. As was mentioned earlier, astrology is essentially about time—and different kinds of time.

If we fail, somehow—in spite of our endeavors—we have a flaw to eradicate, a lesson to learn. We don't grow from our gifts or our successes; it's more typical to relax and coast along on them. Few of us like change. Growth is sometimes painful. It is necessary to let something die in order that something better may be born. Occult knowledge won't eliminate the pain, but it can illuminate the reason for it. Destiny is primarily the result of character: We can't completely divorce what is or what is going to be from what we are or are willing to become.

According to psychologist Carl Jung, who used astrology, the most important problems of life are fundamentally insoluble—they can never be completely solved, only outgrown. It is best to accept problems as part of the cosmic plan, or as "opportunities in work clothes," as industrialist Henry

Kaiser put it, and then develop further by means of them. Nothing is gained by avoiding or endlessly complaining about life's difficulties, and much may be lost.

To return to the theme in the opening paragraph of this Preface: Of course we want to be "happy," whatever that implies individually, but how many are aware that happiness is more typically a by-product of enlightened living and not an end in itself? It's been said that the phrase "the pursuit of happiness" is one mistake Thomas Jefferson made in composing the Declaration of Independence. (Leaving out any reference to slavery probably was another.) How many concentrate all their efforts on *having* and *getting*, instead of *being* and *becoming*? To seek personal growth and fulfillment is a more realistic and rewarding goal.

Orientals observe that Westerners, especially Americans, are not prepared for pain, that we think we have a right to avoid pain, whereas Orientals know that pain is a condition of life. Someone has said that we are "happy" when we honestly determine what we can hope to achieve and then *adjust* what we think we *require* to attain that objective. Such a process will not stifle ideals but will instead redirect poorly aimed goals and reveal the price we must pay for whatever it is we think we want. Once we learn the price, it's amazing the number of things we discover we can live without.

Since the beginnings of human history, tyrants, murderers and ne'er-do-wells have been born in every sign and on every day. While it may be interesting to point out that a Virgo murderer, for instance, would likely be fastidious in dispatching his victim, it would serve no useful purpose in this book to draw attention to negative extremes latent in human behavior. It is better to point out typical foibles, as well as attributes, that are peculiar to a certain Sun-Sign and number, and where or how they are most apt to surface.

For a truly comprehensive analysis of character traits, it is necessary to have a fully calculated horoscope. A difference of four minutes in birthtime, and whether you were born in Philadelphia, Berlin, Calcutta or wherever, can be very significant in your birthday destiny. Remember, *be sure* to read your *root digit* number if your birthday number is not a single digit (e.g., for August 17, read the description for August 8 *first* and *then* that for 17).

George Nelson has defined "living" as "a group performance of very uneven quality played out in time by several billion amateurs, none of whom ever saw a script or attended a rehearsal." This book, then, is a chance for you to peek at the script. The rehearsing is up to you. Or perhaps *revising* is a better word. Regardless, when you flow with your cosmic plan, you'll find that happiness through personal fulfillment is the result.

As you fulfill your destiny in life, remember these words by William Penn:

Look not to things that are seen,
but to that which is unseen; for
things that are seen pass away, but
that which is unseen is forever.

Lloyd Cope

CHAPTER 1

ARIES

March 21–April 20

RULER: **MARS** NUMBER: **5** ELEMENT: **FIRE** SYMBOL: **THE RAM**

"Grow great by your example, and put on the dauntless spirit of resolution."
—*King John,* Shakespeare

If you were born between March 21 and April 20, you will probably finish reading at least *this* chapter. Not noted for your long attention span as much as for your engaging personality and splendid abilities, you always perk up noticeably when the subject is *you*. It's even better if given situations are exciting, fast-moving or preferably both. Conversely, anything that doesn't pertain to you or your special world can evoke Olympian disinterest. Your eyes glaze over if minutely detailed analysis or protracted listening is an unanticipated requirement of whatever has gained your attention or involvement.

Arousing your interest isn't difficult. Your eagerness to experience something new is one of your many enviable attributes, one that the natives of more sluggish signs could afford to emulate. But your motivation has to be tremendous to see you through to the finish. In short, your ego necessities have to be fully satisfied in order for you to overcome your impatience with the requirements of the long haul.

Never happy in the chorus, you are aggressive and competitive with a lively compulsion to be *first* in one context or another. You attack all obstacles with equal gusto, whether it's your mother-in-law or some brilliant business or promotional venture—or both at once. You're not easily deterred. Like your Capricorn and Scorpio brothers and sisters, you need to be doubly sure of your motives. With your wonderful inborn advantage of that Aries direct, self-assured approach, you will probably get what you want. Or at least what you *thought* you wanted yesterday. Today you may want something else, since you can quickly tire of things. Familiarity breeds indifference; you thrive on change and seem to have endless amounts of energy and inspiration to initiate it.

By the same token, you can be profligate in your waste of vital forces by failing to harness energies and directing them toward completing long-range goals. By developing an overall picture of your life, you can tailor necessary changes into a logical progression toward success instead of just letting random events influence you in willy-nilly fashion. When you neglect fore-thought and careful planning and fail to consider important ramifications, you can precipitate messy dilemmas or downright disaster born of impulsive judgment and naive self-confidence. Your passion for freedom and indepen-dence has positive value pertinent only to the goal in view. It can rebound negatively and become merely freedom and independence from the stick-to-itiveness and responsibility that are the stepping-stones to ultimate fulfillment and happiness. Excessive self-centeredness leads to a prison house of regret. If you think about that—for a minute, anyway—you won't insist on total free-dom and will realize that involvement in, and forbearance with, life's less attractive realities is occasionally necessary and will prove to be rewarding.

In astrology, the mental planet Mercury is the esoteric ruler of Aries. When your magnificent Mars energies and enthusiasms are guided by intel-lectual control and reason, you frequently enter the special echelons of prominence and genius. And how you love it, especially the prominence. The long, brilliant career of legendary conductor Arturo Toscanini (March 25) was a shining example of how this works. The charismatic Italian maestro didn't totally overcome his famous Aries hair-trigger temper, and his propulsive spir-it resulted in some pretty brisk tempos, but the net result was an ennobling contribution of beauty and passion expressed through exciting music-making, to the enrichment and delight of millions of music lovers. His volcanic ener-gies were *mentally* focused and disciplined and given unique directional power.

Many figures of international renown from celebrities to government leaders are Aries-born or have a strong Mars influence in their horoscopes. And they need it. An adamant refusal to be vanquished and the requisite visceral force to overcome adversity propel many of your sign into prime posi-tions in life, which they usually maintain despite the vicissitudes they have to overcome. As you may have guessed by now, the fiery, aggressive planet Mars is your ruler. It is symbolized by the cross of matter exalted over the circle of spirit, which signifies spirit merging with limitation and manifesting as action and desire. Your vitality can be astonishing. You have the willpower to fend off bad health, but it can overtake you if you disregard sensible pacing, not to say sensible living, the outcome of which is physical self-abuse. You can liter-ally drive yourself into a sickbed, but you can also quickly recover. Keep your

Aries competitive spirit under control if you're a physical fitness enthusiast. Otherwise, you can feel that you have to constantly improve your performance, such as your time or distance in your running workouts.

With your raw energy, you can go fast and far and accomplish an enormous amount of work. However, all of it may not contribute to your progress in life. It may just add up to a series of erratic starts or episodes with the parts remaining more interesting than the whole. "Great starters but not necessarily finishers" has become a key phrase for the sign of the Ram. Of all the signs, you can profit most by working a meaningful design into the fabric of your existence.

You usually cram more experiences into one lifetime than other signs do in several, and you may do much of it alone since you may view a partnership as an encumbrance rather than as a strictly necessary element to your success. Who can keep up with you? Your pronounced singularity of purpose can blind you to the advantages of cooperation and compromise. For this reason, you aren't really happy in politics, where diplomatic maneuvering and guile are essential. You haven't the patience for that. You prefer main strength and force to get results, and this works for you in many endeavors. Typical executive functions can also be uncongenial because teamwork is an important governing factor for success in the corporate structure. You thrive best in professions or small, independent business ventures. If you are an employee, you don't take orders comfortably but function best when allowed considerable autonomy to do things *your* way. You will not receive kindly any pronounced interference with your methods or theories. Don't become involved in partnerships or group efforts unless all concerned empathize with your need for central consideration when important questions or issues arise.

If you are a typical Aries native, you are prone to a restless and disruptive development period before you can find yourself, and even then the unfoldment of your destiny is rarely smooth. But once you discover a compatible niche that continues to satisfy your ego requirements, even if the pattern is repetitive, you can remain consistently interested. If activities also include some opportunity for variation within structured parameters, so much the better.

Marriage to an Aries is a shared experience. Your lover is expected to share large chunks of you with the world at large, like it or not. You embrace the confinements of the marriage state with enthusiasm during the first blush of blissful fascination, but restlessness, temporarily quelled, is ever lurking. And then you're off again on a tangent, leaving your mate to wonder if he or she married a person or a roadrunner. "Alice sit by the fire" was definitely not an Aries.

Speaking of the Aries lady, don't ever let her feminine, oftentimes beautiful, and even fragile appearance fool you. The sweet little thing with the will of iron is probably an Aries. So, no doubt, was Scarlett O'Hara, the fabled heroine of *Gone With the Wind*. If not, Aries traits were otherwise prominent in her horoscope, such as her ascending sign. Her name was certainly appropriate. Scarlet, a very bright red, is the color associated with Mars and Aries. In the real world, it should come as no surprise that Gloria Steinem, an award-winning trailblazer of feminist publications and notable causes, is an Aries (March 25).

Since the Ram is never comfortable in subordinate positions, the female of this fiery species has the same basic characteristics as the male, and she can be pretty basic; only the body is different. In fact, because she may resent that her gender places her in a disadvantageous or vulnerable position at the starting gate, she could overcompensate and become disagreeably forceful, a rather unbecoming and unladylike trait.

An understanding partner can complement an Aries woman's life as she envisions it to be. He may even indulge her fiery whims with a resigned and bemused tolerance and will doubtless enjoy many exciting fringe benefits along the way. But he will need plenty of patience, probably in direct proportion to her lack of it. In any case, *her* work is cut out for her, and it doesn't include bossing her mate or anyone else within earshot, although the effort required to soft-pedal this trait may be wearying and seem like too much work, which the issue becomes in her mind.

An Aries woman's work *does* consist of moderating a thoughtless lack of consideration for others, which is more a sin of omission, since a self-absorbed or aroused Aries doesn't mince words or waste time with amenities, especially in times of stress. Since she is frequently the instigator, she is the very one who will profit most by cultivating diplomacy. She can make her mark on her world as she sees it and retain the love and admiration of those in her circle instead of arousing their resentful compliance.

It is doubtful that the typical distaff Aries can sufficiently sublimate her drives into producing success for her mate, unless his sign or sign accent is equally powerful—Scorpio or Aries—or at least a cardinal sign. Working behind the scenes is more common with Pisces or Cancer women. Aries is perhaps too self-oriented and eager for personal recognition.

As you may have surmised, life with an Aries, male or female, is a plunge into adventure. Yours is the first sign of the zodiac. That will impress you as being pretty important, and you like to hear important things about yourself. But the responsibilities are of equal magnitude, a fact that implies considerations that are foreign to your nature. If you are a more primitive Aries, you charge ahead without too much thought of the consequences. Therefore, whether your impact on life produces the deference, status and/or authority that you expect depends on other things.

For instance, if your answer is yes to the following questions, you are on your way to fulfilling the potentials of your sign: Are you a controlled Aries, with restless energies harnessed to a consistent pattern of self-expressive yet meaningful development? Do you maintain an overall goal in your mind's eye and eschew passing whims and happenings? Can you substitute a more self-determinative tune like *"I'll do it my way"* for *"Que sera, sera"* ("Whatever will be, will be")?

Can you control an urge to successively change jobs, or mates, or whatever with alacrity just because you are determined to do so? Do you know when you're just indulging your vulnerability to impatience and merely quelling your restlessness with expedient solutions? (Change and progress are not necessarily synonymous, although the Ram can confuse the two.) In scanning your past, can you find a series of starts with no underlying pattern of completion and strive to reverse it for the future? If you are headstrong and even belligerent, do you know why? If you can separate vital issues from trivialities, you can overcome these negative traits.

If some candid self-analysis reveals a personal inadequacy or two (and all of us mortals have a few), you are on the right track, which, however, may not be the fast track you'd prefer. If you must express belligerence, try turning it upon your inner self. Getting a little angry or impatient with the gaps in your own character is a major step toward effective self-realization. On the other hand, projecting irritation outside yourself and making others the scapegoats for your own insecurities and frustrations will only alienate and drive them from you.

Aries is a cardinal, thrusting, activity-motivated sign. But of what use is Aries constant activity or attempts at progress without insight into your primordial urges and uncertain staying power? The reference isn't to physical energy, for you will most likely have that in abundance until the day you die; the issue is staying power of the *spirit*. Aries only achieves anything worthwhile through endurance of the spirit, the power source that tells you to keep going with a worthwhile task when the going gets tough or the details seem overwhelming and intensify your impatience and boredom (your special nemeses).

Your ego basks in the warm glow of a leadership self-image. But assuming the mantle of leadership, of self-importance, isn't very convincing unless it's based on achievement in terms of the realities of the practical world. That is time-consuming even for a Toscanini. If impatience and boredom are your nemeses, there just isn't enough time to give shape to all the ideas your fertile imagination generates. Many of your brainstorms can be stillborn, but there's plenty of time to revitalize them if you manage them right.

Discipline yields commensurate return for efforts expended—words that aren't likely to turn you on. In fact, they can cool your fiery impulsiveness uncomfortably since your eager expectations are usually disproportionate to the time and effort you think accomplishments require or deserve. The typical rambunctious Aries is more apt to take off like an unguided missile and doesn't like discipline any more today than in ancient times when many astrological truths were first perceived. If you are to profit from your restless expenditure of energies, be sure that the element of growth through resolution is an integral part of your pattern of *busy*-ness.

Aries notables who molded their fiery temperaments in tandem with the nature of the times they lived in included French philosopher Rene Descartes (March 31); Spanish painter Francisco Goya (March 30); Russian composer Sergei Rachmaninoff (April 1); and Thomas Jefferson (April 13), author of the Declaration of Independence and third U.S. president. Their resolution of purpose achieved lasting recognition for them without sacrificing any of their Aries genius. They grew great, undeterred by obstacles or temptations to digress from the mainstream of their intentions to achieve their impressive goals.

The polarity of Aries is signified by Libra, ruled by the planet Venus, the symbol of attraction, balance, compatibility and teamwork. These are qualities and motivations most unlike yours that can help to smooth out your rather agitated approach to life. Your headlong rush into a skirmish of ceaseless action will profit by an admixture of the Libran principles of teamwork, equilibrium and diplomacy with your need to succeed on your own terms. But remember, you might not sit still long enough for unsought opportunities to find you and can thus miss some great chances to prove your worth. You're probably off somewhere, busily seeking new worlds to conquer. On the other hand, your inborn drive and stamina, when judiciously and productively directed, can put you out in front of competitors, enabling you to thrive on your fight-to-win spirit as you race ahead to success.

ARIES BIRTHDAYS

Judgment of whether or not a birthday is propitious can be considered from two points of view: complementary or challenging. From the standpoint of personal progress and fulfillment, your destiny may flow more comfortably if your birthday is, or reduces to, an *inner* root number such as 1, 3, 5, 7 or 9. For career drive and achievement, your progress may be enhanced if your birthday is, or reduces to, an *outer* root number such as 2, 4, 6, 8 or 22 (master number); the *outer* root numbers are less comfortable, more obstructive for you to contend with, but they are potentially very conducive to outstanding resourcefulness in order to integrate it with the meaning of Aries.

Remember, if your birthday is two digits (excepting master numbers 11 and 22), be sure to read the *root* digit or number first. For example, if your birthday is 29, read the 2 (2 + 9 = 11, 1 + 1 reduces to 2) birthday profile first and then read the special profile for 29. If your birthday is 14, read the 5 (1 + 4 = 5) birthday profile first and then read the special profile for 14, and so on. If a description in a "special" section contradicts information in the "root" digit (root number) analysis, the "special" interpretation applies more specifically to you.

The first planet in parentheses following your birthday number is *your Sun-Sign ruler;* the second planet (or Uranus/Saturn for number 8)is *your birthday number planetary equivalent.* Subsidiary planetary influences (if any) are bracketed.

Each birthday profile includes celebrities who share the same birthday.

YOUR BIRTHDAY PROFILE
April the 1st (Mars, Sun)
(and root digit for March 28, April 10 and 19):

You will find many opportunities to express the initiative so dear to your heart. Since standing on your own two feet is the principal requirement, the more preparation or skills you can bring to the task the better. The frustrations or limitations you may feel in your very active adolescence are nature's reminders to build something substantial into those early years. Your ascent up the ladder of success will depend on how much power is structured behind you when you arrive at the threshold of your most productive years.

You will have many chances to develop your own resourcefulness and individuality. You frequently see what's wrong with things in a flash, but, with your typical Aries impatience, you might have difficulty carrying out improvements if they turn out to be time-consuming. You can assume that your ideals, plans and concerns are of absorbing interest to all, which may not be the case. Conversely, the problems of others may be of little importance to you unless you become spiritually oriented; then you can become a powerful and constructive force in your regard for universal welfare. As a result, your sympathetic insights can shed light on others' perceptions of human frailty as well as the will to press on. In any case, you are a survivor.

Bold, original and independent, you have big dreams but tend to procrastinate. You will profit from asking yourself if you are being original to improve something or merely novel to get attention. In more mundane pursuits, you can be vigorously self-promotive. In any case, you're likely to be one of kind; at your best, perhaps in some creative realm, you will have a chance to leave your mark on the world. If marriage isn't a bed of roses, it might be because keeping up with you isn't easy.

Debbie Reynolds (actress), 1932

Lon Chaney (actor), 1883

Prince Otto von Bismarck (German statesman), 1815

Special to March 28 (Mars, Sun [Moon/Uranus/Saturn]):
Your straight-ahead ways are aimed at the big picture of success. Although you may have impressive credentials to flaunt, you're not the type to rest on your laurels. With your talent for leadership and sizable enterprises, you may wind up at the helm of some vast or prestigious organization, or you will simply manage your own affairs, large or small, with impressive efficiency. While you restlessly seek new worlds to conquer, it may play havoc with your personal life. You were probably born into an advantageous background or your talents were exhibited early, perhaps through family auspices. You have the ability to attract the right opportunities.

Very gifted artistically, you will need to overcome impatience and emotional instability in order to be creative and reasonably contented at the same time. Otherwise, trying to touch too many bases too quickly can drive away the fulfillment and affection you seek. Your unions may be unconventional but idealistic. Avoid jobs that can make you feel as though you're in a rut (which, in your view, is the same as a grave with both ends open). Your flair for knowing what the public wants and is willing to pay for, if properly directed, can easily gain you entry into the winner's circle and financial independence.

Reba McEntire (singer), 1955
Edmund Muskie (political figure), 1914
Paul Whiteman (bandleader), 1891

Special to April 10 (Mars, Sun):

You're not likely to be left at the starting gate, but whether you win or lose the race in your quest to reach the finish line ahead of the crowd depends a lot on your staying power and your stomach for details or slow-moving projects. You typically start out early in life to seek adventure and fortune, pausing along the way to digest a variety of interesting experiences that may or may not determine your eventual line of endeavor. In your haste to get ahead, however, your initial willingness to tackle any immediately appealing objective can propel you up a meaningless alley or two—or more, if you're really hell-bent for quick results, like wanting to reach the top yesterday!

To say that you're self-assured would be like calling the rain that fell on Mount Ararat a drizzle. It would take a lot to shake the strong belief you have in yourself, your point of view or estimable abilities. Having to take orders or wait in line for anything appeals to you about as much as a root canal session or watching the grass grow. You may be delayed, or even suffer a temporary setback, but your enterprising spirit, courage and physical energy propel you ever onward and upward to some worldly goal that marks you as a person to be reckoned with.

Steven Seagal (actor), 1951
John Madden (sportscaster), 1936
Joseph Pulitzer (publisher), 1847

Special to April 19 (Mars, Sun [Sun/Pluto]):

If you do not strive to expand all your abilities, limitations will become an annoyance. Miserable when restricted, you will need much endurance. You tend to run the gamut in your quest for power, scattering energies and emotions with equal gusto, garnering your share of disappointments in the process. More capable of consistent (if occasionally interrupted) effort than is typical of your sign, your life's saga can begin early, develop considerable momentum and end late. You will profit from cultivating balanced control of your adventurous proclivities, at the same time eschewing any tendency to be controlling in relationships.

Your ambitions are on autopilot; anything that advances your interests is on your green light list. When you are inspired by a larger vision, you can take the lead in establishing new standards of excellence that bring you the recognition you deserve for your abilities. You have a knack for knowing the right people and being well rewarded for your talents and services. And nothing will activate your adrenaline as much as the prospect of coming out ahead of the competition in any given situation, including an amorous conquest. You may be too impatient for the standard educational process and conclude that hours spent in classrooms just delay your urge to get going with your worldly ambitions.

Al Unser, Jr. (race car driver), 1962
Dudley Moore (actor), 1935
Jayne Mansfield (actress), 1933

April the 2nd (Mars, Moon)
(and root digit for March 29 and April 20;
April 11 is a master number, see end of chapter):

Your sensitivity is centered around the lack of easy response to the expression of your ego. You have a remarkable flair for tuning in to changing trends and for influencing or cashing in on public taste. Your usually pleasant disposition, sometimes enlivened by an appealing twinkle in your eye or a knowing glance when you deliver a witty or ironic comment, can be a bit misleading for the unwary listener who may be oblivious to the real purpose for your congeniality—the furthering of your ambitions. Your creative efforts can be something more crucial to society than wine-tasting. However, despite your laudable efforts and expectations, people, situations and enterprises may not flow the way you have in mind.

After some burdensome experiences in your growing-up period, you are likely to find that you must cooperate in all situations and let others be heard in order to get anywhere. Resorting to exasperation or moodiness when you're stymied won't gain you one extra inch. Your birthday number requires an approach that is least characteristic of your basic Aries nature. This can either be challenging or annoying to your ego; either way, it can prod you to overcome frustrations that impede your impressive success potential.

While you usually want to get on with things, the necessity for broad considerations and tactfulness can slow you down. Although you enjoy sentimental expressions of affection, you may forget that others also need inspiration. Not as singularly forceful or ambitious as the typical Aries, you frequently find it advantageous to combine forces with others or will find an emotional appeal an effective ingredient in giving persuasive expression to your creativity and originality. Just because others usually see you on the go, your need for a haven to think, plan and recharge your restless energies may not always be apparent; you are more in tune with a settled environment and family warmth than people might assume you to be.

Emmylou Harris (singer), 1947

Alec Guinness (actor), 1914

Hans Christian Andersen (writer), 1805

Special to March 29 (Mars, Moon [Pluto]):

You have an instinct for the secrets of nature and know how to capitalize on your muted, even folksy, but compelling charisma to arrive at some position of prominence or independence. Overcome any tendency to scatter your energies or to waver in the face of obstacles. When you start something that you determined beforehand was a sensible idea, you should vow to finish it. You have a knack for getting rid of the deadwood in your life, which clears the decks for new ventures.

With your keen sense of which way the wind is blowing and how soon it could turn into a gale, you have the edge on most competitors. It helps that they rarely know what you're up to until it's too late. And with your knack for sizing up rivals and their prospects, it would be folly for them to get into a power struggle with you, for you're able to turn the tables and come out ahead. Although it isn't your natural style, if you become involved in a crucial or threatening situation that ends in a stalemate or contest of wills, you can sit things out for a long time. You know your own worth and are quietly confident.

Lucy Lawless (actress), 1968

Sam Walton (merchant), 1918

John Tyler (10th U.S. president), 1790

Special to April 20 (Mars, Moon):

Sensitive to conditions around you and expressive in ideas, you're likely to be a lot more confident than you sometimes appear to be. Home and domestic contentment are important to you, but your success comes through your ability to move with ease in the outside world and the variety of contacts you make. You have an inborn knack for networking and should capitalize on it. If you initially lack originality, you can quickly latch on to an already successful concept or idea to get the ball rolling. Then, as your success builds momentum, your individuality gradually emerges and sustains your achievement on your own merits.

Creatively gifted, you're more talented for the commercial side of the arts and, in particular, should develop any literary, dramatic or artistic ability you have. With a timeless instinct for trends and tastes, you will function well in any business or career milieu that serves the public. Your talent for putting out feelers, observing body language and reading between the lines of subtle feedback can keep you in the driver's seat and on top of most situations. If modesty and tact mask your Aries drive, people will be quite surprised at your courage and go-get-'em spirit.

Daniel Day-Lewis (actor), 1957
Jessica Lange (actress), 1949
Ryan O'Neal (actor), 1941

April the 3rd (Mars, Venus),
(and root digit for March 21, 30 and April 12):
You are in a creative and socially fluent vibration, and your energies and enthusiasms can make dynamic expression a reality. Whether in your public or private life and whether because of your potent magnetism and/or winsome ways, you attract attention. Talented and imaginative in many areas, you will find a chance to exhibit your natural abilities. Since you are popular and not restricted by opportunities, you could easily scatter and waste energies through restless pleasure-seeking. You will excel at promotion, managing, teaching and verbalizing anything.

Because number 3 birthdays (and numbers reduced to 3) aren't as favorable for learning once you are on your own, you will be more fortunate if you have extensive and thorough preparation in youth. The span between your early twenties and early thirties is a cycle of expression, the success of which will be in direct proportion to whatever has been mastered by the time you begin to establish your place in the world. When you have faith in anything, including yourself, you are a convincing salesperson and can go far. You are likely to have excellent taste and may have a natural, latent flair for art, especially in its practical applications.

With your Aries Martian energy, your love life is likely to be exciting and stimulating, but Mars is not noted for diplomacy or tenderness. You may have to learn to relate harmoniously during your first impetuous romantic escapades. Whether or not you manage to outgrow your youthful exuberance, your affectional or love experiences are likely to be blighted at some point through conflicting passions, emotional tension and/or separation. When your innate interest in beauty and pleasure is misdirected, it can result in personal indulgence and inconstant affections. Likely to be a great crowd-pleaser, your gifts are the kind that bring in money—but you like a good time and can be good at spending it, too.

   Marlon Brando (actor), 1924
   Doris Day (singer, actress), 1924
   Washington Irving (essayist), 1783

Special to March 21 (Mars, Venus [Moon/Sun]):
You're very capable of fulfilling positions of responsibility, but you may be better off working for others or in a structured environment . . . if you can stand it. Very expressive, you may lack the patience to master the technique of an art form. If you persist, however, the results could be prodigious. Your career experiences can cover a lot of ground. You like people and can be quite adaptable if that's what it takes to keep things moving in a way that is progressive and pleases others as well as yourself.

   You have a strong sense of justice, history and the social order, and a genuine talent for rounding up congenial teamwork for projects that may serve cultural or other worthwhile public needs. Close personal relationships may have to play second fiddle if they threaten to interfere with the mainstream of your intentions to spread the gospel of beauty, harmony and fair play. Be receptive to the give-and-take in relationships that stems from the necessities of everyday living, or you're likely to marry more than once.

   Matthew Broderick (actor), 1962
   Rosie O'Donnell (talk show host), 1962
   Johann Sebastian Bach (composer), 1685

Special to March 30 (Mars, Venus):
It's a toss-up whether your flair for easygoing, high-spirited socializing or your aptitude (possibly genius) for making money contributes more to your success capabilities. They probably work hand in hand, enabling you to rub shoulders with upwardly mobile types who recognize a kindred spirit in your fondness for beauty and gracious living. Adaptable, versatile, popular and flirtatious,

lovers tend to come and go. Along with your ability to charm admirers, you're well suited for public life, especially in the creative milieu. You're bright, talented, gregarious and a willing worker, all assets that come in handy as you work your way up in the workforce, business world or a profession.

With your Aries independent streak, marriage may not be one of your easiest accomplishments. You love the pursuit, the glamour and the exhilaration of romance. Your interest is in significant fun. The "thrill of the chase" and the conquest can be more rewarding to you than the continuity of a relationship. A dazzling paramour or inamorata could just be a l'amour trophy for you to show off to envious friends. If there are any pitfalls to avoid, among them would be simply getting by on your charm, overdoing the pleasure principle or letting money slip through your fingers.

Celine Dion (singer), 1968

Warren Beatty (actor), 1937

Vincent Van Gogh (artist), 1853

Special to April 12 (Mars, Venus [Sun/Moon]):

Talented, persuasive and versatile, you have a flair for advertising and selling. You're also a whiz at tooting your own horn. You are adaptable, resourceful and socially invigorating. Whether affluent or not, you know how to entertain in grand style. If necessary, you can make a little go a long way and could show the rich how to live. Your congenial personality and ability to express yourself are the keys to your climb to the top in the business or entertainment realm, or in a creative or kindred worldly pursuit, but you could just trade on them and get along in life on pleasantries if you're not ambitious.

Stimulated by the new and unexpected, you are quickly bored by the thrice familiar, which enhances your own endeavors in any creative field with a special incentive to keep your work fresh and distinctive. Artistically, your efforts certainly won't be humdrum or run-of-the-mill. If not a technical innovator, you will bring wit, originality and vigor to your work or career. In a similar vein, you wouldn't be a prize catch for someone seeking taken-for-granted emotional security or dependable (to you, boring and repetitive) routine in his/her love life. When you turn on the charm, though, you'll have no trouble winning a popularity contest.

David Letterman (talk show host), 1947

Ann Miller (dancer, actress), 1923

Henry Clay (orator/statesman), 1777

April the 4th (Mars, Saturn)
(and root digit for March 31 and April 13;
March 22 is a master number, see end of chapter):

You may chafe at the necessity for dependability, thoroughness, long hours and depth, but, like it or not, this is the only way you are going to achieve your worldly goals and get anywhere with the 4 vibration. Consequently, there may be times when you feel as though the workweek is all Mondays and no Fridays. Forget overnight success. Slow but sure is the way for you, but since it isn't typical of Aries, you're lucky if you somehow see things that way. You will realize your abilities best by channeling your efforts into endeavors requiring the long pull and steady development. Your associates may seem stolid and unimaginative, but they have values essential to your progress. You will learn from them if you are patient—not your outstanding trait.

Avoid all superficial objectives and any resentment of the need for careful, painstaking work. The goals you should aim for aren't the kind you can attain in a jiffy. If you should happen to gain success by swift and easy means, you may meet with periodic setbacks, such as health problems, and it could be necessary to start over again from square one. You can't convincingly assert your Aries penchant for importance except through forging solid foundations—discipline and self-control being the primary requirements. That's your key to success. Unless other indications are strongly contrary, variety will be inimical to you and any insistence on it may only contribute further delays to your progress, the potential for which is considerable.

Your consuming desire for success and leadership may cause worry that interferes with their realization, but the ultimate outcome of your endeavors can be significantly rewarding. Always protected, your determination and practicality can overcome any obstacles; your potential for a truly impressive contribution is great. Your name can be indelibly imprinted in the annals of professional or commercial achievement.

Anthony Perkins (actor), 1932

Arthur Murray (dance entrepreneur), 1895

Maurice de Vlaminck (artist), 1876

Special to March 31 (Mars, Saturn [Venus/Sun]):

Very mentally oriented, you have truly progressive ideas. You take ample pride in your accomplishments, which are, no doubt, hard-won and stem from lots of painstaking effort, persistence and discipline. You may have moved frequently in your early years, possibly the result of parental changes or vicissitudes beyond your control. In any case, you were probably forced at an early age to rely on your own courage, ingenuity and resourcefulness—which may have been difficult but was excellent training for the opportunities for achievement that come your way as your life unfolds.

You're more inclined to the artistic milieu than the competitive struggles of the business world, with a tendency to specialize in some distinctive way that enhances your leadership potential. Your admirable talents qualify you for any field of endeavor where taste, popularity, sales ability and sustained effort can be creatively fulfilling as well as rewarding in prestige and earning power. If stolid, unimaginative coworkers do their job admirably and efficiently, they may exemplify values essential to your progress; you can afford to take a page from their book. One or more marriages may be in the picture before you settle down to a contented domestic life.

Ewan MacGregor (actor), 1971

Richard Chamberlain (actor), 1935

Herb Alpert (band leader), 1935

Special to April 13 (Mars, Saturn [Sun/Venus]):

Very expressive and articulate, you like people to know what you are thinking. It will be to your advantage to maintain tolerance toward the opinions of others. You are willing to work very hard . . . for a while or for as long as any one or more of your many and diverse interests keep you absorbed. Whether in the arts or humanitarian pursuits, you're capable of channeling a lot of energy into projects you believe in. If yours isn't an easy road to success, it could be a blessing in disguise. You aren't the type to bask in the glory of your attainments if they are modest enough for anybody to match with little or no effort—to say nothing of true grit.

You like the freedom to do whatever you want to do whenever you want to do it, so you will resist any activities that limit you to a narrow or restricted course in life. If there's a central theme at the heart of your dissimilar interests, it expresses one of your most endearing qualities—your ability to make others feel better about themselves. In general, you should avoid glitzy, trendy, superficial pursuits, as well as any resentment of the need for careful, painstaking work. Your charm and personal appeal may bring notice for your abilities more quickly than you expect, but with your skeptical, ironic disposition, you probably won't believe in it.

Rick Schroeder (actor), 1970

F. W. Woolworth (merchant), 1852

Thomas Jefferson (3rd U.S president), 1743

April the 5th (Mars)
(and root digit for March 23 and April 14):

This birthday is probably the most conducive to the natural flow of your Aries energies because it is the numerological equivalent of the fiery planet Mars, ruler of your sign. Daring and confident, you will be attracted to many situations calling for action and freedom of expression. You don't just start things. Given the opportunity, you'll jump-start them. Once past early struggles, the road to success becomes easier, but too much of a good thing can lead to nothing at the end of the trail—although you may cover a lot of ground geographically. As life unfolds for you, probably at top speed, be careful that you don't enjoy and value the journey more than the destination—that is, if you have a significant goal in mind. You're likely to remain active one way or another into your sunset years.

Being self-sufficient, you are not fond of anchors of any kind, including marriage if it's the kind that makes you feel weighted down instead of soaring with joy. On the other hand, with your magnetism, your love life and romantic history could be pretty colorful. You like to keep on the move, the faster the better, but in the process you can spread yourself too thin, at least emotionally, and may find it difficult to establish and maintain meaningful relationships.

You need a creative avocation but aren't as well fitted for an artistic profession. However, along this line there are exceptions; if you can muster determined concentration of the spirit (exceptional for Aries, anyway) and stick-to-itiveness, you have the inborn stamina to succeed brilliantly at endeavors requiring creative imagination. A true child of Mars, you don't like to take *no* for an answer. Unlike 1, 3 and 7, which are rather more stable, you thrive on living life to the hilt or on the edge. What could Aries like better than that?

Bette Davis (actress), 1908

Spencer Tracy (actor), 1900

Sir Joseph Lister (physician), 1827

Special to March 23 (Mars [Moon/Venus]):

Dynamic and progressive, you're a unique combination of receptivity, drive, intelligence, daring and excellent taste. Despite the fact that your ambitious nature instinctively gravitates toward outside interests and getting ahead in the world, another part of you yearns for pleasure, thrills, personal popularity, public acclaim and, to top it off, the comfort of love and a close relationship. However, the complexity of your character can make it difficult for others to adjust to your relationship needs—which are highly individualistic, to say the least. Whomever you marry, therefore, will have to accept you on your own terms; you're most compatible with a partner who shares the courage of your convictions.

Your basically cheerful, outgoing, energetic disposition enables you to capitalize on your social popularity to promote your career goals. Despite your occasional feelings of doubt or insecurity, you're likely to come out on the right end of a setback. Win, lose or draw, you keep right on trying—and with your intellectual vigor, job expertise, charm and awareness of public taste, you are capable of memorable achievement. Conscious of how you look and the impression you are making, you might spend money on your appearance and temporarily forego expenditure on something you may need more. This could be a rare occurrence, though, since you are likely to be financially lucky.

Joan Crawford (actress), 1908

Erich Fromm (psychoanalyst), 1900

Dane Rudhyar (astrologer, artist, composer), 1895

Special to April 14 (Mars [Sun/Saturn]):

When you've learned by experience (the hard way) that your impulses don't always work out, you will find it's better to choose projects that have a chance of being completed once you've started them. If you have a message to get across, you'll attempt to do it with the fervor of an evangelist. Forthright and practical, you can be the peacemaker between opposing factions and promote productive teamwork.

Even if you're not the most charismatic personality on earth, your ideas, expertise, concentration and sincerity can carry the day. You take pride in your ability to overcome obstacles through your well-directed energies and patient persistence. At your warm and engaging best, a dynamo when sufficiently inspired, you can be a compelling force in making the right things happen. People won't fail to be impressed when your forcefulness is backed up by discipline and thorough preparation. As time goes on, you're very likely to go on even longer, probably keeping busy with your career or other productive activities well into later years that find less hardy souls than you enjoying retirement.

Julie Christie (actress), 1941
Loretta Lynn (singer), 1935
Sir John Gielgud (actor), 1904

April the 6th (Mars, Jupiter)
(and root digit for March 24 and April 15):

You need love and companionship—and you have many ideals concerning their fulfillment. With enthusiastic risk-taking augmenting your Aries restlessness, you are not averse to changing partners in your quest for blissful perfection. It may not occur to you that some foible of your own is the barrier to realizing a rapturous, perfect union and/or a happy family life. For instance, an initial youthful tendency to impetuous amours and an exaggerated, uncritical opinion of yourself will bear investigating. Unlike your Aries 5 brothers and sisters who haven't the time for such things, you may tie and untie the marriage knot a time or two (or more) in your search for meaningful fulfillment through a relationship.

Change, like charity, begins at home, but it is admittedly less trouble to change partners (an outer effort) than to change oneself (an inner effort), which is unsettling and time-consuming and could even be traumatic for you. You are rarely displeased with yourself for being the way you are. There's a bit of Don Quixote in you; you're always ready to climb the next hilltop to see what lies beyond, hoping that it will be an exciting new experience that beckons. An adventurous, optimistic spirit motivates you, and you have plenty of energy, stamina and enthusiasm for your voyage of discovery in life.

You are likely to be mentally, musically and/or artistically gifted, as well as financially lucky. You impress others with your protective qualities and attract support and encouragement. Your magnetism, adventurousness and fun-loving proclivities make you an ideal love partner for someone who is in tune with you emotionally and who shares your lively outlook and penchant for spontaneity. Until you've found that one special person, though, you do tend to look around a bit. Now, if you could just find happiness . . .

Merle Haggard (singer), 1937
Billy Dee Williams (actor), 1937
Harry Houdini (magician), 1874

Special to March 24 (Mars, Jupiter [Moon/Saturn]):

No matter how much teamwork is involved or necessary, you like to be in the driver's seat and to have your own way; if you're in charge of the purse strings, your chances improve considerably. You are likely to be working right up to the end of your life. "The spirit is willing, but the flesh is weak" aptly describes the only way you can be stopped—and an example for all to admire. Nervous and touchy, you're not the one to cross. Instead of compromising, especially when a principle is involved, you say what you think and not always tactfully. Achievement through hard work, persistent enthusiasm, common sense and public responsibility is your credo—which you may exemplify in the arts, business or a profession.

A strong believer in family life, property and tradition, you're a good marriage prospect and are loyal to friends. Instead of compromising, especially when a principle is involved, your idea of diplomacy is to bring others around to *your* way of thinking. Although you attract your share of critics and opponents, many of them could wind up with grudging admiration, respect and support for you before the final curtain descends on your activities.

    Steve McQueen (actor), 1930

    Malcolm Muggeridge (writer, journalist), 1903

    Andrew Mellon (financier), 1855

Special to April 15 (Mars, Jupiter [Sun/Mars]):
With your excellent memory, talents and exceptional gifts for recognizing quality, you'll enjoy advantages as you travel far and wide in search of experience and success. You don't waste time dithering over what to do and delight in challenging the establishment, particularly if you're crusading for a cause. You probably had a lot to think about as you grew up and, hopefully, learned the value of careful judgment and thoughtful action in the onrush of early experiences. It's fortunate that you're apt to be youthful, enthusiastic and energetic well into your sunset years.

Capable of firm personal loyalties, you can also be very outspoken in your opinions of colleagues, friends and rivals. Although the targets of your devilish sense of humor may not always appreciate your wit, they can't deny the benefits of your wisdom, with or without the wit. Possibly very creative, you can do well financially, but you can also be a genius at getting rid of security as well as other things. And you don't like to be told that you're not prudent. In fact, you don't like to be told anything. Sorry, the stars and numbers know . . .

    Emma Thompson (actress), 1959

    Henry James (writer), 1843

    Leonardo da Vinci (universal genius), 1452

April the 7th (Mars, Mercury)
(and root digit for March 25 and April 16):

Your opportunities will materialize along lines calling for mental depth and specialization. You will gain more from observation and the school of experience than from formal study, for which you might not have much patience. You may have learned the lessons of survival early and can capitalize on the kind of smarts you don't learn in school. You can be a picture of charm, but if people, especially potential competitors, were to ask you what you're thinking or what your plans are, they're apt to get a tightlipped smile with perhaps a hint of calculation. Nobody's going to pull the rug out from under you if you can help it. Your grasp of intricacies, fast insights and financial judgment are lucrative assets.

In the artistic or entertainment field, your endeavors are apt to be informative and enlightening as well as entertaining. Knowing how to squeeze the last drop of effectiveness and impact out of any career situation greatly contributes to your success potential. Your leadership abilities can become known far and wide through your novel ideas and can set new standards in fields that demand the utmost in experience and expertise. The hardest thing for you to do is search for the quiet voice within. You are splendidly equipped for deep mental analysis and meditation, provided that you can remain still long enough (not an Aries trait). You tend to be incessantly active mentally and/or physically.

Since your thoughts are singular and reclusive, your mate or lover may feel lonely at times. Don't tie up with anyone who requires constant togetherness. You yearn for love and home but are somewhat aloof, passively positive and frequently preoccupied with *your* interests. If you develop your introspective faculties, your passionate individualism broadens and becomes an enviable asset. Then, since Aries is typically more concerned with the projection and expression of self rather than the examination of self, this birthday number can constructively impede the feckless onrush of your impetuous instincts. By conforming to the need for concentrative capabilities, your impact can be rare and memorable.

Jackie Chan (actor), 1954
James Garner (actor), 1928
Billie Holiday (singer), 1915

Special to March 25 (Mars, Mercury [Moon]):

You like a good polemic, have a dynamic personality and can play an influential role in the area of cultural enrichment. You're probably streetwise and hard to fool. Trying to put something over on you, especially in your area of expertise, would be a waste of time. Your way may not be the only way, but it's likely to be worthy of consideration and respect or even popular acclaim, and you know how to argue the fine points of an issue. Finding out what makes other people tick is one of your talents for getting ahead; knowledge, news, information, even gossip are grist for your mill as you climb the ladder of success.

Possibly a precocious child, your impressive mental abilities are forged in the crucible of conflicts between instinctive action and structured knowledge. Your razor-sharp mind is just as apt to stem from the school of experience as from academic training; either way, you have an instinct for capitalizing on what you learn. Home and family life appeal to you (when you find time to enjoy them), but your restless urge to be on the go interferes with domestic tranquillity.

Sir Elton John (singer), 1947

Aretha Franklin (singer), 1942

Gloria Steinem (feminist), 1934

Special to April 16 (Mars, Mercury [Sun/Jupiter]):

Very determined, ambitious and frequently gifted, you expect your efforts to be well rewarded in pay or recognition, preferably both. Not the type to sit still, you're usually in motion. When you're not, you're probably enthusing over an inspirational or creative idea that stirs up your restless energies. All the colorful variety of the grand pageant of living appeals to you, and very little escapes your attention. Your inborn pride, self-confidence and optimism come in handy to get you over any rough spots during your childhood or developmental period.

Once you discover an ego-satisfying niche that allows you to express creatively your superb communication skills, you can remain consistently interested and rise to the top. You like career situations with a certain amount of freedom, where you have room to maneuver and maybe to wheel and deal. Your enthusiasms are easily aroused, a trait that will benefit you more if you control the impulse to act too fast or before all the ramifications of a situation have sunk in. Blazing new trails, initiating new concepts and projects, promotion (personal and otherwise) and selling are among your special talents that can pave the way to success.

Kareem Abdul-Jabbar (basketball player), 1947

Henry Mancini (composer), 1924

Charlie Chaplin (actor), 1889

April the 8th (Mars, Uranus/Saturn)
(and root digit for March 26 and April 17):
This can be the most satisfying of the "outer" numbers for an aggressive Aries because the results are so inwardly gratifying. Your opportunities will involve executive functions, mastery of fundamentals and the transformation of your skills and knowledge into the requirements essential to crown an entrepreneurial venture with success. Your talents, pioneering spirit and initiatives can lead to the top in business or the creative fields. Although you give people the impression you can accomplish anything, you may need to submerge some of your innate Aries traits, one of which is your pronounced independence.

Teamwork in one context or another will be an important skill for you to develop; learn to coordinate diverse elements into a smoothly working whole. When you do, there's no limit to the heights of success and fame you can attain, enabling you to rub shoulders with other estimable achievers or dazzling celebrities. You have the power and substance of 4, doubled and juxtaposed into the vision of 8, for you to make broadly comprehensive and practical progress.

Negatively, you could flounder in vast schemes. Even though rich in farsighted ideas, you may lack the patience and comprehension to carry them through to completion with authority. You're not easily influenced once you've made up your mind. Watching and waiting while a slow-but-sure plan develops and finally succeeds can excite you about as much as watching and waiting for paint to dry. In a large corporation, you function best in an autonomous position. Stay clear of a job where there is little chance for advancement or an acceptance of your progressive, not to say grand, ideas. An excellent promoter, with an eye always on profit, you should learn to delegate routine details to others once you've familiarized yourself with the essentials necessary to keep the wheels of commerce turning. You're tops as the initiatory brains of a project, but you should then let someone you trust take over the daily management while you supervise the enterprise and protect your interest in subsequent rewards.

Betty Ford (First Lady), 1918
Sonja Henie (ice skater), 1912
Mary Pickford (actress), 1893

Special to March 26 (Mars, Uranus/Saturn [Moon/Jupiter]):
With your enterprising spirit and wide-angle lens view of life, much of your luck will be self-created. However, that doesn't mean that you won't benefit

from being born with certain advantages. Ever alert to the main chance, the big picture of achievement motivates you. Your instincts are broad and adventurous, and you're likely to start your upward climb to reach lofty goals early in life. Your carefully reasoned personal philosophy, independent view of justice, feeling for public trends and confidence that the risk-reward ratio is in your favor are among your distinctive assets.

Always with an eye on the future, ready to break with tradition or to launch a new one, you have a knack for on-the-spot inspirations and improvements. Whether you change from one job or profession to another in your quest for status and independence or stick to one line of endeavor, your persistence, optimism and sense of responsibility will pay off. For some of you, success in one field or context serves as a stepping-stone to new vistas of opportunity in other areas, including the special role you're equipped to play in the world of affairs.

> **Diana Ross (singer), 1944**
>
> **Tennessee Williams (playwright), 1914**
>
> **Robert Frost (poet), 1874**

Special to April 17 (Mars, Uranus/Saturn [Sun/Mercury]):
If you're properly motivated by your enviable birthright, no one can accuse you of lacking in ideas and vision, especially if they put you into a major entrepreneurial role or the spotlight. Vigorous, confident and ambitious, you're likely to be more disciplined than is customary for Aries. With your keen intelligence and alert powers of observation, you're always ready to blaze a new trail and might travel far and wide in search of fulfillment. In the process, you may very well land on top with a large helping of material security. You're inclined to have scant (or no) tolerance for the opposite viewpoint in a dispute. To say you have a mind of your own would be an understatement.

With your Aries lack of patience for fuss and bother, you know how to get right to the point and avoid activities that blunt your enthusiasm and stifle your initiative. Whether or not you're in business or government, or in the arts or a profession, you are fully capable of protecting your interests and personal privacy. Your articulate, genial manner can mask an impatience with people who don't talk your language or get your message, but you do have your limits and can be brusque and tactless when exasperated.

> **William Holden (actor), 1918**
>
> **Nikita Kruschev (Soviet premier), 1894**
>
> **J. P. Morgan (financier), 1837**

April the 9th (Mars, Pluto)
(and root digit for March 27 and April 18):

You are motivated by a sort of smoldering, relentless ambition; if you discipline yourself effectively, you can be very successful in any job or line of endeavor that makes appropriate use of your resourceful capabilities. Many changes are in store for you; therefore, a purely personal approach to life is apt to be disappointing. The world and its needs are grist for your mill; you're liable to cover a lot of ground, emotionally as well as geographically, in your quest for personal fulfillment. You are strong-willed and not partial to accepting advice—but then you seldom need it. Right or wrong, you can become very stubborn if a principle you stake your life on is threatened. You may become brooding and resentful if you have to struggle too long to attain a goal, whether it was set by yourself or others.

The manner in which you project your intense personality can be a determining factor in the degree of your success . . . or failure. With a strongly introverted self-will, the same one you utilize to carve your niche in the world, it's not easy for you to compromise, which you disdain. Your antipathies are subliminal and difficult to rationalize.

While you might forgive, or appear to, you'll never forget a humiliation or a defeat. Although you can make a name for yourself one way or another, there may be controversy or jealousy in connection with your achievements because of their political or moral implications.

You profit by cultivating a more impersonal attitude toward business or professional associates. You can develop talents in writing, music, business or politics, any field where public approval is the hallmark of success. You're not the type to give up, but if circumstances force you to admit defeat, you're capable of building a wall around yourself and shutting out the world until conditions improve and you're able to get back on track. Your bedrock of inner conviction is tempered by your pungent wit; when things get sticky and the atmosphere is thick with tension, you have a way of breaking the spell with a clever remark, plus getting an ego-satisfying barb in edgewise at the same time.

Hugh Hefner (publisher), 1926

Linda Goodman (astrologer, writer), 1925

William Fulbright (U.S. senator), 1905

Special to March 27 (Mars, Pluto [Moon/Mercury]):

Good-natured, versatile and an energetic go-getter, you are always alert to the main chance. You have a broad outlook but not when it comes to contrary personalities; the atmosphere is happier if people don't oppose you. You think for yourself and frequently say what you think, not necessarily with due regard for your listeners' sensibilities. At your best, you can come up with inspirations, ideas or conclusions in the form of subtle insights that change your own and others' lives. In the process, you can cover a lot of ground, literally or figuratively.

You have a reformative talent, part instinct and part shrewd thinking, for combining traditional materials with unrelated elements in ways that produce new concepts or creations—new wine in *new* bottles—with little or nothing of the old remaining except the original theme or function. You're always ready to shed the trappings, if not the spirit, of the past, which may include leaving a relationship or two (or more) strewn in the wake of lifestyles (and friends or lovers) you've discarded.

> Gloria Swanson (actress), 1899
> Sarah Vaughan (singer), 1924
> Michael York (actor), 1942

Special to April 18 (Mars, Pluto [Sun/Uranus/Saturn]):

You have to be given a free rein and be allowed to discover your own rhythm and inventive insights relating to your personal or career activities. Although you can be somewhat spasmodic, you're very determined and unlikely to stray far from your chosen course, which is to make a success of one venture or another. You're not apt to recognize any limitations to your abilities or ambitions or acknowledge any boundaries to the scope of your vision. Your impressive self-assurance stems from deep wells of emotional strength.

You're good at recycling past experience to get fresh mileage out of it. In one manifestation, this skill can surface as your personal kind of humor . . . but with a twist; you can make people laugh and at the same time settle an old score. When you can't get your way with typically aggressive Aries tactics, you'll resort to subtle persuasion (or manipulation) if that's what it takes to win. And since you're shrewd at it yourself, you also know when the power of suggestion is being used on you. Your own unique brand of charisma and expression is an estimable asset in the professional and business worlds.

> Conan O'Brien (talk show host), 1963
> Leopold Stokowski (conductor), 1882
> Clarence Darrow (lawyer), 1857

April the 11th (Mars, Neptune [Moon/Sun])
(master number):

Your birthday is the signature of the dreamer and prophet, a Ram who may encounter disappointment from seeking purely personal rewards or humdrum business world satisfactions. Adjustments on the material plane may prove difficult, as this birthday is more concerned with intangibles and selflessness. You seldom recognize any limitations to your ambitions or any boundaries to the scope of your vision, yet you are likely to find yourself in some highly specialized or circumscribed niche in life. Whether you're dreaming of creating the 20th century equivalent of the Mona Lisa, seeing your name in lights on Broadway or making a killing on Wall Street, you may have to downsize your unrealistic ambitions to fit within the framework of practical possibilities.

Through the transcendental promise of 11, you are dramatic, bright, psychic and nervously responsive, possibly setting a splendid—not to say unique—example as a teacher, performer or leader in a creative field. When thwarted and your Aries ego is not allowed full sway, you can go to extremes and become confused. Instead of the compassionate Ram, you can become, through egoistic escapism, the sacrificial lamb. You can waste much time and energy playing hunches that satisfy or salve your ego and accomplish little or nothing else and might even lead you up a meaningless alley or two. When your motives are sensible, however, your psychic antenna is usually on autopilot and comes to your rescue to provide the solution to a dilemma.

Generally averse to mysticism, you may frequently find yourself in situations where your beliefs, dreams, aspirations and concepts of an ideal world are tested for their practical worth. Relinquishment of the personal ego, a prime tenet of esoteric faith, is foreign to the highly personalized Aries temperament. To be well rewarded for your services is more gratifying to your ego; but if you follow the path of enlightenment, other values will be worth your consideration, something that may be difficult for Aries to comprehend or accept.

Joel Grey (actor), 1932

Oleg Cassini (designer), 1913

Paul Douglas (actor), 1907

(Note: This master number implies a variable alternative response influenced by the strength or passivity of the planet Neptune in your horoscope. If you don't feel you are responding to the distinctive vibratory power of 11, you are instead expressing the more conventional qualities of 2, which you should read.)

March the 22 (Mars, Uranus [Saturn/Moon])
(master number):

Whether you're a diamond in the rough or someone with highly cultivated talents, you can have something to say that people want or need to hear. Your claim to fame is likely to stem from initiating a fresh trend in the arts, business, technology or government. Nervous and overstimulated, you may constantly need to strive for a balance between subjective desires and objective realizations. You can gain recognition, even worldwide fame, from large-scale projects that in some way enlighten, entertain or benefit humanity. However, the need to focus your energies into endeavors of broad scope presupposes a patience not native to your fiery, restless temperament. You tend to gravitate toward a mobile, stimulating, novelty-prone, more avant-garde milieu. A job, business opening or profession that is trendy in terms of new and different ideas and fads, eclectic lifestyles, humanitarian interests and tomorrow's cultural breakthroughs will appeal to you.

The opportunities you encounter will challenge your creative urge and qualities of leadership, the results being in direct proportion to the integrity of your motives. If they are farsighted and/or altruistic, your originality can enhance the values and the vision you espouse to enlighten others in some unique way, to broaden public awareness and to brighten and/or improve world conditions. You'll have the chance to demonstrate your right to the freedom of action and the individuality you covet, and you will succeed if you soft-pedal any tendencies toward self-absorption, cynicism or fierce independence.

Inclined to be high-strung and impetuous, nervous overload can cause you to waste time and energy and to be dogmatically resistant to helpful suggestions from others. In achieving your place in the world of affairs, you can enhance the benefits of your distinctive Aries qualities by being receptive to persuasion or compromise. You will discover that worthwhile advantages accrue from cultivating flexibility, which helps to achieve your own as well as shared goals. Although there are exceptions, you aren't cut out for marriage—but that may not dawn on you until you've tried it several times. You don't like to feel restricted and eschew a life that is slipping into a predictable, monotonous pattern.

Sir Andrew Lloyd Weber (composer), 1948

William Shatner (actor), 1931

Sir Anthony Van Dyck (artist), 1599

(Note: This master number implies a variable alternative response influenced by the strength or passivity of the planet Uranus in your horoscope. If you don't think you are responding to the distinctive vibratory power of 22, you are instead expressing the more conventional qualities of 4, which you should read.)

CHAPTER 2

TAURUS

April 21–May 21

RULER: **VENUS** NUMBER: **3** ELEMENT: **EARTH** SYMBOL: **THE BULL**

"One touch of nature makes the whole world kin."
—*Troilus and Cressida*, Shakespeare

As a Taurus-born, you have more natural affinity for the genuine joys of this Earth life and of living on this planet than any other sign. This doesn't mean that your enviable attachment makes you automatically happy or contented, but you can be freer of many of the draining resentments that beset the other signs. Facts and figures don't make your eyes glaze over as they might Aries, Gemini or Sagittarius. Complications that arise from the inept handling of life's basic practicalities, such as tasks that for others can assume the proportion of drudgeries, flow easily and naturally for most Taureans. Your pragmatic inborn radar doesn't need storm warnings to function accurately or to sound an alert. This instinct enables you to sense, know or familiarize yourself with the nature of obstacles in advance of encountering them or during the planning stage of anticipated involvement in activities or projects.

To life-of-the-party types, you may seem too stodgy, complacent or conservative. While you are paying off your mortgage or your rent to your landlord when due with predictable regularity, your witty friends may be using their nimble wits to invent clever excuses why they are late with theirs. The main reason is that they don't have the instinct you do to "mind the store." With you it's first-things-first where practicalities are concerned. The earth signs find involvement with basic necessities rather more congenial than the rest of the zodiac. While your sign is the least complicated of the three earth signs, the fact that you are the most elementary and intense does raise other issues.

As indicated by your ruling planet, Venus, you are motivated by an instinctive appreciation of the beauty and immediacy of the physical world. Your primal awareness of the pleasures that it can provide and your ability to make them a reality in your life are thus the measures of your security. You rest your case on your ability to handle and order the basic material sufficiencies. You like a beautiful and, at the very least, comfortable home, land, acreage and all nature generally. Greenery, flowers, sculpture, jewels—all eye-catching objects of earthly or aesthetic beauty—are welcome as complements to your surroundings or decor. Your preference is for furnishings that are substantial and luxurious, but not necessarily antiques (these are more the province of the Cancer-born). Taurus likes the physical presence and comfort possibilities of beautiful possessions first; whatever historic or emotional connotations they might suggest would be secondary. You are more interested in comfort and quality than in status or tradition. Whereas Aries and Gemini thrive on a city tempo, you are generally happier in a country, suburban or rural area. But you can do wonders in a city apartment with a terrace or patio where you can have an assortment of plants.

You can more naturally escape financial worries than the other signs; you are most apt to be materially secure and even well off. You are motivated by the instinct that the currency of the realm or possessions that could be converted into currency can be for you a source of rock-solid, worry-free security and/or profit potential. This enviable advantage naturally and dependably provides the wherewithal for the pleasures, continuity and ease of your preferred lifestyle. Since your values are the sturdy ones, you are more likely to automatically achieve financial and physical security through acquiring and possessing things than any other sign except Cancer. A quote from Luke 12:15: "A man's life does not consist in the abundance of his possessions" will help to keep your proclivities in perspective. Like many a collector, you could discover that possessions can own *you*.

Not especially gregarious socially, you are amiably absorbed by the good things of life, which you are willing to share with friends, and you prefer an atmosphere of plenty and conviviality. As a guest at a party, you may be the one quietly seeing that everyone is well supplied with refreshments while your earth cousins, the Virgos, scurry around collecting empty glasses and keeping things tidy. The twittering chatter won't especially interest you, and the sly innuendo or sophisticated double-entendre may slip by you or miss the mark.

Your affability and generosity do not usually extend to the point of sacrificing your own comfort, however. In fact, your concern for yourself in this regard can extend instead to self-indulgence, to your considerable detriment. When life doesn't turn out according to the vision stemming from your values or some happenstance prevents you from meeting your needs, you can give vent to your frustrations by indulging in food and drink, all the physical appetites. Your *body* then accumulates more expanse, instead of your unique Taurean instincts giving form, beauty and substance to something *outside* your physical self. Your body then becomes the expansive repository for the misdirected consequences of your needs. Circulatory difficulties, whence the word "veinous" (Venus), are a common result for your unwise behavior.

Your fondness for ease and the status quo can lead to a lassitude of spirit or body if the effort necessary to feel relaxed and contented or to extricate yourself from a rut is too unpleasantly comfort- or habit-shattering. You prefer to preserve your position in your milieu in a passively assertive manner and can concern or irritate others with your apparently benign acceptance of conditions not to your liking. Unlike Aries—all fire and brimstone at the drop of a hat or pregnant remark—you can adhere inflexibly to a rather narrow channel through which you have chosen to be an unyielding phlegmatic Taurean. At such times, you don't express a dynamic vitality but instead reveal your great reserves of strength and endurance by the deliberate pacing of your energies as you go about in your unruffled way performing whatever tasks the world sends in your direction or that you can't avoid.

At your best, however, you are substantial and determined, an anchor or pivot on whom others in your environment feel they can rely. You don't go to pieces in a crisis. The urge *behind* your motivations is to sustain "what is" and to resist being goaded into action before you "feel" ready. Repetitive patterns don't bother you. You don't mind life in the slow lane as long as it gets you where you are going. When you are tired, you are physically exhausted and not a misspent bundle of nerves. Even then you manage to emanate an inner glow of self-containment, security and calm power; to those in your environment who may be more nervously organized, you can be either an inspiration . . . or maddening.

As a native of Taurus, you prefer to flow with conditions, not just because you believe they are right but because complaining about them or stirring up a ruckus wouldn't be worth the personal discomfort it might engender. That doesn't mean that you are a pushover or that you don't have your outer limits. You can become very dogmatic when you are aroused or your sense of security is threatened and even violent if pushed beyond endurance. But you have to be extremely annoyed because the emotional exertion, turmoil and attendant discomfort would violate your inner yearning for stability and repose. For this reason, your manner of giving vent to your antipathies is direct and simple. One way you react is to give the object of your indifference or disdain the silent treatment. If you don't like someone or something, that's that! Not for you any Machiavellian schemes of reprisal or just plain "getting even," more typically negative proclivities of your opposite polarity, Scorpio.

You enjoy getting along with people. When you encounter the perfectly human complications that arise from personality conflicts, you aren't as disturbed about them as the other Venusian sign, Libra, to whom *relationships* are the test of life's success. If you are materially and physically secure and reasonably comfortable, the people who blend into your characteristic Taurean pattern (as you envision and develop it) are quite satisfactory and you will have few pangs of regret over those who don't fit in.

Your love needs are conditioned by proximity and demonstrativeness. You would never be happy composing love poems to your beloved over great spans of distance and time. Forget it. You crave the warm fuzzies. Whatever is near is most apt to be dear because of the physical requirements and immediacy of your affectionate instincts. You like to touch, pet, caress and hug the one you love, and you're happiest when your approach arouses a touchy-feely response from your lover. The beauty of love is not lost on you—quite the contrary—but your response is more earthy than poetic. Your aesthetic sense is locked in matter. An affectionately impoverished Taurean is not likely to write poetry; on the other hand, your reverence for material things can bring on self-defeat.

If you can look at a barren piece of land and visualize the house of your dreams, why can't you learn to know the person in your mate's body? You smother your mate with creature comforts and may be unwittingly suffocating his or her spirit. Your approach is fine if you are building an estate, but you tend to treat a loved one like a possession, an extension of personal adornment or pleasure, another item to be shown off on the shelf or an investment with a profitable return. You can't polish a loved one and show him or her off like the family silver; you can destroy what you love and be beaten at your game. You can drive your mate to a point beyond which he or she finds *you* attractive. You help him or her to outgrow you!

You are usually as deliberate about marriage as anything else and as likely to pick a time or reason for wedlock as you are to zero in on a person. Not apt to be impulsively swept off your feet by any particular person, emotional obsession or inspiration, your patient and thorough consideration for taking vows can delay it. Whether a passing fling or more serious attachment, you will be attracted to someone who exemplifies your concept of beauty—either physically—or who gives evidence of an ability to mold a sense of beauty, cultivation and pleasure into the fabric of his or her life and, ultimately, yours.

When your emotional interest has been aroused, you may become more quiet than is customary even for you and for good reasons. First, you are seriously enjoying yourself. The arousal of your love instincts is naturally soothing to you, so you are finding pleasure in one of life's most important experiences. Second, you never reveal your hand until you've fathomed all the possible hurdles. That's what all those silences are about; anxiety and restlessness disturb your placidity only as the time nears for avowals or commitments. And that day may be a long time in coming unless cardinal signs or other potent elements in your particular horoscope emphatically outweigh your typically Taurean reserve and composure. As a fixed-sign child of the earth Venus, you are noted for loyalty in love. You will notice the word "marriage" wasn't used; you will remain faithful as long as the *love* fires keep burning.

As a Taurus-born, you are more responsive to tactile and visual impressions than aural ones; whatever is sensed makes a more indelible impact on you through the faculties of touching, looking or reading than through hearing or listening. In fact, when individuals have something on their minds that they want to get across strongly to you, they should put it in writing as simply as possible because you instinctively concentrate with the eye; verbal communication—sometimes even invective—can go out both ears, making little or no impression on the gray matter in between. The fact is you often hear only what you want to hear; you nod and smile like a spinster who's turned off her hearing aid. Music is another matter, however, especially the music of praise; you can hear that two rooms away.

At times you are inhibited by self-generated resentments and fears or boredom. It may help to remember that we can't always have things the way we would like them in life; it is more prudent—not to say gracious—to develop some liking or tolerance for what life expects of you as your part of the bargain. Life doesn't always send us what we want; it does send us what we need. And rare are those souls who find what they want *and* what they need in the same package. Since you are the least adaptable and changeable of all the signs, this could be your most important lesson.

As always, the key to the principal contradictory trait of any sign is revealed through a knowledge of its polarity. For Taurus, this is Scorpio, another sign of great stability and feeling but with far different motives. Scorpio is co-ruled by Mars, the planet of initiative, energy and change, and Pluto, the planet of regeneration. The motivations thus symbolized are the direct opposite of Venus in meaning. Just as Mars or Pluto as rulers of Scorpio can be excessively forceful or controlling, Venus—the planet of attraction—as ruler of Taurus can overdo its phlegmatic and sedentary tendencies, its love of ease and pleasure.

To observe that you have a compulsive attitude toward the inevitability and rightness of your choices is partly true: compulsive but not necessarily inevitable or right. You could be on the wrong path, but you don't like to change because that takes effort of mind and spirit plus the candid admittance that the wellsprings of your motives and inspirations are not operating effectively in tandem with the real world or your cosmic plan. The unpleasant inference is that if you know you are in error, perhaps drifting in an uncharted direction, it's foolish or lazy not to act to effect changes. You subtly sense that your metabolism would have to shift into a possibly uncomfortable frequency and that potential changes beginning as fresh judgments could well end up as big physical exertions and upsets affecting your customary or preferred routine. You realize inwardly that if this potential expenditure of energy is to accomplish something constructive rather than just pleasurable or convenient, it's going to be spelled *effort*, uncomfortably above and beyond your habitual daily quota. And, as has been noted, your habits are difficult to break. By reverse process this can generate more inertia of the spirit. It isn't exactly part of your nature to find relaxation of spirit, as well as body, uncongenial.

As your ruling planet, Venus exemplifies the earth qualities of Venus rather than the airy Venus of Libra. Since your sense perceptions are more sensitively tuned to the visual impact of things, you are generally more limited in intellectual outlook and interests. Mental glibness and facility thus may not be as swift as in the more articulate signs (Gemini, Virgo, etc.) but can be a lot more profound. If you should decide to ponder the meaning of the universe or some other weighty enigma, you can, through your relentless determination, pursue a thought to its most remote conclusion. Patience is characteristic of your mental approach to imponderables, on the order of Taureans Immanuel Kant and Teilhard de Chardin. If you aim for distinctive creative attainment, you tend to write the longest books, are inclined to dogmatic penetration and yet are more apt to be a novelist, dramatist or performer than a philosopher. Because Taurus rules the throat and neck, many singers and actors born in your sign have gained fame, and their careers tend to endure.

Flights of fancy, instantly articulated, are not your forte. Your methods are slow but sure, better fitted for the traditional fine art approach, the artistic trades or applied arts, or pursuits requiring the long pull, physical aptitude and endurance rather than aesthetically original achievement. You are too down-to-earth for ivory towers.

You are more executive and administrative than creative, and you fit well into organizations. Although you might seem subservient in the face of unfair authority, you really are only patiently waiting for the moment that, confident of your bridge of security, you can move out of a bad situation and into a more congenial and auspicious one.

Ireland, with the sensuous verdancy of its gently undulating terrain, is vividly symbolic of Taurean attributes and is in fact astrologically identified with Taurus. There's a dark side, however, and the key is the *ire* part of Ireland. Look up *ire* in the dictionary: wrath; anger. On the bright side, a joyous response to life is gently or lustily celebrated in song, dance, prose and poetry on that green island. The basic pleasures of beauty, humor and the earth run the gamut in that fascinating, paradoxical land, from irresistible colleens to mischievous leprechauns. Or worse. Of equal fame are the brawling Irishmen. You are indeed fortunate if they are no more than stubborn and withdrawn when aroused! The not undeserved celebrity of their temper, with their spirit not unlikely to be distorted or inflamed by "spirits" of the liquid variety, typifies the extremes of belligerence or violence to which an enraged Taurean can go. But you have to be pushed to the point of sacrificing your basic desire for inner peace and tranquillity before you reach that stage of behavior. Your unleashed rage is overcompensation for your stored-up preference for the easygoing status quo as you see it, and you then become the destroyer instead of the builder.

Since your habits are difficult to break, it is to your definite advantage to deliberately cultivate as many sterling ones as possible; attempting that, and perhaps falling short, you'll at least wind up with quite a few good ones. This is especially pertinent to the training of Taurus children. Habits formed in childhood can last a lifetime. There is no use remonstrating with the little ones when they are aroused; they will only become more obstinate and retreat further into themselves. Better to bring up the issue later when you can discuss it calmly, accompanied by an appeal to their affections, thus employing a principle of Taurus's planetary ruler, Venus.

Diligent and loyal, you can be equally self-willed, stubborn and jealous, a master of "won't-power." Just as in childhood, issues should be resolved by you when free of interference and excitement. Whereas Aries is active with a vengeance, you are *reactive*, fulfilling a logical sequential function in the cosmic order of things. Aries rushes into activity when confronting issues, but you more typically stop to evaluate whether expenditures of energy will lead to a practical result. You thus gather things to yourself as they come your way rather than go after them willy-nilly.

In any association, you can be a very stabilizing influence. When everyone else is ready to wilt, you hang on *beyond* the bitter end. It is hard to do physical damage to yourself, but if you do wear down or diminish your psychic or physical reserves, the same principle works in reverse. It takes a long time for you to recuperate because your vitality is slow in restoring itself.

You have very good memories because information is received and relayed into the deep wells of the unconscious and there distilled in the subliminal matrix of your primitive instincts. Results thus obtained accrue as your brand of wisdom. Since this ingestion is a gradual and lengthy process, you are not usually verbose. You prefer to keep your findings to yourself until a sensible reason for expressing them materializes. You know where you're at and are confident about it. Amiable, not to say mindless, chatter does not provoke the most responsive stimulus for your thoughtful participation. You and Scorpio are the least transparent of the signs. You never give away your inner thoughts by your visible reactions. You naturally inspire confidence because you don't give the impression that you are going to gossip frivolously.

Your symbol, the Bull, is associated with Dionysus and Bacchus, the mythological gods of fertility and wine—a fun combination that you can take too literally. If the taking of the wine was more of a sacrament than a frolic, as is commonly thought, shouldn't the same reverence apply to other things? Your symbol was worshipped as Pan in ancient Arcadia, whence you derive your bucolic temperament. He was the Lord of the Wood, which explains your affinity for trees, greenery, all nature in general and spirits aged in wood, as well as spirits of the woods like leprechauns, elves, fairies and goblins. Pan's function was to make the flocks fertile, and it is not uncommon for some Taureans to become fathers well into their vintage years. Dionysus, Bacchus and Pan were occasionally ill-tempered. If you think about Ireland (and *ire*) again, you will see how zodiacal affinities are born.

So what has all this to do with Immanuel Kant, Harry S. Truman and Bing Crosby? Immanuel Kant was the epitome of Taurean probity and fixity, especially fixity: In all his eighty years he never left his native Konigsberg, in Prussia. (Imagine someone never leaving Harrisburg, or Wichita, even a Taurean.) He was curious about far-off places, however; when he wasn't pondering imponderables—which he was most of the time—he was entertaining himself with travel brochures—or their 18th-century equivalent. Only a Taurean, like Kant, could write at the age of twenty-two, "I have already fixed upon the line which I am resolved to keep. I will enter into my course, and nothing will prevent me from pursuing it." And with the determination worthy of any Bull, he persisted and startled the world of thought thirty-five years later with his *Critique of Pure Reason*.

Harry Truman may have failed in business early in his career, but he didn't fail at the business of being president. He is now considered one of the better ones. He must have been instinctively aware of Taurean health rules: He kept his physical equipment strong and healthy with all those brisk morning constitutionals, leaving reporters much younger than himself who followed along panting for breath.

Bing Crosby exemplifies someone interested in things other than philosophy or becoming president with an insightful difference: Instead of writing about philosophy, he went ahead and lived his and, from all appearances, with enviable success. He may not have become president, but he was the kingpin of various enterprises that produced more income than the president's salary. And his job lasted a lot longer.

Although moving on to non-security-threatening new experiences or a more productive or progressive lifestyle could be to your distinct advantage, you can be as immovable as the Rock of Gibraltar when it comes to resisting change, adapting to shifting circumstances or accepting the suggestions or opinions of others. Getting some thrust and flexibility into your spirit could compare to attaching wings to the Rock of Gibraltar. Anything is possible, however; if the wings, especially of the spirit, are big and strong enough, metaphorically speaking, even the mightiest of rocks can be reduced to pebbles.

TAURUS BIRTHDAYS

Judgment of whether or not a birthday is propitious can be considered from two points of view: complementary or challenging. From the standpoint of personal progress and fulfillment, your destiny may flow more comfortably if your birthday is, or reduces to, an *outer* root number such as 2, 4, 6, 8 or 22 (master number). For career drive and achievement, your progress may be enhanced if your birthday is, or reduces to, an *inner* root number such as 1, 3, 5, 7 or 9; the *inner* root numbers are less comfortable, more obstructive for you to contend with, but they are potentially very conducive to outstanding success. The 11 (master number) would be variable, favorable for creative achievement, but it generally would require more understanding and resourcefulness in order to integrate with the meaning of Taurus.

Remember, if your birthday is two digits (excepting master numbers 11 and 22), be sure to read the *root* digit or number first. For example, if your birthday is 29, read the 2 (2 + 9 = 11, 1 + 1 reduces to 2) birthday profile first and then read the special profile for 29. If your birthday is 14, read the 5 (1 + 4 = 5) birthday profile first and then read the special profile for 14, and so on. If a description in a "special" section contradicts information in the "root" digit (root number) analysis, the "special" interpretation applies more specifically to you.

The first planet in parentheses following your birthday number is *your Sun-Sign ruler*; the second planet (or Uranus/Saturn for number 8) is *your birthday number planetary equivalent*. Subsidiary planetary influences (if any) are bracketed.

Each birthday profile includes celebrities who share the same birthday.

YOUR BIRTHDAY PROFILE

May the 1st (Venus, Sun)
(and root digit for April 28, May 10 and 19):

You will attract opportunities for leadership that are compatible with your admirable qualities of endurance, purpose and inner power. The willingness to make changes that are so necessary to even the most carefully measured success pattern may need cultivating. Otherwise you may achieve a degree of leadership, find the requirements reasonably compatible with your comfort needs and go no farther. Because the effort of spirit required interferes with your need for domestic ambiance or with your reluctance to make changes that unsettle the measure of security already attained, you can become self-satisfied in a pattern of complacent self-esteem and romantic or social popularity.

Your confidence enables you to overcome obstacles: You don't relish the stress involved, but you can't resist a challenge. You can set your goal as high as you like because you have the fortitude to reach it. Your home is an important domain to consider: Your tendency to want things your way may need to be controlled if personal relationships are to be harmonious.

Your earliest environment was probably one of family warmth, domestic felicity and shared responsibilities. You live by your version of the Golden Rule: "Whoever has the gold makes the Rules." You don't like other people telling you what to do or how to do it if it's not what you have in mind.

Judy Collins (singer), 1939

Jack Paar (TV host), 1918

Glenn Ford (actor), 1917

Special to April 28 (Venus, Sun [Moon/Uranus/Saturn]):

Your affectional and emotional tendencies are strong. Your exceptional talents qualify you for recognition. You would be excellent in music, sculpture or architecture, and your magnetism works to assure practical return for your efforts. In the business world, your executive abilities are beneficial if you overcome some inconsistencies; you may be erratic through touchiness or have a tendency to dissipate your energies. You are informative and genial on subjects that interest you and may have a phenomenal memory, the raconteur par excellence. Very capable regarding the business ramifications of artistic endeavors, you have a talent for promoting the efforts of others as well as your own. Whatever career path you follow, you can become completely immersed in it to the extent that it's no longer just a job. It can become your life.

Jay Leno (talk show host), 1950

Ann-Margret (actress), 1941

James Monroe (5th U.S. president), 1758

Special to May 10 (Venus, Sun):

You can benefit from directing your strong will into channels where it is a constructive force in the business or creative world. It will be to your advantage to become more relaxed regarding people and possessions. If you develop another kind of confidence, you will become less absorbed in the visible symbols of success and less dependent on them for security. Working well with others, you can assume the duties of leadership to good effect, as long as you're given free rein.

Work, any reasonable or respectable effort that turns a buck, is to you a means to an end, even an artistic goal. You won't hesitate to indulge in what some might view as crass commerciality if it paves the way to achieve or support a loftier aim.

Paul Hewson (Bono) (singer), 1960

Pat Summerall (sportscaster), 1930

Fred Astaire (dancer, actor), 1899

Special to May 19 (Venus, Sun [Sun/Pluto]):

Flexibility, curiosity and unusual awareness are the keys to realizing your potential. Your gifts are splendid in a creative or professional field, to which you bring subtle insights and the power to give them form in the world of reality. You have a strong sense of justice and can be a charismatic leader, whether in the arts, business or government. Your concepts are impressive and can cast a wide net. If the price of carrying them out, in personal satisfactions, is heavy, you have the endurance to persist to the end—and the rewards are great.

Not inclined to bluff your way through life, you're more apt to put your cards on the table, especially if you know you have a winning hand. With your ability to turn a challenge into an opportunity, projects and enterprises of broad scope will appeal to you.

Malcolm X (religious leader), 1925

Ho Chi Minh (Vietnamese leader), 1890

Dame Nellie Melba (soprano), 1861

May the 2nd (Venus, Moon)
(and root digit for April 29 and May 20;
May 11 is a master number, see end of chapter):

Your cup can "runneth over" where domestic happiness is concerned. The conditions that prevail as you begin to make your way in the world are most compatible with your capability for blending the needs of all in your circle. If you can remember to be the fulcrum with passive subtlety, never insistent or domineering, you can always avoid personality conflicts that bring out your wayward moods and touchy intransigence. By thus blending your Venusian congeniality and patience with others' foibles, the principles will rebound in your favor and bring you the popularity and affection you thrive on.

You can entertain some pretty unrealistic notions about love and sentiment; if you allow yourself to indulge in emotionalism and extreme sensitivity, you will create an atmosphere where only pettiness can thrive. You may have felt isolated as a child—materially secure but emotionally unsettled and reclusive. On the job or in the career milieu, you instinctively tune into public trends, tastes and issues and can capitalize on your distinctive skills and personal appeal.

You can be self-absorbed and at times very stubborn about real or imagined slights. However, at your best, you will see that your mate has any creature comfort desired that is within your power to provide. Loyalty and a desire for luxury and prominence are important to you; you should prosper financially. You may not be emotionally absorbed with home, family or property, like Cancer; it's just the most convenient and comfortable place to celebrate your self-satisfaction and inertia when you're in the mood to relax.

Bing Crosby (singer, actor), 1904

Dr. Benjamin Spock (pediatrician, author), 1903

Baron Manfred von Richthoven (German World War I aviator), 1892

Special to April 29 (Venus, Moon [Pluto]):

Your impressive abilities, combined with Taurean practicality, equip you for popularity and success, which contribute nicely to the achievement of your determined ambitions. You will profit by resolving differences as they come up in life; holding them in only builds up inner pressure for your tendency to be extreme in your reactions. You can become too absorbed in your needs and rather grumpy and withdrawn to the detriment of relationship harmony.

Fast moving, with your far-reaching influence, and not always inclined to live strictly by the rules, you're likely to roam far and wide in the process of fulfilling your destiny. If and when troubles block your progress, you're resourceful and know how to bounce back and rebuild your fortunes. Some of your success in life can be attributed to your being "streetwise" as much as to your formal education or training, which may have been of the hit-and-miss variety.

Rod McKuen (poet, singer), 1938

Emperor Hirohito (Emperor of Japan during World War II), 1901

Duke Ellington (composer, orchestra leader), 1899

Special to May 20 (Venus, Moon):

Talented, and especially practical, you have insights into the unseen laws behind experience. You have a strong sense of self-importance and would not be content in a subordinate position. You are more acquisitive and possessive than may be good for you, and your Taurean resistance to change can stand in the way of your progress. If you learn to adapt and flow with the cosmic plan, success is assured.

With your easygoing personality, you can charm the birds out of the trees or will convince people that you could if they're thinking about hiring you for a responsible position or venture. At times hesitant, you may seem diffusive, but you're really just thinking carefully about what you're going to do or say. Whether it's with the public or just one other person, you're an expert at sensing what is needed and then in your quiet, reassuring way, providing it.

Cher (singer), 1946

James Stewart (actor), 1908

Dolly Madison (First Lady), 1768

May the 3rd (Venus)
(and root digit for April 21, April 30, May 12 and May 21):

Since you are not naturally as flexible and yielding as might be required by circumstances as you begin to make your way in the world, your other Taurean traits can be a balancing asset. Magnetic and charming, a pattern of beauty and/or fluent social expression can make your life artistically rewarding whether in the business or domestic milieu. You are creative and diplomatic. Your background probably included an element of protection or affluence; if not, your practical nature sensed at an early age the value of aiming your sights on rising above humble beginnings.

Whether through necessity or ambition, you'll probably begin working or establishing your career direction early in life. In any case, it will be to your advantage to be well educated or skilled by the time you are in your early thirties, because discipline and your need to express freely do not blend well. With your vivid imagination, combined with your practical nature, you can turn creative pursuits into impressive successes. Your gifts function well in the applied arts or any field where return is more consistently commensurate with effort.

When an issue is at stake, your toughness comes to the fore to strengthen your chance for victory. Your strong sense of irony enhances your flair for personal drama and candid expression. You are emotionally intense and should avoid making personal decisions when under duress. You may feel entirely different a short while later and wonder what you were so upset about; you wouldn't want to be held to a decision made under such conditions. As a consequence, your romantic liaisons may be many, with a marriage or two or a separation along the way.

James Brown (singer), 1928

Sugar Ray Robinson (boxer), 1920

Golda Meir (former Premier of Israel), 1898

Special to April 21 (Venus, Mars [Moon/Sun]):

You combine your Taurean practicality and perseverance with the gifts of expression and quick perception. You function best in a milieu where activity is continuous and assured but where the application is varied and lively. Although marriage can be a successful venture, relationships that aren't too confining may be more satisfactory for you. Your youthful experiences stimulated mental subjectivity as you matured; the result of this process can warp relationships if feelings are allowed to dominate your thinking.

With a little bit of luck, you can build a career, brick by brick, on a solid foundation, and your bank account, dollar by dollar, until there's a sizable heap of money. On your upward-bound trajectory, your versatile entrepreneurial instincts enable you to extend the boundaries of any good fortune that comes your way. Patience, good humor (with an earthy slant) and genuine appreciation for life's benefits are among your creditable attributes.

Tony Danza (actor), 1951

Elizabeth II (queen of England), 1926

Anthony Quinn (actor), 1916

Special to April 30 (Venus, Mars):

You have the courage of your convictions and like to exercise authority, but you may not be willing to accept the responsibilities that go with it. You also like to manage and are well equipped for it. But don't just depend on your winsome ways. Be sure to set an example of good, hard work for subordinates; your Taurean nature isn't sympathetic to too much exertion. Your growing-up period was mentally reclusive and subjective. Your thoughtful conclusions can be an asset in teaching or literary pursuits.

Whether you're taking great pains in the care of elegant possessions, expressing a talent or demonstrating your flair for the pleasures of the table, you're always ready with convincing, not to mention forceful, arguments to back up your tastes and opinions on any topics that interest you. And, when not in your sociable mood, some of them might be unpublishable.

Willie Nelson (singer), 1933

Alice B. Toklas (writer), 1877

Franz Lehar (composer), 1870

Special to May 12 (Venus [Sun/Moon]):

You are happiest with a house and land. Exceptionally artistic and versatile, your Taurean steadiness will help you to center on a specific activity and to achieve notable results. You are expressive, sensible, genuinely aware and concerned with universal values as well as satisfying mass tastes and needs. Beauty and fulfillment, whether intangible or material, and the ability to express or provide it, are the keynotes of your pattern.

More articulate than the typical Taurean, a droll sense of humor enlivens your comments or conversation. An expert at common-sense diplomacy, you're ready to shake up tradition-bound institutions to pave the way to a brighter, more secure future. Studies and education interest you, especially the kind that pay off in one way or another, such as in money or prestige (preferably both). Bold and adventurous, you're able to carve a particular niche for yourself and to stick to it, finding in your work as much enjoyment as in a hobby.

George Carlin (comedian), 1937

Yogi Berra (baseball player and coach), 1925

Florence Nightingale (founder of modern nursing), 1820

Special to May 21 (Venus, Mercury [Moon/Sun]):

You're an effective combination of artistic, intellectual and interpretive abilities. Exceptionally articulate, not to say passionate, about the beauty you find in nature or various areas of creative achievement, you're able to arouse similar feelings of appreciation or inspiration in work associates or the public. You're excellent at spreading the word about the enjoyment to be derived from a knowledge and familiarity with the great literature, music, art and architecture of the present and past. Personable and popular, you can talk people into almost anything.

Well qualified for a job in government, industrial design, education, writing and publishing or the business world, you are capable of mounting a crusade against plans or projects that you judge to be substandard, impractical or in poor taste, and you can be quite vocal and convincing in your opposition. Even your critics might have to grudgingly admit that you are well informed, forthright, determined and, whether right or wrong, honest in your opinions. You like to win and feel that if you work hard and do things right, the truth prevails. Marriage and affectional ties should be rewarding.

Raymond Burr (actor), 1917

Harold Robbins (novelist), 1916

Robert Montgomery (actor), 1904

May the 4th (Venus, Saturn)
(and root digit for May 13;
April 22 is a master number, see end of chapter):

This is a most congenial birthday for the most basic of the earth signs. You will find association with hardworking, serious, responsible coworkers or companions very compatible with your nature. Repetitive patterns, efficiency and depth will be required of you, and you can deliver in full measure. Once your course is set, you stick with it. You might deviate slightly, but any alteration would be about as perceptible as a change in the House of Lords. The danger is that you can become bogged down in a rut of details; you need to be certain that projects you become involved in are worthy of the endless attention you are willing to bestow on them. Try to see beyond your perseverance and concentration to be sure that you are not missing anything.

Your goals will be very important because you will go to any length to achieve what you want. The more difficult it is and the longer it takes, the more determined you will be in your efforts. This works identically if you lack inspiration: Your measure of devotion to a cramped outlook is equally impressive, your negative attitude difficult to change. You will profit by choosing an objective born of the spirit—one worthy of your endless persistence.

Your growing-up period was probably unsettled, without clear purpose and direction. You may have chosen, or been the pawn of, a disconnected pattern out of desperation or indifference, just to satisfy your need to seek a semblance of substance and faith in the future. In marriage and other key relationships, your intentions are good, but your high expectations may be a barrier to happiness or beyond your partner's ability to live up to your idealistic standards.

> George F. Will (newspaper columnist), 1941
> Audrey Hepburn (actress), 1929
> Horace Mann (educator), 1796

Special to May 13 (Venus, Saturn [Sun/Venus]):
Your inflexibility and willfulness can undermine the advantages of good mental equipment. Willing to share the fruits of success, which you usually achieve, you are not averse to hard work, especially if it includes a sense of mission, but you should avoid becoming obsessed with the trappings of prestige and prosperity. The quirk of restlessness behind your devotion to duty or a cause can provoke displays of temperament. If you go to extremes in your feelings of compassion for the downtrodden, you could inadvertently cause more harm than good.

You are a natural for the real estate or merchandising field, and your creative or inspirational flair (while it may not seem substantial enough to you as a source of support) can prompt a rewarding avocation. With your gift for organization, you can stick to a line of endeavor or proceed toward a goal with tanklike inevitability, especially if the reward is status and/or a loyal following. And you wouldn't be bothered if it also didn't include money or other tangible rewards that translate into material freedom. Meanwhile, remember, all work and no play . . .

Stevie Wonder (singer), 1950

Joe Louis (boxer), 1914

Daphne Du Maurier (novelist), 1907

May the 5th (Venus, Mars)
(and root digit for April 23 and May 14):

You are blessed with a personal magnetism that ensures an enduring popularity and romantic appeal. The circumstances of your productive years require a more gregarious approach to life; fortunately, your fervent disposition combined with your natural earthy appeal add up to an irresistible force. You are very congenial—and more versatile, articulate and adventuresome in spirit than the typical Taurean. Your natural disinclination to physical change and initiative, in conflict with the compulsive need to blaze new trails, combines to add a peppery quality to your nature. You are that Bull restlessly pawing the earth.

A domestic base is important but only on your terms. You are strongly ambitious for material success; it provides the freedom so essential to you. However young or old you are, once you tasted the good life, you saw the future. It did not include poverty.

Articulate and productive, the episodic pattern of artistic or theatrical pursuits appeals to you. Indulgence in diversions will be kept in check by your practical nature. You decided early in life that you "wanted to be somebody," or circumstances nudged you into a pattern that called for personal assertiveness and fortitude. You can range far and wide in pursuit of your goals, among which is a happy marriage and family life.

Tammy Wynette (singer), 1942

Tyrone Power (actor), 1913

Karl Marx (philosopher), 1818

Special to April 23 (Venus, Mars [Moon/Venus]):

Very practical, your intuition and insights can be helpful to those in need of health advice and care. You are confident and independent, with an instinct for sensing inner needs and getting along with a variety of people. With just a little bit of luck, you'll have opportunities to move mountains and find pots of gold at the ends of rainbows.

Your business or professional success and wide public recognition are likely to stem from your flair for originality and/or the depth of your insights into the human condition. As a leader, teacher or manager, you leave your distinctive creative imprint on your endeavors. There can be a note of irony, however, in the record of your achievements. Home and family are important to you; you need someone to love and with whom you can share your feelings and environment. Your relationship pattern, though, is likely to be episodic.

Shirley Temple Black (actress), 1928

James Buchanan (15th U.S. president), 1791

William Shakespeare (dramatist, poet), 1564

Special to May 14 (Venus, Mars [Sun/Saturn]):
Behind your restiveness and versatility, you combine the need for patient application with the desire for ego satisfaction. You can become the seeker on the sensual plane through physical restlessness, or you will seek to achieve a goal through a restless, questing spirit. Thoughtful, perhaps profound, your independence works better in a profession than in business.

You gradually realized as you grew up that you weren't going to settle for a nondescript role in the workforce, sensing early the power that accrues to those who find a showcase for their distinctive abilities. A long-distance runner rather than a sprinter, you probably laid the groundwork for your career or work activities before you finished your schooling, and you may have chosen courses that you thought would come in handy on the job. You also knew or learned early that the way to win your place in the Sun was through special or superior skills, industry and dependability. You're not especially gregarious socially, perhaps because you don't always have the time or energy. If there's something to be gained, though, you thoroughly enjoy mixing business with pleasure.

George Lucas (film director), 1944

Bobby Darin (actor, singer), 1936

G. D. Fahrenheit (physicist), 1686

May the 6th (Venus, Jupiter)
(and root digit for April 24 and May 15):
You will find shared experiences, as well as circumstances that call out all your attributes of diplomacy, willingness and/or necessity to compromise and to accept the responsibilities for others' welfare or their guidance, as your main adventures in life. Whether in the domestic milieu or at the corporate level, the give and take of relationships will be a decisive ingredient determining success or failure in your life pattern. At your best, you are well adapted to marriage and may sense a strong lack of fulfillment if you haven't

tied the knot. If you haven't, your caution and desire to experiment and procrastinate in search of an ideal may always prevent it. If you have, and things go wrong, you'll probably resist divorce as long as you can, even if disillusioned. You don't like to admit defeat but may eventually resign yourself to it.

Having some highly idealistic notions about unions, you can be restless with the realities that prevail in relationships, but you have the innate patience to deal with them. Be sure that you base your judgments and expectations on life as it is, not as you wish it were. Taurean women born on this date are very steadying influences for their mates. As Taurus is a feminine sign, however, men with this birthday aren't as securely anchored. In any case, early conditions that may have made you disillusioned and sensitive as a child should not be permitted to hamper your desire for happiness through union in your adult years.

Though usually courteous, you do not shrink from controversy, some of which can be self-created. Your juxtaposition of diverse elements in relationships can create a new vocabulary in the creative realm. In business, politics or the arts, you know how to convincingly convey your ideology. Whether or not one yourself, you have a flair for mixing with celebrities. You like to get involved in group and/or public activities. Your *joie de vivre* is great for living life to the hilt, but it is a disadvantage if it spills over into the business realm, where a cavalier attitude can clash with the bottom line. You may rely too much on the old saying, "Whom you know is as important as what you know," especially if "what you know" means getting down to the nitty-gritty financial issues to which you may be inclined to give short shrift.

   Willie Mays (baseball), 1931

   Orson Welles (actor, director), 1915

   Rudolph Valentino (actor), 1895

Special to April 24 (Venus, Jupiter [Moon/Saturn]):
Knowledge is the key to your development and to forming your sense of values. You can be too impressed by the visible trappings of status. If your confidence isn't based on more solid virtues, you are vulnerable to disappointments, especially in relationships. Sensitive to criticism, you tend to magnify your personal reactions to everything, especially when annoyed, which can bring out your disagreeable side. Personally attuned to the law of the survival of the fittest, your willingness to work hard, especially if it's directed toward improvements and progress, contributes to your success.

Along with your flair for planning, administration and/or seeking the spotlight, you're a real people person and can be very sensitive to the feelings and needs of others. You have plenty of patience for any intricacies or complexities that the creative process might entail. Whatever you do, whether small- or large-scaled, can attract appropriate popularity as well as respect. At your best, your determination to become someone to be reckoned with is tempered by a gentle spirit.

Barbra Streisand (singer, actress, director), 1942

Shirley MacLaine (actress), 1934

Anthony Trollope (novelist), 1815

Special to May 15 (Venus, Jupiter [Sun/Mars]):

Capable of strict self-discipline, you can be annoyed and restless because material advantages so dear to your Taurean nature have to be earned through persistent effort. Reacting to the vicissitudes encountered in finding your way, you might knock around a bit before settling into a productive groove. You're not happy or contented until you live in attractive surroundings. Partnerships could provide some of the advantages and gratification you seek, but the price may be unsettling. You thrive best in a profession; your business sense is good, but your taste for responsibilities is limited. Nevertheless, with your willingness to pay your own way to support loftier ambitions, your birthday is ringed with dollar signs.

You are not limited, however, to one dimension in the creative realm; beauty in all forms gets your adrenaline going. Whether artist, musician or writer, your taut concentration and coiled energy, combined with an ingratiating touch, make you or your output popular with the public. Similarly, when you speak, it's usually because you have something worthwhile to say; your low-key, cultivated manner and resonant voice draw listeners in more readily and deeply.

George Brett (baseball player), 1953

Joseph Cotton (actor), 1905

Katherine Anne Porter (writer), 1890

May the 7th (Venus, Mercury)
(and root digit for April 25 and May 16):

You will learn valuable lessons from experience; but since you are not naturally gregarious and instinctively rather resistant to novelty and change, the process may be slow. You tend to follow the path of least resistance. An awakening to realizations about your life's purpose could be delayed. On the other hand, with conscious effort and awareness of your passive acceptance of whatever comes your way, you can profit earlier rather than later from your experiences. This more rewarding approach would enable you to weave the valuable results into the tapestry of your life during your formative period (between your early twenties and thirty) when it would be more timely and useful.

For you to give concrete form to the values that Taurus exemplifies is more difficult because the basically mental nature of your particular abilities doesn't blend easily with your down-to-earth orientation to life. The communicated emotion, the written word, the idea imparted to others in a useful way, always as a result of your considered judgment, are the most congenial areas in which you can function. You'll thoughtfully weigh all the pros and cons of a situation before acting, or will seem to, but there is a difference between concentration and unfocused musings.

As life unfolds, you have plenty on your mind, but you don't give away your inner thoughts by your actions. Mercury, the planet of mental facility, complements your sign, as does Saturn, planet of conscientious application. If you have expressive or creative gifts, you have the endless patience to go to dogmatic lengths with your inspirations and theories. Your early fluency and sociable or scattered upbringing may have left you unprepared for the deep mental probing required to fulfill your destiny in a meaningful way. Nevertheless, you're an expert at the waiting game, and, through shrewd maneuvering and your congenial persuasiveness, you can attain whatever goal you set your sights on.

Eva Perón (political leader), 1908

Gary Cooper (actor), 1901

Tchaikovsky (composer), 1840

Special to April 25 (Venus, Mercury [Moon/Mars]):

Your Taurean need to establish security may not be satisfied as soon as you would like. You have impressive abilities for creative pursuits that flourish best within a mental framework. Ambitious for status and comfort for all in your milieu, concentrated effort may be required to make your desires a reality. With your independent spirit and eye on the fast track, though, focused effort may not be easy for you to sustain.

You are a firm believer in the work ethic, however, and are determined to get everything that's coming to you. You're willing to start at the bottom, but you won't stay long in a poorly paid or dead-end job if it's at all possible to get a better one. You can do equally well on your own or working for an employer, especially if fringe benefits are included. But if it doesn't look as if the direction you are headed in is leading anywhere, you'll soon get that itch to switch and move on to greener pastures.

Al Pacino (actor), 1940

Ella Fitzgerald (singer), 1918

Edward R. Murrow (news commentator), 1908

Special to May 16 (Venus, Mercury [Sun/Jupiter]):
You profit from gearing your actions to your reservoir of experience. You learn more from observation than from deliberate study. Rather self-oriented, you depend on the encouragement and approval of others. You are inspired, dramatic and perhaps flamboyant, but you can make the most secure progress by subjecting all matters to careful mental analysis. Lucky financially and conscious of appearances and surroundings, your attitude is good-naturedly competitive. With your ability to take setbacks in stride, you're not likely to stir up animosity in pursuit of success. If you are in the arts, a sideline business is a good outlet for your reasoning powers.

Your warm friendliness comes across in a natural loyalty-inspiring manner, assuring you long-lasting success. Ordinarily congenial, you can bristle when your moral sense is offended. However, anger is so unlike you that, when aroused, it's likely to catch the target of your irritation off guard. If you develop appropriate skills, your perceptive earthbound instincts are practically a guarantee that you have a far-better-than-average chance to achieve whatever goal you choose to accomplish. If marriage is one of them, however, that could take considerably more effort, patience and understanding.

Janet Jackson (singer), 1966

Liberace (entertainer), 1919

Henry Fonda (actor), 1905

May the 8th (Venus, Uranus/Saturn)
(and root digit for April 26 and May 17):
Yours is the most congenial and possibly the most satisfying birthday of the Taurus born. Enterprise, administration, promotion—all along big lines—produce the money and bountiful security you find so rewarding. You will gravitate toward the atmosphere of big business, corporations, public relations, fame and so on, but turning circumstances to personal advantage will require an expansive outlook, vision and the willingness to make important

changes, not your strongest trait. If a woman, you are either very ambitious or will marry into success. In any event, the misuse of these powerful traits is extravagance. The money still flows—but out faster than in.

You agree wholeheartedly with Emerson, who said, "Money, which represents the prose of life, and which is hardly spoken of in parlors without an apology, is, in its effects and laws, as beautiful as roses." Another of his observations will keep everything in perspective: "Riches well got and well used are a great blessing." Enough said. The rest is up to you. You probably had an early struggle or a period of patient application as training for the time between your early twenties and early thirties when you begin to make your way in the world. Its practical lessons were not lost on you.

Whether or not you flourish in the higher echelons of business, government, academia, the arts or even religion, your ability to get your message across can make you very influential. When money talks, you're ready to listen. Fringe benefits of your success enable you to live life in the limousine lane. In your effort to raise public consciousness and to establish standards for progress and improvement, your influence and effectiveness touch life's movers and shakers as well as the masses.

Don Rickles (comedian), 1926

Roberto Rossellini (film director), 1906

Harry S. Truman (33rd U.S. president), 1884

Special to April 26 (Venus, Uranus/Saturn [Moon/Jupiter]):
Strict mental training should have been stressed in your early years, but the conditions prevailing then were more conducive to expression of gifts than disciplining them. You don't suffer opposition gladly, lacking the patience for argument. You are very interested in success, however, and have a lot of patience for that. Home, domestic ambiance and relationships in general are very important to you, and you will focus your efforts constructively in order to fulfill your objectives.

You are usually sociable and congenial. If there's one thing that's guaranteed to put a frown on your face, it's money coming in at a slow trickle. But that's not likely to happen or could be a rare occurrence for you. With your talent for reducing things to their essentials, the megadeal with its appropriate remunerative return is grist for your mill. A go-getter in whatever field you choose to pursue your goals, your attention never strays far from the big picture. However, you can be a loser in the personal and/or family sacrifices you make to get to the top.

Carol Burnett (comedienne), 1933

Anita Loos (writer), 1893

Eugene Delacroix (artist), 1798

Special to May 17 (Venus, Uranus/Saturn [Sun/Mercury]):
Upward bound and entrepreneurial, you might study the *Financial Times* as if
it were scripture. Good at organization and finance, you can satisfy your
Taurean need for money but may be inclined to imprudent extravagance.
Positions of authority and the big picture should be your constant aim.
Whether or not in a creative field, you aren't inclined to accept the veracity of
things unseen; your Taurean nature can be too pragmatic and skeptical for
that; you're only satisfied with concrete, visible results.

In the game of life, money can be a terrific way for you to keep score. Be
careful of what you want; you'll probably get it. With your thoughts fixed on
using your brains to get ahead, you're likely to come out a winner in the
success and financial sweepstakes. Love and family life are important to you
and should provide happiness.

Sugar Ray Leonard (boxer), 1956

Birgit Nilsson (soprano), 1923

Eric Satie (composer), 1866

May the 9th (Venus, Pluto)
(and root digit for April 27 and May 18):
During your childhood or adolescence, which was probably unsettled or in
some way disruptive, it may have been difficult to plant your feet firmly on
the ground or to feel a sense of security or continuity. This could have denied
you one of your sources of power when you begin to make your way in the
world. As you try to get your bearings, you may be irked by the many adjustments necessary to your progress. Though the world is your stage, you are
personal and subjective and bring the qualities of emotional intensity and creative ability to your efforts to get ahead, but whether or not it works to your
advantage will depend on how you apply your tremendous willpower.

If it is used to sustain you in periods of stress and change, when you can
feel decentralized and isolated, it will add strength, courage and unflappable
confidence to your spirit—valuable ingredients for your efforts to succeed. In
this context, problems to you become opportunities in work clothes. On
the other hand, if your willpower is used negatively, to dogmatically resist the
changes you must make, you will spend your energies in disappointment and

emotional excess. This birthday and 11 are the least compatible with Taurean qualities. The role you fill best is so comprehensive, nonpersonal and episodic that you can feel like the square peg in the round hole until you come to terms with the broad-based requirements necessary to achieve your unique potential.

The best outlets for you are along lines requiring industry, scientific or creative expression, universal application, sympathetic service and completion of whatever task you choose. As a Taurus woman with this birthday, you will either find yourself in a career with the foregoing requirements or married to a partner whose far-flung, widespread responsibilities could make the union difficult to hold together.

Tony Gwynn (baseball player), 1960
Billy Joel (singer), 1949
Mike Wallace (TV journalist), 1915

Special to April 27 (Venus, Pluto [Moon/Mercury]):
Ardent and affectionate, you need home and a haven but are apt to be absent-minded regarding your part of the bargain. You might be off somewhere fulfilling the demands of leadership, perhaps neglecting or taking for granted your mate or lover. Your sins are more those of omission. Happiest in a profession, especially one that requires intellectual aptitude, activities geared only to making money would depress you. You probably had a good education, which, combined with the school of experience, taught you much about the practical necessities and the rewards of discipline as you grew up.

You are a firm believer in freedom of speech and the right of others to be heard. Intellectual prowess, moral courage and broad-minded tolerance are among your estimable traits, which make you popular with people in all walks of life. Conversely, what you would be intolerant about are barriers to the free flow of ideas. Vigorous, direct, as well as scholarly in your judgments, you embody the principle of fairness.

Sandy Dennis (actress), 1937
Ulysses S. Grant (18th U.S. president), 1822
Samuel F. B. Morse (artist, inventor), 1791

Special to May 18 (Venus, Pluto [Sun/Uranus/Saturn]):
Overemphasis of your Taurean dependence on material values can get you into troubled waters. If you form unions for reasons of expediency, obstacles will thwart your attempts to dominate. If your only motive is gain,

restlessness and uncertainty could be a source of difficulties in your career endeavors. Your growing-up period was active and changeful, instilling in you a taste for variety and freedom. You will find your contentment in seeking fulfillment through the meanings behind the veil of appearances.

In the real world, however, what really matters is generally money, and you're likely to wind up with your share—perhaps lots more. So whether yours is a tempestuous story of rags to riches or smooth-flowing efforts to reach a pinnacle of success, you have the requisite inborn potential to rise considerably above average. And in the process, you can attain your share of public recognition and/or fame in proportion to, or appropriate to, whatever you've accomplished.

John Paul II (pope), 1920

Perry Como (singer), 1913

Frank Capra (director), 1897

May the 11th Venus, Neptune [Moon/Sun])
(master number):

Your birthday is concerned with ideals, mysticism and selflessness, not easy requirements to blend with your instinct for practicality. You can be rigid and extreme if you insist on gratifying only the personal side of your life. Your psychic insights can get lost in the density of your makeup as you try to translate them into commonplace realities.

Nevertheless, they come in handy in even the most ordinary job or task. If you aim for outstanding achievement, your power is one of broad-based illumination and humanitarian purpose rather than the narrow path of personal gain and freedom from responsibility.

One way to realize your unusual potential is to enhance the emotional sustenance, spiritual enlightenment and general well-being of others. However wide your interests, they are most rewarding when sympathetic and idealistic; otherwise you can invite bewilderment or confusion. You are a channel for unique revelation; unless you release these potent gifts in a way that improves or edifies the lives of others, at whatever level, you can become an eccentric frustrated misfit.

The extent of your perception, acceptance and understanding of forces unseen will determine the use or misuse of your special gifts and/or mission in life. Tone down Taurean skepticism regarding anything that can't be seen, touched or heard. Indulgence in eccentric or bizarre activities or behavior reflects your penchant to stand out from the crowd; it might be personally titillating but tends to trivialize your exceptional potential. You'll probably cast around a bit before you find your true avenue of expression and/or decide which skills to develop to the highest level of accomplishment. While you can be a considerate friend, love relationships can be more intense or erratic than permanent, like a flame that burns brightly but briefly.

Mort Sahl (comedian), 1927

Martha Graham (dancer, choreographer), 1894

Irving Berlin (composer), 1888

(Note: This master number implies a variable alternative response influenced by the strength or passivity of Neptune in your horoscope. If you don't feel you are responding to the distinctive vibratory power of 11, you are instead expressing the more conventional qualities of 2, which you should read.)

April the 22nd (Venus, Uranus [Saturn/Moon])
(master number):

The broad vision of the 22 birthday can be transformed into an impressive mastery of the potential inherent in concrete things. Whether in the arts, business or an administrative capacity, your stoicism and down-to-earth resourcefulness are at the disposal of a restless spirit. And whether it simplifies a mundane task or a creative inspiration, your remarkable intuition enables you to envision farsighted improvement or refinement expressed in practical terms. It's your challenge to make the products and benefits of planet Earth more useful, accessible or uplifting to the greatest number of its inhabitants.

More high-strung than typical members of your sign, you're likely to view life through an unconventional lens. When mishandled or misused, the dynamic universal force flowing through you for expression can convert Taurean patience into irrational won't-power. Beware that the resulting bottled-up anxiety doesn't find an unfortunate outlet in the projection of frustrations, with those nearest and dearest to you perhaps the most convenient targets.

If you wrestle with the big problems of mankind, you'll bring the ones in your own backyard down to size. Steer clear of ill-advised shortcuts and doubtful ethics in business or any other sphere of activity. Possibly more fluent, visionary and expressive than other birthdays in this sign, you add the ultimate dimension of practicality to highly original creative ventures. At your best, your unorthodox spirit will find a laudable, and possibly memorable, outlet as your life unfolds, probably in your job, a distinctive career direction or in community activities. You learned the meaning of discipline as you grew up, the necessity for concentration and application, which strengthened your self-reliance and chance for success in nonconformist relationship fulfillment.

Jack Nicholson (actor), 1937

Nicolai Lenin (communist leader), 1870

Immanuel Kant (philosopher), 1724

(Note: This master number implies a variable alternative response influenced by the strength or passivity of the planet Uranus in your horoscope. If you don't think you are responding to the distinctive vibratory power of 22, you are instead expressing the more conventional qualities of 4, which you should read.)

CHAPTER 3

GEMINI

May 22–June 21

RULER: **MERCURY** NUMBER: **7** ELEMENT: **AIR** SYMBOL: **THE TWINS**

"To be merry best becomes you; for out of question,
you were born in a merry hour."
—*Much Ado about Nothing,* Shakespeare

- Do you open a book from the back to find out how it ends and then flip through to the front to find out what the fabulous ending was all about?
- Do you see yourself as you really are? Or do you spend your life living your image, keeping your real self under wraps?
- Do you give a direct answer to a question? Or do you say, "Let me think about it" or reply with a quip?
- Do you keep reinventing yourself, sometimes by the hour, since the possibilities are so numerous?
- Do you see yourself as you wish you were and then have to live with yourself as others see you?
- Does the question "Did you get the car washed?" turn into an epic tragedy? Does anyone really want to know about the car . . . or if you have the ability to get things done . . . or whatever?
- Do you hate to be pinned down? (To you it's the same as being impaled, like a butterfly on display.)
- Do you think that marriage is like a dull meal, with the dessert first?
- Do you like a fresh shoulder to cry on because you have a passion for novelty?

If the answer to all the foregoing questions is "yes" and "no," you are responding in typical Gemini fashion. Being the masters of small talk, you relish question-and-answer openers, crossword puzzles, charades, any and all mental or verbal gymnastics and gossip. You are lost without newspapers, magazines and the Internet. Even almanacs and encyclopedias can be fun for you to browse through. You probably have a collection of "clippings" or reminders about one thing or another yellowing and gathering dust in a closet or drawer somewhere. Your favorite television or radio programs are "talk" shows, quizzes, newscasts and interviews with scintillating celebrities.

To those who assume that truth is revealed only in ponderous garb, your gabbiness might be considered that of a featherbrained lightweight—an unfair appraisal. The assumption that something of great length, size or duration is *ipso facto* more significant than something brief, witty and to the point is a popular misconception. With your irreverent sense of humor, you could probably find something funny in the *Egyptian Book of The Dead*. But just because you are witty, effervescent, creative and adaptable to almost any situation, you may irritate dull-witted types with whom you must rub shoulders in the world of serious affairs.

The drones of the office, at the coffee break, will view you with a jaundiced eye. They harbor little grudges about your doing half as much work as they do and big jealousies because you are the center of attention with your impudent, sometimes hilarious, parodies about the boss. Actually, you may be doing more work in less time, and you just aren't as overawed by authority figures. Not sympathetic to the pattern of routine and grim monotony necessary in building a solid niche in the world of work, you deflate the boss for two reasons: It's amusing to the lower echelons, and it bolsters your own ego to poke fun at attributes you may lack.

On the other hand, colleagues tend to underestimate the importance of your trenchant contribution to the life experience, to dismiss you as inconsequential and, at best, replaceable. So what's wrong with being entertaining? It is just as human as being solemn, and it certainly appeals to a wider audience. The ability to inject color, badinage and satire into the pattern of everyday living is a great gift: The truth that can be communicated with levity can be as effective as through the hollow ring of solemnity. As an old English proverb has it: "Many a true word is spoken in jest." The enduring popularity of Oscar Wilde's plays and epigrams is proof of that.

Your orientation to life, with your brilliant mental equipment, is restless, alert and inquisitive. You can give the effect of "six senses in search of an experience." Your ruling planet, Mercury, the principle of *conscious* perceptions, is the most pivotal in the zodiac. For instance, your planet is the esoteric ruler of Aries, the first sign of twelve; when the function of your sign is allied with the qualities and initiative of Aries, the results can be of a magnitude to produce genius. Aries-born Arturo Toscanini was an outstanding example of this. The Moon, ruling the emotional sign Cancer, is the principle of *instinctive* perceptions. The functions of these two facets of consciousness are sharply differentiated. Mercury, ruling Gemini, is the one you will need to understand because it explains you.

The crescent of soul consciousness above the circle of divine spirit, combined over the cross of matter (earth life), is your planetary ruler. Mercury is thus the instrument of your spirit-mental equipment. It registers sense impressions just as the Moon does; but instead of reacting instinctively, Mercury submits the impressions gathered by experience to the memory bank of knowledge stored within your brain. It then decides its value and usefulness in terms of whatever frame of reference you have fostered and accumulated—or from the standpoint of reincarnation, brought over from past lives. If this explanation sounds complicated, it is also necessary, for it illustrates an important point to be made regarding Gemini: In becoming mesmerized by the exhilarating *act* of thinking and verbalizing, your life can become filled with fascinating *process* and empty of *substance*, much like a beautiful machine whirring away but not attached to anything. "I think; therefore I am" is your cry, and it is echoed by members of Mensa and other high-IQ types. In your partly justifiable enthusiasm, you forget that Aries-born Descartes thought *about* something! Of all the signs, you will profit most by holding on to moral convictions, by cultivating bedrock principles. Failing that, the frothy pleasures of the social milieu, the tissue that binds life together, can beguile you more than the substance of life itself.

Because brevity is "the soul of wit," it does not follow that it precludes depth or significant accomplishment. Ralph Waldo Emerson and Frank Lloyd Wright were brilliant examples of your sign. Emerson found the shorter essay form a more comfortable one through which to express his timeless thoughts. Are *your* concepts deep, linked firmly to an anchor of absolutes and stability? Or are they fastened to a cork, bobbing along on the surface at the mercy of the currents? Do you become resentful and increasingly restless when something depresses you? If so, you miss the value and purpose of difficult times. Life is trying to tell you something, but your instinctive reaction is to find a willing ear for your woes. Gemini, a talker, is likely to think that talking about them is the same as thinking about them. You pass the buck but learn, to your dismay, that it keeps coming around, growing more insistent with each return visit.

You may ease into little self-deceptions like pouring out your problems to any sympathetic stranger willing to listen; typically likable and sociable, you have little trouble finding one. The reason? Your friends have already heard all of them as well as all your rationales (a euphemism for excuses) for failing to come to terms with life's dilemmas. You've begun to sound like a broken record; your friends are still sympathetic but understandably apathetic—and maybe a little impatient.

You may have trouble learning lessons from your experiences; your tune is familiar to your circle, so you frequently resolve the issue by changing people instead of changing your attitude toward your problems. You may eventually run out of people, but you will find that problems aren't so accommodating. They just don't seem to go away when you pretend they aren't there. It's easier for you to change practically anything—your mate, job, locale—but not yourself. In truth, the typical Gemini doesn't have a lot of patience with deep self-analysis. You might wonder why people insist on wanting to know themselves so thoroughly . . . when it's hard enough to know what to wear.

You can get an inferiority complex from comparisons, possibly very inaccurate ones. You see the tiny visible part of the iceberg, and you don't dwell much on the bulk beneath the surface. You can identify with part of a popular cultural symbol, and you feel hopelessly inadequate through your failure to include *all* the package in your appraisal. The tragic glitter that surrounded Judy Garland and Marilyn Monroe, both Geminis, is an example of the extent to which psychic dysfunction and disorientation can affect your life.

Don't let the title of the Tarot card that is identified with Mercury, and with you, mislead you. It is known as "The Fool," and it masks a deep significance for your sign and for Virgo—the other sign ruled by Mercury. In Gemini, "The Fool" signifies the values that you glean from life as you venture forth in the world of experience—values that are the seeds of future wisdom. "The Fool" is the pictorial statement of the *one* force, the *no* thing, yet *everything* of experience: eternal energy—boundless, measureless and infinite. With a satchel on a stick over his right shoulder, "The Fool" is poised at the edge of a precipice. He is carrying the stored-up knowledge of universal memory—and the burden is heavy. On the threshold of the supreme adventure—that of passing through the gates of experience to reach divine wisdom—he is about to descend into the abyss of manifestation, of earth life. All must journey forward, must choose between good and evil, especially Gemini; if you have no bedrock philosophy, you are "The Fool" and the victim of your besetting nemesis, an identity crisis.

Your idealism can be based on the glittering possibilities of your sign, while you can lose sight of its symbolic aspects. The two theatrical masks—one of comedy, the other of tragedy—offer salient insights. Comedy comes from the Greek *komoidia*, a revel in celebration of marriage. In Gemini, it symbolizes the marriage of the two aspects of self. Conclusions are not reached through comedy, which is interruptive and avoids conclusions. That's why it's easier, when finding fault with yourself, for you to make clever, self-deprecating excuses; summoning the determination to free yourself from life's vicissitudes, by implementing the significant changes necessary within yourself, isn't your characteristic solution. You will find that, while comedy is informative, it is not necessarily reassuring. There is hope in tragedy, believe it or not, but no future in comedy. It's only a revelatory pause in the inexorable rhythm of destiny. Think of the holocaust and the "never-again" resolutions made by mankind as an outcome of that tragedy. Comedy is fond of twins, because identity is spiritual and denied by the body. Comedy, dealing in commonplace matters, depends on familiarity. Since wisdom isn't so common, you inwardly shy away from it. It isn't as easy to communicate, and the audience for it is smaller (and you do like an audience). Since comedy is another part of the entity commenting on involvement, Gemini can be the cynical charlatan. Your deepest self knows truth and reality; you would have to in order to make fun of it.

Taurus-born William Shakespeare explored the meanings of appearances versus reality, finding an effective theatrical device in twins and double images. In *Twelfth Night*, there is a set of twins; in *The Comedy of Errors*, the confusion is compounded by *two* sets of twins—a subtle use by the Bard of multiple mixed identities in order to illuminate truth. In *Much Ado about Nothing* and *Measure for Measure*, mistaken identities reveal the truth that things looking the same on the surface can be profoundly different underneath.

Gemini doesn't like solitude, so you are not apt to be a nonconformist. Genuinely independent behavior would set you apart from your fellows, with whom you have a constant compulsion to communicate. Can you imagine a Gemini without an ear to bend? Whatever is trendy and part of the popular mold is apt to be espoused by you, because active participation in the hubbub of life is promised thereby, while taking an unpopular stand might result in isolation. You may have to, however, to realize your ideal. "Who so would be a man, must be a nonconformist . . . never imitate. The great man is he who never reminds of others," in the words of Emerson. Since you require a forum where you can articulate your thoughts, and you like to receive recognition for your gift to express yourself fluently or cleverly on the topic of the moment, your words can have that "certain ring of familiarity."

Even though the substance of your judgment may not win support, your manner of expression can still persuade others. Experiments prove that if you talk enough, and convincingly enough, you can assume the mantle of leadership, even if you are completely wrong. Adolph Hitler, a Taurean, is an irrefutable example of this unfortunate reality. Gemini knows that almost any point of view can be rationalized. With so much artifice at your disposal, it behooves you to think things out thoroughly because your brilliant powers of persuasion, logic and perception can be put to the service of trivial diversions or questionable ends.

It was Leo-born Napoleon Bonaparte who said, "I fear three newspapers [Gemini-ruled] more than a hundred bayonets." The pen has exerted more influence on civilization than the sword. A political leader without the gift of speech is like a fish out of water. Such diverse figures as Winston Churchill (Sagittarius), Adolph Hitler (Taurus), Franklin D. Roosevelt (Aquarius) and John F. Kennedy (Gemini) were all famous for this ability, and the obvious differences in their characters are excellent examples of how this facility is detached from the more profound considerations of ethics, values and moral substance.

You have one of the most powerful weapons in the zodiac at your command: the gift of speech. It can make you a truly consequential person, but there is more self-waste in Gemini, through scattering, than in any other sign. You, and others, can become more entranced with the sound and manner of your voice than with the content of your utterances.

If you are a typical Gemini, you won't do well at tasks requiring industrious and continuous application. Your greatest asset is mental clarity, agility and expressiveness. Writing, public speaking, journalism, teaching, selling, reporting, music and acting can all be your forte. As you can see, yours is vocationally the most talented and versatile sign of the zodiac.

You should never be out of a job, thanks to your remarkable adaptability, and you are willing to try anything once. When things get sticky, you can usually discover a way out, adjust to new circumstances and even manage to gain somehow. Unless there is some strong stabilizing ingredient in your horoscope, such as earth or fixed signs prominent, you will try everything and will usually have the most varied work history.

You can become a restless drifter, vulnerable to every shift in the wind. By stressing education and gaining thorough knowledge early, instead of indulging in endless diversions, you can best prepare yourself for a meaningful life. You will always attract adventure and variety anyway, but it will be difficult to pick up the skills later, especially after thirty, when you will have great need for them. Your best period is likely to be when you are in your twenties and thirties.

You can turn on an inordinate amount of charm and can be the delight of assembled multitudes. If *joie de vivre* could be bottled, you'd make a fortune. An attractive asset in any social or romantic situation, you are rarely boring, or bored, at least at first blush. Being so high-strung, however, you are very susceptible emotionally; although yours is not a water sign, you are frequently at sea in affairs of the heart. Failed relationships are more apt to arouse apathy than enmity in you because attachments may not interest you long enough for them to stir any deep or dogmatic feelings or resentments. Last year's love is apt to become just another friend in a long list of pleasant acquaintances, and one with whom contact is casually maintained. Very perceptive, you know the precise moment for the clever riposte, the devastating comment. You are a natural for keeping things fascinating and bubbly. Will you use your wits to think up countless clever ways to keep your partner happy, or use your cleverness to mesmerize countless partners—and keep yourself romantically titillated?

About as unlike as possible, the natives of Gemini and Scorpio have one outstanding characteristic in common—an identity crisis, and the clever or expedient solution won't be adequate to overcome it. With your brand of Gemini logic, you can turn things around, switch the emphasis and convince yourself—and maybe a lot of others—that it means something else. Being aware of the response sensitivity that is possible from perceptions, you can manipulate the desires and evaluations of people subliminally. You know that people can be influenced to think in terms of what they are confronted with. The medium as the message, public relations in general and subtle manipulative techniques are facets of our culture that Gemini is only too well acquainted with. By convincing others to believe a conceit, even about yourself, you can come to believe it too, at least for a while or until the facts prove otherwise. You may find that you've cast yourself in an ambivalent role, one that you can't back up in performance.

You tend to fear age and can think up all kinds of clever ploys—such as associating with older people—so that you seem younger than you really are. Try studying them instead of using them to keep your youthful illusions intact, especially the ones who've accomplished something. You won't fear age if you anticipate it with confidence born of wisdom, and look at it as the period of when you can harvest the crops from the seeds you have sown. If you fear it, it's because you sense that a void may be in store for you: Knowing inwardly that the carefree values of youth are sophomoric and insecure when confronted with the needs of maturity, if your choices have been trivial, the specter of reaping a lean harvest can fill you with apprehension.

The light touch and brilliant facility that enhance your appeal in human relationships can be your nemeses in material things. Unless you were lucky enough to have a good, solid background in childhood, or had parents of substance, the drifting you may fall victim to can cause troublesome problems where responsibilities are concerned. You don't think much about rainy days except as more challenging tests of your wits. Money pressures can grind into your nervous system like sand in a watch and can make you dismally anxious and discontented. The negative side of those socially valuable gifts is that they can cause you to be evasive in the face of responsibility. It all looks pretty stern to you. You want to be free of such impediments, to flee the boredom of routine (which can be anything that you don't want to do), so that you can go about being spontaneous, clever and entertaining.

You may make many changes before you discover that *one thing* that sufficiently intrigues you that you can go along with its accompanying nitty-gritty. You will profit by cultivating friends who are paragons of stability and patience. Instead of poking fun at their "stodginess" (your euphemism for serious purpose), you can gain more by letting some of their attributes rub off on you. Don't worry about them having any dulling effect on you; you are too irrepressible for that. Let osmosis do you a favor; you might just acquire some firmness of purpose in the process. In sum, don't let champagne and *savoir-faire* become your *bêtes noires*.

The message of the zodiac for Gemini is contained in all the symbols of your sign: the Twins, your ruler Mercury, "The Fool" of the Tarot, the Greek masks of comedy and tragedy. Comedy comes easily for the typical Gemini; the serious side of life is a tragedy for you only if you interpret it that way. Essentially, the figurative meaning behind the Twins, or the two masks, is an important consideration for you to ponder: They are both exactly the *same size*.

Your zodiacal symbol, the Twins, depicts the duality of Gemini, your ceaseless gyrating between life's comedies and tragedies, and all the points in between. Your ruler, Mercury, the winged messenger of the gods in mythology, signifies communication, eloquence, cleverness and travel—and, in a less attractive context, swindlers, pickpockets, card sharks and various other ne'er-do-wells who live by their wits. Mercury makes its imprint on your nature not only through thoughts and ideas that come as swiftly as the speed of light, but also with a matching physical inclination to do things quickly and to move through life like a shooting star across the night sky.

GEMINI BIRTHDAYS

Judgment of whether or not a birthday is propitious can be considered from two points of view: complementary or challenging. From the standpoint of personal progress and fulfillment, your destiny may flow more comfortably if your birthday is, or reduces to, an *inner* root number such as 1, 3, 5, 7 or 9. For career drive and achievement, your progress may be enhanced if your birthday is, or reduces to, an *outer* root number such as 2, 4, 6, 8 or 22 (master number); the *outer* root numbers are less comfortable, more obstructive for you to contend with, but they are potentially very conducive to outstanding success. The 11 (master number) would be variable, favorable for creative achievement, but it generally would require more understanding and resourcefulness in order to integrate it with the meaning of Gemini.

Remember, if your birthday is two digits (excepting master numbers 11 and 22), be sure to read the *root* digit or number first. For example, if your birthday is 29, read the 2 (2 + 9 = 11, reduces to 2) birthday profile first and then read the special profile for 29. If your birthday is 14, read the 5 (1 + 4 = 5) birthday profile first and then read the special profile for 14, and so on. If a description in a "special" section contradicts information in the "root" digit (root number) analysis, the "special" interpretation applies more specifically to you.

The first planet in parentheses following your birthday number is *your Sun-Sign ruler*; the second planet (or Uranus/Saturn for number 8) is *your birthday number planetary equivalent*. Subsidiary planetary influences (if any) are bracketed.

Each birthday profile includes celebrities who share the same birthday.

YOUR BIRTHDAY PROFILE
June the 1st (Mercury, Sun)
(and root digit for May 28, June 10 and 19):

You can be very successful if you choose a field of endeavor where your ability to articulate, synthesize and organize can find individualized expression. Careers that are episodic and varied are best; even then, you may feel restricted by any routine. Your need for self-esteem can be the ingredient that stabilizes your approach, but if your restlessness remains unfocused, you frequently change people, places, direction or whatever, until you settle into a productive groove.

Whether you're the head of a family, a corporation or independently creative, you will profit from the realization that leadership, efficiency and a managerial position are end products of self-control and of a willingness to accept responsibility. Excessive self-promotion made easy through the combining of glittering mental gifts with an egocentric power complex is a pitfall to be avoided. If you don't, you may feel frustrated that life's rewards aren't as munificent as you've conceived to be your due.

Although your natural Gemini facility enables you to get by with a superficial approach, you're more apt to scale the heights by adding depth to your typically expressive, versatile, ambidextrous skills.

The awkward constrained conditions of your growing-up period would have included many opportunities to distinguish between transitory and permanent values; you would have had much to think about that would influence your decisions on the threshold of your career endeavors.

Marilyn Monroe (actress), 1926

Andy Griffith (actor), 1926

Brigham Young (Mormon leader), 1801

Special to May 28 (Mercury, Sun [Moon/Uranus/Saturn]):

You're not the type to sit back and watch the world go by. If, by chance, you are, you won't be wasting your time, for you'll find a way to capitalize on your observations and conclusions. More typically, though, you're apt to be found near the front of the passing parade, as likely as not on the cutting edge of any new trend of the moment that strikes your fancy—and for you the list is long and varied.

Independent and promotional, all ventures that promise freedom, variety and a lively pace will appeal to you. You express best along mental or vocal lines. Possibly a compulsive workaholic, you have a talent for getting information out of people before they know what you're up to. Working for depth will help to restrain your Gemini tendencies to scatter.

Rudolph Giuliani (mayor of New York City), 1944

Randolph Churchill (journalist), 1911

Ian Fleming (author), 1908

Special to June 10 (Mercury, Sun):

The cultivation of inner strength, and dependability, will lend needed stability to your restless, changeable disposition. Any unrestricted pursuit of a mental nature is more congenial for you and will enable you to maximize your estimable potential. You need variety and public involvement to alleviate your tendency to boredom.

Able to muster considerable brass and bravura, you go your own way and don't much care what people think about it. You have plenty of confidence in your expertise because you've gone to plenty of trouble to acquire it. A good planner and administrator, if a mistake occurs when you're in charge of a project, it's your way to take full responsibility and see to it that it's unlikely to ever happen again. You would also have few qualms about dismissing people you think fall short of your standards, which some might consider arbitrary.

Elizabeth Hurley (actress), 1966

Judy Garland (actress), 1922

Philip Mountbatten (British prince consort), 1921

Special to June 19 (Mercury [Sun/Pluto]):

Dissatisfied with many things, you are more aggressive and tenacious than the typical Gemini. When you are more philosophical and understanding, and minimize your subtle controlling instincts, it improves your partnership prospects. Lacking that, you might find sharing your life with another and the requisite give-and-take uncongenial. You may prefer to live alone. Significant, heartfelt fulfillment can be yours through finding values in situations beyond what they offer on the surface. Self-reliance might be your greatest asset, but it may be inimical to the need for compromise necessary in successful relationships. You are too expressive for any routine tasks.

If you were born to good status, you'll mix easily with the affluent and powerful. If not, your ability to live by your wits and a flair for upscale socializing will enable you to attain career or vocational success and to live in a style that your early years would not have promised. You know how to size up people and situations and then employ subtle strategies to capitalize on your impressions and conclusions.

Kathleen Turner (actress), 1954

Louis Jourdan (actor), 1919

Wallis Warfield Simpson (Duchess of Windsor), 1896

June the 2nd (Mercury, Moon)
(and root digit for May 29 and June 20;
June 11 is a master number, see end of chapter):

Your mind power—what you do, say or create—can find it's most productive outlet in the public domain. Receptive to stimulating new trends, you're most effective when articulating them and then encouraging others to keep the ball rolling in new directions in art, music, writing or some other adventurous development. Success for you in one context can produce interesting offshoots that open windows of opportunity in other realms. Then, being a Gemini, it's no problem for you to adapt to different but related activities that are not only more lucrative, but also enable you to capitalize on recognition for past efforts and to make fuller use of your talents.

With your mental flexibility, you are able to familiarize yourself with new conditions quickly and to make speedy adjustments. When you find yourself in situations that seem boring or that impede the free flow of your natural manner of expression, your instinct is to move on to greener pastures. If you can avoid becoming self-insistent, touchy and easily offended and instead always look for the grain of humor in sensitive situations, you will develop a flair for cooperation and diplomacy that can be invaluable. You tend to collect things—unmindful of any ultimate use they may have.

You like material comforts, but the singular drive and concentration of purpose necessary to acquire them may not be congenial to your nature. Fluent and expressive, you are happiest with an audience. You can become a powerful advocate and/or communicator for improvements in the creative fields. You might champion the highly original—perhaps initially strange—concepts of others that break new ground and ultimately enhance public awareness and taste for striking achievements.

Marvin Hamlisch (composer), 1944

Stacy Keach (actor), 1941

Hedda Hopper (columnist), 1890

Special to May 29 (Mercury [Moon/Pluto]):

You are versatile and adaptable and are inclined to be nervous and bored unless you have at least two interests. Your energy and cleverness are assets in public life. Absorbed in your own aspirations, you are not easy to live with, although a domestic anchorage or a semblance of family life is necessary for your contentment. Your inner thoughts were much stimulated by conditions in your growing-up period; the results of your observations and conclusions can lend valuable insight to your utterances when you begin to make your way in the world and climb the ladder of success.

Your irreverent wit and barbed ripostes can make you a social asset—or, if you're not discreet, a social liability. Typically expressive, versatile and ambidextrous, you can juggle two jobs, two identities, two homes, two lovers or two (or more) of practically anything else with aplomb—if not always with due consideration for the consequences. With your great gift for witty self-deprecation, for puncturing the pompous and for sharp one-liners, you are likely to be one of a kind in your circle.

Annette Bening (actress), 1958

John F. Kennedy (35th U.S. president), 1917

Bob Hope (comedian), 1903

Special to June 20 (Mercury, Moon):

Clever and versatile, you function well before the public. Adept at talking your way into or out of practically any situation, it's best if you keep your feelings under firm control, otherwise you can resolutely get on the wrong track and pursue a mistake to the bitter end. Success in your endeavors and life in general is more assured if you cultivate objectivity and contain your aspirations within reasonable limits. Lacking the patience for the long pull, duties or ventures that are cyclic or varied are more congenial and gratifying for you. You may be hard to pin down in a relationship, especially marriage.

Beware of hazards if you are drawn to public affairs and causes, for committed participation in them can lead to personal difficulties. Although a part of you is self-effacing, another part won't take "no" for an answer if a principle is involved. In the realm of controversial ideas or activities, you can reach a fervent pitch of emotional conviction in proclaiming or defending your honor or opinions. Right or wrong, however, your intentions are admirable; you can be generous to a fault where the common good is concerned.

Lionel Richie (singer), 1949

Errol Flynn (actor), 1909

Lillian Hellman (writer), 1905

June the 3rd (Mercury, Venus)
(and root digit for May 30, June 12 and 21):

This birthday number is one of the most compatible for Gemini. You should have a good education and be trained in some creative field, although this is more apt to occur with the May 30 birthday. You, as well as a Gemini born on June 12, will probably have a more disorganized upbringing, which could make it more difficult to qualify, unless thoroughly prepared, for the positions for which you are so naturally gifted. Skills can still be acquired or completed in the late twenties or early to mid-thirties, but initiative, ventures and determination will be difficult to sustain after that time.

The opportunities you attract will be more for expression than for perfecting. You have a vivid imagination, have great creative possibilities—especially literary—and can be very popular with coworkers as well as the public. You're the salesperson par excellence and could sell ice to an Eskimo. With more restless vitality than driving ambition, you'll have little trouble in finding a niche into which you can conveniently settle . . . for a while. You can cover a lot of niches in a lifetime.

All self-expressive activities, whether theatrical, intellectual, musical or literary are most congenial for you. You may have to contend with a diversified and spasmodic pattern when you begin to make your way in the world, which can, however, reinforce your determination to succeed in the realm of your choice. Lacking that stimulus, and the incisive lessons provided by the school of experience, you may have more difficulty attaining a level of significant achievement.

Curtis Mayfield (singer), 1942

Allen Ginsberg (poet), 1926

Tony Curtis (actor), 1925

Special to May 30 (Mercury, Venus):

Very imaginative, intuitive and popular, you enjoy out-talking and out-jesting work colleagues, friends and other associates. Although typically Gemini in that you love a good joke, you probably sense that you won't profit from playing with knowledge; therefore, you can be deadly serious when it comes to job or career matters. Nevertheless, because you are easily bored (but rarely boring!) and will probably start working in your teens, you are likely to have a varied vocational history. But with your adaptability and ingenuity, you'll always find work or a career that provides you with a living—or very possibly a remarkable success.

Beware of impulsive conclusions that can be inaccurate through inattention to fundamentals—although you may insist you are right. Not always partial to diligent application, your excellent abilities for communicative pursuits may be only partially developed; take the high road if you are ever tempted to be satisfied with facile results. Where relationships are concerned, you need someone to be there, someone with whom you can argue, bounce around new ideas, compare notes, share jokes and witticisms and make plans for the future.

Wynonna Judd (singer), 1964

Keir Dullea (actor), 1936

Benny Goodman (bandleader), 1909

Special to June 12 (Mercury, Venus [Sun/Moon]):

Easy mental brilliance and swift perceptions can be your blessings—or curse. You can get by in life on your wits. A virtuoso conversationalist, you have a healthy respect for learning and talent. The arts for you, however, may be more of a hobby than a livelihood. Occasional financial limitation or the specter of continuing uncertainty can lead to an overemphasis and dependence on material values. Prestige is important to you, but you may have to cultivate the patience necessary for true achievement. Although tempted, refuse to compromise and settle for the visible trappings of success or a lesser goal. You are articulate and prolific—tremendous assets if you channel your restless energies into self-development and the sterner virtues.

While you have your adventurous, unpredictable side and might seem to be a maverick to some, you're an able troubleshooter when maximum diplomacy is required. A dependable upbringing or comfortable background, combined with a good education, prepares you for success in any occupation or career that makes use of your leadership potential and special way with words. What you say gains from your way of saying it.

Vic Damone (singer), 1928

George Bush (41st U.S. president), 1924

Sir Anthony Eden (British prime minister), 1897

Special to June 21 (Mercury, Venus [Moon/Sun]):

Controlling your tendency to scatter energies and emotions and overcoming the dejection that follows disappointments are the keys to realizing your splendid possibilities. If moodier than the typical Gemini, you're capable of sulking without letting the people around you know what is bothering you. Or, always ready with an acid remark, you'll air your share of grievances, petty or otherwise. Your home, a dependable income and a strong partner can be an important anchorage and inspiration if you can adjust to the tie that binds. Relationships for you have a way of starting out light and ending up heavy.

Your vivid imagination and nervous disposition can find a constructive outlet in the literary, educational or creative fields. Articulate, entertaining and very versatile, you can do very well in public life. Usually on the move, preferably upwardly mobile, you sense that anyone who stands still on the job or in business can be left behind. Several job or career possibilities might be sampled before you settle into a particular groove. You will profit by cultivating an impersonal outlook, stressing objectivity and patience.

Nicole Kidman (actress), 1967

Judy Holliday (actress), 1922

Jane Russell (actress), 1921

June the 4th (Mercury, Saturn)
(and root digit for May 31 and June 13;
May 22 is a master number, see end of chapter):

This is one of the best birthdays for Gemini, but like so many things that are good for us, the contribution we must make to gain the benefits might not be so congenial. When you utilize your enviable resources of cleverness and adaptability just to get by, a strategy that always succeeds to a degree, you may nevertheless feel thwarted in your quest for position and solid accomplishment. To gain ultimate satisfaction with this birthday, it's best to refrain from any of the Gemini tendencies to scatter or to bend whichever way the wind blows. You can only realize your great promise by emphasizing depth, industry and concentration in whatever job or career you direct your energies.

Your opportunities may not be varied, but they can be enormously satisfying. If you're not as dogmatic in your views as you are in your determination to apply yourself diligently to something deeply useful, enduring and financially rewarding, it will be a big step in the right direction. Choose a skill not easily mastered or a career goal not easily attained. When you find a worthy match for your tireless energies, which are mostly the nervous variety, you will discover that the "tiredness" that comes from victory over a difficult mental challenge is surprisingly rejuvenating.

The conditions that prevailed in your childhood would either have stirred your ambitions or made you egocentric and dismissive regarding obstacles or discipline. At your cleverest, your way out of a difficulty can usually, if not automatically, be a way up as well. If you rise to public prominence, be careful of misguided judgment that could jeopardize your position. Although Geminis are noted for their sense of humor, this birthday can be noticeably lacking in unbridled hilarity.

Noah Wyle (actor), 1971

Robert Merrill (singer), 1919

George III (British king), 1738

Special to May 31 (Mercury, Saturn [Venus/Sun]):

Mental as well as emotional satisfactions are important to you. If an involvement provides opportunity for progress and improvement, you can become very absorbed; otherwise, you will drop it and go on to something else. You seek practical and substantial results, especially in financial security. Although you like travel and change, fulfillment in love and a home or family that you can return to are essential to you.

Talented in several directions in the arts, and whether a wunderkind or a maverick (or a unique combination of both), you can expand the frontiers of knowledge. You're able to detect promising sparks of life in the most mundane or commonplace situations, and you can find a way to inject an unconventional, controversial or cryptic note into your opinions, artistic revelations and intellectual activities. With your thoughtful, sagacious, wide-ranging command of style, the creative force you generate can have a lasting effect if you're lucky enough to find the right milieu in which it can flourish.

Brooke Shields (actress), 1965

Clint Eastwood (actor), 1930

Walt Whitman (poet), 1819

Special to June 13 (Mercury, Saturn [Sun/Venus]):

Restless, you can be annoyed with the amount of effort necessary to gain your objectives. Of all the Gemini-born, your birthday may be the one that most necessitates getting serious about life's nuts-and-bolts realities. You want to be free to express your ego, but you will find true freedom only through the acceptance of discipline. You are suited to the professions, but you can also profit from creative talents. Funneling your mental restlessness into worthwhile challenges will help to reduce nervousness. Home and marriage are a source of contentment.

You are gifted in business as well as the professions. Any literary pursuits, such as the spoken word, publishing, promotion or advertising would be congenial for you. Good with language skills, you might put your facility to clever use, such as by arguing as a way to gain knowledge or an edge advantageous to your own purposes. A talented, highly motivated leader when found in an executive position, you know how to attract or employ gifted associates who augment your skills and enhance your own prestige.

Mary-Kate and Ashley Olsen (actresses), 1986

Tim Allen (actor), 1953

William Butler Yeats (poet and dramatist), 1865

June the 5th (Mercury, Mars)
(and root digit for May 23 and June 14):

You will have many opportunities to either utilize to the full or to fritter away your distinctive Gemini traits. The bon vivant par excellence, you thoroughly enjoy being on the go, whether locally or in distant locales—in short, living life to the hilt. But to what purpose? For example, your sign's duality can come to the fore; whether you cover a lot of ground intellectually or geographically, you're capable of assimilating and capitalizing on your experiences in order to hone your job skills and forge a notable career. If you have something to sell and a social occasion offers opportunities, you know how to "work the room." The downside is just skipping along on the surface and not taking advantage of circumstances conducive to substantial worldly success, such as using a daytime job to pay for classes at night to get ahead. As a result, you'll enjoy vivid memories and very little else at the end of the trail.

The conditions of your early environment may have left you confused: You might either desire to escape reality or, more constructively, to give tangible form to the visions and inspirations of your growing-up period. Although you may never settle down emotionally, you are likely to have plenty of experience in that department. You crave action and freedom but can misuse both if you don't set your sights high enough and sidestep any tendencies toward trivial self-seeking.

This birthday can be peculiarly quixotic for Gemini. With your exceptional gifts, dynamic personality, adaptability and popular appeal, you could innocently coast along and enjoy life with no particular goal in mind. The issue you must consider involves distinction, distraction and the easy way out. Which will you choose? Are your Gemini energies restless because you are bored . . . because you haven't made substantial progress . . . because you lack the solid kind of know-how that wins respect in the world? There may be many dissatisfactions or obstacles to overcome until you fathom the difference between durable and transitory success.

Kenny G (musician), 1956

Bill Moyers (TV journalist), 1934

Tony Richardson (director), 1928

Special to May 23 (Mercury, Mars [Moon/Venus]):
Full of the simmering juices of life, no grass is likely to grow under your feet. You're interested in anything and everything that makes the time pass more quickly. Restlessly on the go, ready for the next adventure on the horizon, you seem to express the secret of perpetual motion—in body, mind or spirit. You're not likely to be happy in the boonies. You need plenty of street life and diversions to keep you from being bored to death. If you're found there, participation in a little theater group or other diversion blunts the edge of hinterland frustration. Mentally and manually dexterous, you may need to develop consistency and discrimination in order to realize success from your impressive talents. Your personal magnetism makes it easier to fulfill your career ambitions and usefulness to people.

One of the professions is the most satisfactory outlet for your drives. You decided early in life that you wanted to "be somebody," and it would take a lot of discouraging setbacks to stop you. Like your June 3rd birthday brothers and sisters, you're exceptionally persuasive and could probably sell oil to an Arab. Cheerful and upbeat, you can attract your share of lively types for friends, people who like to stir up the social pot and keep it bubbling. Naturally flirtatious, your flair for levity and brevity carries over into your love life, which, to your way of thinking, should be fun, not a burden—which is the way you might also view marriage.

Joan Collins (actress), 1933
Rosemary Clooney (singer), 1928
Douglas Fairbanks (actor), 1883

Special to June 14 (Mercury, Mars [Sun/Saturn]):
When your mental gifts and marketable skills are combined with your no-nonsense attitude, you're likely to land either a coveted job or assignment or will wind up in the big leagues of career success. Among your capabilities is the natural insight necessary to profit from your experiences, which can be varied and many. Your choice of associates and ability to attract support for research or interpretive projects are other important assets you possess. Absorbed by your propensity for adventure and for knuckling down to gut realities, knowing how to tap into the power network to promote your aspirations and make your mark in the world is a further advantage.

You're likely to range far and wide in the pursuit and attainment of your career goals. A great champion of ideals, you can be very convincing when you express them through your professional activities or interpret them through your deeply felt creative output. In your determined search for truth in the human condition, very little will deter your efforts to gain your laudable objective. Meanwhile, your career priorities may make it difficult to sustain home or married life.

Yasmine Bleeth (actress), 1968

Bobby Darin (singer), 1936

Burl Ives (actor), 1909

June the 6th (Mercury, Jupiter)
(and root digit May 24 and June 15):

Persuasive, gutsy and popular, your contagious enthusiasm makes it easy for you to get along with people. If you take advantage of your ample quota of staying power, you're destined for success in the arts, business world or government and can be a popular favorite in any field that brings you before the public. In the process of achieving your place in the sun, you can roam far and wide as opportunities beckon to express your distinctive style and skills. You can also be very conscientious and opinionated; you're not shy about voicing your exemplary standards—and consequent distaste for human failings such as self-serving hypocrisy, influence peddling or behind-the-scenes "fixing," especially in public figures. Be careful that your attitude doesn't ricochet. If you're not scrupulous, whether or not deserved, a devious adversary could turn the tables and make you the target of such appraisals.

Although possible financial ups and downs can make you fretful and apprehensive about severe lacks that aren't apt to materialize, you are either reasonably or well protected in material things. Part of you tends to shy away from responsibility; at the same time, you want love and family warmth, the protection of a stabilized environment. If you're not contented, don't self-righteously put the blame somewhere else. You know where it belongs.

Success in ventures is more assured through personal contact. Your early background may not have contributed much to your sense of responsibility, but it was probably great fun, in addition to stirring up your expressive or creative instincts. If you displayed exceptional childhood talents, you could get onto the career fast-track early and jump-start your travels on the road to success in your teens or early twenties.

Bjorn Borg (tennis player), 1956

Sandra Bernhard (actress), 1955

Thomas Mann (novelist), 1875

Special to May 24 (Mercury, Jupiter [Moon/Saturn]):
Your career success is more likely to materialize through business or a profession, especially film or the theater, than through other creative ventures. Your reactions to life are very personal and important to you and tend to be on the sober side. With your fidgety, inquisitive Gemini nature, you will never lack for an interest, which is good. You're likely to have some sort of job or work at something right into old age. Keeping busy is a blessing for you; it keeps you young and functional—even after Social Security time rolls around.

The hazard of boredom is your nemesis in any relationship; for the tie that binds to remain secure, you'll require a mate who provides ample mental rapport—someone who can keep your mind continuously stimulated—and with whom you'll enjoy matching wits and sharing domestic responsibilities. You'll find love, marriage or other close relationships delightfully romantic when channels of communication are humming, when plenty of mutual interests abound and when lighthearted companionship blends comfortably with love and commitment.

    Priscilla Presley (actress), 1945

    Bob Dylan (singer, composer), 1941

    Victoria (queen of England), 1819

Special to June 15 (Mercury, Jupiter [Sun/Mars]):
A mantle of protection surrounds you. Your remarkable gifts and career absorption can bring recognition and material success, with music a special possibility. Home is necessary and may be your career or vocational base. You prefer an exciting tempo to responsibility, a profession to business—the more independent and vigorous the better. Your early life would have been more conducive to creative expression than to discipline. Your freestyle approach enables you to function impressively, if not brilliantly, in an art form without having to learn traditional academic techniques. In the business milieu, however, which is not so receptive to mavericks, you're able to function successfully within conventional guidelines. Either way, your unswerving initiative can lead you right into the winner's circle.

Not driven by ambition, your ability to attract or to make money is more the result of luck stemming from your personal enjoyment in your endeavors, rather than from deliberate hard work with financial reward in mind or from expert fiscal management. If you can convince the latest candidate for your heart in the great romance sweepstakes that he or she must walk a tightrope between being always available and not cluttering up your life, your relationship will be filled to the brim with happiness.

Courtney Cox (actress), 1964

Helen Hunt (actress), 1963

Edvard Grieg (composer), 1843

June the 7th (Mercury)
(and root digit for May 25 and June 16):

Your birthday has tremendous possibilities; depending on your motivation, they may or may not—or just partly—be realized. You run the gamut from the dour pedant to the popular public figure; the restlessness of Gemini doesn't always blend comfortably with the 7 requirement for serious concentration and the solitude that goes with it. Your powerful mental potential might instead be directed into objectives more pleasantly gratified, like skittering along on your nimble wits to enjoy social pleasures and/or easily gained public acclaim for your talents. You could be an information junkie. If your keen analytical powers lack sharp inner focus and become homogenized, you'll simply employ them in ordinary (albeit legitimate) ways instead of using them to plumb hard-won intellectual or spiritual depths.

You think a lot—but about what? Capable of the most efficient mental probity, your mind won't yield maximum results unless you focus more on noteworthy accomplishment and less on diversions, which may get the upper hand when you're lost in thought. Possibly a tremendous force for enlightenment, your utterances, whatever their content, can be very effective, authoritative and taken seriously whether or not they deserve to be.

With your pointed wit and formidable command of language, you're a whiz at word games and similar pastimes, and you can be outspoken and blunt when in your irascible, critical mode. However, depending on whether you're self- or conventionally educated, or mainly streetwise, an IQ test could stump you. If involved in an art form, you're able to think with your heart and feel with your brain. Your mind can function like a fluoroscope, providing an inner X-ray of basic components that purifies the creative (or recreative) process. Your upbringing would make you either resentful of discipline or enlightened as to its value. You need relationships, but they may have to fit into whatever convenient slot you're willing to grant them.

Prince (the artist formerly known as) (singer), 1958

Tom Jones (singer), 1940

Paul Gaugin (artist), 1848

Special to May 25 (Mercury [Moon/Mars]):
You may be the philosopher, or the doubting Thomas, or stage-struck and a bit of a ham. With your inventive turn of mind, you use your brash energy to maintain whatever advantage you manage to gain. You see to it that you get your way and let the chips fall where they may; if you make mistakes, you're clever enough to be sure that you have a way out. You're not apt to settle for whatever is expedient and popular; if you do, you could undermine your credibility and dissipate your exceptional promise. With your thirst for news or information that keeps you mentally stimulated and/or physically active, you could be an information junkie.

Ambitious, literate, career-minded, good at self-promotion, you'll probably have dabbled in several occupations by the time you're in your thirties. After that, however, if you haven't made your mark or set your course, it's usually more difficult for you to knuckle down and make any meaningful changes. Nevertheless, there are occasional exceptions. If you persist, you can pursue a childhood dream until you turn it into a practical reality, even if it takes until your middle years or somewhat past them. Handy with money, you're likely to accumulate your share. Whether or not a celebrity, your personal tastes and private inclinations may deviate considerably from your public image.

Lauryn Hill (singer), 1975
Anne Heche (actress), 1969
Gene Tunney (boxer), 1898

Special to June 16 (Mercury [Sun/Jupiter]):
Independent without being aggressive or overly ambitious, you function well in efficiently organized enterprises where people talk your language. You need home and love, but you may have a lot to learn about them; you tend to think them your due, forgetting that they may have to be earned, or at least deserved. When properly focused, your reasoning powers are exceptional and can bring you rewarding job advancement or recognition in your chosen field. If the temples of knowledge are your preferred habitat, however, you don't crave public praise for your accomplishments and would be just as satisfied with the respect of colleagues.

You can be the life of the party—clever, witty and entertaining—and can enjoy enviable popularity as a host, guest, friend or companion. In family situations, you're likely to be someone's favorite sibling, niece, uncle or cousin. If you encounter delayed success or rough patches in life, your innate confidence, quiet pride and share of luck always seems ready to bail you out and get you back on track.

Joan Van Ark (actress), 1943

Erich Segal (novelist), 1937

Stan Laurel (comedian), 1890

June the 8th (Mercury [Uranus/Saturn])
(and root digit for May 26 and June 17):

With your mental attributes of perception, intuition, innovation and objectivity, you're a natural for any job or career activity involving communication and/or mass-audience appeal; publishing, advertising, distribution, academe, fund-raising or the Internet are possible areas that enable you to capitalize on your broad-based talents. An effective advocate for whatever cause you espouse—whether in business, the entertainment world or public affairs—you are capable of harnessing your versatile gifts and then directing them into productive, widely influential, moneymaking channels. Otherwise, you could fritter away your restless energies through attempting too varied or bustling a schedule or pursuing an ill-advised goal in an effort to escape boredom and/or to satisfy your itch for change, adventure or public esteem.

Motivated by your desire for power and/or material freedom, you are likely to get an early start on the road to success. If you find marriage or other ties that bind congenial, it is because your partners are as willing as you to pull up stakes and go where fresh opportunities beckon. You think big but not always steadfastly; if you become bored with routine or lengthy preparation, remember: "Rome wasn't built in a day," and neither will your fortunes be!

The change and variety in your childhood was not the best preparation for the stick-to-itiveness essential for the success you envision when you begin to make your way in the world. You need to carefully guide your high-strung Gemini proclivities, or your quest for power, money and authority can adversely affect your health. Relaxation techniques are worth a try if your occasionally frazzled nerves could use a rest.

Alexis Smith (actress), 1921

Grant Lewi (astrologer, writer), 1902

Frank Lloyd Wright (architect), 1869

Special to May 26 (Mercury, Uranus, Saturn [Moon/Jupiter]):

Essentially creative, your success is more assured if you have a good educational foundation or early career training; the business world and its responsibilities, however, may be a practical compromise. You will profit from overcoming any tendencies to be self-satisfied with easily acquired knowledge, skills or attainment. The discipline or restrictive conditions of your early background left you with either a distaste or a compulsion for application and thoroughness. You know how to deliver a withering comment when it's score-settling time.

Expressive, fluent, artistic, possibly precocious and/or ambitious growing up, you could start early on the road to fame and fortune, or at least your version of security. In any case, your career antenna is always raised to alert you to upwardly mobile job or career opportunities. And you know how to commercialize your diversified talents into significant success. That antic gleam in your eye signals would-be admirers that you're both amusing and sexy, a combination not easy to pull off. Family life provides an appealing anchor for you.

Peggy Lee (singer), 1920
John Wayne (actor), 1907
Al Jolson (singer), 1886

Special to June 17 (Mercury, Uranus, Saturn [Sun/Mercury]):
Whether conventional or creatively brilliant and intense, you run the gamut between strengthening and furthering traditions or establishing innovative new forms of creative expression. Or you might find a way to successfully blend the two. Not short on ego or personal confidence, you can be self-satisfied where knowledge, artistic trends and your opinions are concerned—which singly or combined you know how to commercialize. Strong-willed, you like independence and authority but may need supportive associates, especially to handle details.

Your aptitude for professional or creative pursuits can bring you recognition as well as financial success; the requirements of the business milieu are congenial to your Gemini flair for promotion, publicity and sense of public taste. Whatever your occupational status, you're capable of painstakingly preparing, and adapting to, practically any job or career assignment.

Barry Manilow (singer), 1946
Dean Martin (singer, actor), 1917
Igor Stravinsky (composer), 1882

June the 9th (Mercury, Pluto)
(and root digit for May 27 and June 18):
Versatile and magnetic, your lust for life can propel you to the top of any job or career effort that capitalizes on your prodigious mental agility,

penetrating insights and amusing insouciance. For instance, if you're in research, the academic world or industry, you'll be popular because of your ready (if sometimes barbed) wit that lightens the sober atmosphere. No slouch when it comes to exchanging bon mots with colleagues or the glitterati, you can be equally humorous at the checkout counter of your local supermarket. You're not snobby about levity. But people you deal with should be forewarned; there could be a method to your sly comments and/or breezy charm.

Although conditions can be a bit disconcerting on the threshold of your job or career strivings, life is not likely to be dull. You may be driven more by dissatisfaction with the status quo than by authentic ambition. You know what you don't want but may have to endure some trial and error missteps before you discover what you do want. Travel broadens your outlook and can inspire creativity. You're not likely to be happy in the boonies unless you're involved in an exciting, time-consuming vocational objective; otherwise, you could be bored to death.

After an upbringing surrounded by the protection, comforts and requirements of family relationships, you can feel decentralized when you begin to make your way in the world. You may sense a personal loneliness—you against destiny. You could find that you have many diverse elements and changes to contend with, which will require much of your time and patience. You have executive ability and authority, but you may have to overcome suspicion and nervousness to function with total success in that capacity. Will you recognize the need to cultivate broad viewpoints, patience and the perseverance to triumph over obstacles and disappointments to complete whatever worthwhile project you attempt? Or will you opt for expedience, clever dead ends and uncertainty?

Michael J. Fox (actor), 1961

Jackie Mason (comedian), 1931

Cole Porter (composer), 1891

Special to May 27 (Mercury, Pluto [Moon/Mercury]):
Independent in your beliefs, determined but somewhat erratic, you love a challenge, work-wise or otherwise. And when you are successful, you want to be paid for it, as generously as possible. A shrewd judge of public tastes and opportunities, you find subordinate positions uncongenial; along with the money, you want recognition for your expertise. Your Gemini versatility and perceptiveness are excellent for leadership in a broad range of careers,

such as in the arts, theater, education or government. You will have learned adaptability from the change or uncertainty of your childhood.

Loaded with subtle charm, you won't suffer fools gladly. If you become irritated and impatient with a dimwit or have a bone to pick, you know how to express it with a veneer of goodwill, which adroitly covers an unmistakable subtext of elegantly worded bile. It wouldn't be unlike you to spend your life escaping boredom, not because you're bored but because you don't want to be. You're happiest when you have a steady companion who shares your interests, but it may not always be the same companion, or the same interest.

Todd Bridges (actor), 1965

Vincent Price (actor), 1911

Isadora Duncan (dancer), 1878

Special to June 18 (Mercury, Pluto [Sun, Uranus/Saturn]):
Gifted mentally, with a flair for self-promotion, your Gemini traits can lead to distinctive success based more on principles than financial gain—although you'll do well financially. Your aptitude for the big picture in ventures is exceptional; as you go about achieving your aims, your efforts will include much change, activity and/or travel, not an uncongenial agenda for your mercurial disposition.

Your yen to better yourself in business or a profession knows no bounds. You are more tenacious and ingenious than the typical Gemini. When you pursue an occupational strategy or objective, especially if it breaks with tradition, you're able to capitalize on your dauntless competitive spirit and thorough preparation. With your sharp intelligence, you're also good at caustic jousting when your integrity or initiatives are questioned or opposed. If you don't break the rules, you might occasionally bend them a bit. Unsettled conditions in the domestic sphere may prove inimical to partnerships.

Isabella Rossellini (actress), 1952

Paul McCartney (singer, songwriter), 1942

E. G. Marshall (actor), 1910

June the 11th (Mercury, Neptune [Moon/Sun])
(master number):
You are perhaps the least typical member of your sign. Instead of being mentally logical or analytical, you are more susceptible to or guided by your feelings as your life unfolds. The wanderer in spirit as well as geographically, you can give the impression of not being anchored to a base of recognizable,

permanent reality. When your potent hunches are sound and on target, you can swiftly and successfully bypass the usual Gemini thought processes to function in your own special way to achieve your objectives. Whether in the arts, a profession, the business world or science, you have a remarkable ability to articulate your instinctive mix of ideas, psychic impressions and inspirations with sensitivity, conviction and compassion.

Mentally responsive to nebulous stimuli, your initial efforts to find fulfilling outlets for your imaginative intellect and avid curiosity might stir up confusion or uncertainty. The veil is lifted, however, once you are able to assimilate your dreams, your ventures into the unknown and other accumulated experience into knowledge comprehensible and enlightening to yourself and to the world at large. However, your sensitivity and ability to explain phenomena or experiences only vaguely perceived by others (advantageous in a creative, communicative or educational context) can carry a price: It can be disconcerting or discouraging when it dawns on you that the average person or the mass public in general doesn't talk your language. When thwarted in attempts to get your unique message across, you can fluctuate between the heights and the depths if you allow feelings of frustration to escalate.

Whether in the creative or interpretive realm, you are very gifted for artistic expression and could blaze a new trail in one context or another. In any case, whatever your job or career accomplishment, it could stem from an unusual or distinctive inspiration that tests fresh horizons and/or deepens established standards. You would be especially qualified for any industry or pursuit involving medicine or healing (or writing about it); oil or water; film in photography, cinema or in other areas of the media or entertainment world; or any activity dependent on illusion. You would also have a keen sense of the fluctuating public mood and uncertainties of economic swings as they affect stock market and other investment trends globally as well as on Wall Street.

The material security of your early environment may have lulled you into an acceptance or appreciation of a conventionally secure lifestyle that obscured the lofty level of your unique possibilities. Your psychic power, enhanced by your creative fluency, makes you very sensitive to sights, sounds and odors but you may need cultivation or rigid self-discipline in order to capitalize on it.

Gene Wilder (actor, writer), 1935

Jacques-Yves Cousteau (marine explorer), 1910

Richard Strauss (composer), 1864

(Note: This master number implies a variable alternative response influenced by the strength or passivity of the planet Neptune in your horoscope. If you don't feel you are responding to the distinctive vibratory power of 11, you are instead expressing the more conventional qualities of 2, which you should read.)

May the 22nd (Mercury, Uranus [Saturn/Moon])
(master number):

Yours is among the most inventive, not to say brilliant, minds in the Zodiac. Your potential to be a highly successful popularizer of serious as well as avant-garde ideas is exceptional. It may not be easy to bring your multifaceted gifts into productive focus, but if you achieve just half of what you are capable, you will be an individual to reckon with in any field of endeavor.

You can play an important role as life becomes increasingly sophisticated and technological, particularly in regard to phenomenal communications breakthroughs. Mercury, your ruling planet, combined with Uranus, The Awakener, produces miracles in the computerized Age of Aquarius. News, information and transactions are flashed on business or home computer screens in volumes and ways undreamed of by prior generations. The information superhighway, voice-activated word processors and other technological advances are among today's wonders that no doubt will soon be old hat. The creative possibilities, combined with your mercurial originality and farsighted vision, are unlimited.

Whether by way of the written or spoken word, you can become a dynamic force for enlightenment through your high-voltage, thought-provoking ideals and inspirations. Nervous and temperamental, you may struggle to find a mold that can contain your outsized, futuristic and sometimes arbitrary speculations—which may arouse entertaining, thought-stimulating or even unsettling reactions in others. You might need the help of practical associates to avoid material difficulties; your swift insights can race over a multiplicity of possible irons in the fire with nary a thought as to their practical ramifications and/or how easily you can get burned.

You can become overstimulated and exhausted by the pace of your mental exertions. If your work or career doesn't provide an appropriate outlet for your highly charged nervous energies, an intellectually challenging hobby could relieve tension. Whether a project requires scholarly erudition or extraordinary creative (or recreative) insight, however, it can gain from your throwaway brilliance.

Sir Laurence Olivier (actor), 1907
Sir Arthur Conan Doyle (novelist), 1859
Richard Wagner (composer), 1813

(Note: This master number implies a variable alternative response influenced by the strength or passivity of the planet Uranus in your horoscope. If you don't think you are responding to the distinctive vibratory power of 22, you are instead expressing the more conventional qualities of 4, which you should read.)

CHAPTER 4

CANCER

June 22–July 22

RULER: **THE MOON** NUMBER: **2** ELEMENT: **WATER** SYMBOL: **THE CRAB**

"Let us not burden our remembrances with a heaviness that's gone."
—*The Tempest,* Shakespeare

Naturally cautious or reticent, yours is the most personal and instinctive sign in the Zodiac. Your emotions and sensitivities run deep because your governing principle is the very root of the life force: procreation. In its most obvious form, this is symbolized by motherhood, protection, nurturing—and a sense of permanence, history and tradition. Typically family-oriented, Cancerians, more than the other signs, are frequently interested in antiques and other collectibles, family trees, restoring old houses and nostalgia in general. Possibly apocryphal, it's not an unlikely story that one Cancerian, when asked where she lived, thoughtfully replied, "...In the past." You're usually loathe to throw away anything for fear that you'll have a future use for it. Some of you are perceptive collectors, while others are merely accumulators.

As a water sign, ruled by the Moon, you have a vivid imagination. For instance, Cancerian children, tucked in for the night and on their way to slumberland, sometimes see (and can be frightened by) illusory images or creatures of the night on their bedroom walls. These scary visions are nothing more than shadowy projections of rustling leaf patterns made by trees or other forms in the path of the moonlight or a street lamp as it glows through a window. The child's anxious imagination fills in the rest.

Fortunately, as you grow up and make your way in life, most of you leave your shyness and fears behind, if not all your fantasies and insecurities. In maturity, focused on your objectives, it's to your advantage that your inborn feelers are always out, not only to warn of possible hazards, but also to be keenly receptive to opportunities for promotion, possession and expansion—which can lead to impressive material freedom. Although a typical Cancerian will depend on a domestic base for inner support and strength, your knack for management, efficiency and publicity can reward you with positions of power and authority. "Onward and upward" (but occasionally sideways, like your symbol, the Crab) could be one of your main themes in life. Nevertheless, with your self-protective instincts, you're not inclined to go out on any flimsy limbs in order to get ahead in the world. You'll typically play it safe, generally moving up one rung at a time on the success ladder. And you will make sure that you have a safety net of security in case things don't quite work out as planned.

However, although finding yourself in unfamiliar surroundings or venturing too far from a sheltering haven can arouse anxiety, you are not likely to be really content to remain in a self-protective or self-satisfied rut whether in your birthplace, home, job or career—even a career as a devoted spouse, parent or homemaker. In the latter case, a part of you will, if nothing else, instinctively yearn for a bigger or better home, more creature comforts or adorable children (or grandchildren) who are shining examples to continue a family heritage, enabling you to bask in some parental reflected glory in the community.

Protectiveness, fertility and tenacity motivate you: You're the paragon of the tribal instinct. Frequently prophetic, as well as highly imaginative, you have very sensitive feelings that can get you into hot water. For example, since your symbol is the Crab, it's not inappropriate that people around you think you "crabby" when you become edgy or upset. Another variation finds you sullen and evasive when loved ones or others try to pry out of you the reason for your occasional pouting or touchiness, an exercise in futility (if you or they remember what a crab's shell is like).

Whether or not you're a dedicated homemaker or have a culinary flair, most of you appreciate the pleasures of the table. And whether you live in one room or a multi-room palace, you need a place you can call "home" that at the very least provides a sense of security.

Cancer, however, "senses" the impermanence of the visible trappings on which the conscious part of you depends for confidence. To feel secure, you must find true permanence and, therefore, inner peace in other values.

"He is happiest, be he King or peasant, who finds peace in his home." With those words, Virgo-born Goethe provided the key to fulfillment for the Cancer-born. You have several "homes," however, that have to be in order before you find security and repose from the buffetings of life. Your home may be, literally, the most gracious, most comfortable one for miles around. It may even be by the sea and as snug and cozy as human effort can make it. However, you are still going to be vulnerable to anxiety unless you have attended to something that you may not have thought much about: a properly nurtured psyche.

That's a part of you so personal that you more or less take it for granted. You know about *your* psyche from those deep responses, from the way it hurts when others have so thoughtlessly trampled on your feelings. You sense that you are quite clearly functioning as a normal Cancerian, so why bring up something so obvious? Well, your psyche is one of those "homes" we mentioned earlier—and the pivotal one, metaphorically speaking, if you are going to gain mastery over your feelings and a measure of control over all your various environments.

The first "home" you become conscious of, as an infant, is the one that contains you—your body and the blur of environment surrounding it. Later on in childhood you became more aware of your dwelling and its atmosphere—the effect that it and other people in it (parents, siblings) are having on you. Surely you remember: Outside in your pram, snow was on the ground, a wintry chill made your eyes glisten and your fingers tingle, but your inner imagery dispelled any discomfort. Thoughts of cozy rooms and enticing aromas wafting in from the kitchen were there outside with you. Your trusting reverie was private but very real to you. Your mind, body and feelings were comforted by the glow of anticipation, by your sense of permanence and protection. Assured that your haven was close by, warmly enveloping most of the time, sparked your innocent pleasure and became imbedded in your memory. As your development continued, you became conscious of environment in the larger sense: your community, your country, your world. With the Aquarian Age upon us as the 21st century unfolds, the farthest reaches of the global village edge ever closer to your door by way of your television screen or computer monitor.

The last, most important, but least understood "home" (that fundamental master key previously referred to) is the one that you are most sensitive to—your own psyche, the subterranean nucleus of your subconscious self. That's pretty deep within you, the primordial core of your being, but that's your ultimate frame of reference for life's critical issues. That won't be news to anyone who has basked in the nuances of your devoted and protective concern—or, in your less attractive moments, to anyone who has tried to pry you loose from one of your fearful, petulant or phlegmatic moods. At such times, you may be affected by something trivial, but the feelings aroused in you won't be superficial. That's why your powerful emotions are such a remarkable asset when constructively channeled into matters worthy of their depth. Your subconscious is the refuge to which you retreat when one or all of your "homes" are in upheaval or downright intolerable.

Your finely tuned sensitivities are barometers for the slightest variation in the emotional atmosphere. As unpredictable as the weather, you can be a rather complicated individual to adjust to. And this is how it works: Others must go at least halfway in the process of adjusting. Affected by the powerful pull of the Moon, it's difficult, if not impossible, for you to control the ebb and flow of your moods; they govern your responses to life. If you are a good actor, you may be able to discipline the projection of your moods and the effect they have on others, but inwardly you remain at their mercy. For this reason, two Cancerians probably shouldn't live together unless they (or one of them) can be very impersonal and willing to forego his or her inmost self-protective instincts when necessary, the exact reverse of typical Cancerian traits. However, when your subconscious "self" is in harmony with the world around you, you are the warmest, most compatible of people, the delightful pivot around whom all domestic felicity revolves.

Your attributes generally lead to success, according to the world of appearances so important to society: You easily acquire a home, a vocation, a mate, a car, whatever you desire (not necessarily in that order). Your chances are thus excellent to satisfy your need for emotional security through your natural acquisitiveness; your anxiety can be pacified by establishing as many roots and comfort as your environment can be made to physically provide. Crabs (Cancerians) and Bulls (Taureans) wouldn't seem to have much in common, but you share some highly desirable inclinations: You both do the best financially and materially of all the signs.

The United States, the wealthiest nation in the world, is a Cancer Sun-Sign country. According to a 1998 study, women, symbolized by the Moon generally, hold the U.S. purse strings. They control 80 percent of all household spending; they purchase 65 percent of all new cars; they buy 53 percent of all stocks. If this trend continues, women will control most of the money by the year 2020. The Cancer-born don't collect clippings, like Gemini; you are instead disposed toward homes, antiques, art objects and stocks, all things that are convertible into cash—and with your luck and instinct, probably at a profit. If you clip anything at all, it's likely to be coupons on tax exempt bonds.

You are a firm believer in property values but not so much for what they represent materially, as with Taurus, as for what they physically symbolize— continuity, roots, a link to the past. This sense of history, of tradition, induces within you a warm, comfortable feeling that, at some point in time, all was well and protected. With your vivid imagination, you subtly infuse the breath of life into objects that are inanimate to anyone else. They become props in the drama of your life. A yearning to sense permanence through things, a need to feel life's indestructibility, is gratified by you in this elementary way. If a house, a chair, a painting has survived man's and nature's foibles for centuries, you feel that there is surely hope then for life itself. You identify subconsciously with former occupants and owners, and you draw vicarious strengths that transcend time from these symbols of enduring continuity. No wonder you can feel edgy in a strange place. You have to feel at home wherever you are. Your moods can thus be tranquilized by the familiarity of your physical surroundings, a subtle benefit inherent in your sign.

The planet Saturn is the main culprit behind all those things that disturb your treasured peace. Ruler of Capricorn, the polar opposite of your sign, its meaning can become a heavy weight on you. It undermines your inclination to live in the past because it is the planet of the present, of inevitable periodic accountability. It can shatter conditions that you are comfortable with and may bring fresh responsibilities or an urgent necessity for changes into your life. You like to feel that life has permanence, that time can stand still. Saturn, the planet of aging, reminds you instead of the inexorable passing of time—that conditions *must* change. What mother, for instance, between loving her newborn infant and her subconscious knowledge of her offspring's inevitable departure from the nest can bear the thought of separation from this part of her own body, even though she is aware of that certainty sometime in the future? Saturn is the pressure that severs the umbilical cord.

"Men are what their mothers made them," according to Gemini-born Ralph Waldo Emerson, a statement that exemplifies the potent power of the maternal and nurturing instinct. The inexorable march of civilization is the collective biography of man. The evidence is impressive that the lunar influence is second only to that of the Sun, the giver of life. From the individual mother to the collective "mothering" or procreative instinct in humankind, each is a variant of the same force quietly coursing through all of nature.

Your ruler, the Moon, the symbol of instinct and emotion, is the mystical reflection of the solar light. It relates to the psyche or soul (from *solar*), just as individual men are the evolving reflection of the universal man. Not all women desire to be mothers, but those who do, even in signs not noted for maternal warmth, will have a possessive identification with their offspring. This is the ultimate response to the wellsprings of life, the joy of living and loving, the act of bringing forth into being; it is the subliminal step in the process of *becoming* and is particularly acute for Cancerians.

This deep awareness of thus being the instrument of life itself carries with it the awesome burdens of the past, as unconscious premonitions. Perhaps a submarine is missing: It isn't in the news yet, but a Cancerian can sense it. The notable memories of the Cancer-born are of two kinds: those garnered from conscious perceptions (accumulated from experience) and those that are instinctive. The latter are inherited and troubling to the soul (the imbedded recollections of past experiences) and are the strongest. Your forebodings are so powerful that you can't be reasoned with while under their sway. Experience and friends tell you that submarines are safer than automobiles, but an anxious Cancerian can remain unconvinced.

That famous statement of Sagittarius-born Santayana, "Those who do not remember the past are condemned to repeat it," has special poignancy where you are concerned. You remember the past on many levels. You never forget an emotional experience: your first love, your first disappointment, your first transgression, your first triumph, your first hate. You remember your emotional anguish, after your first brush with Cupid, when you finally decided to call it quits, when your liaison faded into history. You still have the snapshots or that book of poetry, however, and the memories have mellowed. In retrospect, you know that those were among your happiest times while they lasted.

Being psychic, you may feel like you have lived before. In a more subtle context, you remember large chunks of other *pasts* and would prefer not to repeat them. Instinctively knowing man's vanities and weaknesses—not to say insanities—and resultant destructiveness, you are made apprehensive by suspicion and mistrust of man's future and his ability to mold it safely. And who can blame you? Collective subliminal memories of departures and separations haunt you: parents; siblings; friends; lovers taken from the fold, some never to return. Sometimes the reasons seem so logical on the surface, but if you can never obliterate memories of man's barbaric madness from one epoch to the next, at least you can psychically emphasize the progress that has been forged out of suffering and travail and feel some comfort and hope from that. If you keep in mind that the planet of wisdom and spiritual quest, Jupiter, is exalted in your sign, you have an encouraging solution to your misgivings.

Jupiter is the symbol of faith, hope and belief. At home in Sagittarius, it is even more potent when its rays add the fire of enthusiasm to your nurturing qualities. You are strong on belief, but, being tenacious, you cling to those beliefs that have been etched into your mind and soul as satisfactory and comfortable, those that most likely stem from tradition and continuity. That's fine as far as it goes, but it is easy for you to get into a rut, to repeat past formulas in your personal life, because that is a course you feel to be the safest. New patterns, new meanings, new horizons should be included on your agenda. It will not profit you to repeat the downside of the traits you were born with, to settle for limited goals. While it is assuredly sensible to establish a dependable home and/or family life, are you droning away at the same level in the vocational or business realm or are you moving sideways from job to job? Are you overweight like mother because you are eating the same starchy foods that she favored while you were growing up? Or are your moods a weapon to intimidate your mate or lover because that is how you got your way as a child?

We begin our life with the traits of Cancer, Scorpio and the others, but they are just that—a beginning. They are the basic inclinations from which we forge character in the crucible of experience. As we develop dimension, comprehension and fresh perspective, so do we individually make our contribution to evolution. Cancerians can awaken us to new functions that assure the perpetuation of the race. Traditional environmental concepts may be shattered. You may feel lost and long to perpetuate imageries that you're more comfortable with. The thought of children being raised by day care instead of mothers and the possibility of cloning humans can depress you. That might be your initial reaction, but your spirit has its adventurous side, too, and your gift of imagination is formidable. Remember Jupiter? If you find a way to free your hidebound protective instincts from personal bias, the procreative principle, enhanced by vision, can immeasurably enrich your function in the broader context of the Aquarian Age. The alternative is stagnation, an unattractive process particularly identified with water, your element, so you are especially vulnerable.

Your ruler, the Moon, is astrology's procreative principle in action—or to be more accurate—reaction. The effect it has on the tides and the menstrual cycle is common knowledge. In a horoscope, it functions like a mirror: It is the fluctuating image of our inner self's need for expression and ego security, the reflective side of the solar power. It instinctively registers the extent and quality of the positive or negative impact we are making on life. Whatever our conscious ego is driven to seek, the Moon transmits the soul's evaluation of our status pertaining to that quest. This subtle and restless process is akin to the digestion of food in the stomach. Instead of food, however, the Moon mirrors the digestion of experience. The results are given back involuntarily, without your seeking them. Oftentimes, when your moods are blackest, you may think it isn't doing you any favors!

However, it works this way: If your adjustment to life is satisfactory, the inner image being reflected is flowing smoothly along with whatever you are reaching for in the outer world. The outer actuality and the inner reflection are complementary. When the inner image and the outer actuality clash, however, you have the genesis of emotional dysfunction. The attempt to bring these two factors back into alignment can prompt serious inner conflicts. The distortion you must live with during the process is "psychic" indigestion and can be more uncomfortable or excruciating than physical pain.

Psyche in Greek means "soul," so you get the message: When your soul hurts, you feel it at the very core of your being. The exact reason may vary or be difficult to pinpoint—or it may be a combination of things. In any case, the reflected ego takes refuge by retreating and withdrawing from the arena of experience to console and repair its disjointed inner image. This triggers those famous Cancerian "moods." The degree of lunar effectiveness in other signs depends on other factors.

The Moon, then, mirroring the ego, is the subtle barometer of inner psychological conditions. It represents the hidden side of the consciousness, the inner recesses of the ego, which we project as *feelings*. You might describe it as the reverse polarity of your conscious ego (your Sun-Sign), much like the relationship of the film negative to the actual print. The moods and temperament we externalize (along with our Sun-Sign traits) are the result of the "print," of this sensitive lunar function. On an entirely different level, for example, we define our solar potential through the values of our Sun-Sign, which we exemplify by our lifestyle: how we want our lives to turn out; the deep-rooted values we emphasize by our choices as life unfolds.

Because it has such powerful sway over *your* Sun-Sign (*your* lifestyle), this formative function of the Moon is especially important for Cancerians to understand. This means that you are poised somewhere between the negative and the print, to revert to our analogy. This is why your moods fluctuate so noticeably: You restlessly seek a functional center somewhere between the two, to resolve what you interpret as distortion. The Moon sends a message, which may or may not coincide with your Sun-Sign's intentions. As noted, protection, nourishment and growth are the processes that motivate you. Out of the raw materials of experience, your psychic digestion is continuously contributing to your inner image. Since you can't control the outer world, you can modify its impact on your inner world by screening out harmful influences and instead ingesting values that help you to understand and adjust to the complexities of living.

If your inner resources are healthy and optimistic, as with Cancerians Helen Keller and Mary Baker Eddy, your outlook is going to inspire growth through emotional faith. Your formative function will still be personal, but it will transcend the protection and nourishment of mere self. By linking your anchorage to universal concepts, your inner image isn't as vulnerable to mankind's petty foibles. Your inner image of yourself is strengthened. Instead of reacting apprehensively to disturbing experiences, your psychic response then supports and replenishes. The formative, procreative principle of the Moon is thus positively fulfilled, fortifying you with a reservoir of psychic security.

You wouldn't knowingly put the wrong food in your stomach, and what you select to digest emotionally is even more important. You can't change your emotional susceptibility, and you have no reason to. What *is* important is the interpretation you put on your feelings. Your possibilities for fulfillment are great. Your characteristics have produced impressive milestones in the panorama of human evolution.

What comes across the centuries in a Rembrandt painting? *Depth of feeling.* Motherhood, or a variation of it, is the subject of many of the works by this celebrated Cancerian. He evoked the beautiful mystique of nature's procreative power through his emotional insight. His paintings record his penetrating estimate of the nobility in human character. The images on his canvases resulted from the truth of his inner psychic reflections. He found the release that Cancerians seek, *his* peace, in his artistic creations. They were his true "children," and they still survive and continue to inspire millions of people.

Dedication to art and creativity is optional on many levels, although Cancerians are notably blessed with exceptional capabilities. However, dedicating yourself to the art of *living* is *essential*. Through a familiarity with the tremendous power of your ruling planet, the Moon, success is more easily attained. It will give you an inner calm, a contented adjustment to the world you live in, that can withstand many a storm.

With such a powerful force ruling your Sun-Sign, you can imagine the effect it can have on your disposition and general outlook. Cancerians are especially vulnerable to uncongenial conditions. You can be very exasperating to others in your circle. When something is bugging you, your adroit and indirect tactics are fascinating. Instead of coming out and voicing your grievance, you approach the target with an oblique maneuver, just like a crab. You come on sideways and become crabby about something else, driving everybody up the wall because no one can figure out just *what is* bothering you. You are testing the waters to see how far you can go. Your psychic antenna will tell you if the climate is favorable for your power ploy and if you are operating from strength. If so, you can unleash your pent-up emotions with impressive effect.

Your inherent dynamic range is unparalleled. That gentle, silver-haired paragon of sweetness and light in the Paris Louvre museum, à la Cancer-born Whistler, is the idealized "mother" symbol we all treasure close to our hearts. Forget her. She's a cliché. The real article is more exciting. Historic models, from the Virgin Mary to Clytemnestra and Medea, cover a broader range— from the Immaculate Conception all the way to vengeance, murder and infanticide. Of course, *you* wouldn't hurt anyone. When you're frustrated, you might just clam up for a day or two—or for several weeks—while you're mulling things over. That's *all*, hopefully. You can become so immersed in your own introspections that you are oblivious to the pinched atmosphere directly attributable to your mood.

Your enviable ability to stick to a course or a plan is an asset, but it all depends on how you apply it. The principle can work in reverse when you stick to something long after it has outlived any constructive usefulness. But being a water sign, sensitive to currents, you do know the value of an anchorage; the typical Cancer man and the typical Cancer woman have a central theme in mind—a home.

Emotions and love are the accompaniments to satisfying this deeper urge, the feeling of having roots somewhere. In the love, romance and marriage departments, you are affectionate, sentimental, exceedingly romantic and capable of great devotion and tenderness. In particular, Cancer men can be more than usually dependent on their mates, steady dates or live-in companions for approval, emotional support and attention.

In general, Cancerian feelings can run the gamut. After a deep dive into emotional waters and your feelings get hurt a few times, some of you will retreat into your shell and become super self-protective, which you eventually realize doesn't really solve anything if you still yearn for a soul mate. Once you distinguish between sentimentality, infatuation and love, however, and the right person comes along, your potential for happy togetherness and/or a rewarding marriage is great.

On the other hand, you may see marriage as the opportunity to build with a partner your brand of security, but you may not find the responsibilities that are part of the package so palatable. You encourage the complete devotion and closeness of your loved ones, but if you become preoccupied with other things, you can be annoyed with their indifference to sharing the load or helplessness without your guidance. As a result, you can be very dependent and at the same time variable and resentful if you've had to contribute more than your share to the common cause of marital and domestic bliss.

When emotionally insecure, you can find solace in all the sensual overindulgences, especially eating. Cancerians tend to become overweight as they age. Food is an agreeable substitute for the more mature emotional outlets, and the real source of frustrations or conflicts is thereby neatly sublimated or avoided. Your feelings are rightfully important to you, but if they are exclusively centered on serving *your* needs, you may wind up alone, a victim of your own emotional introversion. If your outlook is narrow, you will live on an emotional island, tenanted by trivial and selfish satisfactions. When your emotional outlook is broad, your feelings are as sensitively tuned to the needs of others as to your own. Then they become a miracle of warmth and comfort, a magnet attracting the love and understanding that you crave because others sense your protective concern for *their* well-being as well as your own.

At your best, then, you're the happy homemaker, the loving mate, the doting parent, the conscientious worker, the supportive executive, the sympathetic friend and the culinary expert *par excellence*. Whether it's the ambiance of your surroundings, suggesting a peaceful haven far removed from the worldly *Sturm und Drang*, or your caring manner and traditional values, you generally have a soothing effect on those lucky enough to bask in the warm glow of your love and solicitude.

CANCER BIRTHDAYS

Judgment of whether or not a birthday is propitious can be considered from two points of view: complementary or challenging. From the standpoint of personal progress and fulfillment, your destiny may flow more comfortably if your birthday is, or reduces to, an *outer* root number such as 2, 4, 6 or 8. For career drive and achievement, your progress may be enhanced if your birthday number is, or reduces to, an *inner* root number such as 1, 3, 5, 7 or 9; the *inner* root numbers are less comfortable, more obstructive for you to contend with, but they are potentially very conducive to outstanding success. The 11 (master number) would be variable but generally harmonious with the meaning of Cancer.

The 22 (master number) would be favorable for originality and recognition but generally would require more understanding and resourcefulness to integrate with the meaning of Cancer.

Remember, if your birthday is two digits (excepting master numbers 11 and 22), be sure to read the root digit or number first. For example, if your birthday is 29, read the 2 (2 + 9 = 11, 1 + 1 reduces to 2) birthday profile first and then read the special profile for 29. If your birthday is 14, read the 5 (1 + 4 = 5) birthday profile first and then read the special profile for 14, and so on. If a description in a "special" section contradicts information in the "root" digit (root number) analysis, the "special" interpretation applies more specifically to you.

The first planet in parentheses following your birthday number is *your Sun-Sign ruler*; the second planet (or Uranus/Saturn for number 8) is *your birthday number planetary equivalent*. Subsidiary planetary influences (if any) are bracketed.

Each birthday profile includes celebrities who share the same birthday.

YOUR BIRTHDAY PROFILE
July the 1st (Moon, Sun)
(and root digit for June 28, July 10 and 19):

Your pride is based in your ability to keep everyone and everything together and contented at home or in business. If you aim high, and don't allow your moods to undermine your purpose, you are destined for prestige and leadership in one context or another. You are well suited to established institutions, business houses, mercantile industries or any calling for which success depends on sensing or adapting to public moods and trends. You have outstanding creative talent and an instinct for the professional care and guidance of children or for family counseling. In a leadership role, the enduring quality of your endeavors can survive, and many generations will come to appreciate your genuine empathy for people and the human heart. With your sensitive feelings, however, you tend to take any criticism—even constructive—too personally. Consequently, it's to your advantage to develop sufficient self-confidence and the willpower to overlook the inevitable slights or negative feedback encountered in positions of prominence, competitiveness or authority.

When you meet with frustrations, you can't afford to be petty or churlish with those in your environment, for you may alienate someone in the most strategic position to provide the emotional security you seek. Since you must express yourself strongly to achieve, be sure that the self you put forward leaves shyness and fears behind and instead projects an image that reflects your inner reserves of quiet strength. It might take you longer to attain your objectives because you rarely risk safety to gain recognition. You may balk at changes that are vital to progress; you can procrastinate or put up a lot of negative resistance. If you are a stern taskmaster in a management role, it is offset by your flair for encouraging and showing off others' abilities to excellent advantage.

Much as it isn't your natural way, cold reason and logic might be necessary to put across your inspirations, which can have a brilliant effect. Your hunches can correctly tell you if something is or is not for you and if the time is right, but they may not be reliable where cool analysis and organization are the deciding factors between failure and success, such as in writing a play or a novel. Your growing-up years were in an atmosphere of material freedom, or your plans were aimed toward achieving it. Although you like luxuries, your income may not consistently support them. Make sure that it does.

Liv Taylor (actress), 1977
Diana Spencer (Princess of Wales), 1961
Carl Lewis (Olympic track star), 1961

Special to June 28 (Moon, Sun [Uranus/Saturn]):

Whether an issue concerns an individual family or the family of man you tend to be outspoken as well as enthusiastic in your liberal views about equality. You take a dim view of a society that lacks the courage and moral resources to reform itself. Personally, however, you can be brilliantly resourceful in carrying out complicated plans. Strong-willed and opinionated, responsibilities and the mantle of leadership in whatever field rest comfortably on your shoulders. People will probably never know by your confident facade if you're susceptible to Cancerian forebodings. When beset by uncertainties or frustrations, your typical reaction is to project a positive image; that's the kind of impression you make, which certainly doesn't hinder your success potential. Your remembrance of your birthplace is so ingrained that, even if the memories aren't all that pleasant, your attachment to it remains strong. In your job or creative efforts, you combine psychic and intuitive flashes with practicality—a formula for meaningful fulfillment, the kind that identifies with the longing for permanence and happiness in the minds and hearts of those nearest and dearest or in the public realm. You are affectionate and do not suffer restraints gladly; if you're preoccupied with achieving your goals, however, you won't have time for dalliance and are likely to be consistent in your affectional ties and love life.

John Elway (football player), 1960

Richard Rodgers (composer), 1902

Henri Rousseau (artist), 1844

Special to July 10 (Moon, Sun):

Efficient, effective, or inspired could be among the words most often used by friends, coworkers or an appreciative public to describe you. Your Cancerian caution and restraint are apparent in your careful choice of words when offering an opinion or making a decision. Protective of your estimable standards, you're ready and willing to stand your ground when the integrity of your work or a project is threatened. However, if throwing in the towel is occasionally necessary and/or costly, it can also be a stepping-stone to bigger and better things.

In your sometimes sideways, sometimes upwardly mobile climb to success, you may have less and less time to enjoy domestic ambiance and the comforts of family life. In which case, your home could become primarily a haven from the cares of the day, a sanctuary for emotional sustenance, the management of which you willingly leave to others. You are very determined and find plenty of time for your own pursuits, however, and are well equipped to handle complexities, as well as people and the public in general.

Arthur Ashe (tennis player), 1943

Saul Bellow (novelist), 1915

Marcel Proust (novelist), 1871

Special to July 19 (Moon, Sun [Pluto]):

Along with your Cancerian caution and reserve, you're also likely to be secretive under your deceptively calm, sphinx-like exterior. Whether you're pondering the mysteries of the universe or harboring a clandestine scheme, you know the advantage of keeping motives, conclusions or strategies under your hat until you are ready to spring them. Once you're set on a course of action, particularly a private indulgence or satisfaction, you couldn't care less about others' opinions or reactions to it. You would probably dismiss any suggestion to explain or justify your personal proclivities. Your ideas about family values and the social order in general can run the gamut from traditional to extreme and controversial.

Charismatic, adventurous, experimental, occasionally provocative, pride in you home and/or family life and a compulsion to have things your way can almost become a phobia. You are very self-protective and can be suspicious, cagey or controlling, especially if you think people are poking around in your private affairs or questioning your motives. When gifted in the creative fields, your subtle stylistic insights convey a remarkable understanding of the human condition.

Anthony Edwards (actor), 1962

A. J. Cronin (novelist), 1896

Edgar Degas (artist), 1834

July the 2nd (Moon)
(and root digit for June 29 and July 20;
July 11 is a master number, see end of chapter):

You will find plenty of opportunities to express your motives and feelings with this birthday, but be careful that you don't drift in a sea of sentiment or accommodation and then resent the consequences. You should strive to live in the present and be as positive as possible because you are exceptionally receptive, particularly to public trends and tastes. People seek you out and enjoy your company because you are sympathetic and understanding, and you know how to adapt to situations. Your knowledge about your area of expertise, as well as a variety of diverse subjects, can be formidable, not to say profitable. Nevertheless, your personal appeal could contribute as much to your success as your skills.

You have a flair for diplomacy and a generally conservative outlook, and you are willing to give important support behind the scenes. You can be patient and gentle to a fault. If people seem to take you for granted, the solution is not to withdraw into one of your moods and sulk in your protective shell but to get busy and capitalize on your progressive instincts and initiate some affirmative action. Avoid depressing surroundings whenever possible because, like a blotter, you are supersensitive and tend to absorb the atmosphere around you.

You like material advantages and comforts but are not inclined to disturb your safety, much less go out on a limb aggressively or recklessly to gain them. Not naturally competitive, you prefer familiarity and contentment to adventure but can be very enterprising if gains are possible and action is called for. You have universal insights and a humanitarian outlook, which may be the result of a decentralized childhood. Talented as an instructor or leader, you have excellent custodial instincts and should do well financially. You are not likely to risk basic security. You are either an accumulator or a discerning collector, or a bit of both. Your home or base of operations is more likely to be welcoming or cluttered than bare bones.

>Dan Rowan (comedian), 1922
>
>Thurgood Marshall (U.S. Supreme Court Justice), 1908
>
>Franz Kafka (author), 1883

Special to June 29 (Moon, Pluto):

Magnetic and fascinating, part of you always remains hidden from your family or others. If necessary to protect your privacy, you'll shift into your controlling mode, a trait that, at its most objective, is most rewarding in connection with your job or business management abilities. Avoid becoming too preoccupied with emotional complications. Your Cancerian needs for domestic protection and security are strong, but your intensity and self-absorption could hinder the enjoyment of relaxing relationships and warm affectional ties. Your occasionally enigmatic moods are not easy for others to adjust to, in which case you'll need an understanding mate or partner. Just remember that the emotional pendulum swings both ways. You enjoyed an atmosphere of material freedom in childhood, or your childhood visions centered on ways of making your ambitious dreams come true.

Whether in the creative fields, the business world or government, you bring formidable expertise and experience to your efforts. If you start with an entry-level job, your subtle capabilities and unswerving inner drive eventually enable you to reach the top. You would excel at any job that requires reformative skills, a clean sweep and a fresh perspective. Along the way, cultivate easygoing rapport with coworkers and capitalize on your enviable ability to stay calm under pressure.

>Nelson Eddy (singer, actor), 1901
>
>Luisa Tetrazzini (singer), 1871
>
>Peter Paul Rubens (artist), 1577

Special to July 20 (Moon):

With a wide range of possibilities to choose from, you could do well in a variety of ventures, preferably in an atmosphere of cooperation and protection. The lunar influence on your birthday isn't as narrowly or effectively focused as for some Cancerians, but the broader scope of your interests, initiatives and experiences provides ample compensation. You have the advantage of a keen sense of mass taste, trends and fads, so any occupation or profession that deals with the public or serves its needs, whether directly or peripherally, would be one in which you could flourish. Although you have numerous available options, you're not inclined to jeopardize your security in order to get ahead in the world.

Without becoming a "clinging vine," you express your emotional nature with sympathy and affection. Your Cancerian interest in home and family may be more detached or impersonal than is typical of members of your sign. This may stem from a disorganized childhood that curtailed hearthside warmth and togetherness and may have given your education short shrift, leaving it up to you to acquire mental discipline and knowledge from the school of experience.

   Natalie Wood (actress), 1938

   Diana Rigg (actress), 1928

   Sir Edmund Hillary (mountain climber), 1919

July the 3rd (Moon, Venus)
(and root digit for June 30, July 12 and 21):

You will have opportunities to give creative form to your emotional insights and intuitions. You have great flair for any artistic endeavor where your imagination and feelings can be freely expressed. Your inspirations can be splendidly rewarding in the decorative arts field (tasteful colors, furnishings, fabrics, etc.), perhaps better than in the fine arts.

When in one of your sulking moods, your aversion to frivolous badinage can make you antisocial and inarticulate. But that isn't typical; you are usually sociable and charming. In fact, too much so when your feelings get the better of you, and then you can go overboard, becoming overly solicitous, compliant and sentimental in your affections. Charismatic and personable, you function well with the public, but you won't function well in a job or career that too erratically disturbs your need for a peaceful haven. The security of a comforting home or family life contributes to your success. You are likely to attract a good income, will probably spend freely on your home, its decoration and creature comforts and could somehow profit through your heredity.

Your Cancerian penchant for acquisitiveness is accentuated: You can be too concerned with materiality. Emotional restiveness and overdoing the good life can hamper accomplishment if your energies aren't disciplined and directed into productive or expressive channels. As you grew up, you were conscious of the need to develop your individuality in some distinctive way, to stand out from the crowd. You'll probably leave your birthplace environment before you are thirty and will establish a base elsewhere.

Tom Cruise (actor), 1962

Tom Stoppard (playwright), 1937

Stavros Niarchos (shipping tycoon), 1909

Special to June 30 (Moon, Venus):

You can be very effective in the arts and music because of your combination of determination and receptivity. You have a decided bent for civic or community service or leadership. You can participate very productively in any cause or pursuit that brightens life for others or makes them feel secure and their feelings deserving of respect and fulfillment. Your interest in history, education or parental concerns could influence your choice of vocation or profession.

When an opportunity attracts you, there's nothing superficial about your contribution to the success of a group or community project. In fact, your coworkers or those who benefit from your job efforts and nurturing instincts are likely to consider you an irreplaceable force for progress and enlightenment. Like the crab, once you get a hold of something, you don't let go. This is great if your choice is intelligent and not just a passing fancy. If you've unwisely gotten into a negative situation, however, you can just as persistently hang on instead of facing the truth and admitting your mistake. You'll find happiness by externalizing your quest for truth and beauty through worthwhile accomplishment, rather than personalizing it self-indulgently.

Mike Tyson (boxer), 1966

Lena Horne (singer), 1918

Susan Hayward (actress), 1918

Special to July 12 (Moon, Venus [Sun/Moon]):

You can find the most rewarding expression of your Cancerian traits in articulating as well as living your deeply held feelings about family values, housing and environmental conditions in general. Whether it's an addition to your domicile, a new building from the ground up or some sort of cultural project, you are receptive to change and progress and are an apt spokesperson. The past, present or future of design or construction techniques and architectural history could intrigue you and benefit from your perceptive artistic insights. Possibly a visionary where the human family and the cultivation of its highest potential are concerned, you can be a source of farsighted encouragement and/or nurturing opportunities to make life more productive and fulfilling in whatever sphere of endeavor.

Your background can be a source of pride and inspiration, prompting you to follow in the footsteps of family forbears who have set an example of achievement for you to emulate or surpass. An expert negotiator when conflicts occur, your nurturing instinct as well as your sense of humor shine through effectively when neighborhood or community issues, such as complaints about air and noise pollution or conflicts among personalities, need settling.

Bill Cosby (comedian), 1937

Van Cliburn (pianist), 1934

Kirsten Flagstad (singer), 1895

Special to July 21 (Moon, Venus [Moon/Sun]):

Your magnetism and creative gifts are notable assets if you choose a public career. In any occupation or profession, you are an invigorating influence. Protective and generous, you are more self-promotive and assertive than is typical for Cancerians, which, if you're not prudent, could be a frustrating drawback, especially in a leadership role. Whether or not it alienates associates and hurts your cause, you're not shy about stating blunt home truths. Of course, if you can find a way to express your firm, and perhaps controversial, opinions and gutsy enthusiasms more diplomatically, your honesty and experience are distinctive advantages and can carry the day in a dispute.

Very receptive to beauty, your tendency to become nervous and moody when you find yourself in a discordant environment needs a constructive outlet, such as giving your ideals and creative imagination practical expression; that way, any unaccountable aversions to things or people (or both) can be minimized because you won't have the time or energy to dwell on them. When things take a turn for the worse in any situation, you know how to assess the prevailing feelings, stem the tide and initiate the rebuilding process.

Robin Williams (actor), 1952

Isaac Stern (violinist), 1920

Ernest Hemingway (novelist), 1899

July the 4th (Moon, Saturn)
(and root digit for July 13;

June 22 and July 22 are master numbers, see end of chapter):

You are determined and persevering and, willingly or not, could find yourself saddled with more than your quota of domestic or other responsibilities. You may have to work harder than other Cancerians to establish your rightful place in the scheme of things. If at first you don't find your most promising niche in the job or career realm, you will either keep plugging away until you do or drift into a rut of emotional discouragement from which it may be difficult to extricate yourself. On the job or in a matriarchal or patriarchal role, you might be responsible for the preservation and smooth-running efficiency of a group or organization that depends on facts, diligent effort and strict guidelines for success. Material security can be an issue, making you cautious with finances and wary of risks or gambles.

Not typically expansive in your thinking, you might consider hard work, even laborious effort, to be the key component for the success of a creative of business project. On the other hand, your enterprising spirit can overcome obstacles that (perhaps naively) you're unaware of until you encounter them. You have the power to reshape artistic or commercial concepts and bring forth new forms. You were probably more sensitive than the typical Cancerian child, and your ambition might be fueled by childhood memories of hardship or struggle and/or an underprivileged family background.

You would be unhappy without a challenge and would find something else to resent. At least a worthwhile challenge can be productive and rewarding. You may come to realize there are many factors in running a home or enterprise successfully besides strict scheduling and dedication to chores. You will generally feel at home with industrious coworkers, although at times their monotonous attention to details can depress you. Make time for relaxation and cultivate a lighthearted attitude. Taking yourself and the world less seriously goes a long way toward making your life more fulfilling. At your best, you are a very inspired, even compulsive, achiever and can accomplish memorable results in the creative, professional or business worlds.

George Steinbrenner (baseball team owner), 1930

Neil Simon (playwright), 1927

George M. Cohan (actor, dramatist), 1878

Special to July 13 (Moon, Saturn [Sun/Venus]):

Security, a supportive haven, pride in accomplishment, time-consuming thoroughness and feelings of continuity are very important to you, but you may find it difficult to make the adjustments necessary to attain them. If your susceptibility to temperamental moods gets the upper hand, it may be due to forces pulling you in different directions; then willpower can turn into willfulness or won't-power. Your restless ego and your desire to express yourself unencumbered by obstacles could meet with setbacks that have little regard for your sensitive feelings.

Conditions in your home or work environment don't always seem to encourage the course that you feel is best for you. Be sure you have thought out everything carefully before you place the blame on fate or are tempted to settle along lines of least resistance. Practical, you do well in an administrative capacity or in any area where dogged determination, nurturing and conserving your own as well as the group spirit are essential for success. When absorbed in an artistic or commercial project, you're not put off by diverse complexities or a workload others might consider drudgery. When at your best, especially in a strategic role, you set an inspiring example with your eagerness to pitch in, get on with it and get the job done.

Harrison Ford (actor), 1942

Dave Garroway (TV program host), 1913

Sir Kenneth Clark (art historian), 1903

July the 5th (Moon, Mars)
(and root digit for June 23 and July 14):

Your outgoing urges and/or opportunities conflict with your emotional and indrawn nature. You're not always in the mood for action and change or for home and family life at full throttle, but you may as well get used to it. You will realize your estimable potential by finding a central focus for the contradictions in your makeup. A born traditionalist, with strong feelings for family values and/or real estate, you could simultaneously maintain or be involved in several homes or properties. A wily tactician can lurk beneath your pleasant facade, enabling you to cultivate diverse interests and be adaptable along lines that don't threaten your domestic anchorage too much. You like travel and fresh experiences but are happy to return home.

If a you're typical Cancerian, certain traits may need to be restrained. For example, you should live more in the present and be willing to discard much of the past, which, however, doesn't preclude taking advantage of auspicious family roots or connections. Having to face many changes that spell the difference between progress and retrenchment, you sometimes will be in a quandary because change can require an uprooting, basically something Cancerians dislike. You will profit by considering the past as a point of departure rather than a comfortable haven in which to retreat to nurse your anxieties. More likely to lead an active outdoor life than the average

Cancerian, you need the security of love and a home, but your attempts to attain them could be more adventurous than deeply satisfying.

If you flow with swift-moving currents, poised and assured, instead of stewing in the backwater and eddies, you will gain remarkable success and independence. Whether or not you're well prepared by your heredity, environment or training, your aggressive energies and gutsy will-to-win enable you to travel far on the road to personal fulfillment and achievement. If there are detours or defeats along the way, you could, with your spunky instincts, probably find a way to profit from them.

   Huey Lewis (singer), 1951
   Jean Cocteau (author), 1891
   P. T. Barnum (circus producer), 1810

Special to June 23 (Moon, Mars [Venus]):

Self-sufficient, practical, sociable and independent, you find many satisfactory outlets for the realization of your Cancerian traits. Medicine, the law, music or a custodial position can provide constructive outlets for the expression of your ideals and sympathies. Whether or not your rise is from humble origins, an inferiority complex stemming from one childhood source or another could be the psychological quirk that propels you toward accomplishment of your goals. You'll probably get an early start in the world of work, acquiring job skills, learning valuable lessons about self-reliance, creative discipline and responsibility along the way.

You have plenty of grit, energy and ambition to overcome discouraging obstacles in your climb to success. It takes a lot to get you down; your drive and determination to achieve may be low-key, perhaps comparable to an inner flame of religious fervor, but it is just as effective as the more agitated or more obvious efforts of competitors. In your restless drive to get ahead, however, you may need to carefully control your physical activities instead of allowing them to control you and deplete your reservoir of emotional strength and energy, which could jeopardize your health and vitality. While you may be a model of achievement, don't assume that others have equivalent talents to follow in your footsteps; you could be a widely acclaimed original.

   Frances McDormand (actress), 1957
   James Levine (music director, Metropolitan Opera), 1943
   Bob Fosse (dancer, choreographer), 1927

Special to July 14 (Moon, Mars [Sun/Saturn]):
Very receptive to appeals to your feelings and sympathies, you feel that you are lucky and are willing to gamble. You learn well from experience, especially how to organize large groups of people to your own as well as their benefit. You never plunge lightly into the fray; your vigorous initiatives stem from, and are anchored to, well-thought-out motives. Your personal changes may be prompted more by nervous discontent with the present than from having a positive plan for the future. If you allow ambivalence or negative emotions to get the upper hand, your vulnerability to discouragement can impede the realization of your ambitions.

Your tireless energies can provide inspirational stimulus for a wide audience. In a creative context, you are able to articulate the problems as well as the achievements of your own and prior generations with understanding and conviction. You sense of humor is likely to be the self-deprecating variety. In your view, the principal purpose of creative efforts is to keep the public interested in salient ideas. Your quietly affirmative philosophy comes through in your dedication to continuing a worthwhile tradition, gratitude for life's rewards, appreciation for every step up the success ladder and penetrating insights into family, cultural and historic relationships.

Ingmar Bergman (director), 1918
Gerald Ford (38th U.S. president), 1913
Irving Stone (writer), 1903

July the 6th (Moon, Jupiter)
(and root digit for June 24 and July 15):
Yours is the perfect birthday for domestic felicity, but that doesn't mean it will be handed to you on a silver tray. You can be dominated by your yearning to relate and protect and thus defeat your purpose by becoming too smothering in your attentions. If for any reason you lack emotional security, you can become meddlesome and self-righteous. However, you are the ideal person to handle burdens and responsibilities graciously when you extend, and are in turn surrounded by, the love and domestic warmth and protection you treasure.

Your home, your mate, your children, your parents, your country, your God, all the relationships that gratify emotional yearnings, are sources of maximum fulfillment for you. You may satisfy your basic values broadly, blending your career, custodial or nurturing instincts in a combined effort involving many people or more simply in marriage and children. Your inner core of optimism and benevolence is your safety net; you're likely to attract conditions that favor security and generally protect you from want.

If you choose a creative path, although your skills will be well grounded, you will express as much or more through self-assured enthusiasm and feeling as through technical brilliance. You easily attract partnerships and support, and possibly an obligation or two (or more), because of the attitude of carefulness, reliability and concern that you project. Your childhood may have been somewhat restrictive or disruptive, but it was excellent preparation for the acceptance of responsibilities when you are ready to make your way in the world.

Sylvester Stallone (actor), 1946

Dalai Lama (Tibetan religious leader), 1935

Nancy Reagan (actress, First Lady), 1921

Special to June 24 (Moon, Jupiter [Saturn]):

Whether or not you ever retire from the workforce, you will one way or another profit from always remaining busy. The choice between pursuing serious objectives or scattering your energies will determine the extent of your fulfillment. Your splendid Cancerian instincts serve you well in a custodial or advisory position. You like comfortable surroundings and are somehow protected. Part of your success can stem from an appealing trait: In the business or professional realm, you're apt to project the warm feeling that you're not just dealing with clients or customers but with members of a family. Public appreciation of this sort of extended personal interaction with people contributes to your evolvement and subsequent impact and success, which can be considerable. You know how to husband your resources and turn them into big financial gains.

A childhood illness or other restriction, perhaps a family-related setback or a rough road to success, can instill in you a strong respect for the preciousness of life and security. An admirer of popular achievers, you have the inborn qualifications to become one yourself, and you might even establish new records of accomplishment and/or acclaim. Compassionate, generous, good at maintaining discipline and working with children, you'll take the trouble to ingratiate yourself with admirers, whether on a personal level or in the public domain.

Michele Lee (actress), 1942

Jack Dempsey (boxer), 1895

E. I. duPont (industrialist), 1771

Special to July 15 (Moon, Jupiter [Sun/Mars]):
Broadly understanding and sympathetic, your Cancerian home-loving and life-enhancing traits are strongly emphasized. With your penchant, and possibly gift, for music, the arts and promoting a supportive atmosphere—and your flair for capitalizing on them—you can attract many things to you that are fulfilling. An enthusiastic worker, you have the stamina, forcefulness and energy to maximize your income potential and aren't likely to do anything that could hinder your pursuit of job, career and/or financial success. You aim to claim your share of the abundance rewarded to middle- or upper-class society members who advocate upholding or furthering property and/or family values.

You are not a willing subordinate and would do best in an independent vocational or career endeavor. That the world of appearances is important to you can mean many things, among them the personal impression you project to accurately reflect or bolster your job or professional credibility. You like to set a good example and may be the Cancerian with the most deeply rooted belief in the nurturing ethos, seeing the burdens of parenthood as your first duty. More athletic than the typical Cancerian, you might have a keen interest in sports as either a participant or spectator.

Jesse Ventura (wrestler and governor of Minnesota), 1951

St. Francis X. Cabrini (missionary), 1850

Rembrandt van Rijn (artist), 1606

July the 7th (Moon, Mercury)
(and root digit for June 25 and July 16):
Governed more by instinct than logic, you can become restless and moody when circumstances require cold reasoning. Because you typically "feel" that something is the thing to do, your experiences can initially be nervously unsettling to your sensitive nature. The fluctuating emotions typical of Cancer are not conducive to relaxed coordination with the cerebral requirements of the 7; but when they are in synch, you can achieve notable results in the arts or a profession, enhanced by scrupulously detailed craftsmanship. In an administrative or supervisory capacity, you are the hub of the wheel and know how to bring out the best in people.

Meanwhile, if you don't come by it naturally, you may as well resign yourself to cultivating mental discipline and depth. In the creative and professional realms, it will enable you to profit handsomely and to tap deep wells of emotional insight within yourself of which you are probably unaware. It is the only sensible way to be prepared for problems when they inevitably arise in your life and when there won't be time for a cram course in intellectual analysis when they are pressing in on you. You may not have the option of "feeling" for answers when you must make immediate decisions, arrived at impersonally, that may determine the outcome of your future.

Personal freedom and a restless nature in your growing-up period led to varied experiences as you actively sought to gratify emotional yearnings. Along with your belief that anything important lasts, or should last, forever, you're likely to have an astounding memory, even for the minute details of events in your life that occurred many decades before.

> Ringo Starr (singer, drummer), 1940
>
> Pierre Cardin (designer), 1922
>
> Marc Chagall (artist), 1887

Special to June 25 (Moon, Mercury [Mars]):

Idealistic and hopeful, you are inclined to be a person of few words. Those few words, however, can carry more weight and influence more lives than all the profuse verbalizing from people less talented, less concise, less informed and less experienced than you. No one could ever say that you're one of those people who talk all the time and never say anything. In a position of authority, you don't say a lot, but what you do say is worth hearing and can prod people into productive action. You can make history in whatever field you excel in. And whatever your gender, you're a sort of nurturing, encouraging "Mother Hen" where budding talents are concerned.

Your home is with you, in your mind, even when you are away from it, which, since you're apt to be pretty active, may be often. You will profit by developing concentration and purpose to counterbalance the tendency to be erratic or impatient and to surrender to your moods. Your talents are as commercial as intellectual; a sense of discipline, if not a taste for it, was acquired in childhood and can be very useful in any career pursuit. With your gift for the well-turned phrase and engaging expressive instincts, you can be an excellent writer, teacher, historian, administrator, director or archeologist. Charitable in your own way, you know how to make money and how to hang on to it.

> George Michael (singer), 1963
>
> Carly Simon (singer), 1945
>
> George Orwell (author), 1903

Special to July 16 (Moon, Mercury [Sun/Jupiter]):
The knowledge, spiritual development, enthusiasm and encouraging insights that can be so beneficial to Cancerians and to those whose lives they touch are emphasized in your birthday. You cannot afford a narrow viewpoint or self-centered introspections. Deliberate cultivation of an interest in others' needs and publicly oriented activities can bring opportunities for remarkable creative expression in the music, theatrical or literary field. Whether on the job, in the arts or the business world, you should do well financially, enjoying the status, freedom and comfortable surroundings that success and money bring. With your skill at rolling out a verbal red carpet, you're a whiz at mixing business with pleasure on home turf.

If you are able to translate your deepest feelings into thoughts or words as convincingly in relationships as in the job or career realm, your ventures in romance, marriage, parenting and/or domesticity will be successful and happy—or at least satisfactory. If not, you may stumble a time or two, settle for an uneasy truce or remain frustrated because you aren't mentally able to bridge the gap that prevents sympathetic understanding of your own or others' emotional expectations or shortcomings.

Michael Flatley (dancer), 1958

Pinchas Zuckerman (violinist), 1948

Ginger Rogers (actress), 1911

July the 8th (Moon, Uranus/Saturn)
(and root digit for June 26 and July 17):
This is an excellent birthday for you. Your protective, nurturing instinct, combined with the opportunity for promotion and expansion, can lead to impressive material freedom. Although you depend on a domestic base for inner support and strength, your instinct for management, efficiency and publicity can reward you with a position of responsibility, power and authority. Since Cancer (with Taurus) is one of the best financial signs, your birthday promises to bring significant cash flow in your direction. It doesn't, however, guarantee security (which is something else). If you are extravagant, money then flows out as fast, or faster, than it flows in.

A well-paid profession, business position, family-related enterprise and career in government are all possibilities that promise the kind of success for which you are destined. With your flair for the common touch, an interest or participation in public affairs can be very fruitful. If you fulfill your maximum career and moneymaking potential, you're more apt to be found in a limousine than on a bus. A Cancerian woman with this birthday might prefer marriage and motherhood to a career—frequently becoming the force and support behind a successful man.

In your natural eagerness to gain objectives, be careful to avoid extremes. You can exhaust yourself by straining the limits of your mental energies and vitality, and you can forget other needs, your own as well as those of your family or other close associates. Your Cancerian feelings need to be flexed. Be wary of emotional rigor mortis because of your intense concentration on the big picture. Your childhood impressed upon you the values of family love and security.

Anjelica Huston (actress), 1951

Nelson Rockefeller (governor of New York), 1908

Count Ferdinand von Zeppelin (dirigible designer), 1838

Special to June 26 (Moon, Uranus/Saturn [Moon/Jupiter]):

If you're excessively dependent on the past and traditions generally, it can be detrimental to the free flow of your development. Very family oriented, you enjoy all the domestic delights—homemaking, parenting, the pleasures of the table. You are talented and expressive and may do best in some creative activity or public function. A job or career that kindles enthusiasm, inspiration and sympathetic public response or that caters to mass tastes and needs will be rewarding. There was much change and activity in your growing-up period, which was excellent preparation for a busy life.

If you feel that you have a mission to fulfill, your creative output won't necessarily have the distinction that your career itself will have. Strong-willed and opinionated, you can attract controversy. In your view, getting the message across and the job done—and affecting as many people as possible—are more important than attention to the style or finish of your work, which nevertheless might incubate in your mind for a long time before you give it concrete form. Whether or not the creative result is absorbing and/or appealing to popular taste, it may fall short of the ultimate accolades of critical acclaim.

Chris O'Donnell (actor), 1970

Greg LeMond (cyclist), 1961

Pearl Buck (author), 1892

Special to July 17 (Moon, Uranus/Saturn [Sun/Mercury]):

You have excellent custodial abilities and a flair for turning your enterprises into profits. This is especially true when you are controlling the adventurous (or erratic) element in your nature, such as when you might choose a different path to pursue than your family background, or start in life, would indicate. You are primarily conservative, but enthusiasms or stubbornness can cloud your judgment, causing you to scatter and dissipate results. At your best, you're able to bring the universal human condition to life in an enlightening way. With your tough mind and kind heart, concentrate on the big picture and leave the grunt work and details to others; there's no use pretending that you have much taste for them.

Whether you rise from the ranks of the aristocracy, or from more humble beginnings, you're likely to become as well known on the job or professionally for your sharp retorts and/or words of wisdom as you are for your skills. With your mental dexterity, you're able to articulate the elemental essence of the basic broth of life, such as the Cancerian love of land and family, and to do it with convincing sincerity.

Diahann Carroll (singer), 1935
Donald Sutherland (actor), 1934
James Cagney (actor), 1904

July the 9th (Moon, Pluto)
(and root digit for June 27 and July 18):

Since concerns outside yourself will predominate in your pattern, in conflict with the fact that you are the most personally motivated of the signs, your birthday can be either exciting or discouraging. You may be very disappointed, as your experiences multiply, when what the world expects of you conflicts with your highly personal Cancerian feelings. Ambitious in a non-flamboyant, low-keyed, persevering way, you don't usually crave the limelight or the kind of top echelon position that invites open, rough and ready competition . . . or public scrutiny.

Because you have a well-developed psychic radar to what goes on around you, you often are able to make in advance the right moves to get ahead, or to protect yourself against possible reverses or take advantage of job market or financial opportunities. You have a sort of sixth sense about money and are likely to accumulate (or inherit) valuable possessions, as well as to shrewdly build up your financial resources and stash them away for the proverbial rainy day.

You long for a cozy hearth and find instead that the world is your fireside, demanding much, or the bulk, of your attention. Your penchant for thorough workmanship brings impressive authenticity and conviction to your job skills or creative inspirations. Your strong will coupled with your emotional depth can make you a sensitive leader, primarily in a profession such as a literary one with an accent on history. The cyclic, disruptive nature of your pattern is inimical to a consuming interest in a purely personal life. The results of a mentally reclusive and subjective growing-up period enhance your prospects when you begin to make your way in the world. You're likely to have few complaints when you reach your sunset years.

Jimmy Smits (actor), 1958

Tom Hanks (actor), 1956

Barbara Cartland (writer), 1901

Special to June 27 (Moon, Pluto [Moon/Mercury]):

Career or personal outlets that emphasize your protective traits will be most congenial for you, enabling you to achieve considerable gratification and influence. Domestic and environmental responsibilities appeal to you, perhaps to excess; you can overdo your role in the home, or at least your voluble comments about your expectations. You are affectionate but independent and somewhat unorthodox. Your upbringing instilled in you a reverence for domestic harmony and the sense of security to be derived from it. You would do well in a job, business or profession that capitalizes on your mental agility and flair for mass psychology and tastes.

A bit like Pisces, you lean toward privacy. You might prefer a background role of influence where you can be an opinion molder, pull strings, let ideas develop and thus progress slowly but surely in your naturally indirect, subtle but persuasive manner. Material stability being one of your must-haves, you'll do a lot of working, planning, maneuvering and even sacrificing (if need be) in order to assure future security for yourself and your loved ones.

H. Ross Perot (business executive, U.S. presidential candidate), 1930

Bob Keeshan (TV actor, producer), 1927

Helen Keller (author, educator), 1880

Special to July 18 (Moon, Pluto [Sun/Uranus/Saturn]):

Having tried many things, you might rise through the training ranks of lower positions to eventually move rung-by-rung up the success ladder to achieve the independence essential to you. Your gift is for administration and efficiency in an activity of broad public scope. As you become less personally motivated and more involved in community affairs, you can be an entirely different person in the latter part of your life. If you begin in the arts, for example, you eventually might branch out into, or include, political or other activities as a result of your proven organizational or leadership abilities.

In workplace or career endeavors that depend on teamwork for success, you like to encourage the feeling of a family involved in pursuing a common, mutually beneficial goal. Whether in independent or group efforts, you combine an earthy philosophy with an innovative twist or broad vision that sets you apart from others in whatever field you choose to function. If family members or others turn to you for advice, you're ready with a solution as warm and reassuring as it is brisk and insightful. You have considerable drawing power in the public domain.

John Glenn (astronaut, U.S. senator), 1921
Nelson Mandela (South African president), 1918
Red Skelton (comedian), 1913

July the 11th (Moon, Neptune [Moon/Sun])
(master number):

Artistic, inspirational, you can be an expert, a connoisseur or a tastemaker in whatever field you choose to showcase your talents. In any job or career context, you have uncanny insights into other people and their feelings. Your magnetism is unusual and subtle; when you believe in a project or a cause, every breath you take and every waking moment can be dedicated to accomplishing your goal as you see it. On the other hand, if your inner goals lack moral purpose and firmness, you can drift along in a sea of sentiment, delusion and parasitical dependence. You will meet conditions in your life that call for illumination and psychic insight that to the uninitiated might seem mystical. You have the ability to provide special understanding in situations where previously none existed and is greatly needed.

You are the specialist—mediating differences between new principles and traditional concepts. Your powerful imagination can convince you of the rightness of your beliefs. If you allow moral principles to become undermined by your desire nature, you can become the victim of aimless debauchery. Strive to be a living example of creative and/or spiritual vision, and give ideals workable form in family relationships, the community, the artistic or intellectual world or the family of man.

You probably felt bereft and decentralized as a child, a sensitive victim of unfulfilled emotional yearnings. If so, that might have been the genesis of your determination to acquire knowledge or skills enabling you to rise above the crowd. You do have your moonswept moods; with your fascination for nostalgia, you could delight in picking over the bones of the past. No matter where you're born, you'll probably pull up stakes and live elsewhere in pursuit of your career goals and then return to your original locale. But regardless of where you live, you'll have ardent connections to home and nature, in body or spirit, underscored by your irreverent wit and candor.

(Remember, if you don't respond to the higher vibration of the 11, you will express the more conventional attributes and drawbacks of the 2.)

Yul Brynner (actor), 1920

E. B. White (author), 1899

John Quincy Adams (6th U.S. president), 1767

(Note: This master number implies a variable alternative response influenced by the strength or passivity of the planet Neptune in your horoscope. If you don't feel you are responding to the distinctive vibratory power of 11, you are instead expressing the more conventional qualities of 2, which you should read.)

June 22 (Mercury, Uranus [Saturn/Moon])
(master number, Gemini/Cancer influence):

The past is your springboard into the future; perhaps an intuitive flash or an accidental discovery will motivate and equip you for specialized activity in the public arena in one way or another. More loquacious than the typical Cancerian, your mind, in your approach to life, is likely to take precedence over your feelings—which you may express in a breezier way. Writing, publishing, communications that blend a contemporary flair with tradition are excellent outlets for your nonconformist thought processes. Recognition can come to you through technical innovation in any line of work, or a distinctive contribution to humanity's betterment—or, on the downside, a lapse in candor or integrity can bring notoriety.

Your exceptional adaptability, a unique blend of advanced thinking and liberated feeling, contributes to the broad appeal of your vocational or creative efforts. If the farsighted Gemini mental force implied by your birthday is not easy to integrate with your Cancerian yearning for peace and permanence, it still can provide you a way to recast your treasured concepts to accommodate fast-moving technological developments.

Insistence on typical Cancerian notions of security could be too restrictive and hampering for you. Trying to satisfy your ego requirements at the purely personal or material level can be misguided and could end in misfortune and disappointment, perhaps involving or adversely affecting someone in the family circle. Your Cancerian vision, whether in the business or medical realms, government or the arts, needs more flexible boundaries for the most meaningful expression and fulfillment—especially since you could be instrumental in paving the way to new concepts of social freedom and equality.

Meryl Streep (actress), 1949

Michael Todd (producer), 1907

Giacomo Puccini (composer), 1858

(Note: This master number implies a variable alternative response influenced by the strength or passivity of the planet Uranus in your horoscope. If you don't think you are responding to the distinctive vibratory power of 22, you are instead expressing the more conventional qualities of 4, which you should read.)

July 22 (Moon, Uranus [Moon/Saturn])
(master number, Cancer/Leo influence):

A home, a housing project, a family to you can be abstract symbols or meaningful realities of warm togetherness, dysfunctional isolation or somewhere in between. You could be concerned with—and may try in your own way to break down—the color, economic or various other barriers that divide humanity into the haves and have-nots, particularly in connection with their living as well as in their working conditions. You are proud to be the family anchor and safe harbor in times of stress and turmoil. You may see it as a step in the right direction when explosives (Uranus, your birthday ruler) are deliberately set by demolition experts to level outdated, multistoried, crime-ridden, inner-city housing projects built for lower-income groups—to be replaced by homey, inviting, single-family dwellings. The planet Uranus also typifies unwed mothers, single-parent households and same-sex marriages—the already-evident family wave of the future.

With your open-minded attitude, the housing and family breakthroughs of the Aquarian Age and the means to implement their acceptability should seem less radical and more understandable to you than to anyone else. Are you capable of transforming the familiar concept or image of a domicile, a home, a family or a neighborhood group into a trendsetting vision of the future? If so, you're in tune with your farsighted birthday connotation and unique ability to blend tradition with innovation.

How will you envision the home, the environment, in the age of interplanetary travel? Your challenge is the greatest for Cancerians. As traditional walls or divisions are altered or come down at home, in the arts or in the workplace, the sheltering limitations and conventional family relationships of the past will eventually yield to the broader communal dynamics of the future. How well you manage possibly jarring or disruptive personal, family, job, community or career developments will be the key to your fulfillment and pride in your accomplishment.

Nervous and idealistic as a child, you probably felt a restless yearning for environmental changes more to your liking than the home or family setting into which you were born—and against which you might rebel. Your extraordinary—not to say brilliant—creative vision, as well as your penetrating emotional insights, are far-reaching assets when you begin to make your way in the world.

Jason Robards (actor), 1922

Alexander Calder (sculptor), 1898

Edward Hopper (artist), 1882

(Note: This master number implies a variable alternative response influenced by the strength or passivity of the planet Uranus in your horoscope. If you don't think you are responding to the distinctive vibratory power of 22, you are instead expressing the more conventional qualities of 4, which you should read.)

CHAPTER 5

LEO

July 23–August 23

RULER: **THE SUN** NUMBER: **1** ELEMENT: **FIRE** SYMBOL: **THE LION**

"Of a cheerful look, a pleasing eye, and a most noble carriage."
—*Henry IV*, Part I, Shakespeare

Love and romance are the essence of your sign—not just personal love and romance, but a love of life and its possibilities for heartfelt fulfillment in the grand pageant of human experience, made more broad and colorful by larger-than-life words, adventures and nobility of the human spirit. "All the world's a stage," and you typically see yourself playing a leading role—and for good reason. The Sun, the life-sustaining center of our solar system, around which all the planets and their satellites revolve, is ruler of your sign, and your symbol is the lordly Lion. Both sign ruler and symbol give plenty of colorful clues to your personality.

Filled with the inner glow of the Sun itself, you radiate charisma, magnanimity, self-respect and courage. You do, don't you? Because if you don't, you're missing the opportunity of a lifetime—at least this one or perhaps several if you believe in reincarnation. The heavenly body associated with your sign, the Sun, is the one that the entire solar system is all about, the cosmic dynamo that vitalizes and illuminates the whole gamut of human experience. That Leo rules the creative urge provides another clue to your enviable Sun-Sign potential. The theater, for example, whether lightly entertaining comedy or darkly informative tragedy, reflects the remarkable drama of life for mass enlightenment. All art forms serve to vividly stimulate our response to experience; the theater shows us universal truths in uplifting, thoughtful or psychologically revealing plots and characters, in intimate, ordinary or spectacular settings.

In general, the typical Leo is the paragon of the inward glow and outward expression of your love of life. Your manner usually sets you apart from other mortals. Your substantial pride, when it's working positively, will generate attention wherever you happen to be. If you don't get it there, you will go somewhere else. Since the exhilaration of the social swirl appeals to you, you won't have to look far. Naturally self-assured, you know how to create an aura of romance, excitement and sex appeal.

You are not partial to drab routine anywhere and have slight tolerance for it in your personal life. You're not fond of details or menial tasks. Although usually courteous, you don't suffer fools gladly. When you're the target of specious criticism, or cornered by a boor, you can adopt the lofty manner of a Bourbon monarch on hearing reports of unhappy peasants. You can be as domestic as Cancer but with a different emphasis: The typical Leo home is the setting for elegant entertaining and for dramatizing personal comforts and attainments rather than just a domestic haven or an emotional link with the past. A beautifully decorated bath or dressing room and strategically placed mirrors would be more important to you than a handsomely appointed kitchen. How you look, the effect you're making or the drama you project doesn't depend much on pots and pans for complimentary feedback. You usually have your share (or more) of vanity. The line, "He never passed a mirror he didn't like," from a Noel Coward play, brings Leo to mind.

Capable of elevating personal charisma to an art form, most Leos tend to be happy and optimistic, with a typically "sunny" disposition and a dazzling smile. You also can have expensive tastes and be drawn to the good life. While the fixity of your sign inclines you to establish lasting patterns in your life, your ambitions and desire to be associated with the elite attract you to the upwardly mobile social crowd. Since you are popular and are likely to entertain glamorously and lavishly, it's fairly easy for you to make a favorable impression and consequent headway in the upscale glitter set.

Your ability to organize and lead, to inspire admiration, equips you for positions of eminence and widespread influence in the world at large. Your contagious upbeat attitude and faith in yourself is one of the powerful weapons at your command. Believing that anything can be done or that your will is stronger than any deterrent has an effect not lost on others. It is the power that brings dreams and missions to fruition, and it is your precious birthright. You can be the great fighter, meeting adversity with strong resolution. Like your symbol, the regal Lion, your carriage and bearing are dignified. Tall or short, thin or stout, you carry your stature like royalty. More apt to purr than roar, you nevertheless speak decisively. It is for you to decide if your dream, like Leo-born Napoleon Bonaparte's, is more extravagant than your capabilities to fulfill it. The ultimate quality and integrity of your quest is the important consideration. Whether you gain the love, devotion and admiration of a family of three or a nation of millions is not the issue for Leo. To have proven that you are worthy of such recognition as a superior sustaining force is ample justification for your pride.

Of course, no Sun-Sign is perfect, and a misuse of your traits, since they are potentially so marvelous, can be equally lamentable. If you are a neglected Leo, you can be sure that you aren't playing your cards right since the deck is stacked so strongly in your favor. If your ego is oversized and warped, you will be more absorbed with the amount of love and attention you are receiving, rather than if you are offering your share or not. Any faults you project stem from a pronounced deficiency of genuine self-love and self-respect. When you aren't convinced of your own worth, painful news for any Leo, your attributes go into reverse and you contrive to hog attention by whatever shallow means available. You can be pretentious and demonstrative far out of proportion to the demands of a situation or an occasion. This gambit, in turn, feeds on itself in a negative way in that you require satisfactions that become increasingly more inflated in direct proportion to the shallowness of your motives.

Leo-born Benito Mussolini is a classic example. Not noted for excessive humility, he had a favorite gambit when deigning to grant an audience. It was shrewdly calculated to dispel any doubts as to his exalted eminence. *Il Duce* received visiting dignitaries in a cavernous Italian Renaissance chamber. His imposingly ornate desk was strategically placed at the far end *opposite* the entrance, across an expanse of floor space that seemed like a football field. There was a studied absence of any other furniture. When the hapless visitor was ushered in, he had to walk the entire length of the room and *stand* as he stated his business. The Great One, naturally, remained comfortably seated, enjoying every malicious, ego-gratifying moment of the encounter.

Rumor has it that more than one distinguished visitor was not just a little bit humiliated by the experience. Of course, few Leos, even the most negative ones, go to such extremes. In the first place, how many of you have rooms that size? And even if you did, there are simpler ways to exaggerate your importance . . . assuming that you've learned the difference between *acting* important and *being* important. Self-estimates are notoriously unreliable, even among otherwise quite rational people. Patience is one of your enviable qualities; can you summon it when your ego is offended? You'll have less need to if you constantly strive to downplay Leo's exhibitionist tendencies, the grandeur complex inherent in your sign. Be wary of any inclination to adopt airs of self-regarding pomposity. In fact, if you *underplay* your estimable opinion of yourself, you offer a smaller target for possible detractors or critics. (Why make it easy for them?) Which brings us to those warped Leos who misuse their enviable attributes. You know the type. They have an inflated belief in their own publicity about how regal, magnetic and sexy they are—and let it go to their heads. In that case, their insecurities are showing, and they become pompous, preening and domineering, to say nothing of displaying their childishness. Did you ever notice the similarity between a throne and a highchair?

There's nothing wrong with wanting to be the center of attention, and you're better equipped than most to carry it off. But when you do bask in the spotlight, try to make sure that you have something worthwhile to offer your audience. Another of your great assets is your ability to develop and maintain a broad sense of humor about yourself. If you can laugh at your own foibles, others will insist that you have few faults and will show less resentment for your attractions. When your personal growth and accomplishments are truly worthwhile, when they stem from unassuming greatness of heart and spirit, your inner glow and outward magnetism will flourish without any need for footlights or applause.

Personalities exemplifying your traits run the gamut—from George Bernard Shaw, Carl Jung and Mae West all the way to the aforementioned Napoleon and Mussolini. If you are conveying to the world the impression of how wonderful you are, be sure that you are backing it up with deserving achievement. You will always be able to bowl over some part of the crowd with portentous platitudes. *Il Duce* did it. But don't forget that "he that loves to be flattered is worthy of the flatterer." The crowd that pandered their love to Mussolini turned on him in the end, fickleness being a familiar characteristic of the general population. You can *earn* recognition or merely *seek* it, but you will only *deserve* enduring love and long-lasting power if you justify them.

Leo's greatest asset is purity of motive and the power of *love*, and the amount of faith that you have in its various ramifications. Your faith in other things, like your own importance, can degenerate into mere obstinacy. Your transgressions are frequently so naive that others can rarely bring themselves to totally dislike you. They have to grant grudging admiration for your prowess to mesmerize others through your glowing magnetism, even if the use you put it to is questionable in your critics' estimation. You are intense in your feelings and resent any neglect or offense to your pride. Slights or harm to your loved ones can arouse as much fury as if they were aimed at you.

You are capable of great achievement. The pages of history are replete with names of the Leo-born. Fame is not partial to any sign, but you can be sure that those who achieve recognition in their own era or fame that transcends centuries have a strong Leo emphasis in their horoscopes, if not actually born under the sign. There are a disproportionate number of stage personalities, dramatists and literary lights of the romantic persuasion born under Leo. While all of you can't be famous, you won't languish in ego-deflating obscurity if you can help it. You will be drawn first to glamour situations, like the entertainment world, where you are completely at home. Any of the professions will appeal to you because the eminence possible through achievement satisfies your pride. What you do "in person" has the greatest impact. You gain more that way than through a letter or phone call.

The urge to dramatize the self is strong in Leo. You are not receptive to outside interference. You cannot be dictated to by anyone and can be directed or guided only by subtle suggestion or persuasion. Individuals who try to put you into a slot according to *their* specifications will experience your majestic indifference. They'll find that it's like trying to budge Gibraltar with a toothpick. Your orientation and your happiness must come from within. Your ego will grow and bloom without nourishment, but building your character is another matter.

Any reformatory process must take place within you. Only the most evolved Leo would ever admit that there is need of help or room for improvement from another mortal. Your pride can make you unyielding. If you go back on an opinion, it makes your judgment questionable. So what? That Lion is only a symbol. And you're still only human.

You can't afford the pride that is false, that interferes with integrity or honesty. You are willing to call on deities since they aren't mortal and don't prick your ego. As a positive and truly inspired Leo, you can spread the spiritual or creative message with a fervor and sincerity that win many to your cause. You capture their hearts. Your eyes glisten with their own distinctive brightness; their light comes from the source of all light.

You are very steadfast and can win through your ability to sit things out. Your patient and unflinching espousal of well-chosen values is not lost on others. They conclude that there is something special about you: You symbolize worth because time does not wither your enthusiasm for your beliefs; they only seem to strengthen and glow more magnificently. Your vitality flows out to others, and they in turn draw strength from you.

People appeal to you socially. As friends who are bright, witty, talented

and versatile, they can provide abundant levity and understanding to lighten
your mood when you are down. They in turn respond to your warmth, confidence, talent, charismatic aura, loyalty and generally cheerful demeanor. A
faithful friend or associate, you can also be demanding in your loyalties. As
a buoyant asset to any social occasion, be it with one person or an illustrious
group, your charm, natural authority and flair for theatrical effect draw people to you like bees to honey. Needless to add, you'd have very little patience
with constant whiners and other wet blankets.

Most of you have a desire to lead or, one way or another, to find a niche
in the limelight you can call your own. You are not too happy in a subordinate job. However, if neighborhood or leisure-time activities (community
theater, arts and crafts, club programs, etc.) provide you with opportunities to
lead, showcase your talents or otherwise inspire accolades, this can compen-
sate for a lack of professional outlets or an upper-echelon job. Since Leo is the
sign of show business, and very few are fated to be the next Hollywood,
Broadway or TV discovery, you need a job or avocation where you can truly
shine and feel admired, respected and appreciated. Managerial positions come
to mind, but you do need the requisite skills and qualifications to be the
leader of the pack.

You'd think that since yours is the sign of love, you would be a fine marriage partner. It's possible, but you are very idealistic about the beauty and
integrity of romance and can be thoroughly disillusioned when results fall
short of expectations. If you become enmeshed in the web of false pride, your
powers of sustainment will be misdirected. Your interest will focus determinedly on how *you* are being treated, instead of what you are contributing
to the cause of connubial happiness and stability.

Intensely romantic and passionate, you're inclined to dramatize your
amours even more than other areas of your life. With your penchant for theatrical expression, the distaff Leo could see herself as a great lover or, at the
very least, a *femme fatale*. Leos are drawn to paramours and inamoratas they
can be proud of; you delight in the reflected glory of an impressive catch.
When this initial requirement is satisfied, you are capable of an intensely personal love. You also tend to idealize the one you love, sometimes to the point
where the ideal you adore bears little resemblance to the real-life object of your
affections. You dream and fantasize about love, but as you are a doer as well
as a dreamer, you invariably try to make your dreams a reality.

Your innate optimism and self-confidence can work against you in
romance; when you fall in love (and it's always "all the way"), you assume that

you're a prize catch or the other person wouldn't bother and that your ardor will be reciprocated with equal fervor. When, heaven forbid, it isn't, your pride as well as your feelings are deeply wounded. When love goes well, however, it becomes your guiding star, your reason for living, your music, your very heartbeat.

With Aquarius, the sign of freedom and independence ruling your solar seventh house of significant partnerships, you don't especially care for the discipline and restrictions of marriage. It's a beautiful and idealistic arrangement as long as everything goes smoothly. On the other hand, there may be rough times that require you to swallow your pride, when compromise and compassion are necessary. And they frequently are, when you must consider and adjust to another's moods and egos. But when connubial bliss prevails, the whole world can come alive for you through the attraction of the loved one and happy togetherness. The potency and depth of your emotional expression has its basis in your love life, so the "love of your life" can be exceptionally lucky. Then your most positive and magnetic qualities soar upward, and the Sun shines brightly. In the meantime, while basking in the leonine glow of your impressive attributes, try to keep your hat size the same.

LEO BIRTHDAYS

Judgment of whether or not a birthday is propitious can be considered from two points of view: complementary or challenging. From the standpoint of personal progress and fulfillment, your destiny may flow more comfortably if your birthday is, or reduces to, an *inner* root number such as 1, 3, 5, 7 or 9. For career drive and achievement, your progress may be enhanced if your birthday is, or reduces to, an *outer* root number such as 2, 4, 6 or 8; the *outer* root numbers are less comfortable, more obstructive for you to contend with, but are potentially very conducive to outstanding success. The 11 and 22 (master numbers) would be variable, favorable for recognition, but generally would require more understanding and resourcefulness to integrate with the meaning of Leo.

Remember, if your birthday is two digits (excepting master numbers 11 and 22), be sure to read the *root* digit or number first. For example, if your birthday is 29, read the 2 (2 + 9 = 11, 1 + 1 reduces to 2) birthday profile first and then read the special profile for 29. If your birthday is 14, read the 5 (1 + 4 = 5) birthday profile first and then read the special profile for 14, and so on. If a description in a "special" section contradicts information in the "root" digit (root number) analysis, the "special" interpretation applies more specifically to you.

The first planet in parentheses following your birthday number is *your Sun-Sign ruler*; the second planet (or Uranus/Saturn for number 8) is *your birthday number planetary equivalent.* Subsidiary planetary influences (if any) are bracketed.

Each birthday profile includes celebrities who share the same birthday.

YOUR BIRTHDAY PROFILE
August the 1st (the Sun)
(and root digit for July 28, August 10 and 19):
"All the world's a stage," and you see yourself as the star attraction. If you rise to the top in whatever sphere, you are fulfilling your destiny. With this combination of Sun-Sign and birthday, you were born to achieve success and recognition. Doing it, however, is another story, and it is up to you. Nevertheless, with your compelling desire and ability to gain prestige, you can become a public figure of magnetism and authority. Even in a lower echelon supervisory capacity, you have a leadership personality.

However, you can also become proud and overbearing. Your firmness of purpose is admirable. It depends on what your purpose is: Is it constructive or not? If it is to insist on your supremacy and self-importance, you will be frustrated until you demonstrate your superiority in the world of your peers; assuming it is not the same as deserving it. If you don't consciously work at becoming less self-centered, you may wind up impressing no one but yourself and a few die-hard admirers.

With your diligence and strength of character you are suited for responsibilities, although you may find some aspects of them uncongenial. The disorganized conditions of your upbringing would have either enlightened you as to the value of selfless objectivity or made you disheartened or resentful of obstacles that impeded the expression of your ego during your early job or career years. An impish sense of humor can be your safety valve when things get sticky or stressful, but it is welcome in any situation—especially when your ego could stand a boost.

Yves St. Laurent (designer), 1936

Dom De Luise (actor, comedian), 1933

Herman Melville (writer), 1897

Special to July 28 (Sun [Moon/Uranus/Saturn]):

Leadership is your aim, and you are well equipped for it in art, literature, music or the theater. You tend to be dramatic and the center of attention, and you will contrive to be the Sun at the center of your own individual solar system. Love is important to you; in fulfilling this need, you may not conform to all the conventions or predictable expectations, choosing companions or mates who may raise a few eyebrows. Your outlook is broad and progressive, as well as practical, geared to the concepts of excellence you desire to implement. You are from a background of material freedom, or you were awakened to its advantages early in life.

You know how to get other people to do pretty much what you want them to, but you could occasionally be frustrated. If your life doesn't unfold like a beautiful drama of fulfillment, you may be tested until you learn the difference between the love of power and the power of love. When you play a leadership role in your sphere of activity, perhaps as a taste-maker, your flair for originality enables you to set new standards or blaze new trails in the creative, business or professional field.

Sally Struthers (actress), 1948

Jacqueline Kennedy Onassis (socialite, First Lady), 1929

Marcel Duchamp (artist), 1887

Special to August 10 (the Sun):

Creatively and mentally gifted, your most congenial milieu is the business world, professions or administration. You're the kind of person who knows your own worth, and it shows. You don't pussyfoot around where your ego is concerned. Consequently, it could be very frustrating for you if you don't get the credit you deserve for your contribution to the success of a creative, professional or workplace project. Your home is a setting for your hospitality, but you aren't partial to becoming involved in the maintenance of it. Eager for the spotlight and personal expression, you find public life congenial and could achieve your share of renown.

Whereas others might proclaim their desire to be of service when they take a job, you might be bluntly candid and admit you're doing it for the money, status possibilities and dependable security offered by the opportunity. With success as your goal, no one can ever say you're not determined. What you may lack in tact, you make up for in honesty. A go-getter, with any talent or luck at all, you're able to rise pretty rapidly from an entry-level job. Although sensitive, you are loyal in love.

Antonio Banderas (actor), 1960

Eddie Fisher (singer), 1928

Herbert Hoover (31st U.S. president), 1874

Special to August 19 (Sun, Pluto):

With a flair for prominence and excitement, the arts and professions are a rewarding outlet for your originality and creativity. Highly opinionated, the value of your contribution increases in direct proportion to the broadening of your outlook and spirit. You are happiest as chief, but you may find it difficult to focus your personal life. You are more restless than the typical Leo. Personal grievances, dubious ulterior motives or egotism can be the cause of your problems and disappointments.

A realist as well as a pioneer, you might strive to cash in on what others may see as an historic breakthrough or crusade. With your penetrating insights into provocative situations and people's motives, you do the best you can; at the same time you might have to contend with events that may not happen the way you want them to happen. Buttressed by your outsized self-confidence, once you've determined your goals and set your course, you're not likely to waver from your commitments or beliefs. If an unpleasant decision is necessary, you're able to bite the bullet and take necessary, if regrettable, action that is in the overall best interest of an organization or project, solution to a problem or your own reputation.

William Jefferson (Bill) Clinton (42nd U.S. president), 1946

Jill St. John (actress), 1940

Orville Wright (inventor), 1871

August the 2nd (Sun, Moon)
(and root digit for July 29 and August 20;
August 11 is a master number, see end of chapter):

With this birthday, the ego-threatening circumstances you occasionally encounter may require your larger-than-life attributes to be downsized a bit in one context or another. Your Leo nature finds subordinate positions very uninspiring, and any adjustments you have to make will be frustrating. Not unaware of the value of tact and diplomacy, when a situation calls for it, you might take the easy way out and become touchy and distant. You're not receptive to criticism unless it's sugar-coated. Laughter and relaxation are very important to you; while generally good-natured, however, your appreciation of jokes about yourself can be limited.

You like the pleasures and luxuries of life and may think they are your due; you are inclined to expect things without an awareness of the effort necessary to gain them. You are very talented and like to have your way but may find collaboration with others the best outlet for your outstanding abilities. In any case, your participation in joint or independent work or career endeavors will be enhanced by your distinctive personality, forcefulness and mordant sense of humor.

You felt early in life the urge to either rise above your beginnings or stand out from the crowd, and no doubt you soon began to devise methods of satisfying your ambitions. You may seem sympathetic and adaptable, but you are in reality as self-motivated and determined as any Leo. Your impulses and enthusiasms come mostly from within and are little affected by the advice or entreaties of others.

Peter O'Toole (actor), 1933

Caroll O'Connor (actor), 1924

James Baldwin (novelist), 1924

Special to July 29 (Sun, Moon, Pluto):

Inspired and magnetic, your complex personality can bring you recognition in whatever field you select to express your talents. The impressive image you project and your subtle crowd-pleasing demeanor can play as big a part in your success as your attributes and skills, which can be considerable. Your ego, however, prone to be exaggerated, is very sensitive and resentful to slights. You are nervous and suspicious under your apparent composure; if your get-even streak isn't controlled, it can provoke you to go to extremes. You have subtle insights into human psychology and know how to use them to your advantage on the job or in the public domain, especially in the literary and theatrical worlds.

You need to feel the protection of domestic security, but your mate or others may have to indulge your self-absorption, adapt to your view of conditions, and make changes according to your prerogatives. If your early years were decentralized, leaving you disappointed or discouraged, the cosmic purpose was to stir an awakening to values other than ego gratification.

Elizabeth Dole (U.S. presidential candidate), 1936

Benny Goodman (musician), 1909

Benito Mussolini (Italian dictator), 1883

Special to August 20 (Sun, Moon):

Perhaps overly sensitive and conscientious, a conflict may arise between your innate pride and satisfaction in your work and your need to be more discriminating and attentive to details. If people question, criticize or oppose your ideas or quality of your work, they're apt to receive short, blunt replies. With the proper education or other preparation, your rise to the top could be as speedy as it is assured and long lasting. A business, creative or government career and group interests in general are congenial outlets for your estimable abilities, which may have considerable public appeal. Although, as a Leo, you like to be at the head of things, you might do best sharing authority and responsibilities with others.

Because your typical Leo attitude and bearing attract attention—and, hopefully, admiration and respect—your home and family life, and the image it projects, could be on a par in importance with your career achievements. If you are lucky enough to find a mate or lover who puts you on a pedestal, it will intensify your zest for life and ardent romanticism. If a parent, you want to be a proud one and will expect your children to be a credit to you.

Connie Chung (broadcast journalist), 1946

Jacqueline Susann (novelist), 1918

Benjamin Harrison (23rd U.S. president), 1833

August the 3rd (Sun, Venus)
(and root digit for July 30, August 12 and 21):

Your birthday is very congenial for your Leo traits. Your financial prospects are excellent through family connections or networking or your power to express and articulate your creative inspirations. You naturally personify and in turn attract the love and affection so dear to the heart of Leo. A potential leader in any field, you are especially effective with the public. Lovable and generous, you may be too fond of pleasure and personal adornment. The world of fashion is a delight to you. Conceit and extravagance may be the only drawbacks to the generally impressive effect you have on life.

Naturally engaging and demonstrative, your enjoyment of life and pride in your abilities are contagious and contribute to your success. Your demands are reasonable, and, even when inhibited, your Leo nature inclines you to make the best of things. Emotional and sensitive as a child, the feelings that may have been bottled up at the time could be the genesis of your need for a creative outlet or acknowledgment of your skills and worth when you begin your job or career activities.

You're capable of resting on your laurels once you've accomplished a major goal and sitting back in a pleasant glow of self-esteem and maintaining the status-quo. However, midway during your working years, some of you will alter or discard former ideals or beliefs and be motivated to move on into new areas of activity and further achievement. Or what was formerly an avocation could become your new line of endeavor, for which you could receive fresh plaudits.

Martin Sheen (actor), 1940

Tony Bennett (singer), 1926

Rupert Brooke (poet), 1887

Special to July 30 (Sun, Venus):

Desirous of prestige and authority, you are vulnerable to extremes through your vitality and nervousness. You are imaginative, competitive and executive, and you are drawn to ambitious ventures and goals. Adaptable, resourceful and creative, you prefer pursuits that are practical and productive, but you can express your share of "won't-power" when opposed and can provoke considerable animosity in adversaries. Most of the time, though, yours is the kind of personality that makes it easy to get along with people and smooths the way toward the achievement of your goals.

Whatever job, business or professional endeavor appeals to you, you are capable of raising it to a new level of efficiency and popularity. Your strength will lay not only in the commendable scope of your vision, but also in your keen perception of public moods and taste. Very individualistic and independent in your thinking, you might rebel against generally accepted opinions and beliefs, particularly in the creative fields. If the going gets tough in your formative years, when you're acquiring the tools of your trade or professional skills, you could become very disheartened, but your Leo courage will inspire you to stay the course and come out fighting. A spirited raconteur, your social and romantic popularity further enhance your prospects.

Arnold Schwarzenegger (bodybuilder, actor), 1947

Henry Ford (automobile pioneer), 1863

Emily Bronte (novelist), 1818

Special to August 12 (Sun, Venus [Sun/Moon]):

To call you a social asset would be an understatement. At a party, you're likely to be the brightest light by several hundred watts. Male or female, you'll probably have more than one high-octane affair before you march down the aisle. (And possibly a few after.) Your Leo need for l'amour and approbation (or your dramatic version of it) may seek a variety of outlets. Will you scatter your high ideals and sense of beauty in personal indulgences? Or will they be focused on the substantial requirements of a significant accomplishment?

Popular and magnetic, inclined to display, your values tend to be visual. Although your flair for the limelight knows few limitations, you would probably be most successful in the theater or some other career that in one way or another brings you before the public or is geared to mass taste. Your relaxed social verve can find many suitable, as well as profitable, outlets for expression. You would do best in a job, business or profession where your keen intelligence, talents and easygoing charisma will have the most effect. Whether your name is on a marquee, an office door or a union card, you're not likely to be a shrinking violet.

> Pete Sampras (tennis player), 1971
>
> George Hamilton (actor), 1939
>
> Cecil B. De Mille (film director), 1881

Special to August 21 (Sun, Venus [Moon/Sun]):

Creative, original and methodical, you have a compelling need for recognition and a position of authority. Inclined to skepticism, you seek to express and enjoy the truth and beauty that validate your faith in life's pleasurable activities. Try to avoid a conflict between jealousy, pride and conventional mores in your partnerships, or it can make them uncongenial and frustrating. Education, music or anything literary is a constructive outlet for your abilities. You'll find that circulating socially helps to achieve your goals: Who you know, and the effect your personal charisma has on them, could be as or more important than what you know.

Whether or not you gain public prominence, you're able to adapt to less-than-exalted circumstances by maintaining an admirable air of dignity while playing whatever role, even a frustrating one, that life sends your way. In any case, whether in a conventional job or higher up on the career ladder, an ordinary lifestyle is not your cup of tea. One way or another, you'll attract your share of attention.

> Kenny Rogers (singer), 1938
>
> Wilt Chamberlain (basketball player), 1936
>
> Margaret Rose (princess), 1930

August the 4th (Sun, Saturn)
(and root digit for July 31 and August 13;
August 22 is a master number, see end of chapter):

Obstacles and delays are likely to impede the easy gratification of your Leo desire for prestige and appreciation. The job you can be proud of will probably be difficult, because the only effort that will interest you is the kind with one end result: prominence, whether in the public domain or in your particular sphere of activity. Usually a fringe benefit of success for most people, behind money and security, recognition of your worth could be the ultimate objective that keeps you plugging away.

Pride is the root of your character, and you can be resentful of all the effort required to gain recognition for what is already so apparent to you: your distinctive attributes. If frustration has a really negative effect on you, you might languish in lassitude or obscurity and nurse your bruised ego on the sidelines. Or, on your way up the ladder of success, you may have to perform tasks, cool your heels or fulfill functions that irritate your proud Leo nature. However, if you realize that application, discipline and perfection of details (onerous to Leo) will get you where you want to go, you have the willpower and endurance to accomplish any goal.

Authoritative and executive, once your worth is established, you excel in important capacities. Your opportunities are deep, if not varied, which suits you fine. Your early environment may not have contributed much to your respect for discipline or authority. You'll probably have quite an adjustment to make in your late twenties.

Billy Bob Thornton (actor), 1955

Elizabeth (Queen Mother), 1900

Percy Bysshe Shelley (poet), 1792

Special to July 31 (Sun, Saturn [Venus/Sun]):

Not averse to work, association with movers and shakers and creative expression with broad appeal are important elements in your quest to capitalize on your talents and opportunities. With your engaging personality, one-to-one contact with influential people can grease the wheels on the road to achievement. The world of industry, entertainment, the arts and related milieus provide ample proving ground for your abilities. Somewhat inclined to go overboard in making your points, it's to your advantage to cultivate disciplined effort along with a need to focus your energies.

If you have to earn any accolades the hard way, you'll probably give the impression that you don't mind and are enjoying the effort as well as the well-deserved enhancement of your personal prestige and other rewards. No stranger to controversy, you can run the gamut from folksy to fiery in voicing your principles and beliefs. Not as egocentric as the typical Leo, you may be better known and appreciated or remembered for your distinctive accomplishments rather than your personal charisma.

Wesley Snipes (actor), 1962

Jean Dubuffet (artist), 1901

Jacques Villon (artist), 1875

Special to August 13 (Sun, Saturn [Sun/Venus]):

Not given to effort unless you feel it has a practical purpose and is appreciated, your tendency to restlessness and extremes can delay your progress and cause setbacks. The 1 (ego) and 3 (expression and diversions) are behind your 4, the number of perseverance and discipline. When your ego is bruised, you can be temperamental and misunderstood. Articulate, creative and dramatic, you can sulk and be resentful if appreciation isn't forthcoming for your status and the effort that has gone into your hard-won achievement.

If there are any detours on the road paved with your ambitious career intentions, your Leo determination enables you to get back on track. Shrewd in promoting your job, career or business goals, you prefer to be in complete control. If you have to work your way up through the ranks, that certainly won't stop you. While you can turn on the charm and be vividly persuasive if it suits your purpose, your no-nonsense capabilities and true grit will count for more than a winning personality to get ahead in the world.

Kathleen Battle (singer), 1948

Fidel Castro (Cuban dictator), 1926

Alfred Hitchcock (film director), 1899

August the 5th (Sun, Mars)
(and root digit for July 23, August 14 and 23):

Since you are not very objective or broadminded, and your pride is your initial frame of reference, your quick judgments can be unreliable. With your strong love nature, you can mistake passion for love and intensity for depth in your varied emotional experiences. Not inherently partial to change and novelty, you may have to become more adaptable, interested in new things as basic conditions change and willing to discard that which has outlived its usefulness to you.

With your seemingly endless supply of energy and endurance, you can be a dynamo in whatever job or profession you choose to showcase and capitalize on your talents. In addition, your livelihood should pay well or at least provide a dependable income. This is important, because for you, money is a necessity; it takes an ample cash supply to keep you happy and to support your champagne-taste lifestyle. Articulate and ingratiating, you are impressed by appearances. It's important to you to appear to be successful and affluent. Whether or not you achieve really big-time earnings, you tend to be very generous to charities as well as in private philanthropy.

Emotional problems may stem from your need for approval and your refusal to be tied down. After all, you're such good company. With so much fun to be enjoyed and life to be lived to the fullest (and the means to live it), why restrict your opportunities? Humble beginnings could be the spur to your driving ambition. If so, your early environment acquainted you with the value of discipline and the need to make every effort count if you are to have anything to show as a result.

Neil Armstrong (astronaut), 1930

John Huston (actor, director, writer), 1906

Guy de Maupassant (writer), 1850

Special to July 23 (Sun, Moon, Mars [Moon/Venus]):
If "Leo, the light of the soul" describes you in ancient mythology, Leo, the reflected light of the soul may be more accurate for your particular birthday. Perhaps moodier and not quite as confident as the typical Leo, your burgeoning charisma helps to offset latent emotional sensitivities and equips you to effectively dramatize your special insights into the unseen side of the human scene. If you're personally not totally comfortable in the limelight, your warmth and nurturing quality nevertheless shine through and enable you to get your message across, whether in the workforce or a leadership role in a creative field, education or the business world.

Somewhat more home-centered than typical members of your sign, your vivid imagination can inspire wanderlust and/or creativity and send you off on adventures in life that usually have a purpose other than mere pleasure seeking—which doesn't mean, however, that having a good time and doing good works are mutually exclusive. Meanwhile, whether busy with home or family activities or out in the wide, wide world, you're likely to be pretty steadily on the go, keeping busy and productive with whatever interests attract you and provide deep personal satisfaction.

Woody Harrelson (actor), 1961

Raymond Chandler (mystery writer), 1888

Samuel Kress (philanthropist), 1863

Special to August 14 (Sun, Mars [Sun/Saturn]):

Your instinct may prompt you to waver between seeking a steady job or assignment with a dependable income or taking a chance on an artistic or adventurous line of work that is more precarious in terms of earnings and security. However, once you've sampled the rich fulfillment of expressing a latent talent, a routine job won't have much appeal as a way to fill your working hours. Not the type to watch the clock and capable of quick thinking in a crisis, you're more suitable to a profession or speculative project than to a nine-to-five business regimen. The glow of your Leo nature and your sense of responsibility equip you to assume the mantle of leadership in one context or another.

With your commonsense orientation and admirable standards, your instinct tells you that if you can justify self-approval, your work or career endeavors also will be worthy of approval. By the same token, if you deliberately choose the high road, you'll probably find yourself traveling it on your way to success. Early family circumstances may have stirred your ambitions and obliged you to adopt a serious view of life.

Halle Berry (actress), 1968

Earvin "Magic" Johnson (basketball player), 1959

Woody Guthrie (folksinger, composer), 1912

Special to August 23 (Sun, Mars [Moon/Venus]):

You can do very well materially if your let your Leo patience and endurance work for you; security, however, can be undermined by being too generous and/or unconcerned about money. Fortunately (or hopefully), you may inherit, earn or marry enough coin of the realm that a laissez-faire financial attitude doesn't create problems. A profession, especially one in the entertainment field, with combined rewards of prestige, independence and ample financial returns, offers you the most satisfactions. You'll probably overcome any tendency to let obstacles on the road to success discourage you.

You're likely to be highly intelligent and industrious, someone who likes things done properly, and a person of real flair rather than a plodder. You're not deterred by workplace complexities; to you they're challenges. If it looks as though a project or situation out of your realm of responsibility isn't shaping up the way it should, you're ready to plunge in and do it yourself if that's what it takes to get it done right. If your job or career success isn't impressive and long-lasting, it can be blamed on something other than your birthday potential.

Shelley Long (actress), 1949

Barbara Eden (actress), 1934

Gene Kelly (dancer, actor, director), 1912

August the 6th (Sun, Jupiter)
(and root digit for July 24 and August 15):

Relationships, whether family, group or connubial, and how you handle the responsibilities they entail, are key factors in your life. Be wary of developing antipathies toward those who really love you, a reaction that may stem from your impatience, annoyance with criticism (even the best-intentioned) or a lack of approval. You will find happiness when you have a healthy inner glow of self-confidence; then your Leo warmth is turned outward, without the inhibiting fear that love won't be returned or appreciated. It is your greatest asset, and the proper expression of it can bring you the peace, success and fulfillment that you desire.

You can't insist on superiority and approval in partnerships. You may have to accept the idea that others' rights to a hearing and to appreciation are just as valid as yours. Let that Leo inner glow's outward luminescence work its magic for you by becoming the kind of individual with whom you would want to share experiences or your life. Then, with your personable style, you'll have no trouble attracting desirable candidates.

You're not domestic, finding household chores tedious. You may enjoy a stint in the kitchen, with one eye on a fancy gourmet recipe and the other on the dramatic possibilities, but you prefer that someone else does the dishes. Your early environment may have given you a taste for independence and freedom that is hard to control when you start your job or career efforts; properly harnessed, however, it can work in your favor. A shrewd communicator, your success potential is on a par with your impressive ability to provide what an employer or the public wants, to commercialize your talents and to exploit your flair for self-promotion. Whether your output is flimsy or substantial, you know how to put it over.

Andy Warhol (artist), 1928

Robert Mitchum (actor), 1917

Lucille Ball (actress, comedienne), 1911

Special to July 24 (Sun, Jupiter [Moon/Saturn]):

More restless and outspoken than the typical Leo, your compelling desire for recognition can bring you the prestige you require (almost an obsession where you are concerned). You're not likely, even in maturity, to rest on your laurels. You're the type to keep busy, either on the job or with other activities that hold your interest, well into your sunset years. Otherwise, you'll fidget and waste time scattering aimless nervous energy while dwelling on your personal frustrations and sorrows. You're drawn to sporadic enthusiasms, adventures and the arts, but a job or career with a more dependable income, future security and other benefits is apt to be more compatible with your commonsense outlook. Perhaps from early exposure to the advantages of discipline and responsibility, you'd rather count on a tidy pension than a gold watch when your working days are finally over. In an alternate scenario, your financial success, if achieved early enough, could facilitate your involvement in some branch of creative endeavor. Active participation in the arena of public affairs will bring the desired publicity for your efforts.

Jennifer Lopez (actress), 1970

Linda Carter (actress), 1951

Amelia Earhart (aviatrix), 1898

Special to August 15 (Sun, Jupiter [Sun/Mars]):

With Leo's special flair for drama and/or the theater, creative or similar work or a profession that brings you in some way to public attention is the most promising for you. For example, you would be more effective as a colorful trial lawyer than a low-key corporate counselor. Behind your need for a domestic base, you are restless and individualistic. You could attain recognition and prestige as much through your distinctive one-of-a-kind personality as through your abilities, which may be considerable. You're adventurous and energetic, too, and are willing to make many changes to achieve your place in the Sun.

While the job or career you pursue will probably call for teamwork and/or compromise for success, you're apt to be more impetuous than diplomatic. Not one to back off if a principle is at stake, you may have to learn that honey goes further than vinegar when trying to gain support and win people over to your side. Even though you tend to be a bit of an outsider, you'll nevertheless earn the respect, if not the mass popularity, gained by the more easygoing members of your sign.

Ben Affleck (actor), 1972

Julia Child ("The French Chef"), 1912

Sir Walter Scott (novelist), 1771

August the 7th (Sun, Mercury)
(and root digit for July 25 and August 16):

You instinctively sift thoughts, sense impressions, ideas and opinions through a sieve of knowledge or stand them up to a set of criteria that is compatible with or reinforces your pre-established fixed opinions. You tend to reject information, an opportunity or experience that doesn't relate to—or that conflicts with or can reflect unfavorably on—your inborn Leo pride or biases. Try to avoid mental self-satisfaction, and don't permit this mental screening process, especially when you're feeling doubtful or insecure, to obstruct a more broad-minded approach to your opinions, educational goals and intellectual attainments.

If you can be more objective in your thinking and learning processes, you'll be more persuasive and successful in your job, business or professional endeavor. Though you can be rich in ideas, you might, paradoxically, like to be alone with your thoughts while you mull over their validity and/or prospects for impact and acceptance. Not shy about airing your views, you can haggle and bicker if necessary, but you are more apt to be soft-spoken and to appear calm, diplomatic and unflappable. At the same time, however, your low-key demeanor could mask a lot of unsettling agitation in your mind.

Specialization in some line of endeavor is advantageous and should provide the material freedom so essential to you. For example, you would be an excellent teacher of drama or a dramatic instructor of any subject. You can be deeply sensitive to issues, whether workplace or personal, that affect your pride. Your Leo endurance will come in handy when you become impatient if your efforts are slow to yield results as fast as you would prefer. Expressive, with or without a flair for publicity, you'll do well in public ventures or will attract your share of attention. Your early environment would have prepared you for the conditions requiring thoughtful adaptability that you're likely to encounter when you begin your job or career endeavor.

David Duchovny (actor), 1960

Mata Hari (dancer, spy), 1876

Emile Nolde (artist), 1867

Special to July 25 (Sun, Mercury [Moon/Mars]):

Finding a productive outlet for the flow of your natural Leo warmth will have a beneficial, stabilizing effect on your emotions. Although your enterprising spirit and eloquent verbal skill are well suited to politics, the business world or a profession, you might gain more recognition, if not more financial return, in the various artistic fields. When you have a personal agenda to promote, your abundant charisma and energy make a formidable combination. You'll fight for a principle and will forcefully voice your opinion if an issue is at stake. In fact, the force of your personality can be the deciding factor in many a tense negotiation.

You have executive ability and, if not actually as a performer, can function successfully in that capacity in the theater. In any case, you'll certainly do your best to impress people with your talents and well-informed, authoritative style. The many changes and varied experiences of your growing-up period should have broadened your outlook. You probably learned that when you don't get your way, it's better to accept a setback or defeat with dignity than with a temperamental reaction.

Walter Payton (football player), 1954

Walter Brennan (actor), 1894

Thomas Eakins (artist), 1844

Special to August 16 (Sun, Mercury [Sun/Jupiter]):

Whether it's your high-potency charisma or your talent for self-dramatization, there should be no lack of opportunity to fuel your climb to success and/or recognition in one communications context or another. Very curious, your interests run the gamut from cultural activities to educational pursuits to travel in exotic locales to whatever you think is over the next hill and worth investigating. You'll probably seem to the rest of the population to be surrounded by the glow of good fortune; in word, gesture or deed, you know how to capitalize on it. However, don't go overboard with inflated expectations.

In any case, never at a loss for words or enthusiasm, you've a pronounced talent for seeing the bright side of almost any situation or adventure, which is certainly no handicap where your job or career aspirations are concerned. The best way to gain your attention or to obtain a favor is to indulge your ego. Words of praise are music to your ears, but, in a pinch, you'll respond favorably to any upbeat topics that stimulate enthusiastic discussion or activity. A steady domestic base may elude your grasp.

Madonna (singer), 1958

Angela Bassett (actress), 1958

Eydie Gorme (singer), 1932

August the 8th (Sun, Uranus, Saturn)
(and root digit for July 26 and August 17):

With your self-assurance, dramatic flair and ability to organize yourself and others, you are well suited to an independent or executive position. The large outlook is natural for you; not aware of limitations, be cautious about over-reaching, especially if your only motive is self-promotion. Willing to work hard for success, you may have much to contend with, but you're equipped to manage. Some of you will credit the popularity and position you achieve to your childhood, which helped instill the sense of responsibility that set the meaningful patterns in your adult life.

Family ties are important to you and may require more time or energy than you bargained for. You won't mind too much, however; with your fondness for plaudits, you can be amply compensated; your pride is given a lift if those near and dear are a credit to the example you set and your abilities. If you utilized the mentally reclusive conditions of your early environment to analyze plans for your future logically and objectively, your entry into the world of work and accomplishment can be exceptionally promising. Otherwise, the negative Leo tendency to become pretentious and domineering will find you settling for shallow ego-satisfactions.

The accumulation of money and your ability to demand a high salary are as much a matter of your Leo pride as of acquisitiveness. Through your positive power complex, you may become a model of efficiency, responsibility, ingratiating expression and unlimited vision. In your less attractive mode, you could be extravagant, obstinate, scattering and overbearing. If not career-minded, the distaff Leo with this birthday will gravitate toward a successful man and can be an impressive factor in her mate's success pattern.

Dustin Hoffman (actor), 1937

Esther Williams (actress, professional swimmer), 1923

Dino De Laurentis (film producer), 1919

Special to July 26 (Sun, Uranus, Saturn [Moon/Jupiter]):

Versatile, with a flair for distinctive expression and colorful living, you can succeed in a creative or administrative capacity. Regardless of the direction your talents and efforts take, your dream is big, and your aim for the top can pay off in an equally big way. You like power and prominence; whether in the arts or the scientific or business world, you can make a dynamic as well as an influential impact and/or contribution. Mining a vein of expertise and success more deep than broad, achievement in your sphere of activity will provide you with the share of the spotlight you deserve.

To function at your best, you need a steady, comfortable home or family environment or some sort of group or organizational support system. With your eyes on the future and your feet on the ground, your progress in life will depend on, and is likely to stem from, a unique combination of originality and practical application, the end results of which can have wide public appeal or affect.

> Mick Jagger (singer), 1943
> George Bernard Shaw (critic, dramatist), 1856
> Carl Gustav Jung (psychiatrist), 1875

Special to August 17 (Sun, Uranus, Saturn [Sun/Mercury]):
Dramatic and dynamic, your approach is based on the possibilities for expansion inherent in broad-based ideas and ventures that may depend for their success on your ability to communicate their unique potential. Your independence and inventive inspirations, combined with your ability to analyze, can produce the wide public impact and success that you envision for yourself and/or your endeavors. Not so compatible with details, you can leave them to others while you concentrate on the big picture.

Whether you're the star attraction or making yourself indispensable on the fringes, a job, profession or business activity that somehow has popular appeal can also pay well and help you to accumulate an ostrich-sized nest egg for the future. Opinionated, when your pride is offended or your views are questioned, your controversial statements or off-the-cuff remarks leave little to the imagination and can cause friction. Nevertheless, thanks to your intelligence and perseverance, you tend to rise up through the job or corporate ranks. Whatever you do, however, it's essential that you take pride in your work. Otherwise, you'll be unhappy and not likely to last very long.

> Sean Penn (actor), 1960
> Robert De Niro (actor), 1943
> Mae West (actress), 1893

August the 9th (Sun, Pluto)
(and root digit for July 27 and August 18):

Purity of motive and greatness of heart and spirit are attributes native to Leo—and necessities for the successful fulfillment of your birthday potential. Apt to be more quiet, reserved and inflexible than the typical Leo, you may find the changeful conditions or disruptions you encounter as life unfolds uncongenial and could privately resent them. On the other hand, you can be bluntly vociferous when your views are challenged and can balk at unsought alterations in standards, goals or requirements foisted on you in your job, business or professional activities, which you may see as a step backward instead of progress or improvement.

Regardless of trendy popular ideologies, and whether or not they clash with your preconceived opinions, you generally prefer to go your own way. You will profit by adopting an open-minded attitude and minimizing your need for ego satisfactions. By stressing objectivity and the achievement of broad-based goals, your pride will be rewarded, but in ways that transcend ordinary prominence and self-seeking gratification. Whether you're a legend in your own mind or in your own time, your success potential is strong and denotes that creative or business ventures will repay you for your efforts.

Your early environment would have impressed on you the values and advantages of material freedom. And while that could influence your worldly ambitions, the job or career you follow may not be a deliberate choice but rather a random opportunity that possibly wasn't your original intention but that just evolved out of a providential twist or sequence of circumstances. In any case, at your best, you will gain a reputation for integrity, dependability and loyalty.

Gillian Anderson (actress), 1968
Whitney Houston (singer), 1963
Melanie Griffith (actress), 1957

Special to July 27 (Sun, Pluto [Moon/Mercury]):

Vulnerable to discontent through your restless drive for power, you find a subordinate position very uncongenial. You need prominence in one context or another for the full release of your splendid abilities. You know your own mind and at the same time can develop your thinking to accommodate new situations, especially those that enable you to showcase your intelligence, expertise and congenial personality. Consistent in your key relationships, they can be a source of support and happiness.

You won't stay long in an entry-level job; despite a possible detour or two, you're likely to climb steadily, if not rapidly or directly, into a position of increased credibility, independence and responsibility. You're not the type to flourish in isolation. With your distinctive personal style, determination and versatility, you'll have opportunities to carve your own special niche in whatever realm you choose to satisfy your worldly ambitions. In any case, you'll no doubt make many friends and/or attract many admirers along the way.

Jerry Van Dyke (actor), 1931

Norman Lear (TV producer), 1922

Leo Durocher (baseball manager), 1906

Special to August 18 (Sun, Pluto [Sun/Uranus/Saturn]):

Freedom of action and the drive for success are your strongest motivations. With your flair for prominence and personal satisfactions, you are miserable in a menial capacity and cannot comfortably subordinate your interests to those of others. Though farsighted in your outlook, you nevertheless have a practical slant on how to make your reformative visions and plans productive and/or profitable in today's world. The visible trappings of success can influence your job or career choice. And you do like your independence; it's important to you to be self-employed, if you can manage it. If not, an autonomous company position of some sort is a reasonable alternative.

Subtle methods are another one of your strengths. You know how to use your personal magnetism to attract support and to capitalize on a network of confidential information. Your psychological radar tells you what kind of impression you're making in any situation and whether or not your initiative or strategy is going to produce the results you have in mind. If you sense negative feedback in an encounter, you'll adjust your style accordingly to improve your prospects.

Patrick Swayze (actor), 1954

Robert Redford (actor), 1937

Shelley Winters (actress), 1922

August the 11th (Sun, Neptune [Moon/Sun])
(master number):

Your dramatic ideals and tastes could find optimum expression in the inspirational opportunities you attract through your birthday. Whether from humble beginnings or a privileged background, your soaring imagination joined to your lofty Leo pride can be a notably winning combination, if not necessarily a long-lasting one. More nervous than the typical Leo, it may require an extra measure of adjustment to satisfy your need to prove yourself. Determination you have plenty of, an asset as long as it doesn't turn into won't-power; avoidance of any rigidity or extremes in your emotional response is a personal prerequisite for the successful fulfillment of your estimable potential. Save the histrionics for certain facets of your professional activities, where they may be profitably rechanneled and transformed into effects that contribute to your success and prominence.

On occasions when your Leo pride is offended, be wary that your swift and possibly wayward psychic impressions don't cause your emotional affairs to become muddled. Your absorption in personal goals may leave you with little patience for understanding others, yet the challenge of objectivity, difficult for Leo, is an important test if you are to find happiness.

Your exceptional creative potential can be directed advantageously into an artistic, theatrical, literary or visionary commercial pursuit. Your charming personality and quick wit may or may not conceal your basic motivations; you're likely to have a hard-nosed attitude about business, about getting ahead in the world with your talents and skills, and about making money—which may be your primary goals in life.

Jerry Falwell (TV evangelist), 1933
Alex Haley (writer), 1921
E. B. White (author), 1899

(Note: This master number implies a variable alternative response influenced by the strength or passivity of the planet Neptune in your horoscope. If you don't feel you are responding to the distinctive vibratory power of 11, you are instead expressing the more conventional qualities of 2, which you should read.)

August the 22nd (Sun, Uranus [Saturn/Moon])
(master number):

The potential inherent in your birthday runs the gamut all the way from extraordinary abilities and achievements to nerve-jarring discontent caused by unexpected delays, restrictions and disruptions—or from random combinations of these various possibilities. Your upsets have a purpose: Nature is signaling you to be as conscientious as possible regarding your exceptional dreams, your objectives and, in some cases, your genius. Your pride will be most securely justified to the extent that your pioneering inspirations in some way benefit and/or enlighten others, whether individuals or the mass public.

If you are creative, your distinctive originality, professionalism and entrepreneurial flair enable you to make a lasting impact on the world. Your sense of humor can be as sardonic and annihilating as it is spontaneous. If you aren't theatrically, intellectually or musically inclined, organizations, causes or public affairs are excellent outlets for your exceptional capabilities and brilliant flashes of intuition. Whether you're outstanding or just outlandish, given any opportunity at all, you're not apt to languish in obscurity. When you are annoyed with the world or your lack of recognition, you might attract attention to your disgruntlement by visual means, such as conspicuous or eccentric attire or mannerisms, headstrong independence or deliberate indifference to authority. Drawing attention to yourself in this misguided way is a clue to your frustrations where the limelight is concerned; avoid an exaggerated sense of your own importance.

Is your nervous intensity focused on the implementation of your broadest ideals? It may be a hindrance that the conditions of your early environment were more conducive to creativity and expression (perhaps making you a popular favorite) than to discipline, which may have left you unprepared for the force and application essential to the fulfillment of your destiny. At your eclectic best, however, you want to be where the action is and to capitalize on the competitive edge of your uncommon leadership qualities.

Tori Amos (singer), 1963

H. Norman Schwarzkopf (retired general), 1934

Claude Debussy (composer), 1862

(Note: This master number implies a variable alternative response influenced by the strength or passivity of the planet Uranus in your horoscope. If you don't think you are responding to the distinctive vibratory power of 22, you are instead expressing the more conventional qualities of 4, which you should read.)

CHAPTER 6

VIRGO

August 24–September 23

RULER: **MERCURY** NUMBER: **7** ELEMENT: **EARTH** SYMBOL: **THE VIRGIN**

"For there is nothing either good or bad, but thinking makes it so."
—*Hamlet,* Shakespeare

The symbol of your sign is the Virgin, the ideal of purity, venerated since ancient times, particularly by the Greeks. The magnificent Parthenon is the measure of their regard for her. That imposing temple was built as homage to Athena, the goddess of wisdom and agriculture, inventor of the plow and protector of the city of Athens. In astrology, the Virgin is identified with the harvest, the separation of the wheat from the chaff. The Virgo glyph, which looks like the letter M with a line crossing over the base from the lower right hand corner, represents the harvested cornstalks bound together for winter harvest.

Mercury, the planet of conscious perceptions, is your ruler; thoughts are things, and experience is food for thought—tasty, bland or bitter. In your case, the process is involuntary, like the function of your digestive tract, the part of the body ruled by Mercury. For you, as well as for Gemini, a ceaselessly active mind is as natural as breathing—with a big difference: Mercury's Virgo rulership, being in an earth rather than an air sign, has a distinctly practical application. The wheels of gray matter don't spin just for the pleasure of mental brilliance, entertainment, and/or insightful revelations, as they do in Gemini. Instead, your mind works like a sieve; your response to and attitude toward life is sifted through it. And if you had your way, only the finest, purest particles would get through. But life isn't like that. Consequently, your vitality, how you get along in life in general and your ultimate fulfillment will depend on how you digest experience—the whole grand scenario, warts and all. Mercury, the "Messenger of the Gods," is a restless planet, prompting you to be always on the go, whether mentally from thought to thought, physically from activity to activity, or geographically from place to place. You're not the type to sit around and vacantly stare off into space. When you are physically inactive, your mind is probably going a mile a minute, perhaps wondering if there isn't something you should be doing.

One of the wonders of the zodiac, the spirit and significance of your Sun-Sign can be most demanding and difficult to fulfill. It isn't easy to exemplify the perceptive state of evolvement required to make a Virgo happily useful and therefore fulfilled. When you achieve this goal, however, your world—whether it consists of family, friends or career—is made infinitely richer by your having touched it. If your remarkable traits are ignited by the flame of genius, your contribution to the world is extraordinary, admitting few peers. Two of the most richly expressive literary giants of all time, Goethe and Tolstoy, were Virgo-born, and Shakespeare had Virgo rising. That's quite a heritage, and it cloaks your characteristics in a mantle of great consequence.

Since your attributes are used to produce results of such impressive magnitude, misuses can be correspondingly detrimental, with an important zodiacal difference: When a sign of power, Aries, Taurus, Leo and so forth, is misdirected, the consequences can be devastating to great masses of people. Although great rulers and political leaders are born under Virgo, they are rarely, if ever, tyrannical megalomaniacs. You and those in your immediate surroundings—home, job, wherever—are most apt to suffer the repercussions when you misdirect your Virgo attributes.

Just as the Moon digests experience for the Cancerian, the mental planet Mercury represents the assimilation of experience for you. Your capacity to master particulars and to excel at craftsmanship is a disguised form of idealism. You can be married to your work to such an extent that your life gets into a rut and can become swamped in a Götterdämmerung of details.

You function in the sphere of conscious perceptions, like Gemini, but you carry the process an important step farther: You combine intellectual results with *practical* possibilities or ramifications. You are more interested in facts, people and results and with the practical effects of your mental stimuli and processes; Gemini is more spontaneous and inspirational and can be satisfied with abstract conclusions. Your typically nervous orientation to life is due to your highly sensitized sensory faculties. Your reaction to experience is subliminally analytical, and it is impossible for you to function any other way. Whatever you take in, you simultaneously pass judgment on it. Your brain is like a fluoroscope on autopilot. While Gemini can be the lighthearted mental dilettante, you fidget because you must live with a constant awareness of an imperfect world and with your powerlessness to change much of it. What you can profitably change, if your frustrations are compelling (or irritating) enough, is your inner frame of reference. Until you realize that the antennae of most people are not instinctively tuned to spotting and/or dwelling on imperfections, only then will you know that yours is a precious, uncommon gift that must be used wisely and judiciously if you are to maximize its splendid life-enhancing benefits and avoid its drawbacks.

Yours is the sign of work and service, which can mean anything from scrubbing floors to becoming president of the United States, with an endless variety in between. Your potential to make a useful contribution to the world is impressive, yet of all the signs, yours is one of the least understood. That the typical Virgo is more reserved on first contact than the typical member of more charismatic signs is true. In general, you will make little impact on those who are beguiled by surface glitter. Don't feel bad. If you get to know such easily impressed people, you might only find them shallow or their interests trivial. In the long run, by not exuding an overabundance of superficial glitz and charm, you are spared hours of misspent social contacts with people who you would only conclude are tiresome. Your values mine a deeper vein: perfected discrimination, not one of life's most popular pastimes. The downside is that you can back yourself into a corner of social isolation; if you'd peek more from behind your fastidious scrim, you might spot a budding Goethe in the social mix. Be willing now and then to waste a little time to find out whether or not it was a waste of time. And for that rare occasion that it wasn't, you might be eternally grateful.

Your remarkable faculties can work splendidly on behalf of your interests in one context and against them in another. Since you're so great at classifying everything, it's to your great advantage to figure out which is which. And once you have, try using your God-given analytical gifts for some *self*-improvement and progress. Admittedly, none of the signs of the Zodiac suffers from an overabundance of that achievement, but they have a better excuse. They don't have your exceptional talent for analysis and introspection. Meanwhile, it's wise to realize that your ability for instant appraisals may not be received with much joy by the majority of the population. Many don't like to be reminded that there are serious flaws in their makeup, that things are at every turn less admirable, acceptable or efficient than they could be. What's worse, to your dismay, there is a fresh crop of imperfect bumblers born every minute! Mutual disenchantment results when these types are the targets of your criticism. Anyway, you don't have an *exclusive* on spotting faults. You're just faster at it, and they bug you more.

You can be volubly aware of the grime behind the glitter. Of course, your comments can be misinterpreted or lost on those lacking your values and sharp perception. Their comments about your being "critical" or "cynical" are frequently just euphemisms for honesty and reality as far as you are concerned. You see things for what they are, from your point of view anyway. While you're busy cataloguing, are your glasses tinted with malice . . . or mercy?

Since your motivation is to analyze *everything,* your frame of reference should rest on as broad a base of understanding as possible. Otherwise, you will just be one of those persnickety, carping Virgos who are in great demand nowhere. The clarity of your perceptions can be phenomenal. You have the ability to cut through the sham of appearances and experience with surgical precision. Your effectiveness, however, is constructive or disconcerting, or even destructive, in direct proportion to the extent of your objective self-analysis, the depth of your understanding and warmth as a human being. If you unleash a verbal sniping over some insignificant detail or mishap, you are missing the forest for the trees. A negative Virgo is good at forgetting the human equation. Belittling others is a way of boosting the self. Everyone doesn't have your consuming penchant to detect minor, irrelevant flaws or to be annoyed by them. Are you a paragon of brisk, or brusque, efficiency?

Often criticism is what we say about other people who don't have the faults we have and who may have the virtues we lack. This can be the main hazard in Virgo relationships. You turn the penetrating light of your inborn fluoroscope on others, when instead you might profit more from some inner self-probing. You should beware of telling people things "for their own good." As Shakespeare put it, "The words of Mercury are harsh after the songs of Apollo." However, to suggest to a Virgo that you stop being critical makes as much sense as to tell you to stop breathing. You might as well ask a Taurus to forget about money, a Scorpio to forget about sex or a Capricorn to forget about ambition. But at least you can soften your observations with considerate diplomacy. A reminder of the difference between analysis and criticism may help: You tend to see them as one and the same; one is a function, however, while the other is an interpretation of it.

Meanwhile, until a Virgo understands that some things are best left unsaid, you're more apt, despite your best intentions, to encounter people who take your constant striving for perfection and well-meant comments very personally. When you make what you consider a helpful suggestion, point out a fault or propose a way to do something in a more efficient manner, there are those who will feel that you are picking on them, thus the Virgo reputation for nit-picking. By learning to be extremely diplomatic and always compensating for criticism with a compliment, you can change that impression.

The key to the marvelous possibilities of your sign is true self-knowledge. Instead of becoming a nag, you need to lead by example and to make some thoughtful allowances. If you find fault with something or someone, don't talk about it unless it's an absolutely necessary component of a discussion or a crucial decision. Don't use it as a ploy to bolster your own ego. The trouble with an extremely critical approach is that Virgo forgets there are flaws in nearly everything; if you insist on looking for them first, you may unwittingly shield yourself from any joy in life's adventures. Virgo should remember that the absence of faults doesn't add up to virtue and that perfection is sterile. The sieve that filters experience for you is useful and protective, but it needn't be so excessively fine-grained unless appropriate to the matter at hand. Let a few modest lumps through once in a while; otherwise, the range of your participation in life can become too constricted.

You are lucky in many ways; you usually have a level head and good common sense. Since you aren't taken in by the appearance of things, you can avoid many pitfalls. Learn to tap your remarkable gifts. Your neuromental intuition can warn you ahead of time to avoid a project where failure is likely. Pivotal factors can be cautiously evaluated in advance, thus tilting the risk-reward ratio in your favor before you commit time and energy to a cause, but your acuity can be a two-edged sword.

It is not easy to emancipate your thinking from the clichés of everyday living that surround you. The considerate Virgo will develop more patience with inevitable trivialities and petty annoyances, the flotsam and jetsam that assume monumental proportions of aggravation to a less charitable Virgo. Why be imprisoned in a catacomb of critical hang-ups? You will alienate yourself in areas where probably your only intention is to help. You usually have a genuine interest in friends' or other people's problems and are willing to listen and be generous with advice or comments (sometimes, of course, unsolicited). You will learn the gratifying rewards of *serving* when you fully understand the meaning of your role. Ever alert to others' imperfections and inefficiencies, you aren't as sensitive to their lack of warmth. You can live without bonhomie if people will just try to get things as perfect as possible.

One of the sins you are susceptible to is a willingness to sacrifice yourself to drudgery without a goal. Work just "for work's sake" is limiting. If your efforts aren't designed to lead anywhere specific, then you are little more than a drudge. How glitterless can you get? At the end of the road, you can be miserable because you will look back on years of effort that came to a dead end, the result of plodding along without any imagination.

What the negative Virgo lacks is self-esteem, a sense of the dignity and importance of your rightful place in the social hierarchy. The immersion of the Virgo drudge in endless "duties" can be a subterfuge for your insecurities. Those in more happily flowing circumstances are not there by divine right or because they are insensitive to the defects that you find so overwhelming. On the contrary, you may lack their ability to take the world in stride as it is, faults and all, and to make the necessary *personal* adjustments. They are only other human beings who've had the insight to envision themselves on a path of growth, understanding and fulfillment.

Too much humble sacrifice or too much *busy*ness with drone duties is a misguided perversion of a noble instinct; it is a form of psychic masochism that averts the need for moderation in all things. Excessively nervous or fidgety Virgos are the victims of misdirected energies or misguided emphasis of their divine birthright. Extreme humility and conscientiousness can also be a subterfuge for sidestepping the effort of spirit required to try for something better. It is an insidious form of false pride, masking a lack of self-confidence. By not trying, you don't risk exposure as a failure. You may succeed with your ploy, but you will have failed at life.

You can be the apostle of the puritan work ethic; anything that is dutiful or laborious is automatically right and holy. As long as you subscribe to such precepts without question, you can get caught up in the commonplaces of existence, which are a fertile field for Virgo's fault-finding tendency. The fulfillment of your potential lies elsewhere; it is to examine with some of your eternal vigilance all that you accept in your daily routine, what you think of as "your lot." You are on the right track when you free yourself from the notion that anything besides work or of proven purity is suspect.

If you don't seek enlightened self-fulfillment, your life will remain incomplete, no matter how devoted you are to work. Just as an excess of pride defeats the purpose of Leo, an excess of servitude is similarly defeating for Virgo. Your ruling planet, Mercury, is mental, and therein lies an important key: You can never *know* too much, and this doesn't mean just facts and figures. You and Gemini will profit from pursuing knowledge and intellectual attainment but for the somewhat different reasons stated earlier. The one thing you can't afford to do is blunder through life uninformed. Many of you naturally sense this and acquire mental training and/or marketable skills that are put to good use in the field of education or other careers that depend on a well-trained mind or a reasonably accurate facsimile. Your natural interest in biographies and history should be pursued, as well as your curiosity about psychological studies and the like. You should strive for balance between the practical and tangible issues and the spiritual or metaphysical aspects of life in your perceptions and conclusions. Balance is what the next sign, Libra, is about: On the evolutionary spiral, Virgo is the preparation for it. Whatever else happens, your attitude toward work and service will determine the outcome of your life and will have important bearing on your health.

Your reasoning powers can get in the way of your emotions, leading to a singular self-sufficiency. Usually more sentimental and kind than passionate, you can mature late emotionally. You are inclined to love deeply on second thought, or you can reason yourself *out* of any emotion. You like to talk as much about sex and emotions as anything else; they can be just other topics for discussion when the conversation lags. You love to classify, but you can't classify to love. You would never find complete fulfillment in a relationship commitment or marriage with anyone who didn't share your mental interests or who was of inferior social position. You usually opt for the middle ground, avoiding extremes, and have good control over yourself emotionally, perhaps too much—except where criticism is concerned. All this can make you seem bland; you rarely get steamed up over things.

Your sign can be deceiving, however, because some of the most colorful and dynamic personalities in history were born under your sign: Elizabeth I and Charles II of England and Louis XIV of France (the Sun King), to name just the royal ones. They were also typical examples of Virgo emotional and relationship proclivities, with either no marriage or an abundance of colorful liaisons (or both). The long list of theatrical celebrities in your sign is surprising, considering your traditionally prosaic astrological image. Many lead or have led very fascinating, often sensual lives, their adventures providing as much titillating gossip as those identified with signs assumed to be more exciting. Virgo women are far from drab, unless you consider Greta Garbo, Ingrid Bergman, Sophia Loren, Lauren Bacall, Claudette Colbert or Raquel Welch drab. And the same can be said of Virgo men—Sean Connery, Peter Lawford, Maurice Chevalier, George Montgomery, Rossano Brazzi. With no intention to demean respectable occupations, it's time to bury that well-worn cliche in astrological writings that Virgos are short on glamour and ambition and that they are best suited to be file clerks, meter maids, letter carriers, bus drivers and secretaries.

Virgos have a reputation for hypochondria. Many of your illnesses are imaginary; those that do become a reality are generally the result of nervousness and frustration. You will profit by studying the relationship of disease to *dis-ease*. There are health hazards the truly negative Virgo can avoid. For example, from the day you are born, it's drilled into your brain that there's something wrong with everything. The relentless nit-picking and narrow judgmental attitude of the excessively critical Virgo are inimical to psychic digestion, which impedes the healthy flow of the nerve currents. The body then becomes the repository for self-generated nervous agitation, with harmful results. Just as there's a psychosomatic connection between arthritis and rigid attitudes, there's a similar connection between poor assimilation of life's realities, excessive nervous frustration and digestive tract malfunction. One medical outcome of this condition, colitis, is known as the "teacher's disease." Teaching is an occupation of both Virgo and Gemini, both Mercury-ruled signs.

By nature seldom idle, you need to keep restive critical faculties sensibly focused. Otherwise, unless you deliberately relax, your mind can drift aimlessly and not always positively. When you are tired, it may not be physical; you could instead be a bundle of frayed nerve-ends in need of restoration. Plenty of fresh air, physical activity and mental relaxation will provide the best antidotes to this condition. Also the theater, music, any diverting entertainments can be pleasant pastimes for you. Even then, however, it is difficult for you to unwind and enjoy them; you are automatically preoccupied analyzing and appraising, usually very accurately, if not always charitably. Your traits do make the best critics. You could have truly barf-baggy (and on-target) reactions to some of life's idiocies passed off as art, music, theater, literature or even astrology and numerology.

Goethe's Virgo genius was such that the ground he broke enabled Carl Jung and Sigmund Freud to make their greatest discoveries a century later. His *Faust* masterpiece, more than sixty years in the making, presents a central image of Western civilization and a hero who still compares favorably with other modern archetypes. The final lines of the drama could be your credo:

All that is transient
Is but reflection;
The insufficient
Here finds perfection;
What never could be said,
Here it is done;
Eternal womanhead
Summons us on.

The secret of your contentment in life and happy interaction with others is a matter of appropriate emphasis and careful direction (or redirection) of your admirable qualities; *tone down* your heaven-sent critical faculties in your everyday personal life and in regard to people, especially coworkers, and *sharpen* and *cultivate* them in terms of your job and professional goals, vocational skills or wherever else they are more relevant, productive and appreciated.

Your ruler, Mercury, is the messenger of the gods brought to earth—that's pretty important. What do the gods desire? You can tell us. Goethe, Tolstoy and other geniuses of your sign have struggled with the "word" from Olympus. You're naturally gifted with linguistics, but the language of the gods is something special. No wonder you're nervous. The other signs would be, too, if they had a weighty mandate like *that* on *their* shoulders! Let's be honest. If at times you seem a little distant, we should remind ourselves of the remote nature of your quest and be grateful. Who else would dedicate his/her life to seeking perfection?

The materials you have to work with can be frustrating, if not exasperating, and therein lies your key: the *personal* quest for in-depth, broad-based understanding so essential for Virgo. When you operate from your *spiritual* center, you will understand that if the world and the people in it weren't replete with faults, there'd be no need to play your part on the evolutionary spiral. You wouldn't want to be eliminated from the cosmic drama, would you? Just think of all the fun you'd miss, telling people how they can do everything a little, or a lot, better! But if you want your life to be truly effective and meaningful, *begin with yourself.*

VIRGO BIRTHDAYS

Judgment of whether or not a birthday is propitious can be considered from two points of view: complementary or challenging. From the standpoint of personal progress and fulfillment, your destiny may flow more comfortably if you birthday is, or reduces to, an *outer* root number such as 2, 4, 6, 8 or 22 (master number). For career drive and achievement, your progress may be enhanced if your birthday is, or reduces to, an *inner* root number such as 1, 3, 5, 7 or 9; the *inner* root numbers are less comfortable, more obstructive for you to contend with, but they are potentially very conducive to outstanding success. The 11 (master number) would be variable but generally would require more understanding and resourcefulness to integrate with the meaning of Virgo.

Remember, if your birthday is two digits (excepting master numbers 11 and 22), be sure to read the *root* digit or number first. For example, if your birthday is 29, read the 2 (2 + 9 = 11, reduces to 2) birthday profile first and then read the special profile for 29. If your birthday is 14, read the 5 (1 + 4 = 5) birthday profile first and then read the special profile for 14, and so on. If a description in a "special" section contradicts information in the "root" digit (root number) analysis, the "special" interpretation applies more specifically to you.

The first planet in parentheses following your birthday number is *your Sun-Sign ruler*; the second planet (or Uranus/Saturn for number 8) is *your birthday number planetary equivalent*. Subsidiary planetary influences (if any) are bracketed.

Each birthday profile includes celebrities who share the same birthday.

YOUR BIRTHDAY PROFILE

September the 1st (Mercury, Sun)

(and root digit for August 28, September 10 and September 19):

Not equipped by nature for roles requiring leadership or for independent ventures in the rough-and-tumble sense, you nevertheless gravitate toward situations where individuality and initiative are prime assets and a likely requirement if you are to realize your potential. Since these aren't typical Virgo traits, they may need some coaxing. You also like an appreciative audience for your sharp wit and clever abilities; whether or not you're on the stage, you know how to "stage" to advantage your personal appeal and skills. In your shrewd approach to life, sidestep any temptation to give ethics short shrift in your determination to get ahead. If you were born on the 1st, 10th, 19th or August 28th, you are generally more competitive and desirous of recognition than other members of your sign. Critical of small returns for your efforts, you usually can attain a good earning level, if not a fabulous one.

Whether an employee or employer, you're an excellent organizer and a responsible team player, manager or executive; you can bring your enviable capabilities to an authoritative position where analysis, methods, discrimination, communication and willingness to work at causes improving the welfare, understanding and enlightenment of others are central considerations. You should avoid petty or shallow satisfactions and vanity and conceit, which are results of your self-consciousness.

Tending to take good care of yourself, you might be a health faddist. You realized on the threshold of your job or career endeavors that you wanted to be autonomous, to attain a degree of prominence and to be as little under the authority of others as possible. You may be a bit perverse about advice, seeking it and then seldom taking it. Your unprepossessing appearance can be deceiving; many types who come on a lot stronger fade from view a lot sooner.

Goria Estefan (singer), 1957

Lily Tomlin (comedienne), 1939

Alan M. Dershowitz (lawyer), 1938

Special to August 28 (Mercury, Sun [Moon/Uranus/Saturn]):

You basically desire to reach out to others in a supportive, heartfelt way. Your urge to express creatively or recreatively may be somewhat hampered by your tendency to accent details to excessive length, perhaps obscuring the essence of your message or inspiration in the process. Emotional and sensitive as a child, you were made aware early in life of the beauty of artistic expression. It was your haven if your childhood became confusing or disruptive.

Your life could be filled with a variety of rewarding interests, some of them seemingly unrelated, the pursuit of which could take a lot of time, energy, expertise and money. With that in view, you'll realize the practical advantage of a job or profession that probably includes a lifelong demand for a specialized skill, product or service, assuring a cash flow that supports your preferably upscale lifestyle. Your versatility within the context of a chosen field further ensures that you can enjoy more than one source of income. For example, if you become a lawyer, you might also write about it, as well as teach the subject. Destined for such a busy life, there may not be a lot of time for marriage or other close commitments, but there are always exceptions.

LeAnn Rimes (singer), 1982

Shania Twain (singer), 1965

Johann Goethe (poet, novelist, playwright), 1749

Special to September 10 (Mercury, Sun):

More ambitious than the 1 birthdate, you have more determination to rise to a position of recognition and power, regardless of the amount of patience and effort involved. In the creative realms, you could attain prestige and popularity as a writer, performer or artist. Likely to be quite positive in your outlook and manner, the impression of trust, independence and reliability you create eases your way to the top in whatever job or profession you choose to aim for success.

Exacting and sensitive, a quick study, you have high standards, possibly stemming from a tradition of some sort that you admire, wish to perpetuate or want to enrich by adding your own distinctive touch. Along with your decision early in life to be the best, your numerous options and aptitudes could lead to self-made success and independence. Try to be open to twists and turns of fate that can lead you into a line of work or life endeavor that you may not have initially aimed for but that makes profitable use of your Virgo gifts of discrimination, communication and patience for details. A hobby or avocation requiring a special talent or a spirit of adventure could be a constructive outlet for your dynamic restlessness.

> Jose Feliciano (singer), 1945
>
> Charles Kuralt (TV journalist), 1934
>
> Arnold Palmer (golfer), 1929

Special to September 19 (Mercury, Sun [Sun/Pluto]):

Independence, low-key prominence and the power to control the impact and outcome of circumstances you encounter or the message you wish to convey are among your principal aims. Your uncanny ability to size up people and situations in minute detail is to your advantage and assists you in attaining recognition, security and status. Although you might seem acquiescent, it wouldn't be easy to keep you in a subordinate position, where you aren't really content to be.

Your psychic radar is on constant alert to pick up information useful to your knack for pulling the strings, perhaps behind the scenes, that advance your worldly ambitions. More apt to employ shrewd maneuvers than bold or straightforward strategies to achieve your objectives, you know how, if necessary, to weave the power of suggestion into your manipulation of key details to promote your aims. Whether in the arts, a profession or the business world, you can bring imagination and shrewd instincts to your pursuit of success in any of these fields.

> Joan Lunden (TV talk show host), 1950
>
> Jeremy Irons (actor), 1948
>
> Cardinal Richelieu (French prelate), 1585

September the 2nd (Mercury, Moon)
(and root digit for August 29 and September 20;
September 11 is a master number, see end of chapter):

Despite exceptions, the success you achieve may bring more income and security than fame. If you wind up in the limelight, it might be more a natural consequence of your talent and affinity for public interaction than because of any deliberate effort on your part to become a celebrity. Because your birthday reflects lunar inconstancy, your reactions to experience can run the gamut between personal charm and affability to arbitrary standoffishness and seclusion, the latter when you're selfishly protective of your own interests. At your best, however, you're outgoing and companionable, if somewhat selective and diffident in your enthusiasms.

You like to think and act for yourself; if your thinking and acting are too assertive and self-protective, though, you'll elicit a similar response from others. You'll gain more respect and cooperation by earning them than assuming them to be your due. Your need to be adaptable and diplomatic, to adjust sensitively to the moods of others, can be blocked by Virgo's critical outlook; you don't like this or that feature about people or situations, so at times you can find yourself in an isolated position.

Normally quiet, unobtrusive, precise and clever, you can be swayed by your feelings, which can become too pent up through your inability to relax and find emotional release; this may, in turn, becloud your goals and delay the fulfillment of your potential. You might choose a course for reasons of safety and then find that your ambitions are too confined by it. Your work should be varied and interesting, preferably including creative overtones, with writing or anything of a mentally disciplined nature a likely outlet. Probative, conventional, reliable and likely to opt for the middle ground, you usually have good control over yourself. You don't get steamed up over things. Or if you do, you try not to show it unless in one of your hypercritical moods. Then, when negatively aroused, you can overreact and become irascible and/or petty. In your strongly opinionated mood, you can be severe with transgressors, meanwhile blandly oblivious to your own shortcomings.

Keanu Reeves (actor), 1964

Jimmy Connors (tennis player), 1952

Marge Champion (dancer), 1923

Special to August 29 (Mercury, Moon, [Pluto]):

You have the pioneering spirit, and, one way or another, you will gravitate toward a line of endeavor that sets you, or the way you do it, apart from the crowd. In fact, you could spearhead a breakthrough and establish an historic precedent. With your penetrating insights and incisive analysis of the human scene, there are far more important things for you to do than focus your mind on a good filing system. On the other hand, if need be, you're inventive and resourceful enough to quickly whip an archaic filing system into a model of high-tech efficiency. Channeled into commercial directions, your shrewd perceptions and creative imagination enable you to cash in on your exceptional expertise or products that fulfill either specialized or broad public needs.

You're eager and ready to joust with competitors or adversaries, particularly in defense of a principle. You've no qualms about voicing your strong opinions regarding politics, the workforce and the social structure in general. A job or career in government; the academic, creative or scientific fields; or the medical industry could provide opportunities for your abilities. In any case, however you showcase your talents, you have a message to communicate.

Michael Jackson (singer), 1958

Richard Attenborough (actor), 1923

Ingrid Bergman (actress), 1918

Special to September 20 (Mercury, Moon):

Whether you have a good education or learn the hard way from the school of experience, an extensive store of knowledge will be as advantageous as your inborn Virgo critical faculties in the pursuit of your job, business or professional goals. Any field where creativity, cooperation and attention to detail are important factors, particularly in the public domain, would be congenial and progressive for you. You have a flair for recognizing the growth potential of an enterprise and then for guiding and nurturing it until it develops impressively along the lines you envisioned.

With your astute Virgo intelligence, you can be as strong-willed as you are naturally strong-minded, but you are nevertheless adaptable and usually willing to hear the opposite side of an argument. Your prodigious memory for the most minute details of a situation or project and a willingness to trust others' abilities also contribute to your getting ahead in the world. Whether you come from a privileged background or modest beginnings, you know how to shift with the wind and make the most of opportunities that can lead to notable success.

Sophia Loren (actress), 1934

Sister Elizabeth Kenny (humanitarian), 1886

Upton Sinclair (author), 1878

September the 3rd (Mercury, Venus)
(and root digit for August 30, September 12 and 21):

You will do well in pursuits where creativity, ingenuity, beauty and fastidious taste are assets. The downside is that you can be a tad smug about "refinement." Very articulate, will you direct your gift of fluency into picky, autocratic criticism or to lightness, joy and sociability? If your Virgo outlook is rigidly narrow, you will be a poor mixer, full of social aversions. You won't budge an inch from scruples as you interpret them to gain easy popularity; it's true that everything you try not to do is on the list of mankind's tasteless excesses, but you can go overboard, swamped in "don'ts."

Your early environment was probably pleasant, even creative, but it may not have prepared you for the discipline required to achieve the maximum success from your job or career potential. Creatively, as a writer, you lean more toward historical, analytical or scientific themes; there your flair for vivid expression has a congenial outlet. You know how to express Virgo's intellectual rigor and patience for details with the eloquence and sensitivity of a poet. Although you might not discover your true vocation until midway in your academic endeavors, keeping busy with numerous interests occupies your mind in a constructive way. You're resourceful if ever there's a need to make ends meet.

In a lighter vein, at your sociable best, you're a convivial mixer, a delightful raconteur—and at the very least an adept conversationalist, brilliantly able to match wits with others on a variety of subjects. These capabilities, of course, contribute to your popularity if the lecture circuit, the performing arts or a worthy cause becomes a showcase for your expertise and personal appeal. Your prospects for happiness in love and marriage are promising.

Charlie Sheen (actor), 1965

Alan Ladd (actor), 1913

Louis Sullivan (architect), 1856

Special to August 30 (Mercury, Venus):

If you gravitate toward the theater, a literary career, the business world or a related field, your flair for colorful expression points in the direction of rewarding or outstanding success, particularly as a performer. Whether you fulfill your potential in a well-paying job or a notable career depends on how you express your birthday's multifaceted possibilities. With instantaneous communication and broad public acceptance in mind, your actions or opinions are likely to be more entertaining and lighthearted than profound, the latter being a euphemism for boring, which you will assiduously avoid to ensure that your work has wide approval and/or influence. You do have your serious moments, however.

You like to enjoy the good life and to mix and mingle with upper-crust types, especially in the corridors of power. If the high value you place on money is to support your expensive lifestyle, which could involve considerable travel (and you like to go first-class), or simply reflects your ability to accumulate more and more of it to demonstrate your financial prowess, you're apt to have estimable money-making or -saving abilities. However, because your nature is more mental than emotional, personal relationships, especially love and marriage, may not be as important or rewarding as career satisfactions.

Cameron Diaz (actress), 1972

Warren Buffet (financier), 1930

Ted Williams (baseball player), 1918

Special to September 12 (Mercury, Venus [Sun/Moon]):
If there's such a thing as a Virgo-born bon vivant, it's you. Whether on the job or at a party, you don't have to work at it—it just comes naturally. You're likely to be more socially and romantically popular than the typical Virgo, the bubbling personification of a glass of champagne. Though personally you could be familiar with life's setbacks, not to say tragedies, you somehow try to keep the lid on the downside and instead accentuate the positive, enabling the sunny side of your mercurial disposition to shine through. In any area where inspiration, creative ideals, lofty goals and technical know-how are essential for achievement, your success potential is impressive.

With your ability to make a profession out of a business and an art out of a profession, your efforts are synonymous with quality. Knowledge and discipline are the backbone of your capabilities. On the other hand, your gifts need to be constructively directed; talent and brilliance can drift into restless superficiality. The latter then becomes private indulgence and, unless given useful and productive focus, can be a wellspring of sharp-witted, caustic criticism. At your best, however, and in whatever field, your contribution can bridge several generations of professional excellence and leave an indelible impression.

Barry White (singer), 1944

Jesse Owens (Olympic track star), 1913

H. L. Mencken (writer), 1880

Special to September 21 (Mercury, Venus [Moon/Sun]):
With your flair for categorizing, you can juggle several distinct sets of values in the pursuit of progress and profit. If a product or service isn't quite up to your usual standards but fills a need, you're willing to compromise if it helps to achieve and maintain excellence in other areas of your job or career objectives. For example, you might drive a taxi or work at some other daytime job in order to attend law school at night. Or, as a writer, you might turn out fast-selling potboilers under a pseudonym to provide the wherewithal to write a serious play or prestigious historical tome.

Nervous and sensitive, you can talk quickly and think even faster, but you may not care to talk shop, unless it's to promote your point of view and commercialize your talents. Once you attain a certain plateau of success, you will need scant encouragement to express your trenchant opinions, which will have a distinctive ring of authority. Whether or not you get an early start in your job or profession, your childhood interests and/or activities were somehow the stimuli for it.

Bill Murray (actor, comedian), 1950

Stephen King (writer), 1947

H. G. Wells (writer), 1866

September the 4th (Mercury, Saturn)
(and root digit for August 31 and September 13;
September 22 is a master number, see end of chapter):
You will find your opportunities along lines that benefit from keen observation, painstaking detail and an appetite for diligent work, for which you have inborn patience and great ability. Forever conscious of the imperfections in things, your frustrations might cause dolorous or depressed moods from time to time, which, however, could resuscitate dormant ambitions and subsequently spur you on to greater achievement on the job, in business or in a profession. Selective and methodical, you can be the master of a technique that gives perfected form to your efforts in the creative or educational realm or in the world of commerce.

You are inclined to study and reading, particularly about art, literature and communications of a serious nature. Basically conventional and retiring, detesting slipshod methods or mediocrity, you have an innate sense of responsibility, which equips you for situations that require discipline and industry. If by chance your personality initially reflects a fun-loving, cavalier attitude toward life during your growing-up period, by the time you're thirty or forty you're likely to project a much more conservative image. A paragon of stainless steel efficiency, your dependable skills could find a productive outlet in the medical industry or other realms of research or as an archivist.

Your ideas or creative inspirations can be mentally convoluted, verbose, perhaps even a bit pedantic, but brilliantly effective when you know what to leave out as well as what to include. Try to remember that fussiness and excessive concern with details won't serve as substitutes where vision and imagination are equally (or more) important to the success of your ventures. Restrictions in your childhood may have been inhibiting but instilled in you a respect for industry, quality and discipline.

Mike Piazza (baseball player), 1968

Henry Ford II (auto manufacturer), 1908

Anton Bruckner (composer), 1824

Special to August 31 (Mercury, Saturn [Venus/Sun]):
Your Virgo mental proclivities may prompt a tough-minded approach to your job, one result of which may be your inclination to ask troublesome questions—and not always diplomatically. As may be surmised, you're not likely to be a stranger to controversy. However, you're eager, versatile and cooperative, especially when it benefits your ambitions and the quality of your work. Although capable of turning on the charm, you'll probably have your share of detractors among your many admirers.

Once you find an appropriate job or career, particularly one in the public domain, you'll rarely be idle the remainder of your working life. If you cast around a bit before discovering your true calling, you're nevertheless apt to garner your share of life's material rewards along with respect for your integrity and enthusiastic acclaim for your accomplishments. You want relationships to last, so you will endeavor to choose your life partner carefully. Your personal development and your continual refinement of your abilities are more conducive to your success than luck.

Richard Gere (actor), 1949

Itzhak Perlman (violinist), 1945

Alan Jay Lerner (lyricist), 1918

Special to September 13 (Mercury, Saturn [Sun/Venus]):
To you, imparting information is as important as acquiring it, particularly in the field of education or communications. You could spearhead important changes in the way a job is done or how career objectives are classified and integrated. Whether you work in a retail establishment, a business office, a manufacturing enterprise or in an institution of higher learning, your strong sense of responsibility qualifies you to be an excellent organizer, supervisor or administrator. In the theater or other public venues, your versatility could find notable expression (especially in a humorous vein) as a performer, playwright, producer or director—or in a simultaneous combination of these skills.

With your natural intelligence and ability to weigh both sides of a question or issue, and your honesty and high moral standards, you are likely to attract partnerships that are as meaningful as they are long-lasting. No matter what course you follow, you'll want it to provide the opportunity to utilize your unique blend of idealism and practicality. When conflicts occur, confidence in your own instincts could be more important than deferring to someone else's years of experience and/or opposing views. You might even be fussy about the accolades you accept.

Fiona Apple (singer), 1977
Jacqueline Bisset (actress), 1944
Mel Torme (singer), 1925

September the 5th (Mercury, Mars)
(and root digit for September 14 and 23):
Busy with ideas, bristling with mental energy, you are also apt to be very selective about where and how your inspirations are expressed, which preferably should be along lines that can steer you into the driver's seat. If you can be tough, aggressive, resolute and at the same time detail-minded without irritating people, you will be expressing your birthright constructively. In your view, knowing that perfection is an unattainable goal, an ideal compromise is where everybody is slightly unhappy. You can live with that. What's important to you is to get on with it, meaning a job, project, worthwhile initiative or whatever at a given time is attracting your attention or inviting your commitment—and let the chips fall where they may. You can be quick with a jolt of verbal nitroglycerin when opposed or an aggravating type gets on your nerves.

You have many opportunities for variety and for bringing broad experience to a creative focal point. On the one hand, you can scatter your energies willy-nilly, waste time looking for things and in general ignore Virgo's penchant for order and neatness; on the other hand, you can keep everything in its proper place and be well organized to function productively. Either way, you can be a pacesetter and innovator in your field of endeavor. If you're sloppy it might just take longer to achieve your goal; once inspired, however, you're not apt to give up. Highly versatile, adaptable and resourceful (especially in pursuit of your ambitions), you could be as interested and proficient in sports or other activities that involve physical skills and discipline as you are in mental gymnastics; either way you're competitive, out to win, and tireless, perfectly capable of putting in long hours on the job if that's what it takes to achieve a goal. At those rare times when you might have time on your hands, you'll probably wonder if there isn't something you should be getting on with.

    Raquel Welch (actress), 1942

    Bob Newhart (actor), 1929

    Darryl F. Zanuck (producer), 1902

Special to September 14 (Mercury, Mars [Sun/Saturn]):

Your analytical abilities and technical skills are second to none. If circumstances require you to accept a minor job or assignment, one that employs your talents in less-than-top-drawer activities, you can justify a strictly commercial venture on grounds that the income it brings provides the wherewithal to pursue loftier objectives. Regardless of your laissez-faire attitude and whether you function in a creative capacity, the commercial world or the realm of science, you're capable of making a significant contribution and/or a name for yourself in your sphere of activity.

    You will profit from minimizing your skepticism of others' motives; otherwise, relationships may be more of a problem than necessary. Although adept at launching new initiatives, you do equally well furthering or enhancing the prospects of established enterprises. Being curious by nature, where you direct your restless mental energies can be very important. Your instinct for excellence can be an inspiration for colleagues who work with you, so be sure your associates will appreciate and benefit from, and not resent, your expertise and valuable input. Apropos of your high-minded conversation and bravura wit, if a sarcastic edge occasionally slithers into your voice, it only confirms that you don't suffer fools gladly.

    Joey Heatherton (actress), 1944

    Nicol Williamson (actor), 1938

    Zoe Caldwell (actress), 1933

Special to September 23 (Mercury, Mars [Moon/Venus]):
Charismatic, enterprising and competitive, you're more of a congenial mixer and in need of companionship than the typical Virgo; however, your inborn fastidiousness can make you an elitist concerning your social life. You prefer to rub shoulders with well-spoken upscale types who know where they're going and how to get there. A natural for public life whether in the business or entertainment world, you're also handy with a dollar and in attracting and accumulating your share of them as well as making them multiply through shrewd investments. If your idea of maximum security happens to slip through your fingers, however, you will still manage to be comfortable.

Inclined to be skeptical unless you can be shown proof of the value of things, you can be restless and discontented, perhaps thinking change and activity instead of thoughtful analyses are the solution to your ambivalence. When that doesn't work, you could find yourself back to square one. Popular, with a pleasing personality, you like ease and comfort and can be self-indulgent. Be careful that your emotions don't interfere with your opportunities for success.

Bruce Springsteen (singer), 1949
Ray Charles (singer), 1932
Mickey Rooney (actor), 1920

September the 6th (Mercury, Jupiter)
(and root digit for August 24 and September 15):
Your sign is the last of the six subjective initiations. Beginning with Libra, the sign following yours, the need for cooperation, adaptability and compromise in relationships becomes the central requirement. These are important issues for your birthday, too, but take care that your Virgo traits don't inhibit the adjustments necessary for success in close relationships. If you allow a critical and judgmental reaction to emotional or affectional stimulation to combine with your reticence about expressing your feelings, it could distance you from chances for love and happiness that are your birthright through the ties that bind.

You're likely to be an enthusiast for family values and tribal loyalty, but you might expect offspring and other household members to toe the mark while you go your own merry way, living by your own laissez-faire rules. Beware of the dampening effect you can have on your prospects for meaningful togetherness that could stem from a deep-seated critical attitude; you could excessively analyze possible partners in your search for perfection and find, to your dismay, that no one meets your lofty expectations. Likely to long for approval and love, the best way to get your full share is by making allowances for human frailties and by setting a worthwhile example.

The Wheel of Fortune can spin in your favor if you keep your Virgo traits under control. Shrewdly enterprising in business or creative activities or a combination of them, you can build, brick by brick, an imposing influential edifice. When you accent the appealing, optimistic side to your nature, the sky's the limit for your success potential. Usually a stickler for details, try to avoid two possibly negative outcomes: You could either become swamped in minor ones and miss the big picture, or, nervous and impatient, you could trust to luck and slight or ignore your expert skills and consequently not be fussy about the quality of your efforts and final results.

Jane Curtin (comedienne), 1947

Billy Rose (showman, producer), 1899

Marquis de Lafayette (French general), 1757

Special to August 24 (Mercury, Jupiter [Moon/Saturn]):

Resourceful if you have to start making your way in the world at an early age, your Mercurial adaptability comes in handy when you encounter experiences for which you have no prior preparation. Even if things get precarious, your streak of common sense, willingness to tackle almost any job and instinct for survival will see you through any initial (or later) trials and tribulations. Reasonably protected, and in spite of your anxieties, you can expect a measure of success in whatever goal you aim for, probably by the time you reach your middle years.

Unhappy alone, you need a home, but your natural reticence can impede personal fulfillment of your domestic yearnings. In your choice of job or career, you might model your inspirations and skills on examples you admire. However, what you do isn't always appreciated, and you can lack the flair for beating your own drum. Nevertheless, particularly as a writer or speaker, your economy, clarity and far-reaching ideas can have lasting influence. Don't plan to retire; you maintain overall well-being into your sunset years by keeping busy.

Cal Ripken, Jr. (baseball player), 1960

Max Beerbohm (author), 1872

Aubrey Beardsley (artist), 1872

Special to September 15 (Mercury, Jupiter [Sun/Mars]):
Whether by instinct or luck, your talent for being in the right place at the right time is one of life's blessings for which you can be thankful. Propinquity and your flair for leadership can help pave the way for your various steps up the ladder of success. It follows that it would be a good idea (and you have plenty of those) for you to circulate as much as possible with people of power and influence. And with your abundance of physical and mental energy, combined with a generous dash of enthusiasm, you're likely to find a plunge into the world of job, business or professional competition exciting as well as rewarding.

To say that you have the courage of your convictions would be an understatement. Partnerships can be very favorable for you, but you are apt to lose interest if returns, from your critical point of view, are inadequate. Your aggressive assurance works well in many areas of life, but it could be a drawback to finding happiness in love and marriage. It is in your best interest to ease up if you feel a need to be right all the time. Don't insist on having the last word; instead, regardless of what you're thinking (and whether you're right or wrong), try to convey an impression of warmth and compatibility.

Oliver Stone (director), 1946

Agatha Christie (writer), 1890

William Howard Taft (27th U.S. president), 1857

September the 7th (Mercury)
(and root digit for August 25 and September 16):
If criticism was the raison d'etre of the universe, your life would unfold along a well-greased path. You also know how to score a bull's-eye when you shoot from the lip. The muckraker par excellence, you discover early in life that there's plenty of muck to be raked. If you have a tendency to be pedantic or overburdened with details that may be of little interest to anyone else but you, this trait is balanced by an important advantage: You should rarely be out of work. Rational, intellectual, with an encyclopedic mind, you're not especially original, but you appreciate people who are. You have a discreet sense of humor; you're not given to gusty Falstaffian belly laughs, but others can be painfully aware of your lacerating wit.

Conscientious, introspective and resourceful, you should guard against a tendency to be overly fussy. However, thanks to the practical ramifications of your mental prowess, you have an enviable ability to recover from reverses and turn defeats into victories. Generally self-effacing, not partial to display, your desire to be "pure" and "free" of the mistakes of others is commendable: Be sure that you aren't blind to your own or cutting yourself off from life's joys in the process.

The mental aristocrat of the zodiac, you can be justifiably proud of your innate mind power; however, it is to your advantage to use it constructively. When you warm up to a subject, don't make it as repetitious and drawn out as a United Nations debate. Deep mental analysis will be more fruitful for you than aggressively seeking to impose your opinions on others. Avoid melancholy attitudes, for your health could become a problem, or you will attract people who become burdens; misery loves company. You can profitably avoid pettiness and should follow pursuits that require a keen mind. Your reserve and thoughtfulness could stem from childhood experiences.

> Buddy Holly (singer), 1936
>
> Elia Kazan (director), 1909
>
> Elizabeth I (queen of England), 1533

Special to August 25 (Mercury [Moon/Mars]):

You do well financially, but you may scatter resources through your disinclination to stick long with things once you attain a certain level of success. Very assertive and positive mentally, your independence may cause early separation from your home environment or can abruptly end an impulsive marriage. A fast, clearheaded thinker, you can be impatient with the measured pace of things or any inferiority in people or conditions. Although you are generally genial and sociable, control any tendency to intellectual snobbery or arrogance, especially in regard to mass public taste.

Your aptitudes are primarily mental, so any creative endeavor could be overweighted with a cerebral, painstaking approach. Your output will be ample evidence of your sophisticated, complicated, diverse mind and the acuity of your insights. One hazard to guard against is a temptation to coast along on your remarkable talents. Well suited for public life, your enthusiasm for your work can be contagious. Creatively or artistically, you do well in a literary, educational or analytical field, research and related spheres or as a popular performer.

> Claudia Schiffer (model), 1970
>
> Sean Connery (actor), 1930
>
> Leonard Bernstein (composer/conductor), 1918

Special to September 16 (Mercury [Sun/Jupiter]):
Although you can spot flaws as quickly as any perceptive member of your sign, your appraisals can be more constructive and encouraging; you have a talent for offering criticism cloaked in the gift-wrapping of reason, optimism and good intentions—all tied together with the bow of logic. Your Virgo tendency to editorialize can achieve more effective results if you avoid going into mountainous waves of detail when a few words will get your point across as well or better.

Shun any rigid or self-righteous mental attitudes that can inhibit your success potential. Your life will unfold more auspiciously if you're flexible about your objectives and sure of their worthiness and suitability. Your effort to master a subject and acquire the consequent expertise could be exhaustive. When you're enthused about your work, you think nothing of putting in long hours, from early morning until late at night if necessary. In case your Virgo reticence is a handicap, strive for faith in yourself and the attainment of self-confidence through the development of your versatile abilities, which can produce distinctive success in the commercial, educational, musical, literary or entertainment world.

David Copperfield (magician), 1956

Peter Falk (actor), 1927

Lauren Bacall (actress), 1924

September the 8th (Mercury, Uranus/Saturn)
(and root digit for August 26 and September 17):
Not expansive or promotional by nature, your opportunities for fulfillment nevertheless will be found in an enterprise substantial in scope or influence or serving its needs. You will achieve your objectives by developing broad-based vision, skills and talents to a high degree of proficiency; think big, and you will discover a way to win through intuitive insights and patience rather than open contest. The average Virgo will go out into the world to achieve his or her ambitions with either natural or acquired skills or an adaptable attitude. That will serve for your sign in most situations, but your particular birthday number needs a dash of the innovative, farsighted overview, the big picture kept constantly in mind. Hopefully, you will sense this need in your dissatisfaction with routine and/or low-paying jobs. But Virgo, not an assertive sign, can rarely win by storming the battlements of commerce. You usually have to do it by using your head and by being a few steps ahead of any likely competition to fulfill the far-reaching potential of your number 8 birthday.

You can be the paragon of efficiency in your work or job, a meticulous rather than an inspired or daring executive. Since you go mostly on nervous energy, high-flying speculations could make you too jittery. Your birthday is the most promising of all for the highly paid executive assistant of indispensable skills. An excellent team player, your ability to anticipate what authorities, associates or the public needs before even they realize it enhances your professional prospects and can be very rewarding financially.

You can excel in public relations, administration, the entertainment world, government or education, and you have outstanding literary skills. You're interested in practical results, probably stemming from an early awareness of the meaning and advantages of material freedom or especially the lack of it. Since your traits are so valuable in almost any enterprise, make sure they are profitable for you, too.

Patsy Cline (singer), 1932
Peter Sellers (actor), 1925
Sid Caesar (comedian), 1923

Special to August 26 (Mercury, Uranus, Saturn [Moon/Jupiter]): If you live up to your birthday potential, you're likely to have an adventurous life. You can cover a lot of ground literally as well as figuratively before your sunset years catch up with you and you ease up on or gradually withdraw from your busy agenda. Meanwhile, more peripatetic than the typical Virgo, distant locales and cultures will beckon as you go about achieving whatever exemplary goals you aim for. You could be an excellent linguist; as a result of your travels, you'll probably be able to communicate in more than one language and might be fluent in several.

With your abundant faith, courage and sense of responsibility, you're well qualified for a leadership role, which you're able to attain despite possibly humble beginnings. Your ingrained optimism and eye on the future sustains you if that's what it takes to slowly but surely rise up through the ranks. An excellent teacher, writer or researcher, your thirst for knowledge and urge to inspire the same in others probably stem from your formative years, when you had a lot to think about and were no doubt an avid student. You would do well in an artistic career where intellectual facility, simplicity and precision are essential components of creative expression. Home and family life are very important to you, but your itchy foot to travel might preclude having much time to pursue them.

Geraldine Ferraro (political figure), 1935

Mother Teresa (humanitarian), 1910

Albert B. Sabin (scientist), 1906

Special to September 17 (Mercury, Uranus, Saturn [Sun/Mercury]):
Although your freewheeling spirit and independent ideas might not jibe with
the establishment norm, your vision and skills are sufficiently convincing and
valuable to the success of an enterprise to keep you on the payroll. You're an
excellent team player when it's to your advantage, but you're no fan of the status quo and are instead always on the lookout for a new concept or technique
that can accelerate the march of progress. Your principal goal is to accumulate
power and influence and to garner the appropriate financial rewards.

In the creative fields, you can be an exemplar of nuance, wit and sophisticated charm. With your Virgo flair for the editing process and attention
to detail, you're able to refine your efforts to a maximum of essential simplicity and a minimum of creative embellishment. The more trivial the subject
matter, the more you can elevate it to a distinctive level of achievement.
Undaunted when facing a challenge, when you have a job to do, you're able
to size up the requirement, plunge right in and get on with it. Although you
can be amiable and the life of the party, you can also stand firm when
opposed, adopting a take-it-or-leave-it stance when you feel you're right. Very
observant, your talent for mimicry can be wickedly amusing.

Anne Bancroft (actress), 1931

Roddy McDowall (actor), 1928

Hank Williams (singer), 1923

September the 9th (Mercury, Pluto)
(and root digit for August 27 and September 18):
More intense and emotional than is customary for Virgo, you may find the
demands of the world conflicting with and inhibiting to your personal relationships. While pleasantly sociable when you're with congenial companions
and in the mood to mix and mingle, you're not as shy and retiring as you are
annoyed when people try to pry into your private life. That's off-limits in your
view. Ironically, you're curious about what makes other people tick who
intrigue and fascinate you, a trait that doesn't do much for your love life.
Instead of basking in the pleasures of affectional or emotional ties, you may
spend more time analyzing a lover or relationship than relaxing and enjoying

yourself come what may. A busy flow of communications, to say nothing of nervous crosscurrents, can accompany this tendency, which you should curb.

Your life is likely to be episodic, with one startling new phase, a break with the past and perhaps several minor skirmishes. You may arrive at the reason for a drastic turnabout through your subtle mental processes or through circumstances beyond your control. Not naturally inclined to a broad-minded objective outlook, many Virgos with this birthday may need to overcome their fussy concern with details in order to tap hidden power and give their high standards of perfection wider application.

Although you could get started early on the road to success in a job or career that makes best use of your abilities, there might be little evidence at the beginning of your working life of the way you will eventually satisfy your worldly ambitions. Your Virgo skepticism and psychic antenna enable you to read between the lines and come out a winner in a power struggle, an instinct that qualifies you for any sort of investigatory occupation. You would be a whiz at personnel management, especially in a medical facility. In any case, unlike Gemini, you're not apt to flit from job to job and are more likely to stick to a career or line of endeavor once you've made a rewarding choice.

Hugh Grant (actor), 1960

Max Reinhardt (showman, producer), 1873

Leo Tolstoy (writer), 1828

Special to August 27 (Mercury, Pluto [Moon/Mercury]):

You like to be associated with accomplished or powerful people who are a match for your shrewd mental abilities. Although you are not partial to subordinate positions, the subtle observation and accuracy of detail you bring to a job or assignment are very useful to higher-ups and/or the overall success of a project. The power of suggestion is one of your potent attributes, and you know how to select and articulate the words and gestures that contribute most to the success of your stratagems. You are inclined to be unconventional and sympathetic in your beliefs as a result of your independent, probing, discriminating mind.

You have scant patience with shallow drivel, and you will no doubt find many nits to pick as you go through life. In the interest of peace and progress, you may have to learn to bite your tongue when what you're seeing or hearing arouses your most critical instincts. Count to ten before offering your candid appraisal; if that doesn't work, expand it to a hundred. Furthermore, your attention span for ho-hum or thrice familiar topics is short. If someone has an idea or a story for you, he or she had better make it interesting in the first five minutes. Otherwise, especially if you're busy, your eyes glaze over.

Tuesday Weld (actress), 1943

Martha Raye (comedienne), 1914

Lyndon B. Johnson (36th U.S. president), 1908

Special to September 18 (Mercury, Pluto [Sun/Uranus/Saturn]):
You may not flaunt your ambitions, but you know how to promote them and yourself in very subtle ways. Thanks to your shrewd psychic radar, you sense what others think before they say it. And at the same time, people could also reveal privileged information without knowing you wanted it. With your hidden reservoir of personal power, you can achieve notable results through your Virgo mental prowess to select, analyze and refine opportunities that come your way on the material level. You could gain a reputation for impeccable taste, originality and a bubbling sense of humor. You are an efficient administrator of practical affairs, your own or others, and could easily wind up with an ostrich-size nest egg.

You can be distant and resentful if people try to turn your life into an open book. Your fear of surrendering your independence and penchant for doing what you want when you want inhibit but do not preclude close relationships or a satisfactory marriage. Naturally wary, you can suspect there's more than meets the eye in almost any situation. When you choose to harbor a secret, people will never know what is going on behind your impassive visage. Thanks to your seductive charisma, you'll always have your share of admirers.

Frankie Avalon (singer), 1939

Rossano Brazzi (actor), 1916

Greta Garbo (actress), 1905

September the 11th (Mercury, Neptune [Moon/Sun])
(master number):
In your effort to find a practical application or outlet for your ideals of perfection, the wide scope of your ephemeral radar can glide over numerous opportunities that qualify for improvement or advancement. Your mind can be like a magic faucet—turn it on and the ideas flow. Be wary that your inborn skepticism doesn't inhibit the free flow of your imagination. In any situation that attracts your attention, the challenge to make "a silk purse out of a sow's ear" can inspire you to notable heights of achievement. In turn, in whatever

job, career or other field of activity you choose to enhance with your abilities, you can be an inspiration to those who work for you or with you, who in turn benefit from your visions, talents and/or leadership capabilities. Nervously attuned, your energies and desires are apt to fluctuate, prompting you to switch jobs or careers. You react sensitively to all that your mental antennae pick up, and not always diplomatically. Since you can be extreme and controversial, you should watch your health and nerves. Even though personally innocent of questionable activities, your reputation and security can be threatened by the appearance of dabbling in devious strategies or escapes. Always scrupulously adhering to above-board behavior is important to your progress, status and security. You are multitalented and very insightful in any intellectual capacity, and you are especially adapted to the literary field, music and education. You can also make your mark in the world of commerce and industry.

To transmute your splendid birthright into a living reality is a formidable assignment; you will go as far as whatever you are. "As a man thinketh in his heart, so is he" applies to you. Because it is what you think, you reveal your basic values through what you say. It is up to you to emphasize purity and illumination and set an example in your life. If your early environment left you feeling confused and decentralized, at least it would have provided you with a foretaste of the kind of life you don't want to live as an adult.

Harry Connick, Jr. (musician), 1967

Brian De Palma (director), 1940

D. H. Lawrence (writer), 1885

(Note: This master number implies a variable alternative response influenced by the strength or passivity of the planet Neptune in your horoscope. If you don't feel you are responding to the distinctive vibratory power of 11, you are instead expressing the more conventional 2, which you should read.)

September the 22nd (Mercury, Uranus [Saturn, Moon])
(master number):

Uranus, The Awakener and higher octave of Mercury (your Sun-Sign planetary ruler), is the ruling planet of your birthday number. At your best, you are the practical idealist, the efficiency expert of large enterprises, a whiz at getting to the essence of a subject or project and giving it new life. If you're not in the driver's seat, you're the first-class technical advisor or executor of strategies set by higher-ups. Combining your natural flair for detail with innovative concepts, you can inject a fresh slant into already-established work or creative ventures. You're right at home with the intricate gadgetry of the computer world and space-age technology as well as farsighted medical breakthroughs. Your revolutionary approach is particularly effective in a public venue and can result in startling avant-garde results.

Motivated by humanitarian instincts, more advanced and independent than the typical Virgo, you could be the source for progressive ideas in the education field. With other indications in agreement, you can improve whatever you touch and be the innovator in whatever future-oriented projects attract your interest. You may feel as though you live in a state of transition, "on the verge," as it were. Through the exceptional intuition of the number 22, much is apparent to you that escapes the notice of the crowd. You can envision something as an abstraction and then, since you're an earth type, follow through on the practical ramifications. Nervous to begin with, your high-voltage inspirations can make you fidgety and impatient with people who aren't on your intuitive wavelength.

If your willpower predominates over your "won't-power," you can make and keep many friends who are always ready to help, especially in the business or creative world. In general, however, you probably work better alone or autonomously, without close supervision, interference or interruptions. An interest in science, the very old or the very new, is typical of your birthday, along with a fascination for obscurities and picturesque or relevant details. Always try to broaden your scope and viewpoints and be as tactful and considerate as possible in your dealings with people.

Tommy Lasorda (baseball manager), 1927
Erich Von Stroheim (actor/director), 1885
Michael Faraday (physicist), 1791

(Note: This master number implies a variable alternative response influenced by the strength or passivity of the planet Uranus in your horoscope. If you don't think you are responding to the distinctive vibratory power of 22, you are instead expressing the more conventional qualities of 4, which you should read.)

CHAPTER 7

LIBRA

September 24–October 23

RULER: **VENUS** NUMBER: **3** ELEMENT: **AIR** SYMBOL: **THE SCALES**

"Your gentleness shall force, more than your force shall move us to gentleness."
—*As You Like It*, Shakespeare

A silver rose . . . isn't that a lovely thought? You like lovely thoughts. Better than that, you like lovely realities: a perfect mate, a gracious home, congenial friends, model children, tasteful clothes, an adoring mother-in-law, charming manners, marital bliss, *especially* marital bliss—in sum, life with the rough edges removed, like those dainty tea sandwiches with the crusts trimmed.

Picture a beautiful couple in the "City of Dreams." And where is such a place? Why, Vienna, of course. Didn't you know it was a Libra city? The couple is enjoying a delectable dinner in exquisite surroundings: shimmering damask, gleaming silver, sparkling crystal, glowing chandeliers and elegant service rendered in the most mellifluous tones. The atmosphere is one of muted splendor. And in a slender vase glistening in the candlelight is a lovely silver rose. How thoughtful and fitting that it should be there on *their* table.

The silver rose is highly symbolic for the couple, so blissfully happy this perfect evening. It was his inspiration to subtly preface his proposal with a make-believe preview of it, flavored by the glittering rococo ambiance of 18th-century Vienna.

They will attend a performance of *Der Rosenkavalier*, the story of a cavalier, a silver rose and triumphant love. But it will really be about them, a make-believe version of their idyllic dream come true. Enthralled by the "presentation of the rose," the scene where the gallant cavalier affirms his love for his enchanting betrothed by presenting her with a silver rose, their hearts as one with the rapturous music will wing upward in surrender to the heady stratosphere of romantic fantasy.

The evening will end as perfectly as it began: our distaff Libran will accept his proposal, just like the dewy-eyed girl across the footlights. Unlike her, however, she will have to wait until her Lothario gets his divorce and until she gets *hers*. It's really not that much bother for her, compared to the prize she's getting. After all, he's everything a girl ever dreamed of: the ideal escort, courtly, considerate and tastefully groomed. Even though he's quiet and unassuming, he projects an aura of masculine power. He is charming and affectionate, and sharing experiences with him is a pleasure. A considerate gentleman, he instinctively remembers to send flowers or candy at appropriate times. He should have been a diplomat, with his willingness to listen to both sides of a situation and to mediate all differences. And you know that he will be very fair with his soon-to-be-dumped wife, Betty, and will see that she's well provided for.

Of course, she hasn't heard Betty's version of her Libran dreamboat. Back home, his wife thinks that he's just on one of his frequent European business jaunts for his company. Alone in New York, she's wondering out loud if he will ever lessen his work pace or if she will ever see the inside of one of those glamorous restaurants of their courtship days not all that long ago. He's just doing what comes naturally for a Libran . . . *again*. It will be his third marriage.

The couple may be fictional, but your characteristics are not. In the Broadway musical *Candide*, the married state is extolled as "the best in this best of all possible worlds." Candide, the leading character, somewhat unconvinced, asks:

> *Since marriage is divine, of course,*
> *We cannot understand, Sir,*
> *Why there should be so much divorce,*
> *Do let us know the answer!*

The teacher, Dr. Pangloss, replies:

> *Why marriage, boy, is such a joy,*
> *So lovely a condition,*
> *That many ask no better than,*
> *To wed as often as they can,*
> *In happy repetition!*

Of all the signs, yours is the one most likely to paper the walls with marriage licenses. Some Librans, more loath to change, can marry parts of people and spend years wishing for the other parts. Since your expectations are so high regarding unions, it might be well to remember two things: None of the saints were married, and all of the great loves of myth and history were "tragic" or touched by adversity and sacrifice. In case you've forgotten, Tristan and Isolde, Romeo and Juliet, Pelleas and Melisande, Mark Antony and Cleopatra, et al., are among the legendary examples.

The glyph of your sign is a pictograph, similar to an Egyptian hieroglyph, of the setting sun halfway below the horizon, balanced, as it were, between the receding cares of the day and the impending pleasures of the evening. The scales, the symbol of your sign, is found on courthouses, indicating Libra's association with justice, judges and lawyers—as well as with partnership and marriage.

The scales are a clue to an important aspect of your nature. When you exemplify your estimable potential, you are well balanced, fair, impartial, unprejudiced and just. When you are not at your best, however, you can be an extremist playing havoc with everybody else's equilibrium, or you can be a vacillating wishy-washy fence sitter, inclined to postponing important decisions ad infinitum.

When you pursue an initiative after due respect for opposing forces, the middle of the road is usually best for you to move forward in. Noted for your personal charm, diplomacy and gently persuasive manner, you can generally get what you want in a way that makes people like it. You excel at cooperation and compromise, but people should bear in mind that you are not a pushover. Despite your typically pleasant demeanor, you're not all sweetness and light, as adversaries quickly discover when they clash with you and learn firsthand about the "iron fist in the velvet glove." When it's in everyone's best interest, however, your personal rewards are often substantial when you meet people halfway and are unlikely to really give up much when you compromise.

You thrive on cheerful company, sympathy and affection, so you are ever seeking congenial partners who complete your picture of life as an experience of beauty and refinement. Libra is the sign most apt to fall in love with love and make some big mistakes. Your idealized conceptions of mating make you more vulnerable to love's hurts and disappointments. While a Cancerian can neglect the mate for the children, a Libran can reverse the emphasis. Your consuming focus of interest is your mate and your need for constant attentiveness. You won't suffer neglect gladly, even in the face of your children's needs.

Your sign is the one that life's struggles are really all about: the fundamental need to get along with people. It is not to protect them or to dictate to them or to give in to them but just to blend your will with that of another or others with felicity and in the interest of shared fulfillment.

You may be the great achiever, winning recognition as it's measured by the world, but if the net result is a solitary existence, your efforts won't have made you happy. You want enduring love and togetherness, and, if a positive Libran, you will tolerate the discipline and the give and take that goes with any meaningful relationship. You may not see it as a fringe benefit, but the desire to fulfill your essential need is so compelling that you will be reasonably adjustable in the process of maintaining the balance.

Venus, your radiant and brilliant ruling planet, is the symbol of attraction. You are frequently visually attractive; even if you aren't a prize beauty, you project an aura of "attractiveness" that can be more alluring and durable than mere physical charms. Ordinary-looking women in history who have had the greatest sensual impact on men include Cancer-born French novelist George Sand; she was the lover of Frederic Chopin, Alfred De Musset and other notable men of her time. Cleopatra, no great beauty but evidently a great charmer, had passionate liaisons with Julius Caesar and Mark Antony, two of history's powerful, charismatic men. Even if a woman who attracts a prize catch isn't Libra-born, it is the magic of Venus at work, *the* potent factor in *your* life. You are a master of all the delicacies, nuances and sentiments of courtship and romance. The spouse of the typical Libra man needs to be an adoring mistress, an efficient mother, an excellent cook and a fastidious housekeeper. The typical Libra wife expects a loyal partner, a gallant lover, an attentive father and a generous provider. (She likes luxuries.)

You are genuinely considerate of others or you give that impression; either way, you are consequently popular. The typical Libran is unhappy alone; you are most fulfilled in a mutually rewarding marriage or some form of commitment or enduring togetherness. Since that is life's most intimate relationship, your innate gift for being tactful, courteous and affectionate can blossom into full flower. Although you are not immune to physical attractions, beauty for you is truly in the eyes of the beholder. The beauty of the relationship is the thing that counts instead of the visual appearance of the participants. For instance, how you look or your particular personality traits are not the inspiration for those "what does she (or he) see in him (or her)" comments. The consummate union of two minds and of two souls is always intrinsically beautiful regardless of other considerations.

You are the fulcrum that can effect a common center between two or more individualities. For this reason, Libra is the sign of marriage, but don't be misled: Before you become swamped in hearts and flowers, remember that it's also the sign of open enemies, legal fights (like divorce) and war. The polar opposite of your sign is Aries, ruled by forceful Mars. Initiatives begun aggressively with Mars' fiery energies end either in Libra's blending of disparities or in irresolution or separation.

Libra can go for the gloss and forget the gut of experience. You might shy away from taking a justifiable critical stand because it could turn people against you or your cause. Perhaps that's subliminal compensation from dim memories of your Virgo incarnation and the loneliness that resulted from your candid opinions and/or criticism. You can be popular for all the wrong reasons, including compromised integrity. To everyone else, you are charming and agreeable; to someone with unswerving purpose or a moral ax to grind, you can be maddeningly equivocal and even seem spineless. You can sacrifice people or issues to your principle of peace at any price or to your own lack of purpose and integrity. This is why people with fixed or controversial opinions or who are mavericks are not congenial to you: They upset the atmosphere too much for your comfort.

But perhaps you can learn something about decisions and commitment to abstract justice and objective ideals from them. Your approach to the ideal of peace can be overly subjective, such as peace for *you* regardless of the subsequent ramifications. Loyalty, therefore, is not a shining trait of the negative Libran if it means taking an unpopular stand or confronting an issue. You want peace and popularity, so at times you won't stick with one person even if a principle is involved or if it might antagonize others or jeopardize your personal ambitions. You can thus be the fawning opportunist able to turn almost any circumstance to personal advantage. In sum, the negative Libran is not staunch in a moral crisis.

For instance, Aries-born individuals might tolerate the clash, clatter and coarseness that can make you ill and upset your poise; at the same time, they may be expressing integrity, which at least is upright in the midst of their brash assertiveness. Your peace-loving nature can make for too much compromise and evasion because discord, conflict and vulgarity are so unsettling to your finely tuned proprieties. You're born with a legitimate amount of equipoise, but you can further cultivate an abhorrence of discord to an extreme. Not being long on initiative, you can wait for things to come to you. But it doesn't mean that you can just sit and wait, smiling sweetly at the world. Everyone has work to do, on the inner and outer levels.

If you want to get ahead in life vocationally, you will need training and skills, or you are apt to rely on your gift for merely ingratiating yourself. Employers will take a chance on you because they like you and can discover later that you really aren't very qualified for the task they've given you. Then, if you lose a job, you can have a biased attitude about it. You may conclude that the termination came about because the boss *didn't like you*, instead of placing the blame where it really belongs—on your own inadequate job performance. On the contrary, the employer may like you very much as a person and feel considerable regret in severing the business part of your relationship.

You function well in association with others. For example, Libran General Dwight D. Eisenhower, as supreme commander of the World War II allied forces, was the balance for the various factions of the war effort in Europe. He was able to pacify the prickly egos of stage-struck generals without giving in to them or letting them disturb or jeopardize the overall strategy of the war. He exemplified discipline without sacrificing rapport and teamwork. As for his tenure as 34th U.S. president, many speak disparagingly of the "Eisenhower years"; many others would much prefer the headlines of the fifties, however, to the headlines of the nineties.

In another context, Libran Mahatma Gandhi began his career in a profession ruled by his sign by being admitted to the bar in 1889. He was a historical exponent of nonviolent resistance to injustice. Through passive pressures, he was instrumental in securing Indian independence. Of course, it cost two million dollars a year to keep him in poverty, but his value as a spiritual symbol was beyond price. Truly inspired by an unswerving sense of justice, he asserted the unity of all mankind; he preached the equality of Hindu, Moslem and Christian ethics. His powerful influence spread to the United States and elsewhere in the world through the adoption of his nonviolent tactics by leaders of civil-rights movements.

Since you are not naturally pushy or a self-starter, joining forces with more aggressive types can be very beneficial. You are frequently able to advance in life through hearing about openings through others and should always be alert to such possibilities since you aren't strong on creating your own opportunities. Your affable personality, expressive gifts and poise get you through the doorway to success. One way to achieve your goals is through your charm and ability to ingratiate yourself with people affiliated with promising situations. You're not especially stubborn; but when your indecisiveness takes over, you can seem stubborn in your refusal to take a stand.

Libra, or the relationship needs that motivate it, is the sign of secret drinkers; Venus, your ruling planet, governs the kidneys, the purifiers of the body fluids. The life of F. Scott Fitzgerald is a revealing example of the tragedy inherent in Libra when the individual does not strive for true balance.

Fitzgerald's first successful novel, *This Side of Paradise*, is the handbook of the Roaring Twenties, a time of tinsel and tragedy, one of America's periods of great unrest. He was bewitched by the glitter that served to mask the seed of later tragic developments in his life and that of his wife Zelda. Subsequently, when the masks were removed, an alcoholic and a psychotic were revealed, both very talented and insightful but unable to deal with reality. They had strained too hard to believe in their false god—an artificially sustained continuity of gaiety and ambiance that worked deceptively in the twenties when the tide was with them but that was totally unrealistic in the leaden thirties when the tide turned against them. In the end, a downward spiral into a morass of tragic disillusionment was the inevitable result.

An older Fitzgerald was able, even in this disenchanted but still perceptive state, to catch the tragedy of relationships in his novel, *Tender Is the Night*. Although only partially autobiographical, it is an insightful example of Libran catharsis. His early and unquestioning exposure to such amenities as attending fashionable schools and leading a carefree social life seemed to set up all the factors for a Libran destined by fate to be at war with both aspects of self: the realistic versus the idealistic. As any of you who have loved and lost already know, anger and forgiveness, rejection and regret are the unavoidable contradictions churning within the injured Libra psyche. Fitzgerald's attempt at marriage was a failure unless you count the ones to the pen or the bottle. To quote Libran Oscar Wilde: "There are only two tragedies in life: not getting what you want . . . and getting what you want."

You think that your destiny is to find a partner; actually, it's to find and complete the "self" through a partner, but there may be complications to overcome. *Anyone*—Libra or otherwise—*sufficiently disoriented within himself or herself* will find it painfully difficult to achieve a fulfilling relationship at even the most elemental level but especially in a romantic liaison. We hear people say, "If only I could meet *Mr. Right* or *Ms. Right*, I could be happy." Don't you believe it. Instead, the net result will be two unhappy people—the misguided first one and an innocent victim looking for a way out of a mistake. Those expecting answers to life's *problems* through a relationship are just trying to absolve themselves of the responsibility to grow up. There's scant chance that those who aren't already positive within themselves and who don't have an inner core of self-reliance, equilibrium and contentment will find happiness through a partner.

Negative Librans have to accept a certain amount of differences and troubles involving others as a fact of life. That's the great challenge for you in the cosmic experiment. Otherwise, like a Virgo with nothing to criticize, your role would be written out of the cosmic drama. Though negative Librans tend toward it, you can't succumb to moral impotence; if you do, you become the syrupy purveyor of felicity, of preciousness. Elegance then degenerates into bon-bon bilge. Remember: "The path is smooth that leadeth on to danger." Negative Librans should learn to appreciate those opportunities that force them to come to grips with moral objectivity; in that way, they will grow and strengthen their enviable assets, which are useless and undeveloped unless put to the test.

The typical male Libran without relationships doesn't like himself; he's inwardly disappointed for failing at the function for which he was intended. But it goes deeper than that: There's a person submerged within himself that he doesn't understand, and he keeps meeting this other self in the guise of other people, which is why he has difficulty relating. He projects his disorientation onto others. He lacks understanding and has a narrow view of beauty and harmony that few, if any, ever measure up to.

The negative distaff Libran can have a chilly neurosis about perfect beauty in her life; *things* and their care can matter very much to her and can become more important than people, who get short shrift because she's emotionally barren. She goes through the motions of marriage as her part of the bargain; she's fair, but she's "Craig's Wife" when it comes to the trappings. Like the beautiful feminine machine in the play of the same name by George Kelly, she is an antiseptic shrew fussing over a spic-and-span household and schedules and chores. Her home is as inviting as an elegant mausoleum. Visitors are drenched in medicinal hospitality, and, with all the misplaced emphasis, this misguided Libran misses the point of life completely. Cleanliness may be next to godliness, but such extremes are counterproductive. This kind of behavior defeats Libra's purpose because what you want to do is *attract*, not repel. "Lazy Libra loathes a duster" is a traditional phrase that typifies another extreme of Libra, another excessive tip of the "scales." She abhors any menial work and doesn't like to soil her hands even to accomplish an everyday household task.

In any case and at your best, however, you are superbly equipped to perform your Libra function, which is the balancing and constructive unification of various discordant as well as harmonious factors in life. Yours is unlike the intention and purpose of Virgo, which is the elimination of all that is not perfect. When positively oriented, you can adjust to all the parts of a person or situation you're attracted to, imperfections included, and, with the magic of your ruler Venus, can integrate them into a workable meaningful whole. You may wince at some features of the bargain; but when the advantages outweigh the drawbacks, your inner desire and ability to smooth things over preclude remaining uninvolved or a deliberate loner.

By being aware of the fundamental necessities inherent in the ties that bind, you gain valuable heartfelt insights that guarantee the happy fulfillment of your treasured ideals. As for Libra and marriage, once you've found your cherished "better half" and exchanged those bands of gold, you can be a responsible, faithful and loving partner tolerant of the less appealing facets of everyday homemaking and family rearing. Meanwhile, it might help to remember one of the secrets of a happy marriage: *low expectations*.

LIBRA BIRTHDAYS

Judgment of whether or not a birthday is propitious can be considered from two points of view: complementary or challenging. From the standpoint of personal progress and fulfillment, your destiny may flow more comfortably if your birthday is, or reduces to, an *inner* root number such as 1, 3, 5, 7 or 9. For career drive and achievement, your progress may be enhanced if your birthday is, or reduces to, an *outer* root number such as 2, 4, 6, 8 or 22 (master number); the *outer* root numbers are less comfortable, more obstructive for you to contend with, but they are potentially very conducive to outstanding success. The 11 (master number) would be variable, favorable for creative achievement, but it generally would require more understanding and resourcefulness in order to integrate it with the meaning of Libra.

Remember, if your birthday is two digits (excepting master numbers 11 and 22), be sure to read the *root* digit or number first. For example, if your birthday is 29, read the 2 (2 + 9 = 11, 1 + 1 reduces to 2) birthday profile first and then read the special profile for 29. If your birthday is 14, read the 5 (1 + 4 = 5) birthday profile first and then read the special profile for 14, and so on. If a description in a "special" section contradicts information in the "root" digit (root number) analysis, the "special" interpretation applies more specifically to you.

The first planet in parentheses following your birthday number is *your Sun-Sign ruler*; the second planet (or Uranus/Saturn for number 8) is *your birthday number planetary equivalent*. Subsidiary planetary influences (if any) are bracketed.

Each birthday profile includes celebrities who share the same birthday.

YOUR BIRTHDAY PROFILE
October the 1st (Venus, Sun)
(and root digit for September 28, October 10 and 19):

Considering your personal appeal and leadership qualities, it isn't surprising that your birthday number and its derivatives are among the most promising for worldly success. Generally more considerate and cooperative than competitive, people find it easy and usually a pleasure to work with or relate to you. And nothing greases the skids to success quite like that. Your birthday confers the appearance of determination and resolution to camouflage your typical Libra tendency to equivocate. Underneath, however, you aren't always so positive, which you'd rather people didn't know. "Chin up" and all that sort of thing, even if distasteful decisions are sometimes necessary—and they will be in your life.

You are dedicated and devoted to your concepts of justice; be sure that your insistence on "fairness" doesn't stem only from your personal pride and ahead of other considerations. People may be due for a surprise when they discover how intractable you can be behind your pleasant facade. When what you consider to be a moral or ethical issue is at stake, or you find an establishment posture or decision offensive, you won't hesitate to take on the powers-that-be. Whether or not you win, you'll gain admiration for your courage in trying to rectify what you feel is a valid grievance or injustice.

You like to be appreciated and have a flair for attracting public attention and popularity. With your ingratiating charm and 1,000-watt smile, you are a master at getting what you want. The lilting bluntness of a determined Libran is not soon forgotten. In regard to the ties that bind and domesticity, however, you may need to be considerably adjustable. Ardent and sincere, your success in love and marriage will depend on selecting a partner worthy of your affections.

Mark McGwire (baseball player), 1963
Julie Andrews (actress), 1935
Jimmy Carter (39th U.S. president), 1924

Special to September 28 (Venus, Sun [Moon/Uranus/Saturn]):
Relationships are necessary for you to express your affectionate nature, but you can overreact when adjustments are necessary to keep your emotional involvements on an even keel. When serious partnership problems erupt and you face a choice between fight (to keep the relationship going) or flight (to call it quits), you'll tend to choose the latter in keeping with your aversion

to discord and quarrels. Inclined to dramatize everything that concerns your personal life, you may find it difficult (or unnecessary) to sustain a long-lasting intimate relationship when your Libran charm makes it so easy to enjoy off-again-on-again love or marital experiences.

With practical rewards in mind, you may gravitate toward the business milieu. However, since your urge to express yourself is strong, many of you would be happier in a creative or artistic career if you can make it pay. Suave and literate, you exude an air of worldly grace. As a performer, you're sensitive to the most extraordinary nuances and can convey the inner reality of life. Many Librans with this birthday who go into the arts wind up on top. A peripatetic childhood could prompt the wanderlust that lures you far from your birthplace in pursuit of your job, business or professional endeavors . . . or perhaps an amorous adventure or two.

> Mira Sorvino (actress), 1967
>
> Brigitte Bardot (actress), 1935
>
> Marcello Mastroianni (actor), 1924

Special to October 10 (Venus, Sun):

Indecisiveness is traditionally a shortcoming of Libra but probably not in your case. You can be an outstanding exception, capable of making dynamic decisions that put you ahead of the crowd. And fast. You're likely to get an early start with your job or career activities that enable you to gain a position of importance before midlife. Socially, romantically and publicly popular, those attributes have a bearing on your excellent career-related financial prospects. If you don't achieve impressive income and security, you'll attract a mate or partner who fills in that gap.

Very gifted in the arts, you are restless and discontented until you establish an important beachhead. Your need to satisfy your ambitions adds gritty determination to the usually more pliant Libra nature. Whether you demonstrate your abilities in the world of commerce or creativity, you can count on your abundant potential to carve a distinctive niche for yourself. Although successful relationships are possible, you will probably find your career activities more rewarding, or at least more time-consuming, than your personal life. In the wake of adversities, blue skies are likely to smile once again over your prospects for fulfillment and happiness.

> Brett Favre (football player), 1969
>
> Thelonius Monk (pianist), 1918
>
> Giuseppe Verdi (composer), 1813

Special to October 19 (Venus, Sun [Sun/Pluto]):
Being rather independent and bolstered by your undercurrent of magnetism, you're apt to make your own rules in relationships. Your suspicions are easily aroused, so your mate or steady date should avoid even the appearance of straying. More at home in a profession, you are also artistic and can make a creative venture pay. You take pride in your shrewd insights into people and situations; whether it's a job, business or other career opportunity, your instinct for turning on the charm at just the right time aids your climb up the success ladder. You're very security-minded about money and are happiest when you can stockpile it in amounts sufficient to alleviate any fears of scarcity.

You're not likely to waste much time with people who aren't achievement-oriented or who aren't aiming for or don't already inhabit a respectable social level. In addition to admiring and enjoying the company of achievers, you sense that such connections are instructive and important and will be drawn to people of accomplishment or to the milieu they travel in. You may seem hearty and straightforward but underneath you are driven by a powerful force to prove your worth. And you'll resort to whatever ways and means necessary to establish your distinctive personal and creative identity.

Evander Holyfield (boxer), 1962

John LeCarre (writer), 1931

Umberto Boccioni (artist), 1882

October the 2nd (Venus, Moon)
(and root digit for September 29 and October 20;
October 11 is a master number, see end of chapter):
Your birthday signifies a love of home and family and a natural rapport with the public in your job or career pursuits. The success of either one, however, usually depends on some sacrifice of the other. You may drift a bit or follow the path of least resistance until you get motivated and direct your energies into income-producing and, hopefully, status-enhancing work. However, even though you're initially encouraged by a job or profession, you'll be discontented until you've advanced enough to gain substantial material security or see the future prospects of same—and this may take longer than you like.

You're exceptionally adaptable, so your prospects are excellent to succeed at whatever course you choose to satisfy your worldly ambitions. Yours is the kind of ingratiating personality that makes it easier to maneuver your way through the thickets of opportunity that are mixed with disappointments in order to meet people of importance, which doesn't hurt your cause any. Much of your success could stem from others' input or support. Along with your qualities of charm, tact and expressiveness, your cooperative spirit and sense of humor will come in handy when you begin to make your way in the world.

Filtered through your distinctive personality, your exemplary standards and your job or career achievement is an effective influence of unique power and impact. Very sensitive in your response to affectional or emotional stimuli, you thrive best in a happy domestic or community environment of tranquillity and refinement. Since you react nervously to stress, discord or thoughts of failure, you avoid where possible situations that are inclined to be frustrating or depressing.

> Sting (singer), 1951
> Groucho Marx (comedian), 1890
> Mahatma Gandhi (Hindu leader), 1869

Special to September 29 (Venus, Moon [Pluto]):
You may wander a bit before finding the niche that provides the equilibrium you seek. You can be absorbed in your own needs and not be as willing as the typical Libran to make major adjustments; you nevertheless require relationships and are willing to make concessions—up to a point. Nervous and tense without people, they may be nervous and tense with you when you're not at your most winsome and congenial. The entertainment world, art, commerce and government are promising areas in which to demonstrate your distinctive talents, personal credibility and instinct for public popularity.

Life's mysteries and ambiguities intrigue you, and the results of your investigations and experiences regarding them can enlighten the public as well as be personally beneficial. In a similar vein, you have the knack for tapping into mass consciousness, and through your taste and abilities, you can supply the balm that alleviates the complexities and anxieties of modern life. Whether or not you're a performer or you're just naturally being humorous, folksy or serious, you project a remarkably friendly, empathetic, accessible quality to which people respond and that makes them feel relaxed and comfortable. Meticulous about your craftsmanship, you're impatient with sloppy work done by others. Whatever you do, you'll try to make it mean something constructive and are willing to work hard to put it over.

> Bryant Gumbel (TV newscaster), 1948
> Madeline Kahn (actress, singer), 1942
> Greer Garson (actress), 1908

Special to October 20 (Venus, Moon):

You do best by avoiding situations where assertiveness, boundless determination or heavy responsibilities can be requirements for success. A career where sociability, cooperation, popular diversions and ideals are an asset is more congenial for you. You thrive on approval and the collaboration of others. Versatile, you might try your luck at several jobs or careers before you find the one that makes best use of your unique abilities, among which are your deferential leadership qualities.

Competitive for public approval, once you're on the right track, you're comfortable in the limelight or progressing up to a top job because you merit it. However, you aren't always the type to battle your way into prominence. If you're not personally aggressive, you won't mind (and can be eternally grateful) if someone with initiative and daring who believes in your talent and potential does it for you. You have a flair for knowing what the public wants and for cashing in on your personal charm, expertise and popular appeal in ways that fill the demand. Even if you have to share some of the credit, your lifelong efforts can add up to impressive achievement.

Tom Petty (singer), 1953

Mickey Mantle (baseball player), 1931

Bela Lugosi (actor), 1888

October the 3rd (Venus)
(and root digit for September 30, October 12 and 21):

Charm is of use in all things—pleases practically everybody—and you have it in abundance. Since your life is dominated by beauty, whether in relationships, creative endeavor or your appreciation of it in art, music, poetry and so on, you should have few problems in finding suitable outlets to express your talents or feelings. In seeking a pleasurable existence, for instance, you might initially decide to become an artist because the carefree artistic life attracted you as much as the creative possibilities. The connoisseur par excellence, you're able to smooth the way as life's amiable "master of ceremonies" in any touchy situation. It isn't a guarantee of your own emotional contentment, however, because your ideals are so lofty and hard to fulfill.

Fastidious, reticent to offend anyone, you can wince or shudder discreetly at social crudities. Your fluency in dealing with people is exceptional and is a formidable asset as you begin to make your way in the world. You're capable of overcoming obstacles that test your flair for getting what you want and at the same time ruffling few feathers. For example, you can make a highly controversial statement, smile sweetly and dare people to dislike you. It should be easy for you to demonstrate or cultivate the generosity of spirit that is an inspiration to others in whatever job, business or profession you choose to express your talents. Everything you do can have its own special stamp, such as remaining polite even in the most difficult circumstances.

Your intrinsic sense of beauty and of the mutual rewards of collaboration can bring success in the creative or performing fields, and your adaptability is an asset in almost any endeavor. Your impartiality and knowledge come to the fore when you must make a tough choice. You might even find pleasure in the painstaking process of arriving at a decision that benefits you as well as others when an important issue is at stake.

Neve Campbell (actress), 1973
Gore Vidal (novelist), 1925
Thomas Wolfe (novelist), 1900

Special to September 30 (Venus):

Love for your home is important to you, although it may be a burden at times. Your romantic interests are intense, while they last. You have more success with relationships when you control your vulnerability to disappointment by lowering your sights to the level of realistic expectations. In the meantime, you're likely to go your merry way, automatically assuming the best of people whether or not you know anything about them. Your ingenuous enthusiasm assures you plenty of popularity, but it might be more prudent to hold in reserve a bit of your unrestrained sociability and affection until you're better acquainted with new people you meet.

The extent of your career success could depend as much on the impact of your personality as on the extent of your inborn talent and its skillful cultivation. When people have to deal with you in the job or business realm, there could be times when they wonder where the charming person they thought they knew has gone. You know how to fight your way to the top and let the chips fall where they may. Your deep and abiding dedication to causes you believe in is impressive. If necessary to defend a stand you've taken, you'll put on the gloves and spar your way to winning your share of rounds from adversaries who oppose you. With your charm and diplomacy, however, you're able to attract an imposing list of allies to help you put over your favorite projects or come out the winner in many a contest.

Martina Hingis (tennis player), 1980
Angie Dickinson (actress), 1932
Truman Capote (novelist), 1924

Special to October 12 (Venus [Sun/Moon]):

Magnetic and popular, you work best with others and can have an advisory or protective interest in their welfare, particularly newcomers to your chosen job or career endeavor. You have scant patience for restrictions or discord. You can capitalize handsomely on the inborn advantage of your adaptable and congenial nature; when you do, the arts, professions and the financial or business realm are all worthwhile possibilities for your diverse talents and potential for significant success.

Pushy people can get under your skin, but even when you're dead tired you can find a way to squirm out of a ticklish problem with diplomacy. Or if you're involved in any sort of rivalry or contest, your unfailing politeness smoothes over or dulls the lurking hard edge in a competitive atmosphere. When you go over the top with infectious conviviality, people are happy to accompany you. Although not totally immune from controversy, you tend to be attractively ladylike or the perfect gentleman. If your looks or personality are the attention-getting variety, you can arrive at a party, and, before long, everyone is ready to fall in love with you.

Kirk Cameron (actor), 1970
Luciano Pavarotti (singer), 1935
Dick Gregory (comedian), 1932

Special to October 21 (Venus [Moon/Sun]):

An artistic career can be very successful for you, if other testimonies agree. You may seem indirect and apparently nonaggressive as you pursue your goals, but competitors or adversaries learn soon enough that you mean business. Meanwhile, your network of friendships and links to people in powerful positions are very advantageous in attaining a pinnacle of achievement in a job, business or profession. You manage to sublimate disappointments but could need to cultivate discipline when obstacles impede your progress from time to time. Your own subjective aversions to people or conditions may contribute to your difficulties.

While you have your serious side and are an advocate of plain talk, you're usually affable and ready with a witty remark at the drop of a hat and equally ready to get caught up in the whirring fun of the social mix. Whether in your personal life or regarding a career matter, however, and no matter how highly a person or situation is recommended, you'll bank on your own no-holds-barred appraisal before you agree with others' evaluations and bestow your personal approval and/or make a commitment. If you're the source of an unpopular decision, you'll make no bones about explaining how you reached it.

Carrie Fisher (actress), 1956

Dizzie Gillespie (trumpeter), 1917

Alfred Nobel (industrialist), 1833

October the 4th (Venus, Saturn)

(and root digit for October 13;

October 22 is a master number, see end of chapter):

With your gift for managing situations and people, you will find opportunities to put it to the test in the pursuit of your worldly ambitions. You meet reality at every turn; at your best, you're able to ease your way out of stalemates, criticism or defeats through your charm and talent and the ingratiating effect they have on others. No matter which side people see of you, they soon find out about your uncanny ability to play all sides to the middle, which doesn't hurt your cause any.

Your toughness and frankness are masked by a personable manner and a smile that would melt the snows of Mount Everest. You aren't necessarily an opportunist; it's just that obstacles that impede your progress have to be overcome—and if effort, patience and determination won't do the trick, you can turn the charm knob up to high to tip the scales in your favor and win points for any cause you espouse. Despite the pleasant impression you make and the importance you place on getting along with people, you know how to say no, stand your ground and remain popular—the calm in the eye of a storm if one is brewing.

Getting ahead in the world on your terms can take a lot of time, and you may not have much left over for relationship fulfillment, which may have some bearing on the variety or outcome of your emotional experiences. You're likely to get off to an early and probably bumpy or episodic start in your career strivings. The more you're inspired, the harder you'll be willing to work, and the prospect of success is the thing that inspires you most. Capable, calm, cool and collected, more a pragmatic doer than an idealist, it's doubtful that you'll ever become a poet unless you can make it pay.

Alicia Silverstone (actress), 1976

Charlton Heston (actor), 1924

Buster Keaton (comedian), 1896

Special to October 13 (Venus, Saturn [Sun/Venus]):

Inclined to be a little extreme about things, you can loathe interference and limitation and then turn around and be somewhat dictatorial yourself. At least you're usually willing to own up to your own mistakes. Independent-minded yet cooperative with a strong sense of responsibility, you're a valued worker in any job or career situation. You could have capabilities and be talented in more than one direction and might switch careers at some point, using one as a stepping-stone to another that's more prestigious and lucrative.

Although you're artistically inclined, you like a reliable money source and may find the business world more satisfying and/or steadily income-producing than pursuing a creative aspiration or a role in public affairs. Whatever you do, diligent work and pride in the results are in your genes. You know your own worth and like to be appreciated; praising your work is a good way for a higher-up to inspire your loyalty, even if your job category isn't all that inspiring. In which case, with your excellent business head, an avocation or a cause that interests you could be profitable as well as enjoyable. Oozing charm and self-confidence, you're apt to be as popular socially and romantically as you are in your career activities.

Jerry Rice (football player), 1962

Paul Simon (singer, composer), 1941

Margaret Thatcher (former British prime minister), 1925

October the 5th (Venus, Mars)
(and root digit for October 14 and 23):

Yours could be a life of aggressive adventure or a promenade of discovery. More self-propelling than the typical Libran, you can be charming and a dear in your own way. As long as it's your way. When vocational opportunities or other circumstances stir you into action, you aren't always in the mood to be disturbed or challenged, at which times, ever the diplomat, you could be engagingly snappish. In your view, when things are going along placidly, which may not be often enough to suit you, why rock the boat?

But there will be times when you won't have a choice. For example, when you're tired of decisions and just can't face another one, life may not permit you to luxuriate in Libra's limbo of irresolution or peace at any price. Another issue has a way of popping up, keeping you on your toes in perhaps a touchy situation that could generate considerable friction. But then that's why you're there when decisions are important; you have a talent, if not a reputation, for making many right ones.

An astute negotiator, skilled in compromise, you can always find a way to maintain your treasured equipoise in the midst of stress and strain—when everyone else is ready to throw in the towel. In job or career strivings, your ambition and determination lead on to success. Another asset is your flair for arousing the spirit of teamwork in people you work with, or for, or who work for you. You do have your limits for being nice, however: You can be notably outspoken and controversial and won't mince words or spare people's feelings when situations become really fouled up and exhaust your patience. And there will be plenty of those in your lifetime.

Kate Winslet (actress), 1975

Vaclav Havel (political leader, dramatist), 1936

Chester A. Arthur (21st U.S. president), 1830

Special to October 14 (Venus, Mars [Sun/Saturn]):

As a Libran, you will prefer circumstances where things run smoothly and people are cooperative; however, as a tough and dedicated advocate of whatever cause or project has attracted your interest, you have a spine of steel when you have to deal with opposing factions or any difficult conditions. You can be very convincing, with a knack for defusing tension or settling an issue with a trenchant observation or flashes of mordant wit. Training is important to your success; you find mental pursuits congenial. You're not likely to be one of those self-made achievers who failed to get a high school diploma or a college degree.

You are affectionate and like flattery. You know your own worth, but when problems seem insurmountable, you may be unsure of yourself and reticent about tooting your own horn. However, when things get sticky, you are usually able to find a way out. Then, when you've overcome an obstacle or met a challenge successfully that boosts or restores your confidence, you're more self-promotive. If you have to wait a bit for a position of responsibility, you'll be well prepared for it. With your various talents and adaptability, you can wear more than one hat simultaneously.

Harry Anderson (actor), 1952

Roger Moore (actor), 1927

William Penn (American colonist), 1644

Special to October 23 (Venus, Mars [Moon/Venus]):

If professional success is your guiding star, your personal popularity and flair for ingratiating yourself in the power network are not far behind. Generally taciturn and soft-spoken, you nevertheless won't back away from a fight about a principle you believe in. You like change and variety but are very sensitive to discord. Periodically impulsive, you might stir up antagonism when you bypass people who, whether rightly or wrongly, think their input should have equal consideration with yours when an important issue requires a decision. You respond to the artistic and beautiful aspects of life and have creative talent; whether or not this turns into a career, you have the ability to make it pay. Your social life and how you look and the effect you have on others are very important to you; you're likely to devote considerable time, energy and money to making a favorable impression and to attracting the admiration and approval you crave. For this and similar reasons, such as your contiguously extroverted persona and romantic appeal, you should enjoy successful business relationships as well as public popularity, if not as much fulfillment in personal partnerships.

Michael Crichton (author), 1942

Johnny Carson (TV talk show host), 1925

Gertrude Ederle (swimmer), 1906

October the 6th (Venus, Jupiter)
(and root digit for September 24 and October 15):

You tend to see life through a rose-colored filter and won't be happy until you've known the bliss of a fulfilling marriage or other joyful togetherness, which may take a try or two, or until you've had your idealistic expectations reduced to more practical proportions because you thought marriage would offer all the joys of romance and none of the responsibilities of the ties that bind. You're not easily disillusioned, however. In another twist of misguided relationship enthusiasm, you could assuage your romantic yearnings in numerous unsatisfactory affairs of the heart. You have a very low tolerance for frustration and loneliness and may opt for expedient solutions that lead to uncertainty and disappointment.

When your Libran affability, talent and typically ample self-confidence and enthusiasm for life are in full sway, however, you get an early start on a suitable career trajectory that can zoom upward and onward without too much of a struggle on your part. The downside stems from your dedication to achieving your worldly ambition; if you're swamped by irresistible job or career opportunities, you might devote so much time and energy to getting ahead in the world that you could postpone or deny yourself the chance for a loving relationship and lasting happiness.

You dislike anything vulgar or that seems unjust. Most of you find comfort in attractive home or family surroundings that reflect your need for harmony and beauty. However, some Librans with this birthday tend toward high living and a grand lifestyle; in this case, you have something in common with Cancerians. Whereas they can become overweight from emotional discontent, you're susceptible to a reverse principle: You tend to gain weight when you settle into a soothing routine that includes a rewarding marriage, lavish entertaining and general contentment. Too much happiness may not be a good thing, at least for your figure.

Elisabeth Shue (actress), 1963

Carole Lombard (actress), 1908

Jenny Lind (singer), 1820

Special to September 24 (Venus, Jupiter [Moon/Saturn]):
Optimistic, industrious and productive, the lure of a desirable goal will inspire your enterprising enthusiasm, but you are not partial or adaptable to episodic or disruptive changes unless you initiate them. Partnerships are vital to you as well as friendships, both of which you thrive on as you make your way in the world. Your work or the realm of your endeavor is likely to have plenty of public appeal. If things don't always go well, it isn't because you haven't tried.

Although you are inclined to stretch your vocational luck in several disparate directions and can settle for a dependable income-producing job, you might not find total satisfaction in the worlds of commerce and industry. Your appreciation of beauty, social relevance and artistic expression is compelling and can become creative activity in the literary, musical or entertainment milieu, perhaps in some promotional or entrepreneurial capacity. Or one of these fields could become a rewarding sideline. Love and marriage are very important to you, and you won't be happy and content until you team up with the right partner.

Linda McCartney (singer), 1941

Jim Henson (puppeteer), 1936

F. Scott Fitzgerald (novelist), 1896

Special to October 15 (Venus, Jupiter [Sun/Mars]):
With your team-spirit leadership abilities, you have the potential to personify the highest standards in whatever job or career endeavor you choose to express your talents. Although a typical educational background would be a plus for your achievement prospects, it isn't absolutely necessary for your success; you

can learn as much or more from experience, reading and observation than from the standard curriculum and formal study. No matter what you do, however, your efforts are apt to be enhanced by that rare and appealing quality known as "heart," the endearing effect of which is not lost on your work colleagues or the public.

As a distinctive personality on the job, in the entertainment world or the temples of learning, your verve, wit, panache and remarkable insights practically guarantee popularity; your appealing combination of charm and audacity through which you express the foregoing traits is a further guarantee of success in the world of commerce or the arts. Strongly affected and influenced by beauty and proportion in any field of endeavor, you know how to translate and articulate your sensitivity into practical form and creative achievement.

Lee Iacocca (business executive), 1924

Oscar Wilde (playwright), 1854

Friedrich Nietzsche (philosopher), 1844

October the 7th (Venus, Mercury)
(and root digit for September 25 and October 16):

Responsive to the proprieties of art and society in general, you do well associating with tasteful, educated people who are already established and successful. With your inborn mental and creative gifts, you can achieve prominence by capitalizing on those assets. Although you're not typically inclined to dogma or profundities, you will find that really worthwhile work or professional opportunities will depend for their success on how much serious thinking you are willing to do (and you're capable of a lot). There are exceptions, of course; given the right opportunity, you could get by with parlaying your nimble wits and Libran affability into facile, lighthearted success. In any case, with your quicksilver mind and easygoing personality, you're highly adaptable to the needs of the moment and have a knack for surviving changeable or unsettling conditions.

Being an air sign, your orientation to life is rational and analytical but not necessarily studious. Be careful that your habit of judging everything according to your own finicky sensory standards doesn't wear away your feelings. Emotions don't flourish in the mind. Love and affection need to be given free rein if you are to find the happiness you are entitled to by way of a relationship. Your spirit of relaxed equanimity could be the keystone of happiness in your personal life, partnerships and domestic surroundings.

Whether in government (as an expert negotiator), the arts or the entertainment milieu, you have an instinct for achieving public popularity. Whether it's due to typical Libra traits or your own personal magic, you never seem to wear out your welcome or exceptional persuasive gifts. Whatever work you do in a job or a profession, you're capable of putting it over with your own distinctive style, skills and convincing credibility.

John Cougar Mellancamp (singer), 1951

June Allyson (actress), 1923

James Whitcomb Riley (poet), 1849

Special to September 25 (Venus, Mercury [Moon/Mars]):

You can be tough-minded when you're involved in a difficult situation. Even then, your Libran attributes shine through; you're simultaneously able to convey a willingness to compromise that seldom if ever leaves you at odds with people you're dealing with or out on a limb. Once you decide on a job or career path, you can rise rapidly through the ranks to a position of importance. With your quick, facile mind, however, you may need to be wary of jumping to conclusions that can get you into hot water if you've just skimmed the surface of a touchy situation and/or are on the verge of making a serious mistake. Be sure you have all the facts straight before making a momentous decision or a provocative statement.

Although artistically gifted, you may have more success in the commercial or government milieu. A natural connoisseur and communicator, you can succeed in a pursuit that has to do with beauty or entertainment—creating it, expressing it or merchandising it. You're inquisitive and will find that extensive knowledge and information, whether gained from the school of experience or a formal education, will open many a door for you. You'll rarely be caught without an answer to a problem, but there will be times when your adroitness will fail you; you won't be at a loss for words—you'll just say the wrong ones.

Christopher Reeve (actor), 1952

Barbara Walters (TV commentator), 1931

Dmitri Shostakovich (composer), 1906

Special to October 16 (Venus, Mercury [Sun/Jupiter]):

Your abundant energy, lightning mind and eager work habits provide a productive outlet for your questing spirit. You could be a travel enthusiast, not just for pleasure but to acquire firsthand knowledge and information about faraway lands and ancient civilizations; this enables you to reveal, through your work, your expanding intellectual or creative horizons. But whether your travels are literal or figurative, your mind can cover great distances in either your chosen field of expertise or over an ample variety of subjects that may somehow have a central theme such as justice or cultural enlightenment. In any case your perceptive, visionary outlook qualifies you for leadership in the arts, business or government.

Proud of your own worth and capable of handling practically any job with responsibility and distinction, you'll probably do best in a vocation or profession where idealism is a guiding principle. For example, if you're a whiz at writing, communication, research or promotion, you might find most fulfillment working for an organization that raises funds for worthy causes. In your personal life, it could take many years of loyalty and devotion before you discover that a marriage or other close relationship has run its course and that it is time for a change.

Tim Robbins (actor), 1958
Angela Lansbury (actress), 1925
Eugene O'Neill (playwright), 1888

October the 8th (Venus, Uranus/Saturn)
(and root digit for September 26 and October 17):

Contacts are important in promotion and publicity, and your flair for turning on the charm will come in handy when you set out to achieve your goals in life. You know when to stick your neck out and when to duck. You know better than anyone whether you're abundantly or scantily gifted with the requisite skills for your chosen job or career. Regardless of those considerations, however, your combination of gritty determination and instinctive intuition helps you to succeed or, in a worst case scenario, can get you in over your head.

You know what you want, which first and foremost is to rise above the crowd. You're adaptable and persevering; one way or another you'll accomplish your objective. The work you choose, whatever it is, may simply be the one that offers you the most opportunity to get ahead in the world with the least risk. Your gift for expressing big ideas and suggesting projects that can turn into personal as well as monetary gain is an impressive asset where large-scale enterprises are concerned. As long as you don't allow your ambitions to inflate enough to overshadow practical realities, you will succeed. Hopefully, your common sense tells you that the more demanding a challenge becomes, the more likely the intensity and friction will accelerate, which should set off alarm bells for you to keep your distance from ruthless competition and/or the likelihood of failure.

It's Libra's function to ameliorate differences, not shy away from them. As long as what you are doing pays off in prestige and income, you will tolerate irksome side issues. Your charisma and friendliness can attract a lot of public attention and will go a long way in resolving differences in your personal life. Your poised self-assurance combined with your self-deprecating sense of humor will contribute to your popularity. Any career where a charismatic personality, big ideas, pragmatic vision and the ability to win public support and approval are a plus is congenial and profitable for you.

> Matt Damon (actor), 1970
>
> Sigourney Weaver (actress), 1949
>
> Jesse Jackson (civil rights leader), 1941

Special to September 26 (Venus, Uranus, Saturn [Moon/Jupiter]): No matter how affable, happy-go-lucky or accommodating you seem on the surface, you have an underlying need for approval, personal popularity and success. People who oppose you find out that you don't easily yield any ground on important issues or admit defeat without a struggle. When others try to thwart your initiatives, they discover a lot of high-minded idealism, self-confidence and calm tenacity lurking beneath your amiable facade. You may have to walk a thin line between the purists and pragmatists in your job or career endeavors, which can test your gift for diplomacy.

Primarily artistic, you can make a professional and/or commercial success of your talents; and the more broad-based and influential the project, the more enthusiastic you'll become. You wouldn't find the business milieu as congenial. Although you are altruistic and future-oriented, you have an eye out for the main chance and know how to capitalize on an opportunity and run with it, especially if it's an immediate entree into big-time achievement or heads you in that direction. You're happiest when prestige and the appropriate financial returns accrue from your efforts. When you are lucky enough to meet a mate or partner who is as interested in getting ahead in the world as you are, you'll click like castanets.

> Olivia Newton-John (singer), 1948
>
> George Gershwin (composer), 1898
>
> Alfred Cortot (pianist), 1877

Special to October 17 (Venus, Uranus, Saturn [Sun/Mercury]):
Success motivated as well as mentally oriented, you have a flair for acquiring skills and knowledge that can be turned into career progress as well as money. With your relaxed pleasure in your work, you may act and sound amenable, but in the end you are as apt as not to go your own way, which can have an adverse effect on personal relationships. You'll welcome any publicity that enables you to move ahead in the world. You can do well in the creative or entertainment realm, in government or by promoting or merchandising an artistic business venture, such as an art gallery, but you're probably better off alone than in a partnership.

With your work skills, adroit maneuvering and sense of responsibility, you know how to navigate the middle road when push comes to shove and you happen to be on the losing end of an important issue. Regardless, win or lose, the impression you leave behind when changes occur is a vital consideration for your future prospects: However things turn out, you want to be a credit to people who have supported your effort to put across an idea or to succeed in a venture. Your fairness and ability to handle difficult situations as well as anyone could even elicit admiration from people who disagree with your views.

   Margot Kidder (actress), 1948
   Rita Hayworth (actress), 1918
   Arthur Miller (playwright), 1915

October the 9th (Venus, Pluto)
(and root digit for September 27 and October 18):
Your subtle—not to say simmering—magnetism lurking just beneath the surface of your radiant smile contributes to your social and romantic popularity. When various worthy causes stir your interest, you can put your literary and promotional ability to good use and are gifted at bringing people together for mutual benefit. Your talents can be exceptional in music and the arts as well as science and government, but they require strong discipline for their fullest realization. You have a penetrating mind and avid curiosity; nothing gets past your scrutiny that's in your range of experience, especially if it could be useful in promoting or advancing your worldly aims.

With your lively personality, adventurous spirit, strong opinions and impish sense of humor, you delight in going your independent way in pursuit of fun or achieving a personal, job, business or professional goal. Ready and able to proselytize for your principles and beliefs, the distinctive image you project in tandem with your career efforts can have lasting impact and acceptance if your work attracts public attention.

A natural-born rebel, you may not conform to society's definition of morality; as long as it harms no one, you figure that what you do is nobody's business but yours, whether in regard to your personal behavior or in the career realm. You know how to take advantage of opportunities that originate behind closed doors. You could resort to some sort of subterfuge to obtain information that you wouldn't get as readily if your identity were known. With your ready smile and subtle insights, you're able to tap into and capitalize on the conventions or quirks of mass consciousness in ways that impart a distinctive flavor to your creative output and public persona. Although you have the maverick spirit, you nevertheless appreciate the value of establishment academic credentials that help to foster public acceptance of your ideas and activities.

John Lennon (singer, songwriter), 1940

Camille Saint-Saens (composer), 1835

Miguel de Cervantes (novelist), 1547

Special to September 27 (Venus, Pluto [Moon/Mercury]):

You have a sharp mind and penetrating insights and can probably get by in life on your ability to quickly size up people and situations and capitalize on opportunities without too much effort. On the other hand, if you aim higher and apply yourself, you can enjoy outstanding success in a job or a career where mental facility, apt expression, perseverance and your subtle understanding of what makes people tick are requisite assets. You'll probably find the creative or professional realm more compatible with your gifts than the business world, where novelty and independence aren't as welcome as sticking to the tried and true.

Your sensitivity and diplomacy may blunt the edge of your frankness when difficult circumstances prompt off-putting, tension-generating comments, but there won't be any mistake about the meaning of your words. You prefer to be tactful, but you won't hide your contempt of wishy-washy types who will say anything to be liked and who avoid taking a stand, which is especially irksome to you if a moral issue is at stake. A stickler for your own principles, you'll probably never tire of expressing or standing up for them. You have the talent for imparting knowledge and articulating beauty but preferably not in a subordinate position.

Gwyneth Paltrow (actress), 1972
Jayne Meadows (actress), 1926
Vincent Youmans (composer), 1898

Special to October 18 (Venus, Pluto [Sun/Uranus/Saturn]):
You can be a trendsetter in your chosen field of activity, especially in the area of big-time achievement, where you can attract your share of public notice. Although what you do may not be big in physical terms, when you're successful it will reach and have an effect on large numbers of people. Whether or not circumstances sometimes require you to pursue your ambitions on a shoestring, your vision and power of suggestion are compelling and enable you to persuade important people to join forces with you to overcome limiting conditions. Thus with your gift for "working relationships," you're adept at creating, nurturing and capitalizing on collaborative opportunities that can become successful ventures.

Any vocational or professional area that caters to the latest in public needs or tastes would be suitable for you. You may appear accommodating and apparently nonagressive as you pursue your goals, but competitors or adversaries learn soon enough that you mean business.

The change, activity and travel that are part of your job or career pattern can stimulate the latent curiosity and diffusiveness in your nature. Your appealing personality has a lot to do with your success; you're friendly and popular, and you enjoy being "on."

Wynton Marsalis (musician), 1961
Mike Ditka (football coach), 1939
George C. Scott (actor), 1927

October the 11th (Venus, Neptune [Moon/Sun])
(master number):
Your far-ranging imagination and psychic promptings coupled with your insistent drive and exemplary ideals are the principal components of your uncanny ability to spot a trend while it is still a distant breeze. Very sensitive to symmetry, proportion and comparative values, you're likely to get an early start on achieving your job or career aims, but that doesn't mean that your prospects for success will unfold in a logical, progressive manner. Opportunities that offer job, business or professional fulfillment are apt to be more completely satisfying from middle life on; you may not find your true niche until you've dared to dream and allowed your flights of creative fantasy constructive free rein.

Early rebuffs or sidetracked goals, however, only spur your determination to get ahead in the world on your own terms, which include aiming your talents and enthusiasms in the most influential, status-enhancing and/or lucrative direction possible. Whether you're serving the public in some business capacity or lifting people's spirits with your artistic revelations, you like to be financially rewarded for your efforts. You are capable of commercializing your knowledge and inspirations once you come to the conclusion that what you have to offer can raise a new groundbreaking standard of excellence. In any case, your earning prospects are ringed with dollar signs.

You might go to great lengths regarding your insistence on, or your own interpretation of, fairness. Not typically dynamic or combative, you can go to the other extreme and be too soft-spoken, pliant, sympathetic or acquiescent. With your inborn sense of aesthetics, you are sociable and capable of well-deserved popularity, yet you could remain reserved, giving others the impression that you aren't revealing any more than you want them to know. Or, between Neptunian vagueness and Libran vacillation, you can take too long to arrive at a decision and perhaps miss an important opportunity. Prone to romantic fantasy, you could be either the great lover or the great deceiver, or an exasperating combination of both. A negative Libran with this birthday can indulge in gushy panegyrics about how beautiful everything is and resent any realistic criticism. You have great need for a home, but you may not find fullest satisfaction in a partnership.

Elmore Leonard (author), 1925

Jerome Robbins (choreographer), 1918

Eleanor Roosevelt (First Lady, humanitarian, writer), 1884

(Note: This master number implies a variable alternative response influenced by the strength or passivity of the planet Neptune in your horoscope. If you don't feel you are responding to the distinctive vibratory power of 11, you are instead expressing the more conventional qualities of 2, which you should read.)

October the 22nd (Venus, Uranus [Saturn/Moon])
(master number):

You have a lot of self-confidence, the kind that can bring your farsighted ideas, trend-setting activities and timely innovations to the forefront of public awareness. Dynamic, with a personal sense of mission and drama, a competitive or confrontational situation that makes the typical Libra ambivalent or uncomfortable can galvanize your determination to plunge into the fray and come out on top. You may not always win, but you won't back down from a fight when a principle you believe in is an issue.

Libra prefers that things run smoothly. However, with this birthday, you won't sacrifice the need to rectify an injustice (as you interpret it) to your personal preference for peace. You have a broad sense of humanitarianism, with the accent on the underdog, that you would like to see implemented. Either your distinctive originality or your distinctive idiosyncrasies, or a blend of both, will set you apart from the rest of the population. In any case, you are well qualified—if not always motivated—to inspire and lead others. You have a flair for public life, where you can capitalize on your mental and creative attributes.

Society's mores aren't one of your big enthusiasms. Strongly independent, with your penchant for a liberated lifestyle, you tend to live by your own rules where relationships are concerned and are likely to have your share of the unconventional variety. The opportunities that enable you to make your way in the world may prompt some eccentric, even radical, behavior, but Libra innately shies away from anything distasteful unless it serves an ideological purpose. Your remarkable intuition tells you how to turn experience and/or knowledge into power. What you want the power for will tell the ultimate story.

   Jeff Goldblum (actor), 1952
   Derek Jacobi (actor), 1938
   Franz Liszt (pianist, composer), 1811

(Note: This master number implies a variable alternative response influenced by the strength or passivity of the planet Uranus in your horoscope. If you don't think you are responding to the distinctive vibratory power of 22, you are instead expressing the more conventional qualities of 4, which you should read.)

CHAPTER 8

SCORPIO

October 24–November 22

RULER: **PLUTO** CO-RULER: **MARS** NUMBER: **9** ELEMENT: **WATER**
SYMBOLS: **THE SCORPION AND THE EAGLE**

"Keep your fellow's counsel and your own."
—*Much Ado About Nothing*, Shakespeare

As a member of the fixed-water sign Scorpio, you share a distinction with Aquarians: Your sign and Aquarius are the only ones in the zodiac that continue to have two ruling planets. After Pluto was discovered in 1930, it became your main ruler and Mars your co-ruler. However, unlike any other sign, Scorpio also has two symbols: The Scorpion with its deadly sting is traditionally associated with your sign; the soaring Eagle is less well known as the other Scorpio symbol. The Eagle is the modern equivalent of the mythological Egyptian Phoenix, which consumed itself in fire and then rose reborn from its ashes, a symbol of immortality. The Eagle represents the highest potential of your intense nature and the complete subjugation of, or your ability to rise above, the baser instincts symbolized by the Scorpion. Those born in your sign typically have a choice: to surrender to the way of the flesh or to aspire to and exist in the higher realms of purified love—or somewhere in between.

Mars rules the lower octave, the primitive, carnal side of your nature; Pluto rules the higher octave, your transformative potential. Mars normally denotes energy, drive and initiative; if Mars in its Scorpio negative phase holds full sway over your emotional nature, it becomes vigorous physical energy channeled into sexual obsession, rampant amorous experiences and/or erotic depravity. If you decide to use your sexual magnetism as a weapon, you can become a gratification machine or turn others into one, programmed to satiate your appetites for physical and material satisfactions and pleasures as exemplified by the debauched lifestyle of the infamous Gemini-born Marquis de Sade. (The Marquis, whose perverse erotic practices inspired the word "sadism," had a strong Scorpio influence in his horoscope.)

Pluto is the planet of concentrated power, subtle instincts, sensual equilibrium, emotional fortitude, controlled sex drive and the recycling process.

BRADLEY MEIDL

2 9 1 495 4 5 9 4 3

31 = 4

25 = 7

11 - 18 - 10175 - 2004

$\frac{29}{over}$

⑥

Your challenge is to contend with these disparate Mars/Pluto proclivities as they converge in your sign and to purge yourself of Scorpio's undesirable traits if they threaten to become the ruling force in your life. Their struggle for dominance within you has been termed *the battleground of the soul* and is the source of your simmering personality mystique. When you're successful, you exemplify the most laudable traits of your sign, enabling you "to win glorious triumphs," in the words of Scorpio-born Theodore Roosevelt.

With your tendency toward strong likes and dislikes, including love and hate, you can react favorably or unfavorably to an individual at first sight and rarely change your initial impression. Your uncanny psychic antennae enable you to immediately and automatically tune in to other people and their motives, especially their fears, foibles and susceptibilities. Among your other notable characteristics are your distinctive sexuality, potent magnetism, investigative curiosity and financial acumen. When unevolved, you will turn these traits into a minefield of intimidation or revenge, prying vindictiveness or the manipulation of others' assets and/or possessions to your own exclusive benefit. In this mode, you are famous for never forgetting a wrong or a foe and can be the paragon of that famous old Scorpio proverb: "Don't get mad, get even."

At your considerable best, however, when your Eagle- or Phoenix-like traits predominate, you control or overcome the more primitive side of your nature. Then you personify the "free Spirit" of Scorpio with soaring inspirations, idealism, humanitarian instincts and a unique ability for total dedication to a worthy cause. When you typify these qualities, you live by a moral code that channels your magnetism, emotions and acute perceptions into a lifestyle that is a shining example for your family or your community.

As you may have surmised, yours is probably the most provocative, not to say the most powerful and complex, sign of the zodiac. Shrewd strategies, like keeping people guessing about what you're thinking or are up to, are second nature to you. You would make a wonderful detective or spy. You never give anything away by your appearance or behavior. For example, when a problem provokes exasperating or turbulent emotions, it's typical of you to maintain a calm, cool, collected facade that masks what you're really feeling or thinking (or plotting). This impassive demeanor at your disposal is equally advantageous in the rough and tumble business world. For instance, if a competitor (or a colleague who could become a competitor) reveals a plan or unwittingly spills information useful to you, not a flicker of recognition or reaction is apt to cross your face as your mind shifts into autopilot and subtly weighs the possibilities for personal gain from the encounter. In such a situation, your expressionless visage is like the Sphinx—and just as much of an eternal mystery, as though you were born to outlast contemporary conditions and to come out ahead of the game by not revealing secrets.

Keeping your reactions under rigid control, a characteristic of your *fixed-sign* qualities, is an instinctive reflex of one of your well-publicized traits—your secretiveness. You figure that what people don't know about you, or your plans or motives, can never be used against you. And unless you lead the life of a saint, it's a gut reaction that can come in very handy as you wend your way through life's difficulties and rewards. You're a meticulous planner and use all sorts of schemes when mapping out a campaign. And since you believe in being prepared, you are usually ready with a solution or a counterattack for any and all adverse contingencies. This win-win strategy applies to all your transactions, including personal relationships; you usually wind up calling the shots, either directly or indirectly, when conflicts or setbacks occur. Of course, most of you have nothing to hide; your life is a reasonably open book. Still, you'd rather be safe than sorry, in case some of the pages from your past contain items that aren't above suspicion, censure or reproach if they were accidentally disclosed or otherwise came to light. Your soul knows whether you feel genuine love or secret contempt for anyone who must pay, in some way, for your favors—even through marriage. As previously noted, one of Scorpio's specialties is being secretive—only *you* know what you are really feeling. When you opt for an expedient romantic conquest, you can score a victory in a primitive or obvious way, but you will miss the real beauty of love. For Scorpio, the ultimate tragedy at the end of the trail is to have missed the sublime release of emotional ecstasy. *You* always know, at the deepest levels, what the results of your choices are, regardless of surface appearances. You see through pretense or superficiality and are not fooled by it in yourself, even when under the spell of satisfying worldly needs through the most expedient means at your command—your emotional and/or sexual bounty.

A character in an ancient Chinese legend illustrates some basic aspects of your complex nature. Turandot, princess of Cathay, is destined by ancient tradition to become the bride of the first royal suitor who can answer three riddles. Although cold and man-fearing, she is beautiful and much sought after even though the stakes are pretty high: the alternative to winning her hand is the beheading of the hapless contestant. The princess is a dazzling beauty with just enough emotional quirks to inhibit the enjoyment of it. The embodiment of fire and ice, a Scorpio characteristic, she hates men and fears love for reasons too lengthy to elaborate here.

As things develop, a brave young prince accepts the challenge, answers the riddles and wins her reluctant hand. Being a winner and an impulsive risk-taker, he was probably an Aries. At this point, the defiant, tremulous princess pleads with the winner to forego claiming his prize. Surely he wouldn't force her to fulfill her part of a loathsome bargain. Well, again typically Aries, the triumphant prince impetuously offers her an out: If she can guess his name before daybreak, he will release her from her commitment and go bravely, if not cheerfully, to the executioner. This impresses her as it should any frigid Scorpio, and you begin to sense that she might enjoy losing. The way it turns out, she does not guess his name, and does lose. Quivering with ambivalence, she finally gives herself to the prince in a rapturous embrace; from broken goddess to pulsating woman with just one kiss! Her transfiguration is a key to Scorpio's complexities.

You hate to lose power, and you are going to be doubly sure, before you release your passionate Niagaras, that you won't be in a position where mis-placed trust leaves you vulnerable to humiliating personal devastation. Your responses to amorous stimulation are like children of a strict and suspicious parent: You let them out to play but under guarded surveillance. Emotional release, through commitment, can be practically traumatic to you; it's as though you are giving up precious treasure. After bestowing it, the suspicion that you might not be a total winner in the love stakes can have disastrous effect; you just won't stay in a situation where you sense that you can't win. You may linger while you're smothering smoldering frustration or resentment, but inner tension builds and finally surfaces as love turned to ice—or venge-fulness—if you decide you've been emotionally double-crossed. Your break can be clean and final, like a surgeon severing a limb. None of that casual Gemini "just friends now" routine for you. The master of the withering glance, the chilly smile, a Scorpio scorned is an impressive adversary. As the great "get-evener" of the zodiac, you can be vindictive: If you had to die to set-tle a score, you would die happy.

You drive a hard bargain, but your magnetism is so powerful that you have no problem finding takers: You're the specialist at erotic projection. The trouble is, you may wind up with memories of many "takers" and little or none of ecstatic emotional fulfillment. Even though you give yourself, you always hold back a little (and maybe a lot); your pride demands that escape hatch.

You can never be dominated, only tamed, thriving instead on the submission of others; even when married, a part of you remains single inside. Unless highly evolved, you never totally give up your inner self; that would be like relinquishing your ultimate defensive weapon. That's part of your fascination for partners or admirers who want to weaken your resistance, yet the opportunity for sizzling physical union or a memorable clandestine rendezvous draws them into the danger zone.

Since any reasonable "percentage" of you, emotionally speaking, can be equal to "all" of anybody else, few complain of the possible drawbacks. Like Princess Turandot, you are the "ice that burns." Did you ever touch anything so cold it felt hot? Or vice versa? The sense perceptions are numbed, reason ceasing to protect your admirers from pain or danger. It's a centuries-old phenomenon; even Leo-born Petrarch noted in his sonnet #104: "I am fire, I am ice." The ultramagnetic intensity of Scorpio has the same effect, reason disappearing when your formidable assets go into action.

Like Princess Turandot, you aren't moved until you have some proof of the magnitude of your suitor's devotion. In the meantime, partners get to know only as much of you as you want them to know; preserving an element of mystery helps you to retain the upper hand. You are frequently misunderstood, an enigma to others; it's not entirely unplanned—you like it that way.

However casual you may appear to be, your significant attachments are never easy and breezy. Anyone getting that response from you can count on "out of sight, out of mind." You run the gamut from saint to sinner, all or nothing, and can estimate at a glance the price of anything, including a relationship experience. Coquettes or witty lotharios, fun for an evening of entertaining diversion, are not apt to stand the test of time. They will eventually either bore or irritate you or arouse your suspicion. And once you are turned off, they may as well wait for the Sphinx or those faces on Mount Rushmore to smile. Any contact that is provocative at all will elicit a particular response from you. Your eyes tell whole stories, and easy familiarity is not one of them. It is not typical of you, nor is it a part of your strategy, to express your feelings or to gush. For this reason, other things considered, you make a successful, if not always the best, executive. Five presidents of the United States were born under Scorpio—the record.

You mask your motives and inner thoughts so well that you always play from your kind of strength; you're a master of finesse. You may want particular information. You will get it without arousing anyone's suspicion, or revealing why you wanted it, or even giving a hint that you wanted it. Yours

is the most subtle sign of the zodiac, the sign of the sleuth, the spy who infil-
trates foreign governments, the double agent. You like to probe and find out
what others are up to, but you prefer your own motives to remain a secret.

You have tremendous awareness of whatever is going on around you and
are capable of profound insights. Will you employ your powerful gift of perception in the pursuit of commonplace satisfactions? Will you use it to probe
your deepest motives and your reason for being? Will you settle for the trivial
idea that man is born but to die and is just an anachronism between two
voids? Will you accept that we exist solely for the pursuit of "happiness,"
which in your case can be a euphemism for physical self-indulgence? Or will
you view man as the reflected image of the universal spirit, the vehicle through
which the purpose of divine energy is sublimated into awakened awareness of
the loftiest objectives?

You may pose as the crusader, the liberal or the evangelist, but you can harbor intolerance or sanction injustice—and not feel remorse. This is your
negative side, the narrow side that is content as long as the needs of the self are
satisfied. Until you pierce the veil of illusion separating the material and physical aspect of life from the spiritual, you will content yourself with petty
satisfactions that turn to ashes, the literal "dust to dust" result of the shallow way.

You may be very disturbed underneath, but surface poise never deserts
you. You never break down, sniveling for sympathy—that is ruled out by your
pride. Of the three water signs, yours is frozen water, and you don't thaw easily. No matter how tumultuous things get inside, you can maintain your
poise. Pity the poor souls drawn into your charismatic aura and who tangle
with you unwittingly: Are *they* in for an experience! They can come on with
childlike trust and leave as wizened adults, all in the course of an evening.
Boys turn into men, girls into women, or they are dropped like squeezed
lemons. Even when you seem relaxed and happy, there's no guarantee of your
psychic tranquillity. Your pride can suffer when you discover that other values
are just as or more important than the ones you depend on, that there are
other strengths and *other kinds of power.*

While you are basking in the thought that a robust physical body is one of
nature's ultimate achievements, because it serves so well to satisfy nature's sensual
drives and pleasures, remember that Robert Louis Stevenson and John Keats
were Scorpios who overcame physical *frailty* to achieve greatness. They sublimated their energies into the creative realm and still live in the minds of men.

So you don't care about posthumous glories? Your interest is in the *here
and now*. Whereas Taurus, your polar opposite, can be absorbed, you become

obsessed; whereas Taurus is passive, you are impassive, both masking potentially violent reactions. Whereas the Bull's rage is blind, yours can be sulfurous. You can hate as you love, unreasonably. Adding flexibility, adaptability and levity to the glacial depths of Scorpio can thaw out your attitude and broaden your outlook. A sense of humor added to the high seriousness of your emotional urge can be a welcome leaven to its high-voltage intensity.

You can become compulsively absorbed in an impossible quest, wearing down nerves and energies. You can sacrifice yourself with grim determination. You can destroy yourself on the inner plane with subconscious resentment, which can surface later as a physical or psychological problem. Like Libra, who needn't be physically attractive to charm people, neither need you be to weave your magic spell. Your gaze can be hypnotic; you usually attract attention by your appearance, or your walk, without having to try. It's because you project something elemental, that "something" being the Mars-Pluto contest for soul dominance within you. The evidence of this, as it surfaces, is your passionate intensity, the part of you that appeals so strongly to your potential lovers. It follows that something in *their* nature needs to submit to the icy-hot test of the elements in an encounter with you, or they wouldn't be attracted.

You've been endowed with your abundant magnetism in order to challenge your values as life unfolds. Your relationships are vivid, but potentially turbulent, especially when your partner is unfaithful or loses interest. Your jealousy can be easily provoked. A look or gesture directed at a rival by your partner can annoy you greatly. You become suspicious. Knowing your own wandering speculations only too well, you suspect them in others. Your visceral approach to sex and emotional release throws the whole process into high relief: It becomes as grand and impersonal as the elements from which it derives. Nature takes over and returns you to yourself only after the force is spent. Remember that this elemental power is available to you in other forms twenty-four hours a day, all your life; only *you* can determine into which areas of life it will be directed. Needless to add, it can be very constructive, or destructive, unless the less desirable aspects of it are sublimated.

Being the apostle of the power complex, you seek action that gives it expression; you don't like a subordinate position career-wise or socially. You are psychic and keenly analytical; unlike Virgo, satisfied classifying things, you wonder how the results of your analysis can be turned into power. Many scientists are born in your sign. They seek the keys that unlock nature's secrets, with variable results for humanity. The discoveries are fine; man's inability to handle power, however, creates a few problems. If you remember the words of

Capricorn-born Lord Acton, "Power tends to corrupt; absolute power corrupts absolutely," perhaps you will have more respect for the enviable resources at your command. Be sure that the primitive energies of Mars aren't dominating the transformative power of Pluto.

The TV Evangelist Billy Graham of global fame and influence exemplifies the drive and conviction of the soaring Eagle that motivates your sign. He personifies and continues the historic tradition of Scorpio passion and fervor, elevated to the spiritual plane. Hypnotic and galvanic, you can find your assets to be of tremendous benefit in the public milieu or in a less conspicuous pursuit.

Your distinctive traits, however, are especially potent as the means for getting a powerful spiritual message across to millions of people; the principle of regeneration, of rebirth, is thus expanded into a cosmic force—with historic consequences. Mohammed and Martin Luther are brilliant Scorpio examples of this power.

Mohammed conformed to the typical Scorpio pattern by marrying, at twenty, a wealthy widow many years his senior. He no doubt benefited from her ample material resources. At the age of forty, however, he had a vision in a cave at Mecca; this completely changed his life, and he continued to have revelations to the end of his days. Convinced that he was selected by God to preach, he started with three converts: his wife, his son-in-law and a friend. Today there are over one billion Muslims; they not only reject Christianity, they even use a different calendar! Did you think it was 1998 *everywhere* in the year 1998? Wrong! In Mecca, 1998 was 1419 (from March 9 at least). This illustrates the power of Scorpio. You can even measure time your own way and convince millions of people to adhere to it. When you realize how persuasive your utterances can be, you should have better appreciation for your magnetism and invincibility. You're hard to resist, in whatever context.

Mohammed is an outstanding example of a Scorpio with an messianic obsession and the power to communicate it through Plutonian fervor and unremitting conviction. He saw the light and was the oracle transmitting its inspiration to others; many generations later his impact remains undiminished. All Scorpios have this ability to galvanize and mesmerize others, even if you're not, as we've said, conventionally attractive. The uses you put it to will spell the difference between a life cluttered with surface satisfactions or one brimming over with emotional and/or spiritual fulfillment.

While there aren't nearly as many Lutherans as there are Muslims, Martin Luther still made quite a splash. He first studied law, but, like all prophets, he, too, had a religious experience. Following his revelation, he entered a monastery, becoming a priest at the age of twenty-four. By the time he was thirty-four, he began to find fault with Catholic practices. The Church returned the favor, found fault with some of his and excommunicated him as a heretic in 1521. Luther then began a translation of the Bible, among other activities, that took him ten years to complete. He even married a former nun, which makes him seem quite contemporary. The outcome of his Scorpio revelation is that Lutheranism is the state religion of Denmark, Norway, Sweden, Finland and Iceland—leaving the feeling that, had he lived longer, it might also have become the state religion of Italy. Nothing can be put past a Scorpio, once you get inspired. *It all depends on what you get inspired about!*

SCORPIO BIRTHDAYS

Judgment of whether or not a birthday is propitious can be considered from two points of view: complementary or challenging. From the standpoint of personal progress and fulfillment, your destiny may flow more comfortably if your birthday is, or reduces to, an *outer* root number such as 2, 4, 6, 8 or 22. For career drive and achievement, your progress may be enhanced if your birthday is, or reduces to, an *inner* root number such as 1, 3, 5, 7 or 9; the *inner* root numbers are less comfortable, more obstructive for you to contend with, but they are potentially very conducive to outstanding success. The 11 (master number) would be variable, favorable for creative achievement, but it implies an important moral challenge when combined with the meaning of Scorpio.

Remember, if your birthday is two digits (excepting master numbers 11 and 22), be sure to read the root digit or number first. For example, if your birthday is 29, read the 2 (2 + 9 = 11, 1 + 1 reduces to 2) birthday profile first and then read the special profile for 29. If your birthday is 14, read the 5 (1 + 4 = 5) birthday profile first and then read the special profile for 14, and so on. If a description in a "special" section contradicts information in the "root" digit (root number) analysis, the "special" interpretation applies more specifically to you.

The first planet in parentheses following your birthday number is *your Sun-Sign ruler*; the second planet (or Uranus/Saturn for number 8) is *your birthday number planetary equivalent*. Subsidiary planetary influences (if any) are bracketed.

Each birthday profile includes celebrities who share the same birthday.

YOUR BIRTHDAY PROFILE
November the 1st (Pluto, Sun)
(and root digit for October 28, November 10 and 19):

If you have your way (and you're not apt to be thwarted), your ambitious nature will focus on job, business, professional or other activities that provide you with opportunities to express your transformative vision; when challenged by outmoded or faulty conditions, you're determined to improve them or to replace them with ones that assure success. Subtle and incisive, with a strong and commanding personality, your power and influence will be strongly felt whether you're the head of an enterprise or the head of a family (or both). If drastic reform is necessary in the name of progress, so be it. Although you can be sunny and outgoing, your resentment of slights could bring out the brusque side of your nature; anyone who offends your pride had better get used to a permanent cold shoulder.

Intense and dynamic, you're talented at healing, the law or the expressive arts, to which you bring great emotional insight. Your philosophy is that your job or career endeavors should be responsive to whomever or whatever they're intended to benefit, especially if a group or the public is involved. You can turn your curiosity about people and your investigative skill into some sort of job or career advantage, such as in an employment agency or in the executive search field. The price of career independence is that your finances are likely to be subject to variation or extremes—perhaps up for long periods, then down; you should plan to manage your long-range security accordingly and start nurturing your nest egg early in life.

You can be very devoted without necessarily being demonstrative, but your desire to dominate in business can extend to personal relationships, with a tendency toward jealousy and/or possessiveness. Your early background was probably expressive and free, with opportunities that encouraged your creative talent and need for approval. You can be blessed with an infectious sense of humor, remarkable financial capabilities and a zest for life that attracts considerable admiration and support for your integrity and your distinctive career efforts.

Lyle Lovett (singer), 1957
Gary Player (pro golfer), 1935
Stephen Crane (author), 1871

Special to October 28 (Pluto, Sun [Moon/Uranus/Saturn]):
Whether you're highly educated, or simply streetwise, knowledge is important to you. Moreover, it's your key to worldly achievement, whether utilizing your

promotional, administrative flair or demonstrating your efficiency and dependability among fellow workers in a more mundane milieu. Your psychic abilities provide you with insights in advance of the times, so you have a double advantage on competitors; you have a vision of the future, and your tireless energies guarantee that you will always play a leading role in it.

Strong-willed, dominant and tenacious, your orientation to the opportunities that life brings you is highly practical, shrewd and innovative. You're distinctive in what you do and/or how you project your personality, and you instinctively know how to make it pay.

Your dramatic power complex and need for protection from life's vicissitudes feed on the freedom and respect that money and success provide. Even though you are strongly opinionated, you can be very dutiful and self-sacrificing if need be. You will have ample, if not always consistent, opportunities to express the all-important love and affection that will complete the picture for you.

Julia Roberts (actress), 1967

William Gates (software pioneer), 1955

Jonas Salk (polio researcher), 1914

Special to November 10 (Pluto, Sun):

Excellent at research, reformative missions, writing or in the government milieu, be careful that your penchant for subterfuge doesn't backfire. You know how to go undercover to obtain useful information or evidence regarding a cause you're promoting; just be sure that your own activities are always aboveboard and that they don't even suggest a questionable situation that, if disclosed, could damage your reputation. You wouldn't want to jeopardize or diminish your power to favorably impress the public, which is one of the keys to your success.

Fiercely determined in your quiet way, you don't make a lot of noise about your goals; with your excellent vitality, you just set them and then go about achieving them. If you experience a setback, you won't easily accept defeat and fade discreetly into the background; instead, you're an expert at revising strategies and making comebacks. The studied ambiguity and the middle-of-the-road ploy sometimes necessary in dealing with thorny issues are among your other skills. If you pick the right partner, a marriage or other relationship can be lasting and fruitful. The trick is to pick the right partner. This assumes, however, that you will capitalize on your sensual magnetism in ways other than to test your appeal with numerous admirers.

Roy Scheider (actor), 1935

Richard Burton (actor), 1925

Mohammed (prophet), 570

Special to November 19 (Pluto, Sun [Sun/Pluto]):
With your tremendous drive and abundant vitality to fuel your ambitions, you nevertheless know how to husband your resources and pace yourself sensibly as you climb the success ladder. Whether you pursue a key position in the workforce or aim to distinguish yourself in a profession, the arts or in the commercial world, you're likely to be on your way to reaching the top early in life. An apt student, your dedication to mastering a skill or technique can pay off in a variety of ways, including realms as diverse as the aerospace industry, the music world, science or government; your drive is fueled by your indefatigable power to achieve. And you know how to gauge and interpret the public pulse.

Good mental balance is important to you; among other things, it can help to neutralize or control any craving you may have for emotional or sexual variety. You do not subscribe to establishment moral codes and can scale the heights or plumb the depths. You're avid for knowledge, but on your terms, such as a rather narrow range of subjects that can flatter the image you cultivate and your desire to garner approval and/or popularity. Highly magnetic and persuasive, your motivations will determine the extent of your success and ultimate happiness. A virtuous hobby can relax your intense nature.

Jodie Foster (actress), 1962

Calvin Klein (fashion designer), 1942

Indira Gandhi (former prime minister of India), 1917

November the 2nd (Pluto, Moon)
(and root digit for October 29 and November 20;
November 11 is a master number, see end of chapter):
Your birthday indicates inventiveness in many avenues of expression—medicine, business, politics, the theater—and fruitful employment awaits you in the general workforce. You have a distinctive gift for nonverbal communication and body language, and you will typically act first and talk later. One of your potent looks, from charming to withering (an icy smile, for instance), can tell a whole story, and this is an asset that helps you avoid time-wasting involvements and facilitates your climb up to the pinnacle of success.

Whether attracted to you or turned off according to your own intentions, people get your message without your having to put it into so many words. If you're not always clear about what you want, you're very clear about what you don't want: powerlessness and financial lack; the two are synonymous in your mind.

If signs of trouble develop in a key relationship, your glacial calm masks emotional intensity that can run the gamut from simmering to seething without revealing what you're really feeling about the other person or the situation. People who interpret your natural diplomacy as submissiveness are in for a big surprise. You not only don't give an inch—somewhere, somehow, you're secretly plotting a fresh advantage or gain.

When you react uncertainly, even erroneously, to the opportunities life brings your way, you can have a chip-on-the-shoulder pride that makes admitting a mistake difficult. You tend to dominate by indirection in order to obtain the affection and emotional security you crave; when annoyed or thwarted, your words take on a steely-toned edge. Yours is a restless, fluctuating birthday. Unless your emotions are channeled constructively, they may exert more influence over your life than is healthy and cause you to succumb to an endless foray of amorous adventures.

Burt Lancaster (actor), 1913

Warren G. Harding (29th U.S. president), 1865

Daniel Boone (frontiersman), 1734

Special to October 29 (Pluto, Moon [Moon/Pluto]):

Your rare insights into the inner components of plans, projects and people enable you to circumvent the more laborious and time-consuming approach of trial-and-error methods. Whatever you aim for in a job or profession, you will bring a sense of pleasure to your work, an energetic drive and, if in a creative field, a flair for the spectacular. As your life unfolds, a typical Scorpio phenomenon is apt to occur: a radical turnabout in your career choice or direction. For example, you might begin as a performer in the theater or entertainment world and eventually forego that ambition to concentrate on writing. Or you could begin a career as a foreign language instructor and wind up training championship race horses.

Your obsessive curiosity makes you an excellent psychologist, investigator or researcher. The work you excel at, probably geared to achieve ultimate public impact or appeal to popular taste, is likely to involve a high degree of technical mastery. You have the power and inclination for leadership and can bring to yourself and your associates great honor. At your best, you are emotionally sensitive and steady, capable of devotion and loyalty to your mate or other object of your affections. Home and family are important to you, and your partner's absorption in your concerns strengthens your relationship and your chances for success.

> Winona Ryder (actress), 1971
>
> Richard Dreyfuss (actor), 1947
>
> James Boswell (biographer), 1740

Special to November 20 (Pluto, Moon):

When your outstanding entrepreneurial instincts are focused on projects that reflect public moods and tastes, your success potential is exceptional. Although you don't always score a bull's-eye, you know how to come up with a product, skill or target that has wide appeal and attracts support. Very adaptable in the job domain, you're sensitive to what superiors expect or what your position requires and can fine-tune your abilities to provide it and weed out any extraneous complications or shortcomings along the way.

Uncompromising, reserved, magnetic, with a sly sense of humor, you attract your share of love and marriage opportunities or romantic liaisons (the words are deliberately plural). Although you are positive and self-assured, there may be considerable duality in your life: two marriages (or your quota of extramarital activities), two occupations or two halves to your life (such as one prominent and the other obscure). You're excellent in any professional or business capacity where ethics, honor and integrity are important: government, law, education, economics, the ministry and so forth. A dependable worker, performer or executive, you're able to keep any emotional extremes in your private life separate or hidden from your career activities.

> Veronica Hamel (actress), 1943
>
> Dick Smothers (comedian), 1939
>
> Robert F. Kennedy (legislator), 1925

November the 3rd (Pluto, Venus)
(and root digit for October 30, November 12 and 21):

As a writer, artist or performer, or in whatever field or job capacity you choose to express your eclectic ideals of beauty, your skills or creative output can strongly influence cultural trends and the values and tastes of your coworkers or contemporaries. The end-product of your work may not be beautiful in the conventional sense of "pretty"; instead, it's more apt to reflect the prevailing moral or social conditions of a time and place with insight and precision and could be sufficiently candid to arouse uneasy reactions as well as critical approval or public popularity. Technical skills can be far less important to you than a probing eye and spontaneous expression, which inspire you to employ the simplest means to get your incisive message across most effectively.

Capable of deep, enduring love or an enduring love of pleasure, you may find it easy to scatter your romantic or emotional largesse; In your not-infrequent self-absorbed mode, you thrive on the cozy assumption that you're irresistible; you are not apt to be disappointed . . . for a while. You're also vulnerable to a quirky relationship dichotomy: If the object of your affections has a strong will, and he or she resists your controlling instincts or possessiveness, you are going to clash; the problem stems from your having to respect your loved one, yet you don't respect anyone who is weak-willed or easily subjugated. Just as you instinctively can screen out emotional and social duds, you can bypass career ruts when you concentrate on your ambitions.

A variety of interests and a light and articulate social life can vent some of your steamy emotional intensity. The creative and interpretive arts are potent fields for your talents. Your subtle charm enables you to mix and mingle with widely divergent groups of people who may have nothing in common except their mutual admiration for you. If you discover your true métier and get on the right track, you can lead a life of exceptional commitment to whatever course of action inspires you. Whether it's your courage, obstinacy or effrontery, you go your own way in the face of establishment opposition, but your defiant tactics can delay the ultimate satisfaction you savor because you stick to your guns. Your relationship prospects are likely to include more than one marriage or romantic liaison, perhaps a residual tendency stemming from household changes, tribulations or disruptions you experienced as you grew up.

Dennis Miller (comedian, talk show host), 1953

Roseanne (comedienne, talk show host), 1952

Charles Bronson (actor), 1921

Special to October 30 (Pluto, Venus):

The bright side of your birthday is your indomitable spirit, faith in your potential to succeed and an unquenchable thirst to express yourself in some creative capacity. The dark side is that you can lose your way, or worse, never find it and spend your life fighting secret demons and the spectre of failure. In any case, you don't spend lots of time dwelling on the past or contemplating the future; your great gift is living for the moment, at which you are an expert. However, giving in to undesirable solutions that swiftly relieve or paper over problems could invite disaster. When you succeed in the creative arts or the world of entertainment, you can enjoy impressive popularity, which can attract a wide and disparate circle of friends with whom you share comparable levels of accomplishment. Like attracts like, and you're right at home with talented people who fascinate and stimulate you.

Prim and proper is not your style; there's apt to be more than a hint of spice in your personality, and you're a master when it comes to rejoinders or snappy one-liners. Your heartfelt espousal of the values you cherish can be an inspiration to people you work with or for, whether in the business world, the creative arts or the halls of academia. No matter what you do, however, writing and your gift for dramatizing your feelings are likely to be an important component of your expressive abilities and work activities. The ties that bind attract you, but you're apt to exchange vows more than once or live by your own rules regarding marriage. Although fundamentally loyal, your emotional life may be one long vacation from bona fide commitment.

Henry Winkler (actor), 1945

William F. Halsey, Jr. (naval officer), 1882

John Adams (2nd U.S. president), 1735

Special to November 12 (Pluto, Venus [Sun/Moon]):
Whether your star rises in the entertainment world, government, business or a creative field, the charisma you project is equal parts passion, intelligence and charm (read sex). In the eyes of your admirers, you can do no wrong. Socially and affectionately, you are more interested in quality than quantity and are not apt to be a flitting butterfly. Generally speaking, you gravitate toward people who are practical and well organized and who are more apt to be low-key than boisterous. You don't like complications and, given a choice, will tend to steer clear of neurotics, losers, loudmouths and others you would consider misfits or boors. Instead of entering into the general revelry at a party, you might be found off to the side enjoying just one or two people or sizing up the various other guests, especially if you happen to be on the lookout for a romantic conquest.

In a demanding job, business or profession, you're equal to daunting challenges and can win considerable recognition. Bright, perceptive and magnetic, you profit by having a "mission" in life and by avoiding expedient motives or methods. You always know when to doubt others' veracity, but are they as aware of your intentions? With your compelling charisma, you can be the master of diplomatic restraint as well as the power of suggestion. Your subtly seductive charm can get you anywhere . . . from the bedroom to the board-room. You can imply that if others surrender to you, they will be loved faithfully in return. Well, as Barnum said . . .

Sammy Sosa (baseball player), 1968

Grace Kelly (actress, princess of Monaco), 1929

Sun Yat-sen (statesman), 1866

Special to November 21 (Pluto, Venus [Moon/Sun]):

Animated, sociable and musically gifted, any occupation in the expressive arts is your best milieu, where you can rise to an important position and make a name for yourself. That is what your birthday denotes. Once your doubts and suspicions are overcome, your Scorpio drive and intensity are formidable. Very mentally perceptive about many things, you sometimes aren't aware of the extent of your own capabilities. Your keen intelligence and indomitable spirit can see you through many a delay or reversal. You seem to sense that wasting energies on anxiety or introversion will only delay your progress.

You do know how to have a good time and, somewhat against type, can even resort to clowning if that's what it takes to get a laugh. In your more reserved mode, you can unobtrusively fit into any gathering, large or small, if you think there is any reason to be involved. When you want to push the charm button, others easily become aware of your sensuous magnetism. If you didn't complete your education, study and learn from role models in order to acquire the expertise or style that can add a finishing touch to your technical skill in a job or profession or in the business or entertainment world. You hope that some of the magic of successful people in your field of activity will rub off on you. Whether or not you stray from the fold, marriage and family are important to you, and you'll probably try to sustain a commitment.

Ken Griffey, Jr. (baseball player), 1969

Goldie Hawn (actress), 1945

Voltaire (author), 1694

November the 4th (Pluto, Saturn)
(and root digit for October 31 and November 13;
November 22 is a master number, see end of chapter):

Pluto, like Venus, is a money planet, which could impel you to focus your job skills or creative inspiration on work that is likely to promise the most suc-cess and financial abundance. You prefer to gain power and status through conventional methods, but if you can't, you might resort to unorthodox means to attract attention to either yourself or your aspirations and abilities. Whether on the job, in business or in the creative realm, you can find personally satisfying ways to express your independent spirit. You have scant patience with authoritarian restrictions or establishment mores, and you can manage to attain success despite being misunderstood, unappreciated or opposed.

In its highest manifestation, your power complex is difficult to express except through painstaking effort to cultivate and promote your distinctive style and skills. You are proud, want power and may be dismissive of those who achieve success by conforming to popular taste or by just doing what they're told. At the same time, given your achievement potential, you're no slouch at capturing public interest and/or popularity. When you're annoyed with the requirements for getting ahead in life, you bottle up your emotions and find it difficult to express or release them. You're cautious about commitments, which invites disappointment, hurt or frustration. You have to extend yourself and express your innermost feelings. If you don't, you'll have to settle for the technique of love and sex and casual encounters rather than its heartfelt essence.

When you realize that your chance for overall fulfillment in life calls for patient effort, application, forbearance and depth, and that more is expected of you than those who manage easy gains, then your feelings are likely to be relaxed and to flow more smoothly in relationships, which relieves accumulated inner tensions. You may lose a skirmish or two in your battle with life, but enlightened self-knowledge, acceptance of responsibility and discipline and a mastery of skills enable you to emerge a winner in the long run.

Art Carney (actor), 1918
Walter Cronkite (TV newscaster), 1916
Will Rogers (humorist), 1879

Special to October 31 (Pluto, Saturn [Venus/Sun]):

There's a sunny, congenial side to your basically pragmatic, zealous, ambitious approach to your vocation or career and life in general. You're willing to invest as much time and hard work as is necessary to be successful, but you won't insist on the loftiest standards if the struggle to satisfy the severest critics takes the joy out of the job. You prefer to be a crowd pleaser than an ivory-tower genius with very limited public appeal. With that as your credo, you can please a lot of people who look to you for inspiration or guidance. You're willing to fight for a cause that inspires your fervor but not at the expense of cramping your style or your magnetic personality.

An expert at brinkmanship, you're skilled at walking a tightrope between victory and defeat. Possibly ahead of your time in your leadership qualities, you can play a pivotal role in breaking down the barriers to justice and fair play in a situation that would benefit from progressive change. Although your greatest fulfillment may come about through your selfless devotion to a humanitarian cause, your talents could also find effective expression in theology, education, politics or a creative field. Where your relationships are concerned, you can be lucky and meet your soulmate on your first plunge into matrimony.

Dan Rather (TV newscaster), 1931

Chiang Kai-shek (chief of state, China), 1887

Jan Vermeer (artist), 1632

Special to November 13 (Pluto, Saturn [Sun/Venus]):

The way you stubbornly stick to your guns is admirable, but it might prevent you from rising as high as your abilities warrant in your chosen field of endeavor. Whether in business, government or the creative realm, knowing when to come out fighting and when to hold your fire can mean the difference between success and failure, a distinction you might fail to grasp. If your aptitude for compromise is as great as your crusading spirit, you would move a lot more swiftly and surely along the success track. Nevertheless, you're able to give your job or career prospects a power boost whenever you have the opportunity and will no doubt enjoy your share of upward mobility.

Your occasionally combative attitude is offset by your generally warm-hearted manner and deft sense of humor, both of which assure you personal as well as public popularity if your work puts you in the limelight. When you feel compelled to express your opinions in the plainest possible language, you can become difficult and temperamental because you resent the need to resort to patience and diplomacy to put your points across. Your inner complexities may hinder the expression of your strong love nature, inclining you to settle for surface satisfactions rather than deep and lasting commitment. You are gifted in writing, exploring the higher mind and healing.

Whoopi Goldberg (actress), 1949

Robert Louis Stevenson (novelist), 1850

Edwin Booth (actor), 1833

November the 5th (Pluto, Mars)
(and root digit for November 14):

Despite renown for your sybaritic tendencies, you're just as, or more, likely to channel your tireless energies into a notable career endeavor that can bring you wide recognition and an ample income. If you covet financial security, however, you may need to work at it. If you don't, it could be a toss-up between a limousine or the subway, depending on how well you manage your fiscal affairs at any given time. Although especially talented for the entertainment world, you're a go-getter and a valuable asset in any enterprise. Whether in the arts, a profession or the world of commerce, you're usually a vigorous worker and will probably have many job or career changes (mostly upwardly mobile) before you apply for social security. With scant or no patience for troublemakers on the job or off, you prefer to get on with whatever occupies you with as little fuss and bother as possible.

Once you set a goal on something that absorbs your interest, including a close encounter of the romantic kind, you're not easily distracted or deterred. You're from the "all or nothing" school where your love relationship is concerned and are likely to expect the object of your affections to be as completely committed to meaningful togetherness (and plenty of it) as you are. You have your subtle streak, but there's no mistaking your sensual message, intentions or expectations when someone you have attracted finds your magnetism irresistible. When you're completely bowled over by a lover, try not to come on too strong; don't allow your Scorpio possessiveness or jealousy to become an issue and mar your chance for happiness.

Your birthday shows your proclivity to live life in the fast lane. No matter what fate brings your way, which includes your share of trials and tribulations along with fun and excitement, you're not apt to be bored. Mostly, you won't have time for it, even when you no longer have the endless energy that keeps you on the go during your peak years. Whether it's finding a new love, rekindling an old flame or discovering some other engaging interest in your sunset years, there's sure to be some kind of stimulus to keep you motivated and looking forward to each new day with eager anticipation.

Bryan Adams (singer), 1959

Art Garfunkel (singer), 1941

Roy Rogers (singer, actor), 1912

Special to November 14 (Pluto, Mars [Sun/Saturn]):

With your probing mind and yen for travel and adventure, you're likely to roam the four corners of the globe, either geographically or figuratively, in your search for knowledge and fulfillment. When you establish a goal, you can be intrepid, enterprising and indefatigable in your effort to achieve it. Wherever you apply your energies and estimable capabilities, they can enrich the scope and quality of a project whether in the workaday world, the business realm or a profession. You can be aloof and impatient with competition, authority figures or opposition and prefer to focus on overcoming difficulties and getting the job done.

Excellent at furthering causes you believe in, you're able to expand the horizons of whatever field you choose to devote your talents. Your early experiences and first impressions can be very instrumental in stimulating initial interest in your future job or career. Whether or not you complete your education, your exposure to cultural as well as other desirable influences, such as a supportive mentor, sets an example that inspires you to develop your skills and sense of responsibility to the highest level of accomplishment. Becoming too rigid in your ideas and assumptions can impede your progress and land you in a rut; developing flexibility broadens your vision and helps to strengthen your self-confidence. Scorpios can harbor many passions; one of yours is to excel.

    Charles (prince of Wales), 1948

    Aaron Copland (composer), 1900

    Claude Monet (artist), 1840

November the 6th (Pluto, Jupiter)
(and root digit for October 24 and November 15):

Your drive is for power and success, but your need is for family and home. You can be very loyal and devoted to loved ones and friends, and lucky is the person who can count on your encouragement and support. You willingly accept responsibility for those in your environment and will do all that you can to make them secure and happy. Power is your Scorpio birthright; if you can manage to turn it on in the right place at the right time, there is very little you're not capable of accomplishing. It's all a question of priorities, timing and deployment of your energies for maximum effect and benefit, whether for yourself or those nearest and dearest. You're a pillar of dependability in a crisis.

Once you begin to make your way in the world, your inner drive and determination enable you to sustain and amplify your initial success in the business domain or other field, such as writing, music or education, you've chosen in which to capitalize on your estimable abilities. Some of you, however, since you're emotionally oriented, will be inclined to deploy energies according to how you "feel" about things rather than how you arrived at your decisions through abstract, logical analysis. Your intense will-to-win spirit and adaptability are among your outstanding traits. You might be thrust into a position of heavy responsibility at an early age through necessity; at your best, you're equal to the challenge and would come through with flying colors. You know how to improvise to keep a project going.

You cherish independence, but you don't like to be alone. If your idea of power is to dominate your domestic environment, you will live with a sense of loneliness. Others may give in to you but will harbor resentments. You don't like to take orders or be the target of criticism; by living up to the impressive potential of your birthday, you can minimize or bypass aggravations. Your early years either gave you an insight into the advantages of material freedom or the frustrations that accompany a lack of it . . . possibly your major fear.

Maria Shriver (TV cohost), 1955

Mike Nichols (director), 1931

John Philip Sousa (composer), 1854

Special to October 24 (Pluto, Jupiter [Moon/Saturn]):
Your combination of charm, willpower and sex appeal can attract many admirers, but they have to offer more than surface allure to keep you interested. Your gracious, outwardly cool manner more likely than not masks a formidable inner intensity. You may seem never to lose your temper, but people close to you in stressful situations can sense the frustration or resentment simmering underneath your diplomatic facade. Whether in the world of business, government, entertainment or the arts, your tact, determination and expertise enable you to win the day when a ticklish challenge requires deft handling.

Your competitive spirit and personal discipline can attract the kind of opportunities that provide entry into the big leagues career-wise. You achieve success mainly through your own outstanding qualifications, through which you gain the support of people in the power network who are in a position to grant favors. Very family-oriented, you can be just as considerate and protective of coworkers as you are of the folks at home. A digger and a prober, you're apt to become completely immersed in whatever you do, including the nitty-gritty details. You may feel duty-bound to be an anchor of responsibility, discipline and trust; regardless of your motivation, however, those around you will benefit from your concern for their welfare and happiness.

Monica Arnold (singer), 1980

Kevin Kline (actor), 1947

F. Murray Abraham (actor), 1939

Special to November 15 (Pluto, Jupiter [Sun/Mars]):

Your psychic antenna tunes you in to unseen forces, a proclivity that may be involuntary. If you instinctively profit from this ability, you might just label it a good "hunch" and not dwell on it. Nevertheless, this gift can be a promising factor in your success potential; utilizing it in a job or profession offers a subtle advantage. The mysteries of the universe intrigue some of you, which can be a highly personal source of inspiration and knowledge. When this arcane interest colors your endeavors in the arts, the business world or a profession, the depth of your approach, investigative skills and special technique can yield a distinctive style that sets you apart from others in your field.

Your contagious enthusiasm and philosophical attitude imbue your work with qualities that appeal to a wide variety of people. Your pragmatic outlook prompts you to deal effectively with conditions as they are and not as you wish they were. You may feel a sense of mission, an obligation not only to enlighten contemporaries, but also to pass on to the next generation the benefit of your experience and wisdom. You might be regarded as the spearhead of an awakening (or reawakening) pertaining to a business or profession ready for fresh insights, improvement and/or expansion. Patience, persistence, resourcefulness, a grasp of detail and a shrewd sense of how to get things done enable you to better yourself and reach the top if that's your goal. With your aggressive, forceful spirit and drive, an enduring relationship may or may not dovetail with your idea of a fulfilling life.

Sam Waterston (actor), 1940

Edward Wagner (astrologer, columnist), 1906

Georgia O'Keeffe (artist), 1887

November the 7th (Pluto, Mercury)
(and root digit for October 25 and November 16):

It could be an exercise in futility to try to put something over on you. Very little escapes your scrutiny. One of your rulers is The Eagle, and you're a sharp-eyed bird observing what is going on around you at any given time. Some of you are masters of seductive communication; your comments get right to the point, and you voice them with subtle conviction. You're able to move imperceptibly from a tone of faintly whispered secrecy to one of trenchant authority. With your great aptitude for debunking a questionable view or information that arouses your suspicion or pricks your pride in any way, anyone who opposes you in a verbal clash has about as much chance as a slingshot against a tank.

You will have many opportunities that challenge your mental abilities and will triumph according to how well you deal with them. You have an incisive mind, many inner resources, potent silences and an excellent memory, especially about people who have crossed you or tried to. Being a fixed sign, your opinions follow in the same mold (they are not typically flexible). You are unlikely to change your mind once it is made up about something important to you; if you ever do, it is not apt to happen overnight.

Your knowledge, whether derived from formal schooling or experience, should be as broad-based as possible. In that way, your attitudes and decisions are based on something besides personal bias. With your sense of personal power stemming from your acute mental prowess (part learning, part innate intelligence, part psychological insight), you could achieve an influential position as you move steadily along the road to success. In any case, restless in your early years, you're usually smart enough to attain a measure of security through vocational training, scientific research, the world of commerce or the arts.

Keith Lockhart (conductor), 1959
Billy Graham (evangelist), 1918
Marie Curie (physical chemist), 1867

Special to October 25 (Pluto, Mercury [Moon/Mars]):
You expect full return for your efforts, which can lead to significant achievement in business or the creative realm, but you are apt to be bothered or feel hampered by the demands of others in your environment. You have great need for affection; although you attract your share, it may be stymied by emotional turbulence and/or shifting loyalties. Expecting others to toe the mark, you're inclined conversely to refuse to be hampered by supervision or other restrictions yourself. Withal, you are a capable executive, never happy in a subordinate position. Your creative flair is cerebral; the great achievements of the past stimulate your imagination. If you pursue a career in the art world, you are apt to be ahead of your time, startling or erratic as well as innovative.

People who think they can best you in a verbal exchange should think again. With your 360-megabyte memory, you're always at the ready with an arsenal of defensive comebacks. When you're cornered and confronted with a question that you would rather not answer, you know how to fill the air with radar-deflecting particles. On the other hand, you're an expert at getting your own viewpoint across, especially when opposed; to say that you're a good talker is like saying that a shark is a good swimmer. Intense, set in your ways, prolific, an effective fighter, strategist and promoter, there's not much doubt that you'll achieve your goal given any reasonable opportunity. Whether locally or globally, your name can become synonymous with the field you excel in.

> Barbara Cook (singer), 1927
>
> Pablo Picasso (artist), 1881
>
> George Bizet (composer), 1838

Special to November 16 (Pluto, Mercury [Sun/Jupiter]):

If you deal with the public in your job, or if your career flourishes in the limelight, your appeal runs the gamut from brittle honesty (and perhaps biting humor) about life's gritty realities to a folksy philosophy that appeals to people swayed by a gentler, more optimistic outlook. In any case, whether you are easygoing or temperamental, your facade effectively masks your unswerving ambition to achieve success in life on your clearly defined terms. The super-salesperson for the values you espouse, your employer, coworkers and the public find it easy to identify wholeheartedly with your sunny optimism, sharp comedic sense and personal skill, a blend that promises considerable popularity. Your initiatives and personal credibility can epitomize the heart and soul of progressive efforts to improve conditions or to break new ground in your chosen field. The challenge hidden in the opportunities you meet is sincerity, which you seem naturally gifted to personify. Your ability to wax lyrical about mundane or ordinary things in life enables people to feel happy and contented through your help in discovering or accentuating the everyday pleasures that can be lost in the hubbub of life's humdrum realities. You have a firm belief in causes and work well with others. Money and the security it can provide are important to you as your passport to freedom.

> Dwight Gooden (baseball player), 1964
>
> George S. Kaufman (playwright), 1889
>
> W. C. Handy (composer), 1873

November the 8th (Pluto, Uranus/Saturn)
(and root digit for October 26 and November 17):

Broad knowledge and distinctive skills are essential components of your life, and the sooner you acquire them, the sooner you'll be on your way to success; the need for them is interwoven into your estimable gift for administration and promotion, particularly of wide-ranging projects or enterprises. Your dramatic power-complex feeds on the freedom and respect that achievement and prosperity bring. You're more apt to be found in a profession or the creative realm than in business, but wherever you function the canvas of your life will be big, larger than ordinary. Your combined psychic receptivity and intuition provide you with insights in advance of the times, so you have a decided advantage on competitors.

You instinctively gravitate toward centers of power. Although your makeup is intensely emotional, your response to the opportunities life brings you is primarily psychological, practical and innovative. Your special expertise, or a particular flair for putting yourself and your ideas across, makes an enduring favorable impression on people you deal with, and you know how to turn that impact into power or money or both. That's the good news. When you're provoked or opposed, however, your dogged determination to control the situation may make you seem arrogant, brusque, cunning or self-centered to your adversaries.

Somehow your acumen doesn't spill over into your personal life, where you might have difficulty establishing a rewarding relationship. Emotional uncertainty leads to disappointment. Intense, dynamic and productive, perhaps your insistence on complete freedom also keeps you free of love and/or other close alliance that you may tend to keep at arm's length. You can be hard to convince and may have a healthy sense of your own importance; your determination and ample ego, of course, are no handicap to your effort to reach the top, which you usually manage to do in a job or career endeavor. With your inborn prodigious stamina, singular purpose, self-containment and self-discipline, how could it be otherwise?

Bonnie Raitt (singer), 1949

Patti Page (singer), 1927

Margaret Mitchell (novelist), 1900

Special to October 26 (Pluto, Uranus/Saturn [Moon/Jupiter]): With your adventurous spirit urging you onward, you can range far and wide literally or figuratively in your effort to fulfill your singular potential. Your philosophy is very idealistic; you envision a world without walls, where everyone lives in peace and harmony for the mutual benefit of all people regardless of origin. The real world, however, falls short of your standards and can be a disappointment and/or a perpetual challenge. You're likely to feel more comfortable in a profession than in the hurly-burly of the business world. A job in a social services organization, the arts, the law or the medical or related fields would be a congenial outlet for your infectious optimism.

Whatever you do, you won't be happy unless it has broad public appeal or impact and/or improves conditions.

You have your practical side; you like to live well; recognition of your worth and money in sufficient quantities are very important to you. You are anxious to do well, and you appreciate receiving your share of credit for it. With your jubilant personality, you can communicate any ability, but you have a special flair for inspirational activities and the healing arts. Any area where your persevering efforts would encourage a brighter, more affirmative outlook would benefit from your being a part of it. If you expect too much from relationships, you are inviting disappointment. Between youthful curiosity and budding ambition, your job or career strivings probably got off to an early start.

Hillary Rodham Clinton (First Lady), 1946

Francois Mitterand (former prime minister of France), 1916

Mahalia Jackson (gospel singer), 1911

Special to November 17 (Pluto, Uranus/Saturn [Sun/Mercury]):
Your low-key manner may belie your reserves of quiet power and tenacity, attributes that come to the fore when you believe in a cause and decide to put your weight behind it and to fight the good fight. Whether it's your integrity, knowledge, background or impressive self-assurance, you're likely to be someone to be reckoned with. You are popular in whatever circle you move, have a sharp sense of humor, are an excellent observer and conversationalist and take pleasure in indulging your curiosity about any subject that has attracted your interest. Pluto is a money planet, Scorpio is a money sign and 8 (1 + 7 = 8) is a power number, so it's not unlikely that your probing mind will inevitably drift to thoughts of financial power as exemplified by property and security, if not of riches.

Magnetic and deep-thinking, the best milieu for your intellectual agility is a large enterprise, where your probative thought processes can benefit large numbers of people, especially in the public domain. If you change your occupation, it probably will be as much for a position of broader influence as for increased income. You're proud of your 360-megabyte memory, which enables you to recall facts and figures and prior experiences, particularly a setback or a grievance, with remarkable acuity. You're relatively easy to get along with, as long as your mate or partner doesn't try to change you, pry into your affairs or interfere with your personal comforts and lifestyle. You're not likely to mellow with time.

Danny De Vito (actor), 1944

Martin Scorcese (director), 1942

Isamu Noguchi (sculptor), 1904

November the 9th (Pluto [Pluto])
(and root digit for October 27 and November 18):

The primrose path could be the path of least resistance for you. Since you have an obsessive, compulsive nature and an abundance of creative impetus, your life is constructive or destructive, or somewhere in between, depending on where you direct your charismatic personality and seductive emotional power. In its most decadent form, your life will be an endless pursuit of pleasure, with the negative residue of your promiscuity strewn in the wake of your amoral excesses. On the other hand and on a higher level, your interests and hobbies could range from amateur or spectator sports to personal participation in musical or artistic expression, intellectual pursuits or invigorating leisure-time or community-related activities. You needn't be a rocket scientist to figure out which course would yield the most advantageous results as your life unfolds.

In the job and career realm, your informal manners enable you to roll up your sleeves and plunge into the nitty-gritty of your job or assignment with gusto and steady concentration. If you make a mistake while dashing along in high gear, you're able to just as quickly correct it and minimize or deflect negative feedback or consequences. You're not particularly competitive in a business or a profession because you don't have to be to attain success; with your compelling persona, you have a way of simply attracting opportunities without too much effort on your part. Not the type to raise your voice, you're not easily distracted; you have tremendous drive and endurance when preoccupied in a job or career that absorbs your interest and fans the flame of your ambition. Even though Scorpio is a fixed sign, you adjust to changes more willingly if they are inwardly motivated and of your own volition than if you have to adjust to circumstances beyond your control. When life proceeds as you envision it, your energy, progressive spirit, determination and expertise with subtle strategies are practically guarantees of success in whatever job or career you choose to maximize your potential. Depending on your aforementioned emotional proclivities, however, your personal life may be more difficult to bring into focus. In marriage or other close relationship, your partner had better have plenty of strength and diplomacy in order to humor your wide mood swings, to cater to your need for flattery and to give you the feeling that you rule the roost.

Carl Sagan (author), 1934

Stanford White (architect), 1853

Ivan Turgenev (novelist), 1818

Special to October 27 (Pluto [Moon/Mercury]):

With your innate persistence, you can overcome any obstacles that stand in the way of achieving a job, business or professional objective. Wide knowledge in connection with a specialty and thorough mental training will be your prime assets in your endeavors to get ahead in life. Fortunately, you learn quickly, and with your incisive mind and excellent memory, you have an enviable knack for solving on-the-job problems and attaining a position of considerable influence. You also have Scorpio's probing instincts, but you don't have to dig deep to succeed in a job or profession. That isn't to say you won't, but with your facile skill you could skim the surface and get by on your articulate persona, mental agility, expressive talent and swift grasp of workplace situations.

On the other hand, emotionally, you're the classic still-waters-run-deep type. Fulfillment in marriage or other close relationship depends on whether you and someone who cares speak the same heartfelt language. Verbal communication of your amorous feelings can be as meaningful to you as the warm glow of touchy-feely togetherness. Intensely emotional to begin with, you tend to magnify everything that concerns you personally. Your life will flow more easily if you dwell less on personal matters and concentrate more on the world outside and its never-ending challenges.

John Cleese (actor, writer), 1939

Dylan Thomas (poet), 1914

Theodore Roosevelt (26th U.S. president), 1858

Special to November 18 (Pluto [Sun/Uranus/Saturn]):

When you decide to go after something, you'll probably have all or most of the bases covered before you take the first step. Whether pursuing a job calling for particular (well-paying) skills or a profession, your career endeavors will probably involve much change, activity and travel, which will be necessary components for climbing the success ladder and fulfilling your life's objectives. Though your initial efforts may not get you where you want to go or even put you on the right track in business or the arts, you will feel more misguided than discouraged. Scorpios are not easily vanquished, and you'll just chalk up to chance a few missteps in a seemingly time- or energy-wasting direction. You do best in any large field that requires concentration of purpose.

You have a no-nonsense attitude toward establishment expectations and are inclined to go your own way to achieve your place in the Sun. If, for one reason or another, you aren't able to acquire the standard training a job or career requires, you're able to rely on your abundant determination and practical knowledge derived from the school of experience to bluster your way through the challenges you encounter. You have enough dash and bravado to conceal whatever trepidation you may be feeling inwardly. If the occasion calls for main strength and daring, you're not afraid to rush in where angels fear to tread. If you're impetuous, impatient or too independent, people will have to admit that you do get the job done. Very loyal, your affectional ties and/or marriage provide an anchor of stability while you're out conquering the world.

Linda Evans (actress), 1942

Imogene Coca (comedienne), 1908

Paderewski (pianist, statesman), 1860

November the 11th (Pluto, Neptune [Moon/Sun])
(master number):

Whether or not it's realistically possible, your greatest inspiration and potential could be realized through living in a society where total freedom of thought, feeling and behavior can be experienced. If and when these options are open to you, they provide unlimited credit at an imaginative memory bank that can serve you well as your life unfolds. With the extraordinary opportunities the world can bring your way, you'll be either a saint or a sinner, or a provocative combination of the two extremes, to which might be attributed your craving for strict personal privacy. Unless you're in politics, you'll be determined to maintain a wall between you and the public. When at a party, you might look and act as though you wish you were somewhere else.

If you aspire to the creative realm as a career choice, a spirit of make-believe distinctly your own can be uppermost in your work, which may seem inconsistent with your more direct way of dealing with people. Your job or professional interests can run the gamut—from the business world to politics, the healing arts, Wall Street or the realm of entertainment. There are few limitations to inhibit the expression of your talents and abilities. Your strong feeling about any issue that attracts your sympathies is practically a guarantee that it stands a better chance for success than if you didn't get behind it. Whether you start early or late to make you way in the world, you have an instinct for capitalizing on your opportunities and turning each one into a stepping-stone to a higher level of success. At your best, your creative work will be probing, illuminating or even disturbing rather than conventional.

You project a certain magic in the social milieu and in your work with people that translates into personal, public and romantic popularity. Whether or not you're a Tom Cruise or Sophia Loren look-alike with a dazzling smile, you're likely to attract your share or more (possibly a lot more) of admirers and amorous adventures. And whether your charisma glimmers faintly or glows brightly, you're not immune to the lure of exotic (not to say erotic) divertissements; your romantic exploits could rival those of Mollie Bloom, Tom Jones, Lady Chatterly, Casanova, Moll Flanders or Don Juan. Negatively, this Scorpio birthday warns of murky or confused morality and uncontrolled appetites; extreme vulnerability and escapism join forces with sex, death and regeneration, a potent mixture. When you respond positively, the same influences can be the source of great moral, spiritual or creative illumination.

   Leonardo di Caprio (actor), 1974

   Demi Moore (actress), 1962

   Fyodor Dostoevsky (novelist), 1821

(Note: This master number implies a variable alternative response influenced by the strength or passivity of the planet Neptune in your horoscope. If you don't feel you are responding to the distinctive vibratory power of 11, you are instead expressing the more conventional qualities of 2, which you should read.)

November the 22nd (Pluto, Uranus [Saturn/Moon])
(master number):

Scorpio being a fixed sign, you basically resist change, especially any unexpected one forced on you by circumstances; the need to make jarring adjustments can upset you emotionally. And since you're so intense, the personal repercussions can be difficult. If you rise to a position of prominence or leadership, to which you are drawn, you will no doubt have to adapt to, and flow with, conditions not of your own devising. You may not like it, but that's all part of the success package for you, so you can't afford to be inflexible. However, being inventive, you could accidentally discover a dynamic new career direction, upon which you could leave a lasting personal imprint.

Self-willed, self-determined and very independent, you tend to press your theories on others and can become adamant in your insistence on doing things your way. Fortunately, your motives are usually admirable, and you always believe that you are right. The combination of 22, which relates to Uranus (the planet of extroverted self-will) combined with Scorpio (the sign of introverted self-will) is potent. When these forces conflict, the result can be the apotheosis of "won't-power." When redirected for constructive empowerment, however, internal tension can become a refusal to be dogmatic or to maintain trivial, narrow or radical viewpoints. Conflicts then become energizing, if you use them with your acutely penetrating insight and with the intent to overcome obstacles that impede the constructive unfoldment of your life.

Your vision of the future can result in groundbreaking initiatives on the job front (perhaps in some workforce or union capacity), in business, government, science or the creative arts. You might have little patience with colleagues or others who mouth the clichés of conservatism. You're all for new products, systems and devices that produce profound sociocultural transformations, a process congenial to Scorpio. Marriage and a family can provide stability and a haven of rejuvenation to counteract the tension generated by your career activities. One way or another, your climb to success is likely to absorb so much of your time and energy that you'll have little of either left over if you are inclined to emotional dalliance.

Jamie Lee Curtis (actress), 1958

Charles de Gaulle (general, statesman), 1890

Andre Gide (author), 1869

(Note: This master number implies a variable alternative response influenced by the strength or passivity of the planet Uranus in your horoscope. If you don't think you are responding to the distinctive vibratory power of 22, you are instead expressing the more conventional qualities of 4, which you should read.)

SAGITTARIUS

November 23–December 22

RULER: **JUPITER** NUMBER: **6** ELEMENT: **FIRE** SYMBOL: **THE ARCHER**

"I speak as my understanding instructs me, and as mine honesty
puts it to utterance."
—*The Winter's Tale,* Shakespeare

Isn't it great, being a Sagittarian? The world is constantly sending opportunities your way; you know how to capitalize on them, and you have a knack of turning problems into advantages. It isn't? . . . It doesn't? . . . You don't? . . . Your life isn't a smashing success? You've got to be doing *something* wrong! After all, your ruler, Jupiter, the planet of luck, is sending out all those positive rays, and they're aimed right at you! If you're not using them for your benefit, that's your problem—not Jupiter's! The king of the gods, with so many millions of subjects, couldn't possibly give individual attention to each and every one of you. Anyway, you're his emissary as well as beneficiary; you're not just the recipient of celestial welfare! You, too, have your part to do. It could be that Jupiter is sending you too much good fortune, and you're just taking it all for granted.

Your symbol is the Centaur, a creature half man and half horse in Greek mythology. Also known as the Archer, the feet of the animal part are solidly planted on terra firma. Man, the upper half, aims his bow and arrow toward the stars and the spiritual, erudite, optimistic and ennobling aspirations of existence. When living on the higher side of your cosmic birthright, you're able to combine the advantages of heaven and earth and bounce back from almost any setback.

There's rarely a Sagittarian born without some gift and accordingly some measure of luck, and it's often abundant. Even if it's nothing more than contagious enthusiasm and the gift of gab, those at least are the hail-fellow-well-met advantages of the born salesperson. At the very least, you're protected from the worst; the trouble is, sensing this, you can slip into the rut of coasting along on your good fortune and never have your eyes opened to your greatest potential or to the gaps in your makeup that prevent the full

realization of it. We all have work to do: eradicating flaws, building character, cultivating understanding, developing skills and so on, some of us more,
some less.

Propelled by your natural exuberance, the spirit of adventure urges you
onward to seek new contacts, novel experiences, fresh knowledge and deeper
meanings to life—or simply to discover what's around the next corner or
behind the next hill or what makes a new friend tick. If what you find turns
out to fall below your expectations, however, you'll probably be philosophical
about it; it doesn't dampen your eagerness to explore the next stimulus for
your restless curiosity. In this regard, energy, one of your remarkable attributes, can be a hazard. If your body isn't going at full throttle, your mind is.
When you are endlessly active, constantly doing things, perpetually on the go,
the energies of your commendable buoyancy scatter, becoming mere wandering of mind, body, attention and direction. If you become too diffuse and
disorganized, you can wear out others as well as yourself with your zest for life.
Then you are like Stephen Leacock's hero, who jumped on his horse and
instantly rode off in all directions at a gallop. This is why it is difficult for a
disappointed or unhappy Sagittarian to arrive at a mature state of reflection.
When would you have the time?

As a fire sign, you're gregarious and enthusiastic. You also share a few
Aries traits (which may need some restraint)—naiveté, impatience and impulsiveness. Often outspoken, frequently sportsminded, you can range far and
wide in your interests. Most of you have that itchy foot to travel. Being a people person, faraway lands and their inhabitants interest you.

A born gambler, you're not above taking risks that would give others
pause for thought, foolishly assuming that everything will turn out all right.
It doesn't always, of course, and you have your share of ups and downs like the
rest of us mortals. But even the hard knocks and rough jolts rarely destroy
your faith in human nature or your joy from wanting to participate in the colorful pageant of living.

During those occasions when life's grimmer realities catch up with you
and you become moody and depressed, you're likely to retreat to your home
environment or some secluded haven to recharge your batteries. Then, after
thoughtful reflection, you're ready to emerge refreshed by your temporary hia-
tus and will be straining at the bit to get back into harness and the swing of
things.

You have many attributes that enable you to live up to your highest
potential. You can be the crusader with a natural nobility of spirit, diffused in

many directions to implement your acquisition of knowledge and, ultimately, wisdom. You can be the keen student, seeking to gather and learn from the widest variety of information and experience. With the advent of the Internet and websites, you can exchange ideas, news and inspirations with people in the far corners of the globe.

Being the extrovert in action of universal philosophy, you have great expressive force: Where Scorpio internalizes with intensity, you externalize with exuberance. With your self-generated fervor and your buoyant conviviality, you can be socially and romantically popular even when people have little in common with you. You rarely arouse enmity; you suffer most through self-waste, self-hurt.

Your sins are usually those of omission rather than commission. You can assume that your beliefs are their own strengths and forget that practical necessities are required to implement beliefs and give them form in the workaday world. You can ascribe to friends the same virtues that motivate you and become bewildered when the reality is different, when you fail to understand motives less idealistic than your own. Whereas Virgo can become trapped in the commonplaces of life, you may need to give them more attention and respect instead of casual disregard.

You tend to have blind faith, to believe what you want to believe. If you overvalue your assumptions and abstractions, you become perplexed and frustrated by the world as it is, which can be quite different from the way you wish it to be. Divergent opinions and contrary conditions are part of the cosmic plan for you in order to find a common center, learn from it and proceed from there toward a goal. An impatient Sagittarian may not understand the measured pace of the evolutionary process. It's hard for the Archer to lose, but you can be profligate, letting ideas and initiatives dissipate into nothingness after burning bright. You are the sign most apt to forget that the mills of the gods grind slowly. You should learn to trust that—and also that they grind "exceeding well." You can *assist* the process with your insights; you can't eliminate it or speed up the tempo. The values of your sign, no matter how commendable, are not the only ones deserving of the world's attention; there are eleven other signs in the zodiac with as many pathways to the truth, which exists independently of who is right and who is wrong. No one has a hotline to it. Belief systems that include atheists and agnostics, and religions as diverse as those founded by Gautama Buddha, Jesus Christ, Mohammed and Martin Luther are ample proof of that.

Your challenge is the unity of spirit and material values that combine to advance a worthwhile purpose. That isn't easy, but like the Man of La Mancha, you have to believe in the impossible dream. Who gave Columbus the money (a material necessity) to sail west into the New World (his impossible dream) to fulfill his spirit of adventure? It was King Ferdinand and Queen Isabella of Spain, as every schoolboy knows, and Spain is ruled by Sagittarius, as every schoolboy, as yet, doesn't know.

A Sagittarian is usually a great mixer, rarely a social climber, but you can be the *mental* status seeker, a pretentious form of snobbery. Sagittarian courage then turns into cerebral braggadocio or intellectual vanity. You become disdainful of others not so fortunately gifted as you are. With your outstanding mental equipment, you may forget that "the heart is wiser than the intellect." Impatient or annoyed when others fail to get your message and a disagreement flares up, you can become hostile, sardonic and cutting in speech. At such times, a parting of the ways is not an unlikely outcome. To insist on pain of a rupture that someone with a different viewpoint agree with you is to selfishly seek a mirror of yourself in others. The outgoing, gregarious Sagittarian spirit then becomes cramped and shrunken to the size of your own ego, big in this context but decidedly infinitesimal in the cosmic scheme of things.

Your naive and candid demeanor can unintentionally rub people the wrong way; as you bluntly state the truth, or your sometimes heedless and tactless concept of it, others may wince. You can become the lip-service idealist, uttering "platitudes in stained-glass attitudes"; you can clothe clichés with great flourish and miss the essential point of an issue entirely. If you overstress the spiritual component without due thought for the earthbound necessities, you can sink in the quicksand of noble but impractical intentions. However, if you overstress the material, animalistic implication of Sagittarius, your psychic rejection principle goes into action.

The negative Sagittarian who overemphasizes materialism suffers the most. Your spirit craves freedom; if you clog it with ordinary conceits and demands for success, recognition, wealth or possessions, you are no longer master of your destiny. You won't gain the freedom you seek if material gain becomes your consuming interest. You'll never have enough, not because you literally can't acquire vast sums of money, but because of your duality; you can mistakenly interpret psychic anxieties as money fears. Instead of a jovial Sagittarian odyssey, your life becomes a cramped contest with a world of density foreign to your deepest instinct: to be a free spirit.

Not averse to "get-rich-quick" notions, you can find speculating more exciting than value investing. The financial freedom that you expect to gain thereby, however, can become an elusive myth; you could get caught in the trap of worrying whether your stock market choices will go up or down and about the losses you may have to absorb. With your highly charged nervous system, you can become enmeshed in a web of fretful anxiety, which thwarts your urge for liberation.

Being a sign of varied extremes, you could turn negative and eschew *all* efforts to cope with material things and just leave everything to chance. You will adopt the convenient attitude that somehow such concerns are a bore or require too much time and effort. This is merely an excuse for indulgent extravagance or waste and indicates a lack of respect for practical virtues. You become the profligate spender; instead, you should focus your energies on accumulating and conserving valuable resources. Although all signs can fall prey to gambling, alcoholism and other escapes, Sagittarius seems to be especially vulnerable to these lapses, a misuse of Jupiter's gift. The dark side of the Sagittarian principle is celebrated in the glitzy temples of Las Vegas and Atlantic City.

If you want to be a successful Sagittarian, you must be orderly and methodical, especially in a career that provides opportunities for upward mobility and expansion. Otherwise, instead of being on top of things, you're trapped down in them, passively accepting dull routine and the discouraging prospect of being unable to extricate yourself from your predicament. Then you are vulnerable to an inherent pitfall of your sign, similar in effect to that of Gemini, your opposite polarity; you, too, can suffer greatly as you age and your youthful stamina fades. However, if you apply your energies productively and make substantial progress while the going is good, you can avoid disappointment and being resigned to reduced circumstances in your sunset years.

According to Robert Frost, "Most of the change we think we see in life is due to *truths* being in and out of favor." The key words are "the change we *think* we see," because the more things change, the more the essentials of life remain the same. The wise words of William Penn, cited in the Preface, bear repeating here:

> *Look not to things that are seen,*
> *but to that which is unseen; for*
> *things that are seen pass away, but*
> *that which is unseen is forever.*

It's to your advantage to penetrate beyond the sham or veil of appearances, of fashions in thought, to realize that much effort and trial and error are the means of releasing your powerful potential in whatever way or area you choose to function. That is the most productive way to maximize your boundless energy and enthusiasm.

Many Sagittarians have made the world infinitely richer by their diverse contributions. Mark Twain, Maria Callas, Noel Coward, Gustave Flaubert and Toulouse-Lautrec, to mention just a few, have hit the mark and left their own distinctive imprint on the world. As crusaders in music, literature, the theater and the art world, the essence of their triumph has been their heartfelt belief and unique insights that illuminate some aspect of the human condition through their extraordinary creativity. Sagittarians are prophetic, as these examples illustrate, able to envision a new order or to revitalize an old one with an exhilarating fresh slant on age-old cultural issues.

A tradition of literary freedom stems from Gustave Flaubert, just as a revival of interest in the historic traditions of operatic singing stems from the rediscoveries of Maria Callas. When Flaubert's classic, *Madame Bovary*, was published after five years of toil, it created a moral furor. He was prosecuted but won his case and consequent vindication everywhere for artistic integrity. His insistence on realism and truth and his willingness to stake his own reputation on the outcome freed literature from the moral strictures of his time. Who can forget the "blood, sweat and tears" of Sagittarian Winston Churchill? If you tend to overlook the impact of all such notables on civilization, just imagine the world without their respective contributions. It would be much the poorer.

Your sign represents the trail-blazers of the zodiac who can ignite the world with the flame of inspiration and genius. The colossus that was Ludvig von Beethoven, another Sagittarian, posed musical mysteries, the ultimate meanings of which can still elude the listeners and musicologists of today. There is no doubt as to the meaning of his Fifth Symphony, however. The brief but memorable opening notes were the signal for freedom and eventual victory in the oppressed countries of Europe during World War II. Beethoven's musical inspirations began by following the classical mode. Then he passed through a tempestuous period in his composing career, his final inspirations ending appropriately in serene contemplation: a perfect Sagittarian pattern. He broke rules, not to satisfy childish whims, but to restructure musical forms. Sometimes he labored over as many as twenty or more versions of a single passage in his manuscripts. The musical beauties that seem to flow with such consummate inevitability were the result of painful and exhausting trial and error, the agony of endless experimentation and the realization that his genius was struggling against encroaching deafness.

Generally unconcerned about the past or tradition, you are more interested in the future. However, you can profit from a sense of history, a trait more typical of Cancerians. Many there are who proclaim that we know more than the ancients; "Yes, and the ancients are what we know" is the response of Libra-born T. S. Eliot (with a powerful Sagittarius emphasis in his horoscope) to such callow appraisals of history and the geniuses who have cast long shadows through the mists of millenniums past. Four and a half thousand years later, we still don't know how the Great Pyramid at Giza was built. That awesome structure was until the 19th century the tallest man-made building in the world, quite a record for an ancient Egyptian architect. We stand on the shoulders of giants. This truth is a clue for you to scan the width and depth of the past for some of your answers. If nothing else, it could instill in you a sense of humility.

Emotionally, you are a paradox: You're as receptive as anyone to the thrills of joyful togetherness, but marital happiness depends on the mutual give-and-take that can elude the Sagittarian. When self-absorbed in your enthusiasms, you can be frustrating to live with. You tend to do things in fits and starts, instead of steadily and constructively in all of life; you're basically not partial to sustained, patient, everyday cooperation or compromise, which are essential necessities of marriage or any ongoing relationship.

Your innate curiosity is more powerful than your loyalty; you are an instinctive flirt. You can have several attachments simultaneously; you often marry twice or can maintain a discreet, long-lasting attachment elsewhere that satisfies your need for emotional amplification. You're the all-around, fun-loving playmate, without those smoldering wells of emotional intensity characteristic of Scorpio, for instance. Your passions are more abstract, intellectual or casual.

You range from having a sense of humor about sex to being ambivalent regarding your interest in it. Half of you wants to sin, while the other half wants to look pious while you sin. Not constituted for the confines of marriage, you are likely to do as you please. "Don't fence me in!" could be your theme song. Your mate has to trust you and your penchant for freedom; you have no patience with restrictive relationships or suspicious attitudes. Your outlook on love and marriage as a glorious experience can blind you to the underlying necessities; your emotions, exuberant when aroused, are difficult to sustain. In any event, you won't be shattered by a broken marriage. Instinctively nursed recriminations are not your style.

Since yours is a positive fire sign, the distaff Sagittarian is unique, similar in certain respects to your Aries and Leo sisters, only you're more the "pal" type, not so emotionally attuned. Feminine "liberation" movements probably amuse you; you've traveled that route for centuries, with some celebrated examples as your models. Mary, Queen of Scots and Queen Christina of Sweden were two of your headstrong royal sisters, vivid examples of the traits that subconsciously impel you. Possibly there's a message for you in the fact that Mary lost her headstrong royal head to the executioner, and both queens wound up minus their thrones in their compulsion for intrigue and freedom.

You're lucky if you don't lose anything more than gloves, glasses and umbrellas, which you have a habit of leaving in taxis, trains or airplanes, or wherever else you find it convenient to forget life's little details. At such times, you're probably thinking about that controversial book just published, that fabulous new movie or what sight you want to see first when you get to Rome.

You are frequently the hoyden, the coltish, leggy type typified by the high-fashion model. You can also be Alice in Blunderland, due to wool-gathering or faulty hip coordination. You can bump into tables, crash into plate-glass doors or trip over your own three feet if nothing else is handy. Sis Hopkins—with her apple cheeks, arms akimbo and pigtails flying—had nothing on you when you were growing up.

Men with a taste for adventure, mental and physical, can find you a fascinating challenge, if not a domestic delight. You're usually not much intrigued by sinks, stoves or diapers. A Sagittarian of either sex should avoid association with deliberate, moody or slow-moving individuals, for they will never understand you, nor you them, unless there's a mutual willingness to make significant adjustments. You won't acquiesce to dictatorial attitudes or interference with your interests; your nonchalant (and to them, irresponsible) attitude will exasperate such types unless they have the patience of Job. You do, however, need a soothing influence in your life, something warm and real, like an understanding partner, friend, pet or whatever. It will give your mind a rest from its usual restless, roaming preoccupations.

Your attitude toward friends is sincere; with your boundless enthusiasm, you frequently give as much thought and effort to pushing the affairs of others as you do your own. That it can be unappreciated or overlooked is more than puzzling to the Archer; you could find ingratitude downright offensive. Console yourself by remembering that you are the *exception* and not the rule and must make allowances for the shortcomings of others. You won't withhold praise, but people generally earn all that you bestow.

You can think that you are infallible, and you are chagrined and disappointed when your efforts don't succeed. You can insist on the same energetic application from associates. In fact, your constant reliance on your high expectations of others to do things as well as you can become a handicap. You might have an inflexible code, a concept of justice; you like to see transgressors get their just desserts because you feel qualified to pass judgment.

William Blake, the English poet, artist and mystic, is an outstanding example of the Sagittarian universal spirit. He rebelled, like Beethoven, not as a childish ego strategy but because he wanted to give original structure and form to his intense spirituality. He believed that man's soul is, during its time-conditioned life on Earth, a wanderer from the realm of pure spirit. "The man of conventional faith," he said, the too-slavish "reasoning man," has forfeited imagination and daring.

Blake spent fifty years, as poet and artist, trying to open the gateways of his fellow men's perceptions to the glories of the infinite. He was unimpressed with laws, especially moral laws. He pitied and forgave the meanness of others; in his view, forgiveness is the very soul of Christian living. When he regarded common things, he saw through to God's hand within, to essences and eternal forms and demons. Lacking formal education, he distrusted the entire intellectual establishment.

Mystics were out of fashion in Blake's time, and a Sagittarian can be out of step with the world at any time; the trick is to be in tune with the *infinite*, not with transient fashions, and then to translate your findings into a form that the world can recognize and benefit from. You are the emissary for that revelation in whatever context you choose to apply it. You can become the beautifully integrated individual of your ideals through the glorious principles inherent in Sagittarius, with your faith increasing as it is rewarded in the course of living. Then your warmhearted, unfettered, all-inclusive acceptance of the universe becomes sublimated in the unconscious, a golden springboard into your sphere of action, accomplishment and fulfillment.

Blake revealed the essence of the Sagittarian principle with brevity and beautiful simplicity in these immortal lines:

To see a World in a Grain of Sand
and a Heaven in a Wild Flower,
Hold Infinity in the palm of your hand
and Eternity in an hour.

SAGITTARIUS BIRTHDAYS

Judgment of whether or not a birthday is propitious can be considered from two points of view: complementary or challenging. From the standpoint of personal progress and fulfillment, your destiny may flow more comfortably if your birthday is, or reduces to, an *inner* root number such as 1, 3, 5, 7 or 9. For career drive and achievement, your progress may be enhanced if your birthday is, or reduces to, an *outer* root number such as 2, 4, 6, 8 or 22 (master number); the *outer* root numbers are less comfortable, more obstructive for you to contend with, but they are potentially very conducive to outstanding success. The 11 (master number) would be variable, but it generally would require more understanding and resourcefulness to integrate with the meaning of Sagittarius.

Remember, if your birthday is two digits (excepting master numbers 11 and 22), be sure to read the *root* digit or number first. For example, if your birthday is 29, read the 2 (2 + 9 + 11, 1 + 1 reduces to 2) birthday profile first and then read the special profile for 29. If your birthday is 14, read the 5 (1 + 4 = 5) birthday profile first and then read the special profile for 14, and so on. If a description in a "special" section contradicts information in the "root" digit (root number) analysis, the "special" interpretation applies more specifically to you.

The first planet in parentheses following your birthday number is *your Sun-Sign ruler*; the second planet (or Uranus/Saturn for number 8) is *your birthday number planetary equivalent*. Subsidiary planetary influences (if any) are bracketed.

Each birthday profile includes celebrities who share the same birthday.

YOUR BIRTHDAY PROFILE
December the 1st (Jupiter, Sun)
(and root digit for November 28, December 10 and 19):

A paragon of the affirmative spirit, you're always ready to shake the dust from your heels and blaze a new trail. With your inspiring leadership qualities, any project you head has an excellent chance for success. Your endless curiosity and innate optimism enable you to discover ways to survive any lean years when your job or career efforts have slowed down or been blocked. Your combination of enthusiasm, vitality, pride and self-assurance impresses people, and you win them over with your pleasing manner. Talkative, fond of good-humored polemics and of expressing yourself, you have the sort of personality that can turn opportunity into victory, and that's what you're happy to deliver if at all possible.

On the other hand, you may tend to scatter your energies. You must exercise as much patience and singular application to a course of action as possible if you want to attain your goals. Atypically, you don't like making a change unless it appeals to your sense of adventure, so you are likely to shy away from any that is foisted on you because of practical necessity (to which you may have to grudgingly acquiesce) or that in your view is merely capricious or disruptive (which you'll try to avoid).

A socially popular bon vivant, close associations are very important to you; you have a contagious loyalty toward friends and colleagues, and they are happy to reciprocate. Though you can seem breezy and informal, you're willing to work diligently to attain the freedom and independence that accompany material success and can rise to a position of prominence or public acclaim, particularly in the entertainment world. Even when things get sticky, you're protected by a certain amount of material luck. The lessons you learned early in life about discipline, responsibility, restrictions and patience provide firm support for your glowing confidence and gregarious charm, even if others consider you to be a devil-may-care maverick. You can be happy in a marriage or commitment, but you may have to test it several (if not many) times before you find the ideal relationship.

Bette Midler (actress), 1945

Richard Pryor (comedian), 1940

Woody Allen (actor, writer, director), 1935

Special to November 28 (Jupiter, Sun [Moon/Uranus/Saturn]):

In the creative realm of the literary or visual arts, the originality and drama that infuse your work can have considerable public impact and influence. Words, whether spoken or written, are second nature to you. On the job, in business or in a profession, you have a convincing way of expressing your thoughts, ideas and strategies in order to get your views across. Your enthusiasms can run the gamut, from the diverting to the profound, but you're more likely to be found crusading for a worthwhile cause that has inspired you. You're able to translate your own experiences into a sympathetic understanding of kindred souls that makes it easy for you to deal effectively with people in almost any situation. If some find you blunt, outspoken, remote or disinclined to dance diplomatically around sensitive topics, those descriptions of you are just euphemisms for your economical, direct, uncompromising style.

Strong-willed and affectionate, you're likely to indulge your free spirit and ignore conventions if they get in the way of being true to yourself. Typically restless, you aren't averse to an episodic life and will enjoy the fringe benefits. With your resourcefulness, you'll no doubt find a way to avoid nine-to-five workdays (unless of your own volition) in order to keep the money coming in. Although primarily absorbed in your own pursuits, home and family provide an anchor for your restless disposition.

Ed Harris (actor), 1950

Randy Newman (singer, songwriter), 1943

William Blake (poet, artist), 1757

Special to December 10 (Jupiter, Sun):

You are happiest when you have an agenda filled with activities that provide promising outlets for your various interests. You'll never be content playing second fiddle; one way or another, you prefer to run your own show. Even in a large organization, the best way to keep you motivated and enthusiastic is to allow you a certain amount of autonomy. In fact, given the opportunity, you'll thrive most productively in the foreground. Likely to be refreshingly candid, your ideas, comments, opinions and verbal arrows go straight to the mark. Whether or not you're too blunt and outspoken, at least people know exactly where they stand with you.

With your flair for informing people about the trends and events that help them to better understand the world they live in, writing, publishing, education, communications, the ministry or government are among the fields you can be drawn to and excel in. You might tend to overreach, but as long as you remain within the bounds of practical possibilities, your abundant ambition and vitality enable you to achieve your goals in life. As far as marriage is concerned, you can take it or leave it. The ties that bind and a well-ordered home life are not your big priorities. "He travels farthest who travels alone" could be your motto. You're very adaptable regarding your domestic surroundings.

Kenneth Branagh (actor), 1960

Chet Huntley (TV newscaster), 1911

Emily Dickinson (poet), 1830

Special to December 19 (Jupiter, Sun [Pluto]):

More temperamental and probing than the typical Sagittarian, you could also be more independent and authoritative—not to say contentious. You also have your slyly humorous, mischievous, lighter side and enjoy teasing people. You could fancy yourself quite a student of human nature, and you are often incisive in your observations and conclusions. Well suited to public life, you could turn your investigative philosophy into a successful career in the business or professional world. In the entertainment realm, your distinctive insights can win critical acclaim as well as public popularity. Your transformative vision can enhance the impact of any activity you're engaged in, deepening as well as enlarging the scope of either a routine job or a big project.

To call you resourceful would be an understatement. Penetratingly thorough in your work, strong-willed and indefatigable, you know how and where to flush out information or evidence that corroborates or strengthens your convictions about a subject or work method. If you encounter resistance, you might resort to not-too-subtle suggestions or questions to find out what you need to know in order to resolve an issue or to maintain a project's forward momentum. In any case, your style for achieving a goal is a shrewd combination of ambition and progressive, adroit tactics, made more appealing for coworker or public consumption by your faith, enthusiasm and charm. Marriage and/or a comfortable home life provide a welcoming haven from the tensions of your career activities.

Jennifer Beals (actress), 1963

Robert Urich (actor), 1946

Jean Genet (playwright), 1910

December the 2nd (Jupiter, Moon)
(and root digit for November 29 and December 20;
December 11 is a master number, see end of chapter):

Very sensitive to life's inequities and the layers of encrusted tradition that can stifle progress, you could be attracted early in life to a business or profession that is ripe for an invigorating breath of fresh air and sweeping improvement. However, if an exemplary tradition does contribute to community betterment and deserves respect, you will fight to maintain the standards it represents. A possible arbiter of public taste, you know how to capitalize on your under-standing of it; in fact, if you're in a prominent position, you might play a role in molding it. On the job, in business or in the creative milieu, you're ready with your views on what is worthwhile, high-brow, inferior or expendable. You might be more amused than annoyed by stuffed shirts with more money than taste. In any case, you're rarely at a loss for words, especially to express an opinion.

You are willing to make the frequent changes necessary to achieve success. Though you may meet with disappointments and frustrations, your reactions to opportunities can bring out the humor, affection and generosity in your nature. You function best in congenial surroundings and harmonious interac-tion associations, which you personally go a long way toward creating. Be careful, however, not to assume a knowledge you don't possess, for you could find yourself in a position foreign to your nature, or out of your depth, in your efforts to please or to substantiate your views.

You have a knack for doing well financially. Naturally cheerful and opti-mistic, your traits contribute greatly to the harmony and contentment in both your working and domestic surroundings. Being so sensitive to the atmos-phere around you, when it's depressed, your Sagittarian enthusiasm can lift the droopy spirits of your mate, family members or coworkers. With any luck at all, you are a candidate for a happy marriage, but you could find the ties that bind less easy to maintain if you're in the limelight.

Monica Seles (tennis player), 1973

Tracy Austin (tennis player), 1962

Maria Callas (singer), 1923

Special to November 29 (Jupiter, Moon [Pluto]):

You have strong feelings about your likes and dislikes and are ready to back them up with the results of your innate curiosity, firsthand experience or probing mind. With your powerful mix of magnetism and optimism, few can resist you or your inspirations, which are generally worthy of serious atten-tion. Although thoroughly familiar with the differences between right and wrong, you are rarely judgmental, possibly because you wouldn't want the impartially inquiring searchlight beamed on your own foibles. Public relations savvy, passion and tenacity are among your assets. On the other hand, estab-lishment values and mores are not your biggest enthusiasms.

You could be a bit of a mystery or opaque to coworkers or others around you or to the public. Whether in a routine job, a profession, the world of commerce or the creative arts, you might play several roles, playing each one with your own special brand of exuberance. No matter what the issue (or the controversy) is, you can come up with a quip or an insight that will have eluded everyone else. And you have a colorful (possibly off-color) way of backing up your opinions with a contagious enthusiasm that your hearers find hard to resist no matter which side they're on. When you're beating the drum for one of your provocative opinions, you're able to do it with a stylish arrogance. Marriage and/or home life are important, but you're apt to live this part of your existence according to your own rules.

Gary Shandling (comedian, actor), 1949

Jacques Chirac (French politician), 1932

Louisa May Alcott (novelist), 1832

Special to December 20 (Jupiter, Moon):

It's a good thing that you usually have the means to back up your sympathetic feelings and generosity; otherwise, you would have to deal with those wearisome financial aggravations that crop up when outgo exceeds income. If your earnings are the more conventional variety, your self-protective instincts, cheerful disposition and share of Sagittarian luck can help to keep adequate sums in your bank account. Basically, your experiences with money can run the gamut from plenty to little. For instance, you could pile up impressive reserves through your talent for handling funds or real estate. Whether your abilities are ordinary or extraordinary, your abundant self-confidence combined with your remarkable flair for getting along with people is alone a winning formula for success.

Very conscientious, with a nurturing instinct aimed at those less fortunate, you are well qualified for a job or a professional career in the social services. In the health-care field, you can investigate the healing arts, become a lab technician or dietitian or pursue hospital management. Other related areas include taking care of medical insurance matters, becoming affiliated with a medical journal, getting involved in medical training and so on. No matter what you do, however, your best bet is some sort of involvement with public needs, services, trends or tastes, which could include merchandising, publishing, writing, entertaining, advertising, public relations or restaurant management. Hazards to guard against, however, include excessive optimism, gambling tendencies, short-lived enthusiasms and expanding a project beyond practical guidelines.

Anita Baker (singer), 1957

Audrey Totter (actress), 1918

Sidney Hook (philosopher), 1902

December the 3rd (Jupiter, Venus)
(and root digit for November 30, December 12 and 21):

The possibilities for your birthday run the gamut from the pursuit of superficial activities that satisfy a penchant for freedom, exhilaration and pleasure to the exploration of psychological profundities or social philosophies that shed fresh light on human behavior. Sportsmanship, possibly actualized as an athlete, and a sense of fair play are among your admirable attributes. The more you increase in wisdom, skill and understanding, the more you will be able to fulfill your estimable potential, which might in some way, large or small, contribute to the enlightenment of your fellow man. If your highest principles come to the fore, your aspirations will know no boundaries, and you will be able to translate them into practical realities that benefit you as well as people in all walks of life.

Articulate and expressive, you can "charm the birds out of the trees" if you so desire. Among Sagittarius birthdays, yours is one of the most promising for happiness through marriage or other serious commitment. You think in terms of "us" and "we" regarding the ties that bind and are more than willing to meet your mate halfway (or more) when differences intrude on blissful togetherness. For some of you, though, "age does not wither, nor custom stale" your enthusiasm for a good time. With your penchant for adventure (including romantic dalliance), you might try your luck and cast around a bit before you settle down. You could be too eager or impulsive in your affections or emotional reactions. Once you team up with Mr. or Ms. Right, however, it should be smooth sailing on the love boat.

If your Sagittarius traits shine through and you are typically open-handed, upbeat and personable in a routine job at the beginning of your working life, you will project an aura of success and prosperity about you that can attract preferential treatment from the powers that be. If you rise to a management or executive position, you're likely to be a dynamic and visionary leader, popular with colleagues and deserving of the responsibilities and accolades your capabilities merit. You would be impatient with time- or energy-wasting methods (or people); your specialty is apt to be a talent for cost-cutting or other skills that increase efficiency and output. Your gregarious personality provides what it takes to be effective in the workplace.

Jean-Luc Godard (film director), 1930

Andy Williams (singer), 1930

Anna Freud (psychoanalyst), 1895

Special to November 30 (Jupiter, Venus):

Likely to be highly principled, with a well-developed civic and social conscience, you are qualified for government service, writing, publishing and the
arts in general. In the business world, you would be a unique combination of
aggressiveness (with the requisite energy to back it up) and enough compassion to blunt the forceful edge of your workplace or management style.
Although you might begin your work career in a lowly job, you are willing to
apply yourself, learn the tricks of the trade and gradually make your way up
to a position of responsibility and increased earnings in recognition of your
ripening abilities.

The sky's the limit for your creative potential, especially in the literary
field; you're capable of achieving whatever goal your inspiration and vision
can foresee within the range of practical possibilities. Popular, flexible and versatile, you might temporarily mark time with a position related to the
mainstream of your intentions if it seems like a sensible tactical strategy and
then get back on track when conditions again favor your advancement. In the
art world, whether as a gallery owner or manager, artist, publisher or instructor, the theme of social realism could motivate you more than a desire to
display or create decorative pictures. Apt to prefer powerful visual images that
depict societal issues such as the plight of the disadvantaged, your work can
convey a strong political message as well. A marriage, whether or not you contribute your share to its success, provides an anchor of support against life's
vicissitudes.

> Dick Clark (TV host), 1929
>
> Winston Churchill (statesman), 1874
>
> Mark Twain (Samuel Clemens) (author), 1835

Special to December 12 (Jupiter, Venus [Sun/Moon]):

Your Sagittarian independent—not to say hedonistic—streak could be your
calling card in the world of creativity. You have your own distinctive perspective on the values and mores of the social order, and it's more likely to be
provocative than compliant in the way you express your inspirations and public appeal. Articulate, talented and artistic, your tendency to ups and downs
can be stabilized by your dedication to a career, a cause or a mission. Very
expressive, your creations can be brilliant and imaginative, particularly in the
theater or the entertainment milieu. As a Sagittarian, you have a sharp mind
and are naturally active intellectually.

Whether your style is forceful, persuasive or enthralling, you can be influential in whatever line of work you choose to express your abilities. Your career could be not only one that brings impressive achievement, but also one that is notably pioneering and prolific. On the other hand, you enjoy, as Patrick Dennis's "Auntie Mame" put it, "feasting from the banquet of life." You are very pleasure-oriented, thrive on group escapades and are inclined to let the good times roll on forever when there seems to be an inexhaustible supply of revelry. If you don't rise to an appreciable level of success in a job, business or profession, it's probably owing more to your carousing proclivities and a lack of persistent application rather than your capabilities. Especially gregarious and outspoken, you're likely to have an opinion about almost anything and are willing to express it at the drop of hat. You might turn skittish around commitment-prone admirers and be too restless and fun-loving to stay in a marriage for keeps.

Dionne Warwick (singer), 1941

Frank Sinatra (singer), 1915

Edvard Munch (artist), 1863

Special to December 21 (Jupiter, Venus [Moon/Sun]):

Yours is likely to be a life of purpose as well as activity and discovery, which could continue well into your sunset years. With your roving spirit to lead you on, your range of interests is far and wide (whether literally or figuratively), with an admirable stick-to-itiveness for any job or project you undertake. Your extensive travel experiences, which could take you to the four corners of the globe, are a likely source of material for your creative inspirations, particularly in writing, publishing or education.

Well qualified for the world of sports or entertainment, your outgoing personality assures you public, social and romantic popularity. However, there's a serious streak behind your jovial sense of humor and spontaneous laughter, which shines through in your work, where you're more inclined to go by the rules than to follow the freewheeling instincts of the typical Sagittarian. Less scattering, more sensitive and more practical than your easy-going (but sometimes prickly) persona indicates, you are nicely balanced between your mental and physical capabilities. Not a typical homebody—more a roamer at heart—you could be a better friend than a marriage companion. In the latter case, you might keep one eye on the exit signs. You will have your share of romantic encounters, however.

Keifer Sutherland (actor), 1966

Chris Evert (tennis player), 1954

Jane Fonda (actress), 1937

December the 4th (Jupiter, Saturn)
(and root digit for December 13;
December 22 is a master number, see end of chapter):

Your birthday denotes that while you may be lacking the spirited, carefree bonhomie of the typical Sagittarian, you still have plenty of your fire sign's energy and physical vitality. The opportunities you meet serve to draw out your innate benevolence and courtesy, but the patience required to overcome the various challenges that impede your progress and hoped-for rewards for your efforts can blunt your optimistic outlook. You don't take naturally to concentration, but you can develop it instead of becoming fidgety and resentful because of necessary job, business or professional discipline. Fortunately, you do have a whimsical, quirky sense of humor that is your escape hatch when you feel moody or depressed, which can come in handy in the entertainment world.

You will do best by accepting a lifestyle that is not as fast moving as a Sagittarian might like. If you harbor resentment that time-consuming responsibilities are beneath you, it can affect your overall attitude and in turn have a depressing effect on your emotional life, job or career progress and earning power. Avoid a defeatist attitude. Don't count so much on luck; find satisfaction in the knowledge that your hard-won gains will be long-lasting. Capitalize on your excellent abilities for organizing and managing things.

There will be times when you will feel like chucking it all and heading for Patagonia or some other exotic locale, which isn't as far-fetched as it might sound. Likely to be well traveled if given half a chance, you can cover a lot of ground either geographically or intellectually—or both if you translate your experiences into creative work, especially in the literary field. Likely to be a wide-ranging reader, a philosopher at heart, you often ponder the larger issues of life, especially from the historical or cross-cultural point of view. One way for you to manage a happy marriage is to team up with a mate who shares your passion for excellence and who enjoys travel, sports and/or the life of the mind as much as you do.

Marisa Tomei (actress), 1964

Jeff Bridges (actor), 1949

Thomas Carlyle (essayist, historian), 1795

Special to December 13 (Jupiter, Saturn [Sun/Venus]):
Whether your have humble beginnings and learn mainly from the school of experience, or you rise from a privileged background and enjoy the benefits of a fine education, you are capable of becoming an acknowledged expert in whatever line of work or career you choose to follow. However, with your passion for freedom, you are likely to be happiest in a job, business or profession that allows you plenty of leeway to do things your own way and in your own time and with as little supervision as possible. You'll contrive to escape what is, to you, the unbearable dreariness of the everyday world. Nevertheless, if ordinary needs or themes predominate in your work, it can still have a progressive, visionary quality.

Your up-tempo spirits and contagious enthusiasms can make you popular socially and romantically. These attributes can also take you far with coworkers and professional colleagues, from whom you gain considerable respect for your fresh ideas, job expertise, high standards and independence. As broad-minded and firm as you are fervent in your beliefs, you have the power as a leader or mediator to bring people of opposing views or disparate backgrounds together for mutual benefit and enlightenment. You know how to iron out the rough spots that crop up in the workplace, government, the law, the ministry or the halls of academia. You are the outdoorsy type, strive to maintain physical fitness and have a self-deprecating sense of humor. With your productive approach to life, you are a good prospect for marriage and look forward to a devoted family life.

　　Christie Clark (actress), 1973

　　Dick Van Dyke (actor), 1925

　　Gustave Flaubert (novelist), 1821

December the 5th (Jupiter, Mars)
(and root digit for November 23 and December 14):
Your dominant theme is adventure (with a capital *A*). Life is an adventure; love is an adventure; a new job is an adventure; a new home is an adventure; a new car is an adventure—you name it, it's an adventure. The prospect of a new experience jump-starts your adrenaline into high gear. It would surprise no one if you went hang-gliding, climbed the Matterhorn, or joined the Nude, Coed, Bungee-Jumping Club. You like travel and the excitement it offers. In fact, some of you like it so much you don't mind embarking on a trip without a return ticket. Which is the way you see life, too. Getting there is half, if not all, the fun, like a journey on the Orient Express. And getting

back may be another stimulating adventure. You're willing to plunge into life without a safety net.

Your good humor is contagious and highly desirable on the job or in the business or professional world. If you lack financial resources, which is rare, you can usually acquire them with your enviable energy and exuberance. You like to "tell it like it is" with Sagittarian candor and can be a pioneering force in new movements in the arts, industrial design, literature, government, entertainment or education. Your inspirations, many of which are intended for practical public consumption, can win widespread popularity as well as enjoy lasting global impact.

Along with your admirable attributes, however, you can be too busy, outrun yourself and become nervous, high-strung and impatient. Then you live more on the surface and will fail to realize the depths you are missing. All your travel might not be for pleasure; you could do more of it for time-consuming business reasons, an intrusion you may resent. You generally dislike routine and detail. A willing worker, you prefer a job or career that you can have on your terms—which means varied, fast-moving and progressive; you might stifle a yawn or become rebellious when it isn't. Risk-taking lures you, and you can find it as exhilarating as a tightrope walk on a breezy day. However, when you dash ahead into a new venture without considering all the ramifications or consequences, you'll have about as much success as an unguided missile. You're a plausible candidate for marriage if and when you tone down your foot-loose-and-fancy-free lifestyle.

Walt Disney (film animator, producer), 1901

George Armstrong Custer (Civil War general), 1839

Martin Van Buren (8th U.S. president), 1782

Special to November 23 (Jupiter, Mars [Moon/Venus]):
Articulate and expressive, you do well where artistic talent or an appreciation of beauty, combined with a venturesome spirit, is an asset. Although you have plenty of energy and initiative, you won't rush into things or stir up the action if it means riding roughshod over the amenities and/or passing up a chance to ingratiate yourself with the people you're dealing or working with. You like to get on with projects, and with people, in an atmosphere of cooperation and congeniality. You would consider the fast track a hazard to human relations and would rather take time to make a favorable impression for yourself or a cause than win at any cost.

Given your engaging personality, companions (even on first meeting) will delight in discovering someone with whom they have an immediate and fun-loving rapport. You can capitalize on your skill and grasp of organizational work and ability to broaden your appeal in whatever job you're qualified for, be it in business, government or a profession. Ideologically flexible, with deep-seated understanding, you are expert at bringing together people of opposing views or clashing doctrines. However, be careful to practice what you preach. You can't always be on both sides of the fence convincingly. In any case, even when people don't agree with you or your methods, shifting loyalties or enthusiasms, you're nevertheless likely to earn their respect. Not at your best alone, you should find marriage and family life agreeable.

Harpo Marx (comedian), 1893

Boris Karloff (actor), 1887

Franklin Pierce (14th U.S. president), 1804

Special to December 14 (Jupiter, Mars [Sun/Saturn]):
The forces that work for you are inner faith and outer initiative, blended into an acceptance of responsibility, hard work and the need for patience in achieving your goals. Fair play and expertise rank high among your guiding principles. Your good sportsmanship and willingness to contend with the nitty-gritty realities can be inspirations to everybody associated with you in the workplace, in a profession or in the competitive business world. Although blessed with typical Sagittarius energy and enthusiasm, it's not your style to rush things.

Your yen for adventure is likely to be combined with some sort of serious purpose. When you're not fully in control of your estimable traits, your nervous intensity can make you a little reckless and/or indifferent to consequences. Then you could be tempted to expand a project or to overreach beyond practical guidelines, which you should always observe. You prefer to give full rein to your penchant for freedom and independence, but routine restraints will keep you ever mindful of bottom-line practicalities. If you have difficulty learning from experience, you're squandering a great inborn advantage. Marriage and home life appeal to you and can be anchors of support.

Patty Duke (actress), 1946

Lee Remick (actress), 1935

James Doolittle (Air Force general), 1896

December the 6th (Jupiter)
(and root digit for November 24 and December 15):
Outgoing, jovial, enthusiastic and gregarious are some of the descriptions of

your Sun-Sign, which your particular birthday personifies to the hilt. Yours is also one of the best entrepreneurial birthdays in the zodiac, as well as one of the luckiest. Since a healthy outlook is vital to success, you should have few problems. Born wise in that you naturally project optimism, you sense the unseen protection for those who live by fundamental faith in the rightness of things. When life becomes difficult, you probably respond with a "c'est la vie" shrug and look confidently ahead to the future in the belief that "this, too, shall pass."

It is natural for you to communicate your ingrained enthusiasm should you find your way into the arts, writing, publishing, music or the theater. Very creative, inspired and compulsively restless, you could succeed equally well if you aim strictly for commercial success or for a career in academia. But no matter what job or career you choose, you'll do best by exemplifying your commendable ideals in your work, in which case your own striving for excellence can rub off on fellow employees or professional colleagues and motivate them to do their best work, too.

Your mood is usually so "up" that when traveling, you probably won't complain if it rains, the food is awful or your hotel leaves much to be desired; you are more likely to find something interesting to see or do that offsets what to others would be a cause for complaint. A museum to you is as enjoyable on a rainy day as a sunny one. Of course, if you don't live by your positive Sagittarian traits, you can become mentally agitated, nervous, impudent and reckless, causing you to waste time venturing up meaningless alleys or fall prey to the gambling spirit carried to costly lengths. On the other hand, your life can be one of development and enrichment, with your work and accomplishment of each succeeding decade better than the last. However, it may take a few twists and turns of destiny before you settle into the line of work or profession best suited to your talents. You willingly accept domestic responsibilities and can find long-term happiness in love, marriage or a rewarding commitment.

Steven Wright (comedian), 1955

Dave Brubeck (musician), 1920

Ira Gershwin (lyricist), 1896

Special to November 24 (Jupiter [Moon/Saturn]):
Your innate optimism enables you to face challenges head on and is your defense against becoming discouraged or throwing in the towel. Not likely to walk away from a fight, you'll stand your ground in defense or support of an issue that you believe in. Sociable and gregarious, an expert at promotion, you

have abundant appeal to individuals or groups of people and can wield considerable public influence in the information age. In addition to your innate mental facility, you have an excellent marketing flair to bolster the success potential of a creative or business venture. Even your critics concede grudging admiration for your estimable skills.

You profit from association with learned people; although you may be tempted when frustrated, you should always avoid wasting time with trivialities. Literary efforts that reach a wide audience could be rewarding for you, especially if they convey some sort of insightful, uplifting or redemptive message. Your talents can also find a successful outlet in the theater, the ministry, science, music or the law. Nervous, mentally oriented, sometimes erratic, you have a strong sense of responsibility and are willing to work hard. Sensitive and receptive, you profit from choosing associates carefully. You could be inspired to follow in the footsteps of achievers whose devotion to their ideals has impressed you. You'll probably remain active into your sunset years. A successful marriage will be a welcome source of stability.

William F. Buckley, Jr. (TV journalist), 1925
Geraldine Fitzgerald (actress), 1914
Henri Toulouse Lautrec (artist), 1864

Special to December 15 (Jupiter [Sun/Mars]):
An enthusiastic go-getter in every sense of the term, not easily dissuaded once your mind is made up, you might learn more by observation and absorption than from formal education. Or if your academic training was in a specific line of work, your impetuosity can tempt you to forego your original intention and pursue a different career. Your pioneering spirit and confidence in your beliefs are reflected in your willingness to risk your own resources to back up your business or creative inspirations and decisions. Your organizational flair and *joie de vivre* benefit you as well as coworkers or others with whom you collaborate. You like the outdoors and look for freedom and variety in your occupational pursuits.

Able to throw out sparks that get people motivated, or stir up their amorous feelings, your energy and enthusiasm can carry over into your love and social life. Your colorful escapades, romantic and otherwise, can send many an eyebrow into the stratosphere. You're also no shrinking violet on the job, in the business world or in a profession; whether or not you begin at the bottom and/or serve an apprenticeship, you'll be ready sooner than later to call the shots and go your own way, as far out from under the supervision of others as possible. Your home and emotional life are important, but there might be some inner conflicts to resolve before your domestic objectives are attained. You may have to tie and untie the knot a time or two before you make a success of marriage or sustain a commitment.

Don Johnson (actor), 1949

J. Paul Getty (oil executive), 1892

Alexander G. Eiffel (structural engineer), 1832

December the 7th (Jupiter, Mercury)
(and root digit for November 25 and December 16):

Learning is your forte, but you're more apt to be a student of human nature than a devotee of book knowledge, a structured curriculum or statistics and graphs. Likely to be as thoughtful as you are adventurous or gregarious, there is generally a well-defined purpose, if not a clear plan, behind your aspirations or projects, such as contributing your time and energy to promoting a cause you believe in. You're a soft touch for charity. However, if the cause you most believe in happens to be your own success prospects, you have the brains that can turn the entrepreneurial urge into financial success; with your abundant energy, integrity and optimism, you will probably spend little time worrying about money. Despite your cavalier spending habits, you always seem to have enough put aside for a rainy day.

There's a possible hazard in that your Sagittarian impulse for wandering and variety can delay or prevent you from achieving your full potential. You're an articulate verbalizer but not always about matters of any great depth. Nevertheless, you can give the impression of being a cultivated individual, which is mainly what matters in selling yourself and attaining personal popularity or even a measure of prestige in your circle or the public domain. Meanwhile, beware of any flash-in-the-pan success; it may lack durability potential, become unraveled and force you to return to square one to begin your efforts anew.

Although with concentration and determination you could establish a niche in the business world, you would probably do better in a job or career that uses your mind more creatively, such as in the literary field, music, the law, alternative medicine, the ministry or any area where ideals and inspiration count for more than acceptance of cramped day-to-day routine. You can cover a lot of ground both geographically and romantically, meaning that you'll have to quell your restless spirit before you're ready to settle down to a marriage or other long-term relationship.

Ellen Burstyn (actress), 1932

Eli Wallach (actor), 1915

Willa Cather (novelist), 1876

Special to November 25 (Jupiter, Mercury [Moon/Mars]):

A thoughtful idealist, your theories and command of language, whether spoken or written, will have content as well as verve. A dreamer, futurist or inventor, you have a talent for scientific, mechanical, educational or architectural pursuits. If you indulge your intellectual curiosity about the wide variety of subjects that can claim your attention, your research could take you to the four corners of the globe. Knowledge and discoveries that have broad public implication and appeal, as well as humanitarian significance, can spark your interest and bring recognition in a profession or a creative vocation or avocation.

Life in the slow lane is anathema to you; when people around you don't keep up with your fast-track pace or find fault with you or your methods, your verbal arrows can be cutting. And with your optimistic exuberance, there's not much of a time lag between an impulse and your immediate action; beware of misjudging an opportunity that offers instantaneous surface appeal and then plunging ahead unmindful of possible hidden hazards. You're a stickler for justice, see chances everywhere to improve things and are eager to contribute your time, energy and expertise to a worthwhile cause. Likely to be unflappable under pressure, you can prevent a faltering or controversial situation from spinning out of control by keeping everyone involved focused on the essentials and their upside potential.

Joe DiMaggio (baseball player), 1914

Andrew Carnegie (industrialist), 1835

Gaetano Donizetti (composer), 1797

Special to December 16 (Jupiter, Mercury [Sun/Jupiter]):

Clever and intellectual, typically Sagittarian, you are fond of change, travel and amusement, and you don't mind an episodic agenda or a bit of uncertainty in your life. Your adventurous spirit keeps you moving forward one way or another. A world-class talker, upbeat, fast, eloquent and convincing, you know how to get your message across. Fortunately for your income prospects, your ideas, words and the way you choose to make your way in the world can be ringed with dollar signs. Between your pride in your work, your luck and your ambition, you're likely to go far and can win considerable recognition—not to mention fame and fortune.

Restless as a racehorse, you're likely to start early in life to integrate your various aptitudes and resources (ambition, skills, enthusiasm, vitality, schooling) into a working whole. You might even do your share of odd jobs to pay for training that opens the door to a career in government, the law, the business world or the entertainment field. Whether or not you know early on what line of work you want to pursue, you will keep one thing firmly in mind: a practical ideology that enables you to champion a cause and at the same time climb the rungs of the success ladder. You dislike interference, yet your gambling spirit could be tempted by unethical influences that cause you to risk your carefully established reputation. Always steer clear of people or situations that aren't strictly aboveboard.

Steven Bochco (TV producer), 1943

Sir Noel Coward (playwright, actor), 1899

Ludwig Van Beethoven (composer), 1770

December the 8th (Jupiter, Uranus/Saturn)
(and root digit for November 26 and December 17):

Your need to promote, publicize and expand your talents, credibility or ideals in a big way is most apt to succeed when you control or avoid impulsiveness and jumping to conclusions. Since you're one of the Sun-Signs less likely than others to be overtly materialistic, you can be the great spender and be financially irresponsible, but you're lucky in attracting money. You may need to discipline some typical Sagittarian inclinations, such as misguided enthusiasm, ill-advised gambles, careless scattering of efforts or reckless judgment and instead focus your energies and initiatives cautiously and intelligently on wisely chosen objectives and activities and thus avoid unnecessary delays or setbacks on the road to success. There will be enough of those to contend with anyway, so why hazard more?

With your natural zest and jauntiness and other birthday traits, you can win or waste, but the big picture will be what lures you, and you will benefit from concentrating on it. Success is your goal, in the most far-reaching manner possible; with that in mind, you should choose avenues of expression that allow for considerable freedom and amplification. Dead ends are anathema to your Sagittarian progressive spirit. You are creative and innovative, as well as practical, and have excellent organizational capabilities, all of which are valuable assets in any job, entrepreneurial venture or profession. In the business world, the perfect career for you would be as owner or top executive (but not a patron) of a Las Vegas gambling casino.

Your principles are important to you, and you will be most fulfilled in a line of work or activity that enables you to combine your large-scaled worldly ambition with an opportunity to ballyhoo for your visions, values and beliefs—preferably in a way that has public impact. You're particularly well qualified for a job or career in the upper echelons of the travel industry (making VIP transportation arrangements, organizing safaris and other group tours), or in education, politics, the law or the entertainment realm. Wherever you choose to demonstrate your estimable capabilities, you're likely to be a dynamic force. You'll attract your share of admirers, too, but you may need to exercise understanding and not rely on luck to sustain a marriage or other long-term relationship.

Kim Basinger (actress), 1953

James Galway (flutist), 1939

Sammy Davis, Jr. (singer, actor), 1925

Special to November 26 (Jupiter, Uranus/Saturn [Moon/Jupiter]): Likely to travel far and wide in the fulfillment of your Sagittarius aspirations, you typically leave your birthplace and establish a residence (or several in the course of events) at some distance from it. One beneficial outcome of your peripatetic wanderlust is that your first-hand experience with faraway lands and people contributes to the deepening of your humanitarian feelings and the broadening of your philosophical outlook on life. Large ideas appeal to you and are your springboard to research, organize and convey information or to pursue ventures of vast scope and/or historic interest as well as broad public appeal. Your ideal medium of expression is one that transcends language barriers as well as national borders and cultural boundaries, enabling you to play your role figuratively or literally as a citizen of the world.

Anything that challenges your great mental capacity is ideal for you; unless it is a means to an end, steer clear of work that is boring, narrow in scope or an obvious dead end. Instead, capitalize on your ingratiating personality, skills and flair for networking to help you get started on your way to achievement in a job, the business world, the creative realm or a profession. You have the ability to project a sense of fairness, sound judgment and impeccable taste that can garner the respect of your peers as well as popularity in the public domain.

Tina Turner (singer), 1938

Robert Goulet (singer, actor), 1933

Charles Schulz (cartoonist), 1922

Special to December 17 (Jupiter, Uranus/Saturn [Sun/Mercury]):
Whether you depend on your practical philosophy to negotiate life's adventures or live by your wits, you'll rarely be at a loss for words. Capable of being studious and thorough when a subject arouses your enthusiasm, your intellectual attainments, understanding of human foibles and ability to communicate your findings in the written or spoken word can become the basic components for your income-producing activities. Your articulate, expressive personality and affable attitude can pay off in a promising job, a business venture or a profession as long as the work reflects your values and goals.

Proud of your keen mind and confident in your opinions, you don't like a subordinate position or tedious grunt work that ignores and/or fails to utilize your progressive, insightful thought processes. You might view the average job as indentured servitude with measly fringe benefits (like just enough money to pay the rent). Despite your busy agenda, you're able to buckle down when the spirit moves you and win public popularity for a commendable creative achievement. However, the business or professional realm may be more congenial for your nervous, impatient temperament; the insecurities of work and income in the creative fields can be unsettling to you. Unless you come by it naturally, you may have to cultivate mental discipline in order to be a front-runner in the success sweepstakes.

William Safire (newspaper columnist), 1929

Arthur Fiedler (conductor), 1894

Ford Madox Ford (writer), 1873

December the 9th (Jupiter, Pluto)
(and root digit for November 27 and December 18):
Your thirst for adventure can be tinged with a taste for the exhilarating thrills of living on the edge of danger or a fiasco. Your investigative curiosity can tempt you to venture into situations where angels fear to tread. At the same time, you have plenty of personal integrity. With an eye for quality and a firm belief in your ideals and standards, you're willing to bypass a sure thing of dubious merit and instead go out on a limb of uncertainty in pursuit of a loftier goal more representative of your taste, courage and determination.

You can depend on a firm philosophy and your intense emotional strength to see you through difficulties when they occur, an experience that enables you to forge a meaningful design out of the episodic pattern of your life. You can't afford to indulge any Sagittarian tendencies to irresolution or scattering. If you willfully insist on complete freedom of action, remember that it may include "freedom" from domestic comforts, love and affection as well. In the interest of joyful togetherness, soft-pedal your protective veneer of independence that jeopardizes or can eliminate your chances for happiness in marriage or another long-term commitment you could otherwise look forward to.

More intense than the typical Sagittarian, you communicate better with mature, inquisitive minds—people who find it absorbing and informative to plumb the depths of human behavior or to probe the secrets of the universe as they impact on people's lives. In your career activities, your outgoing yet subtle charisma and intellectual sensuality can attract attention and success, particularly in the entertainment realm. However, unless you have the instinct for criticizing your own work with the objectivity that it merits, you may need to develop that faculty to ensure the consistent quality of your endeavors. In that way, your life can become the odyssey of achievement that you envision it to be.

John Malkovich (actor), 1953
Dame Judi Dench (actress), 1934
Kirk Douglas (actor), 1916

Special to November 27 (Jupiter, Pluto [Moon/Mercury]):
Your Sagittarian flair for getting along with people is filtered through your shrewd ability to see problems or irregularities that others miss (or prefer to sweep under the rug) and to arouse interest, if not always enthusiasm, for resolving them. You could play a pivotal role in transforming the operating procedures of a job, business or profession so effectively that you're likely to achieve employment security and a steady climb to recognition and prosperity. You could also be too upfront in your criticism of situations that need to be overhauled in order to meet professional or ethical standards or to reach earnings expectations; in the process, you could get a few noses out of joint when you beam the spotlight on touchy issues and the people responsible for them. At such times, you'll no doubt garner more (grudging) respect than personal popularity, but you will always attract your share of esteem in your area of expertise.

You are versatile and can work at two things at once, such as functioning day to day as an expert in an exacting career and at the same time teaching what you know to avid students. Your instinctive and analytical mental faculties are well integrated, enabling you to draw on your ample reservoir of knowledge, to think fast on your feet and to improvise convincingly and entertainingly if a situation calls for you to wing it. You won't settle for a subordinate position if you can help it, so once past the threshold of your youthful (and probably haphazard) career beginnings, you'll do all in your power to move ahead with enthusiasm and adaptability to attain your worldly ambitions. You're capable of sustaining a relationship; whether you marry early or late, it could easily be for keeps, freeing you to concentrate on your goals.

> Jimi Hendrix (guitar player), 1942
>
> David Merrick (stage producer), 1912
>
> James Agee (film critic, playwright, writer), 1909

Special to December 18 (Jupiter, Pluto [Sun/Uranus/Saturn]):

With your eye on the future and your reformative spirit, you can be an influential force in whatever job or profession you decide to stake your claim to fame. Your willingness to think big, to eliminate anything superfluous and to take a chance on risky large-scale ventures may be the reason the theater, film or other creative milieu is an attractive outlet for your abundant talents. Your radar is sharply attuned to other opportunities, enabling you to function productively in business, government service (especially in an investigative capacity) or the publishing world.

Your approach to life is relatively simple and straightforward. Although you may be ingratiating and amenable on the surface, your demeanor can mask your iron-bound determination to get your way and not settle for anything less than you feel your aspirations, expertise or conclusions deserve. Nor do you think it necessary to defend your ideas, competence or calm self-assurance. With your ability to wear down or outlast opposition or to resist others' proposals, you can turn the power of suggestion into an art form. With your restless spirit, you do best cultivating a talent and/or choosing a line of work that reins in the Sagittarius tendency to scatter and that compels you to concentrate.

> Brad Pitt (actor), 1963
>
> Steven Spielberg (film director, producer), 1947
>
> Betty Grable (actress), 1916

December the 11th (Jupiter, Neptune [Moon/Sun]) (master number):

As the valiant Sagittarius idealist, and despite discouraging evidence, you can believe in the impossible dream. You might even believe there's a pot of gold at the end of the rainbow. But beneath your calm, even folksy exterior, there lies a demanding conscience to settle for nothing less than the best from yourself or others as your life unfolds. If you're in a position of authority, you prefer high-quality subordinates to whom you can confidently delegate responsibility. Your Sagittarian urge to see far-off places may be sublimated into adventures of the mind and spirit that subsequently enable you to break the boundaries of new frontiers in science, government, education or the creative realm. Perhaps not greatly interested in material things, you're probably better fitted for the arts and professions than for the competitive struggles of the business world.

Whether you're a rhapsodic Utopian, a pragmatic dreamer or an authentic mystic, you will follow your guiding star with a sense of mission and apparent inevitability. In so doing, you may neglect a few of the essential details of living, and perhaps blame the personal confusion or disillusionment that can result on the world's lack of appreciation for your cherished ideals. The world may take a different view, however. In other words, you can expect problems if you coast along on your unrealistically optimistic assumptions and give life's nitty-gritty practicalities short shrift. Instead of an impractical, visionary drifter, you need to be a down-to-earth Don Quixote focused on turning an impossible dream into a workable reality.

Capable of great understanding, you are innately prophetic, psychic, receptive to paranormal phenomena. You know how to identify and orchestrate a multiplicity of views, information or facts to determine and then advance the major theme that emerges, enabling you to reconcile incongruities among the seemingly disparate threads that bind all life together. Your knack for tuning in to others' feelings can make you a popular favorite with your peers or the public. You can win plaudits from your contributions to the field of history, politics, literature or education. Your love life runs the gamut from romantic escapades and unconventional liaisons to enduring marital contentment.

Donna Mills (actress), 1942

Rita Moreno (actress), 1931

Aleksander Solzhenitsyn (writer), 1918

(Note: This master number implies a variable alternative response influenced by the strength or passivity of the planet Neptune in your horoscope. If you don't feel that you are responding to the distinctive vibratory power of 11, you are instead expressing the more conventional qualities of 2, which you should read.)

December the 22nd (Jupiter, Uranus [Saturn/Moon])
(master number):

Your birthday combines the extroverted will with the spirit of freedom and adventure, a potentially volatile combination; the dynamic electrical power of 22 can go to extremes in nervous, scattering Sagittarius, resulting in an inventiveness of limitless possibilities—positive as well as negative. You are ambitious, extremely independent and possibly a genius; what you will probably never be is a conformist. If you're in any way conventional, you'll choose the most convenient rules to live by and either ignore or flaunt the rest. In any case, you aren't inclined to accept what "authorities" say about much of anything and typically make up your own mind about important issues; you also tend to suddenly change your mind about an earlier too-hasty decision—to your own and others' considerable chagrin. That can be your problem: not setting any limits and/or not submitting your ideas, initiatives and ventures to the rigors of disciplined thinking before acting.

Expansion, spontaneity and originality are your *betes noires* unless carefully controlled. It would be prudent for you to express your more unorthodox ideas within the framework of an established enterprise, group practice or methodology. That way, they can be immediately tested as to their feasibility. Being fiery and enthusiastic, you like to see your ideas implemented *tout de suite*, but you might race ahead unaware of, or indifferent to, their ultimate implications. If you chafe at being held accountable when one of your brain children founders or produces an unsuccessful outcome, it could mean that it needed discipline instead of unfettered freedom.

The breadth of your vision and impersonality of viewpoint, coupled with individual integrity, can lead to notable success. When you're particularly effective in handling a situation on the job or in the business or professional world (especially in electronics or the media), it's probably owing to a remarkable flash of intuition fueled by your infectious enthusiasm. At such times, you could give the impression of being charged with power that can find no ordinary outlet. As a consequence of your broad range of interests, you seem to have an answer for any problem, which you may be ready to voice at the slightest provocation. Any occupation or career you follow should allow you considerable autonomy and be compatible with your highly individualistic theories and principles. Instant, dynamic, unorthodox attractions could be the dominant factor in your love life (or life of loves) as well as your marital (and divorce) prospects.

Diane Sawyer (broadcast journalist), 1945
Dame Peggy Ashcroft (actress), 1907
Andre Kostelanetz (orchestra conductor), 1901

(Note: This master number implies a variable alternative response influenced by the strength or passivity of the planet Uranus in your horoscope. If you don't think that you are responding to the distinctive vibratory power of 22, you are instead expressing the more conventional qualities of 4, which you should read.)

CAPRICORN

December 22–January 20

RULER: **SATURN** NUMBER: **4** ELEMENT: **EARTH**
SYMBOL: **THE MOUNTAIN GOAT**

Be cheerful; wipe thine eyes; Some falls are means the happier to arise.
—*Cymbeline,* Shakespeare

So you have experienced delays, mishaps, losses, reversals and other stumbling blocks, the kinds that discourage or defeat members of other Sun-Signs. While you may not feel grateful at the time, in your case these deterrents do serve a crucial, constructive purpose; barriers and setbacks are the means by which you rise in life. They are the spur to realizing your potential, and you couldn't function any other way. You *need* something to work against, unlike a Libran, who needs something to work *with*. You frequently find yourself coming face to face with blind alleys or obstacles in one form or another that loom up and signal the need for fundamental changes if your life if is to move ahead steadily, despite a detour or two (or more), in the general direction of success and fulfillment.

When exemplifying your basic inborn attributes, you gravitate toward life's challenges the way a baby reaches out for a teething ring—and for much the same reason; instinct tells you that you need to sink your teeth into something resistant, such as an impediment to your progress, if you're to overcome the bleak prospect of a dead-end future and instead fulfill your promising success potential.

Capricorn is the cardinal earth sign, the Mountain Goat is your symbol and Saturn is your planetary ruler. Frustrated unless you are satisfying your craving for respect through success, your insecurities about getting somewhere in life are thus virtues in disguise when you're not letting them become liabilities. Because of them, for instance, you will tolerate circumstances to which less ambition-oriented types would never give a minute of their time.

Where a proud Leo might feel degraded, an Aries frustrated or a Gemini bored, *you* will tolerate a menial position or an aimless job that has all the earmarks of failure in the eyes of others. But people don't know you—they're in for a little surprise! Your instinct works according to an inflexible formula: You're not tormented by failure, you're tormented by *thoughts* of failure! That's why, when you've taken on a lowly task (with an ulterior motive in mind), it's a small but significant step toward a better future as you go about realizing your cosmic birthright.

When a part of you, such as your body, is occupied in temporary servitude, you have an image, if nothing more than a rough outline, of what you must do. Perhaps you're working as a clerk in a store, thinking how nice it would be to own one, which is the way Virgo-born (Mars in Capricon) J. C. Penney started on the road to fame and fortune. You may even find yourself working as a maid, waitress or waiter, valet or cabdriver, but as you go about your tasks, you'll have in the back of your mind an ambitious plan—however sketchy—for future activation. In the meantime, the modest salary you receive is providing the means to attend law or design school (or whatever) at night. That is what is on your *mind*, while others are busy observing how lowly your job is and perhaps treating you accordingly. It's all to the good, however much circumstances force you to stifle your resentments at the time; your Capricorn instinct is drawing from and simultaneously strengthening your Sun-Sign's *power* base. The more dissatisfied or aggravated you become with your life situation, the more determined you are to break the shackles that bind you.

People are naive if they estimate you according to the position they find you in at any given time; they don't know the Mountain Goat. They'll know better if you wind up owning the business and the same types have to take orders from *you*. They will also learn that you, having been on both sides of the fence, have a flair for leadership, if little tolerance for compromise or a dismal rut. What all this can do to your personality, not too buoyant to start with, helps to fend off the more frivolous conceits of the social milieu, with which you have little patience anyway.

You have an absolute reverence for the material world and, with that as your frame of reference, a compelling need for building an imposing structure that you call a life. Meanwhile, you might forget that life is not a product but a *process*. You have interesting traits in common with Aries and Libra, with strong similarities to Leo and Taurus trailing not too far behind. As we go along on our journey through the zodiac, each sign gathers and absorbs the principles, more than the traits, of the preceding signs, which are then subliminally utilized. Leo, for instance, has a measure of Aries assertiveness now subdued and dignified by the sustaining glow of the Sun; Taurus stability is another auxiliary factor absorbed into the distinctive motivations of Leo.

As Capricorn is the tenth sign of the zodiac, just think of the useful array of principles available to you, and you're good at converting things to your own use. In addition to the Aries and Taurus advantages already mentioned, you have the mental facility of Gemini; the protective, nurturing tenacity of Cancer; the pride of Leo; the discrimination of Virgo; the equilibrium of Libra; the intensity of Scorpio; the adventurous spirit of Sagittarius; and (hopefully) all the virtues of Capricorn's particular characteristics (and again, hopefully, none of the negative traits of all the Sun-Signs preceding yours).

Like Aries, you want to be chief and are ever alert to any opportunities pregnant with the possibility of promoting your advancement in life. Unlike Aries, you are not easily discouraged or diverted from your quest. You're also not hampered by a short attention span. In fact, if positively oriented, discouragement, as previously noted, is grist for your mill. "Difficulties elicit talents," according to Horace, "talents that in more fortunate circumstances would be dormant."

This is why fiery Mars, the ruling planet of Aries, is exalted when posited in your sign. The impulsive, assertive energy of Mars is tempered and made to produce lasting results through the patience, industry and discipline of Saturn. For instance, Aquarian Ronald Reagan was born with Mars in Capricorn; his spectacular rise in life from impoverished beginnings is assuredly a shining example of an American success story and the intensified power of Mars when placed in your sign. In Libra, Saturn, *your* ruling planet, is exalted; the powerful crystallizing effect of Saturn is made more gracious and amenable, more influential for inducing lasting harmony and cooperation in relationships. Your affinity with Taurean attributes is based on your need for material security but not at the expense of power, position or respect. The rays of the Sun, ruling Leo, reach maximum potency at noon, when the day is brightest and consciousness is at its most perceptive and magisterial. However, in this natural house of Capricorn, the tenth in the zodiac, the essential meaning of the Sun (life-giving spirit and sustainment) can be distorted in the noon or Capricorn zone of the zodiac. The solar power can burn fiercely for all the wrong reasons.

The juxtaposition of Capricorn (the zenith), Leo (pride and love) and Saturn and the Sun is a powerful and complicated amalgam of cosmic implications. The energies and principles involved, mixed the wrong way, can result in misdirected pride and a chilly, narrow love for success and status. Instead of warmth and understanding for other human beings, you can seem like an automaton programmed for one function: *getting ahead*. Only the outgoing selfless warmth typical of the glowing Sun can counteract the coolness of Saturn. Genuine love and generous concern for others are ways for you to arouse a heartfelt response from those in your milieu, instead of the grudging respect (but little else) your achievements will likely elicit. When projecting your best self, you become the exceptional human being, worthy in reality, as well as symbolically, of your place in the Sun at the pinnacle of the zodiac.

Those personifying your traits comprise a wide range. You can combine endurance with glamour and powerful charisma, as witness the outstanding careers of Elvis Presley, Marlene Dietrich, Cary Grant and Loretta Young — all magnetic, talented Capricorns who built *solidly*. It's the only way The Mountain Goat can justify glamour and adventure over an ingrained preference for safety and stability.

Whatever your milieu, you are at heart the magistrate. You feel yourself to be a born practical leader, ordained to be at the top in your sphere of life. You like to have your leadership unquestionably acknowledged, and you can become impatient and defensive if your right to elevated status is questioned or doubted. As a positive Capricorn, you are confident of your worth, so you never feel the necessity to boast. The degree of your humility is the essential clue in assessing your achievement, whether you merely flaunt the trappings of success or are truly fulfilled. If the latter, you will rise to the heights without getting unduly excited about it.

If you find it necessary to broadcast your accomplishments and be pretentious about it, you can label yourself an insecure Capricorn. It doesn't always occur to you that authentic recognition might have to be earned according to ground rules other than yours. Your attitude toward others can be condescending or demeaning if their opinions differ from yours, be they about your status or any subject about which there can be a sharp division of opinion. The arrogance, pride and contempt you can summon for adversaries, competitors, underlings or those who have slighted you in some way are impressive. You then become the inscrutable strategist, the formidable foe. If of this latter persuasion, you have primitive means of boosting your own ego simply by implied or candid put-downs belittling others' worth or their achievements as compared to your own.

Although Capricorn is potentially the most civilized sign, it doesn't follow that your attitudes or values are always so carefully cultivated; you can adopt the "end justifies the means" attitude to rationalize questionable ambitions. Someone has said, "Our task is not to make life easier but to make men stronger." The evolved Capricorn doesn't expect or insist on the easy way. When the goal you envision is not easy to attain, you rise to the challenge; you face it, to make yourself stronger by mastering it, even if it makes your ascent more gradual and your victory comes after many delays or setbacks.

Fortunately, yours is the gut-plus-grit reaction of the spirit to experience, translated into persevering effort rather than impulsive action. Capricorn is the captain of industry—your own or in a larger societal context. Since a part of you has one eye on the next rung of the ladder, the idea of a gold watch at the end of long years of labor doesn't inspire you. You don't mind unexciting routine as long as it leads somewhere, preferably *up*. And if others want to see a face turn to stone, all they need do is downgrade your achievements, criticize your ability to manage or twit you about your ambitions. Your outlook is really a sensible one; not expecting too much from things generally, you can be more pleased than most when things go well. Others, especially fire- and air-sign types, with their more buoyant expectations, are more discouraged by disappointments.

Your capacity to endure frustration has its negative side. If you don't get the encouragement of some taste of success, you can fall under the influence of melancholia and an extreme outcome of Saturnian crystallization (inertia). In this instance, circumstances still force you to exercise your survival instinct, but your spirit, your will to overcome, is benumbed. When you deal negatively with misfortune, you accommodate yourself to it; then the cosmic purpose *behind* your saturnine capacity to *endure* a challenge and triumph over it is thus abandoned.

Saturn, the planet of time, rules the latter years of life; careers that require lengthy training, experience and dignity fit the Capricorn temperament. While euphoric attitudes may seem to work in youth, a maturity or old age ill-prepared for can be a nightmare. The homeless derelict is a vivid example, an image that no doubt haunts the inner recesses of the Capricorn soul, which is ever ready to rouse the specter of privation should you relax your drive for security. This gives you an almost neurotic compulsion to succeed, to escape the unspeakable horror—to you—of failure.

In case you've concluded that Saturn is spelled T-R-O-U-B-L-E, there is a brighter (well, not totally) side to the lord of karma: a festival to Saturn. In ancient times, there was a celebrated revel called (of all things) the Saturnalia. It was held in late December (during part of your Sun-Sign period), and remnants of it still linger in the carnivals of Italy and other Latin countries; an understanding of its nature will help you to fathom some basics of your Capricorn heritage.

The idea was to celebrate King Saturn (or Chronos) of mythology, who ruled during the Golden Age. The meaning of this for you—the combination of Saturn's discipline with the golden Sun at its brightest, radiating its maximum warmth at the zenith or Capricorn zone of the zodiac—is highly symbolic. The purpose of the Saturnalia was to pretend for its duration the equality of all. Accordingly, during the festival, class distinctions were abolished; all men had all things in common, as in the Golden Age. The spirit of this Saturnine frolic was remarkably democratic for the times; slaves and masters ate together, gifts were exchanged and civic functions ceased while it was in progress.

Saturn was venerated as the god of planting and husbandry; *your* traditional purpose through the centuries, as a Capricorn, has been to husband your resources. The conclusion of the festival—a return to structured reality, a cessation of its principle of unfettered freedom—suggests the ambivalence of Capricorn and the seed of Aquarius. You believe in equality and liberty, but instinct tells you that, in practice, it would be a mockery of the facts—at least at any stage of man's evolution known to us.

The Roman soldiers at Durostorum, year after year, gave the celebration their own sanguine touch. They chose by lot a handsome young specimen from among themselves, who was then clothed in royal attire to resemble Saturn. Attended by a sizable retinue of soldiers, he went about with full license to indulge his passions, no matter how base or shameful, which sounds like fun for any lusty lad, and, so far, not at all like Saturn. But there was this catch to his holiday of endless pleasures: At the end of thirty days he had to cut his own throat on the altar of the god he was impersonating.

It's not easy to circumvent the principle of Capricorn. And you seem to sense that by seeking shallow satisfactions, by not following the straight and narrow, you only invite embarrassment, like getting caught in a topless bar or at an X-rated movie. At heart, you're as human as the next one; you yearn secretly to taste those colorful episodes you read or hear about but not when anybody is looking; you have your reputation to consider (or protect). That's why certain videos come in plain brown wrappers. You want to participate as a personality, to show that you're not the prude or wet blanket others may think you are, but your soul isn't in it. You're inhibited at the deepest subconscious level, where Saturn has the final word. As appealing as prurient episodes may appear in fantasy, you conclude inwardly, perhaps somewhat wistfully, that they just aren't for you, that there's no future in promiscuous folly.

You know that there is no real respite, either, from the struggle for achievement and that to approach life in a superficial way, even for a time, is to build on sand. And if there's one sign that puts zero stock in flimsy satisfactions, it's yours. The Roman soldier sacrificing himself, after his round of pleasure, exemplifies in reverse the essential "pain now, pleasure later" credo of Capricorn. The ancient victim—doing it the other way around—was a *real* man, suffering a *real* death, in an *assumed* role, ironic and revealing for you. Preoccupation with frivolity and pleasure could only be an assumed role for the typical Capricorn, and it would no doubt fill you with unconscious forebodings and prompt a personal guilt trip. You would desecrate the purity of your subliminal motivation: the mystic union of the Sun and the Earth, a symbolic fertility rite. The climax of some of the Saturnalia included a real union of the sexes, making the permissiveness of today as new as ancient history. As usual, there's nothing new under the Sun, especially when it's in Capricorn; in fact, the untested new only makes you nervous and/or suspicious.

Emotionally, your life is *not* a festival. Though innately persevering and industrious, you will eventually realize that there is *more* to life once you begin to make some headway toward your goals. Then the inner you will want to attract, with your usual caution, a fitting partner with whom you can share the emotions and joys of impending or burgeoning success. Because you tend to structure this aspect of your life, too, it isn't simple to find just the right person. Few people view their emotional participation with another as their useful contribution toward providing the missing parts of someone else's overall picture—in this instance, *your* emotional needs.

Those who interest you will have to meet several important qualifications. However attractive they may be outwardly, their inner attitude toward life had better be serious and their approach to it well organized. If not, they should be willing to let you lend a guiding hand, the success of your efforts depending on your sensitivity and their receptivity; when discipline comes in the door, love can fly out the window. It requires a delicate balance and can only succeed through your patience and understanding. Unless your partner is also a Capricorn, you're the one with strict guidelines no matter how diplomatically disguised, so unless you would be happy with a doormat for a partner, you can expect some opposition and perhaps disappointments before you find someone willing to share emotional fulfillment on your terms.

You are capable of deep fidelity and will stick to a relationship long after it has served any purpose other than providing you with yet another challenge. Capricorn isn't in a hurry to throw in the towel, even when the heart is empty.

You aren't especially sentimental or romantic but more reserved and circumspect, preoccupied with your ideals of what an attachment should consist of. You have a framework for success and can be grumpy when all the pieces don't fit according to your prescribed formula. You like public acceptance of your accomplishments in all areas of life. You are most satisfied with a partner who exemplifies your ability to achieve your relationship goals with enviable success and who reflects your values.

If you are a negative Capricorn, you are likely to have few intimate relationships and can be cold and overbearing. Unlike the Aquarian, you could have a separate manner for people of different stations. You can be condescending or abusive to underlings, perhaps because you see an aspect of *self*, a haunting nemesis, that you instinctively fear or scorn. You can be dismissive of, or oblivious to, the plight of the disadvantaged and, instead, be the fawning flatterer of upper-crust successful people because they mirror what you want to be.

This may be a misapplication of your symbolic governing principle: *time*. Since "hard work" is your middle name, and some of you have to fight for every inch of gain, you don't feel like wasting time on people or projects of lesser importance that are thus automatically disqualified of any usefulness in your climb to success. Being reflective and introspective (the companions of *solitude*, which you don't mind), you tend to be socially impassive but prefer an upwardly mobile milieu. But you don't suffer fools gladly; the innocuous chit-chat of Gemini, for instance, can either bore you or make you nervous and prompt you to wonder why the airy Mercury-ruled individual doesn't switch channels and get on with something serious.

Due to the inherent coolness of Capricorn, you are more comfortable with Saturn's rays if you are a man. As a distaff Capricorn, you can be undemonstrative and aloof, but your partner will usually be spared any silly or gushy behavior. You are typically very loyal and devoted; your ambitions, unlike a distaff Ram, can be sublimated into a remarkable allegiance for your mate and his goals. (He may, in fact, have been your boss during your working days.) When he suffers a crisis, you become his bastion of strength against life's vicissitudes. The only way this could be altered is if his difficulties stem from a serious breach of the moral code. Then your Capricorn principles may be stronger than love, your embarrassed reaction corroding your ingrained sense of devotion.

Capricorn is the sign of the artist. This does not mean that all artists are born when the Sun is in your sign—very few are, in fact. It *does* mean that

Saturn strongly motivates artists, as it does you, instilling in both a drive to achieve and a willingness to endure hard knocks and suffer in the process. In their book *Born Under Saturn*, Rudolf and Margot Wittkower supply ample evidence. They trace the effect that artists had on society and the response of society to artists through nearly two thousand years. That artists are a race apart from the rest of mankind is the basic overall conclusion. The image, the distinguishing traits of the typical artist that are interchangeable with those of the typical Capricorn, is contemplative, brooding, industrious, persevering, solitary and creative.

During the Renaissance, the image was born of the artist as an alienated individual, and Capricorn similarly can be set apart to one degree or another from the mainstream but not because you are misanthropic. The effort required to achieve your purpose is so demanding in time and energy that you generally have little left over for social caprice. However, you generally make the most of your reticent charm in the intervals between periods of concentrated effort.

Renaissance artists, according to the Wittkowers, "recalled the glorious days of antiquity, when, in their view, artists were the favorites of Kings and enjoyed the veneration of the people." As a typical Capricorn, you desire no more than to attain such a democratic plateau and admiration for your accomplishments in your adjustment to the life experience. Theoretically, you're as at home in the White House as you are at McDonald's (but preferably one in Beverly Hills).

In the Wittkowers' book, artists are described as "laboring" and "toiling" in their effort to bring forth their creations, attributes typically associated with the Capricorn temperament. From the artist's viewpoint, it is beautiful to convey the truths of life through creative means. The struggle toward a goal, *your* obsession, no matter how vaguely defined, involves the same energies as bringing a work of art into existence and to fruition. In your case, the work of art is the life you structure for yourself. We drink in the result with pleasure, but the ultimate satisfaction is in the struggle, the victory over formidable odds. You can tell the difference between ivory towers and craggy mountain slopes. That mankind is capable of serving a higher purpose than self is the truth revealed by art through the sacrifice entailed, and it is the ultimate beauty of Capricorn. The same power that can transform paints, brushes and canvas into a revealing communicable experience is within *you*. Life to Capricorn can be likened to the canvas of a work-in-progress: What kind of picture are you painting? Is it the kind that will bring you the happiness and fulfillment you seek? As described in *Born Under Saturn*, the desire for prestige and recognition, so natural to Capricorn, was manifested in artists as early as the 6th century B.C.: ". . .during the archaic period, signatures of artists appear on statues and vases. The presence of such inscriptions—as pride in a successful achievement or as a wish to record the artist's name for posterity, we cannot doubt that these masters regarded a work of art as being distinct from other crafts." You can unconsciously regard your *life* as a work of art distinguished by your special values from all other lives. The analogy between artistic creativity and Capricorn principles is graphic. The motives that impel you to create a life according to your demanding specifications spring from the same source as those required to create a work of art; you may not be conscious of it, but it is at the core of your approach to life. You're not like Virgo, sorting out and evaluating matter. Instead, you go a step further, organizing it and putting it together for productive use; you have plans for it. Instead of an odyssey, as with Sagittarius, a painting, a symphony, an edifice or other enduring accomplishment is the appropriate metaphor for your life; whether or not it becomes consequential is up to you.

Art is ultimately one of mankind's most communicative relationships because it transcends time. We can have a relationship, for instance, with Rembrandt, though his flesh and blood ceased to exist centuries ago. His paintings aren't about the *subjects* that intrigued him; they reveal instead the state of a human soul: the artist's. What Rembrandt divined through his feelings is what is communicated to us. Because there is thus a subtle linkage of souls separated by centuries, the limitations of time are condensed and transcended. Saturn, the urge behind the artist's effort, the ruler of your sign, gives as well as takes away and contrives to purify experience to its ultimate essence. Whatever finally survives when a particular life is finished is Saturn's comment on that experience. The extent of your fulfillment links you ultimately, in whatever measure, with the long tradition of human achievements. Whether you are at the pinnacle of world power, a leader in your community, or simply a respected and substantial citizen, you have upheld your status and dignity or risen above your beginnings; either way you have exemplified the laudable attributes of your Sun-Sign.

Since your governing principle, Saturn, is the one that determines the success or failure of *all* lives, you can appreciate the pronounced effect it has on you as a Capricorn. Those born in other signs, with Saturn powerful in their individual horoscope, are similarly influenced, as are legendary artists. Henri Matisse, John Singer Sargent, Berthe Morisot, Gustave Dore, Maurice

Utrillo and Bartolome Estaban Murillo were Capricorn-born, and Paul Cézanne was born on the cusp of Capricorn-Aquarius. Saturn was the dominant motivating factor of their individualities. It is equally powerful, with a different emphasis, in the creative force of Pablo Picasso, for instance, born in Scorpio. Saturn in Taurus is powerfully placed opposite the Sun in his horoscope, providing the compelling impetus for him to accept nothing less than recognition and success.

Whenever Saturn contacts the Sun, the Moon or Mars (a counterprinciple) in *any* horoscope, it is a critical factor in the life process of that individual, and it has much effect—or can have *more* effect, though through different means—as though the individual were born with the Sun in Capricorn.

The practical idealism of Capricorn glows through many exponents— perhaps never more splendidly than in the dedicated lives of Albert Schweitzer, Martin Luther King, Jr., Pablo Casals and Benjamin Franklin. Albert Schweitzer was a doctor, scholar, musician and philosopher, yet he fulfilled the Capricorn ideal most significantly as a great humanitarian. Martin Luther King, Jr., in the all-too-brief life span granted him, exemplified the unceasing dedication of Capricorn to an ideal: the true freedom of his race. Major breakthroughs resulted from his hard-won victories in the cause of civil rights. Pablo Casals, one of the great musicians of history, had ideals far transcending the boundaries of his exalted profession. This is the kind of man who would undoubtedly rather make music than breathe—yet he could say that no music could justify to him the hunger and death of one child, a simple thought that reveals the quintessential spiritual beauty of Capricorn. Finally, Benjamin Franklin, a principal founding father of the United States, was a man who would have been an extraordinary individual at any time in history.

When you operate from your spiritual center, the rays of the winter Sun are warming. You reveal the promise that is the very essence of Saturn: that behind every effort, the solar power is waiting to break through to shed its rays over your accomplishments. Capricorn has virtues far removed from concepts like "time is money." Reactions to Saturn are usually of two kinds: acceptance or fear. Very few are turned on by Saturn, the Lord of Karma, mostly because they don't understand his purpose. The actual meaning is the most constructive in the zodiac but not from the conventional point of view. If you can imagine a guiding principle that weighs and balances everything with exquisite exactitude, through all eternity, then you can appreciate the meaning of Saturn in its broadest implication.

A characteristic of your sign is to become hardened to defeats.

Unfortunately, in the process, this can permeate your outlook *in toto* without your realizing it. Then people can be turned off by your cool, diffident demeanor, and you suffer innocently. Remembering that all energies have their positive and negative applications can be helpful to Capricorn. You can turn the Saturn principle of crystallization—of hardening—*around*; you can become hardened in your *refusal* to let the traits that contribute so much to your achievements spill over into your personal dealings with people. By avoiding that pitfall, your personality then has its rightful ring of purest crystal, refracting human warmth and love like a polished prism, through all the varied glints and colors of the solar spectrum. You can still be motivated by ambition without being stern or cynical, gaining benefits that make life happy as well as productive. After all, isn't that what your eternal striving is really all about?

CAPRICORN BIRTHDAYS

Judgment of whether or not a birthday is propitious can be considered from two points of view: complementary or challenging. From the standpoint of personal progress and fulfillment, your destiny may flow more comfortably if your birthday is, or reduces to, an *outer* root number such as 2, 4, 6, 8 or 22 (master number). For career drive and achievement, your progress may be enhanced if your birthday is, or reduces to, an *inner* root number such as 1, 3, 5, 7 or 9. The *inner* root numbers are less comfortable, more obstructive for you to contend with, but they are potentially very conducive to outstanding success. The 11 (master number) would be variable, but it generally would require more understanding and resourcefulness to integrate with the meaning of Capricorn.

Remember, if your birthday is two digits (excepting master numbers 11 and 22), be sure to read the root digit or number first. For example, if your birthday is 29, read the 2 (2 + 9 = 11, 1 + 1 reduces to 2) birthday profile first and then read the special profile for 29. If your birthday is 14, read the 5 (1 + 4 = 5) birthday profile first and then read the special profile for 14, and so on. If a description in a "special" section contradicts information in the "root" digit (root number) analysis, the "special" interpretation applies more specifically to you.

The first planet in parentheses following your birthday number is *your Sun-Sign ruler*; the second planet (or Uranus/Saturn for number 8) is *your birthday number planetary equivalent*. Subsidiary planetary influences (if any) are bracketed.

Each birthday profile includes celebrities who share the same birthday.

YOUR BIRTHDAY PROFILE
January the 1st (Saturn, Sun)
(and root digit for December 28, January 10 and 19):

It's possible—anything is possible—but it's extremely unlikely that you will settle for, much less be happy in, a subordinate position. You wear authority, individualism and success like a glove. And you like quality gloves. The job, professional or business opportunities you encounter are a possible launching pad for your attributes of ambition, efficiency and leadership. With your self-assured demeanor, you can be especially successful in business or government, but you have a flair for creative writing, too, with one special requirement: Your output in any of the arts would have to pay off in either a dependable or, preferably, a big way. Practical, versatile and resourceful, you could promote a career as a poet by working as an advertising copywriter.

Although you might hone your aptitudes with a good education, you're just as able to capitalize on natural intelligence as formal learning and could knock about a bit before settling into the productive groove of your work or career choice. Perhaps through sensing that you are destined for the top, you can become so absorbed in the pursuit of your aims that you can seem distant. Being so independent, given more to leading than to following, you can be willful and self-absorbed, with little thought or interest in people outside your immediate circle or range of interests; nevertheless, you can find love and happiness in marriage and family life. At your engaging and imposing best, you impress others with your powerful personality. At the least, you will have an air of self-containment and authority—no matter how modest your job or other attainments.

Wanting the recognition and rewards of your world, you just naturally gravitate toward activities with upscale potential. It's more than mere ambition with you—it's a deep belief, this right of yours to rise above the crowd. Few, if any, will question it. They wouldn't dare. If your organization can't immediately pay you what you're worth, you can be temporarily mollified by a title.

J. D. Salinger (novelist), 1919

Barry Goldwater (politician), 1909

Paul Revere (silversmith, American Revolutionary War hero), 1735

Special to December 28 (Saturn, Sun [Moon/Uranus/Saturn]):
Ambitious, persevering, well organized, with a flair for self-promotion, you're strongly motivated by the need for recognition and success—and if you have your way, you won't settle for less. Upward mobility is never far from your thoughts, which becomes your guiding principle for any of life's important decisions. Your flair for leadership can take various forms. You could become a company official or win your share of public popularity in the entertainment field; you could be a headhunter or trainer of corporate executives; or you could establish a niche for yourself as a communications consultant. And being ambidextrous, you could juggle several careers at once.

When you're sufficiently motivated, putting your nose to the grindstone is as natural as breathing. You don't mind a treadmill of hard work or numerous assignments and can add your own distinctive time- or money-saving touch to whatever job you choose to excel in, or to a business or profession that makes best use of your estimable capabilities. Status to you means community recognition and respect for your accomplishments, and especially freedom from supervision and financial worry. If for some reason you don't rise to the top, it won't be owing to a lack of abundant potential. Although tempted by unconventional unions, you'll probably enjoy your share of marital or other relationship togetherness.

Denzel Washington (actor), 1954
Dame Maggie Smith (actress), 1934
Woodrow Wilson (28th U.S. President), 1856

Special to January 10 (Saturn, Sun):
Typically levelheaded, you're likely to get your bearings early and to head toward a goal. There may be mistakes or detours along the way, but you seldom doubt your intentions to get somewhere in life that matters or to make your mark in a job or career. Whether it's a company title, the right address, professional prestige, lots of money or the starring role in a film, you'll gear your efforts to achieving your aims. While you might endeavor to acquire an education, your first work experiences could make greater demands on your attention and abilities than textbooks; the real test for you is in the real world.

If encouraged by early success, you're so sure of your right to recognition that your dour reaction to intermediate or subsequent rebuffs or setbacks might prompt a cloud of residual ambivalence or bitterness about your prospects and provoke unnecessary alienation with the powers-that-be. Nevertheless, your determination is strong enough for you to establish your own gratifying version of success, even if it isn't exactly what you had in mind. When you opt for a practical compromise to get ahead, it exemplifies your belief in the art of the possible. Excellent as a manager or executive, you are also gifted for the performing arts. It may take a try or two before you settle into a contented marriage or other enduring commitment.

George Foreman (boxer), 1949

Rod Stewart (singer), 1945

Gisele Mackenzie (singer), 1927

Special to January 19 (Saturn, Sun [Sun/Pluto]):

You are ambitious, subtle, determined, suspicious, skeptical and probative, a combination of attributes that, with any luck at all, will produce the topflight, possibly extraordinary recognition and/or success so dear to the heart of the typical Capricorn. A paragon of efficiency, leadership and persistence, you thrive in the business world, the creative milieu, in a government post or in some behind-the-scenes capacity. If getting ahead is about pushing all the right buttons, your aim is excellent, along with your instinct for covert strategies and the power of suggestion to attain your objectives.

Whether or not your gifts are special, you could be an example of someone with average talent plus enormous persistence who will triumph over a person with brilliant abilities but a lack of powerful drive. If you're a rare combination of both advantages, you can be a powerhouse in the achievement sweepstakes—in which case the sky's the limit. You usually seem to know exactly where you're going and why, and probably how to get there and how long it will take. And if anyone looks (and looks again) before leaping, it's you. If an opportunity or a proposal calls for investigation, you'll delve as deeply as necessary to unearth any possible hazards that could be lying in wait to jeopardize your intentions.

Dolly Parton (singer, actress), 1946

Paul Cezanne (artist), 1839

Robert E. Lee (Civil War general), 1807

January the 2nd (Saturn, Moon)

(and root digit for December 29 and January 20;

January 11 is a master number, see end of chapter):

The opportunities you encounter as you strive to achieve your goals will stimulate either your tenacious worship of the Bitch Goddess Success or will prompt you to cultivate a broader outlook toward prestige-related worldly objectives. If your initial forays into the world of work are frustrating, the experience may cause withdrawal, with you retreating to become the hub of your own universe—which can inhibit your future progress. It would be more constructive for you to become less self-absorbed in your outlook and to develop a broader, more extroverted attitude toward achieving your place in the scheme of things.

In your negative mode, you are vulnerable to the sins of omission in your personal life rather than the sins of commission. For instance, you are born with the nurturing instinct, but if you're overly ambitious, you'll be inclined to nurture your career prospects and strivings to the exclusion of other pertinent considerations, such as the protection and comfort of your family or others in your environment for whom you are responsible. You won't deliberately neglect them, but they might get more than occasional short shrift while you're busy elsewhere pursuing your ambitions. Paradoxically, you can be sensitive, and you do appreciate affection and a protective environment, but Saturn-ruled Capricorn usually has to earn or deserve what is desired.

In the creative or expressive vein, whether your slant is traditional or innovative, you're inclined to be very industrious and prolific. One of your greatest assets is your ability to deal with and appeal to the public because you know how to mix your various personality components and yet develop a recognizable style. This, as much as your skills and expertise, is one of the ways you manage to remain prominent once you achieve a certain status. In the arts or in the business or professional world, you can capitalize on your ability to distinguish between vacillating or constant public tastes and trends.

Cuba Gooding, Jr. (actor), 1968
Julius La Rosa (singer), 1930
Isaac Asimov (author), 1920

Special to December 29 (Saturn, Moon [Pluto]):
Rivals may call you ruthless, admirers might describe you as tough, but there would be little disagreement on one point: You could be the archetype of the self-made individual. If you come from literally humble beginnings, you can climb to the pinnacle of success and will probably make a few waves as you ascend ever upward, leaving stymied, bewildered or irked competitors in your wake. If your moneymaking exploits don't manage to acquire the prestige or celebrity of the Fords or Rockefellers in the pantheon of capitalists, you'll nevertheless develop a reputation for solid business acumen and/or for a prosperous wheeler-dealer style that gets results in your sphere of activity.

With your penchant for secrecy and behind-the-scenes strategies, only you know what you're up to when you go into action. You might announce or say one thing regarding your intentions, act in a misleading way in order to throw a rival or a higher-up off track and then do something entirely different when an issue intensifies and push comes to shove. A hazard to avoid: If your insecurities or self-protectiveness gets the upper hand, you could become aggressively pretentious. You need the love and affection that a relationship can provide, but whether it's marriage or an unconventional alliance, a part of you is likely to remain skeptical, uncommitted or isolated.

Ted Danson (actor), 1947

Jon Voight (actor), 1938

Mary Tyler Moore (actress), 1937

Special to January 20 (Saturn, Moon):
Since you place such store in physical and material comforts, it's all part of your destiny that you feel their lack until you make the concentrated effort to secure them for yourself. Discomfort is for you (perhaps more than the other Capricorn birthdays) the prod that pushes you to succeed. If you are a negative Capricorn and look at life through a glass darkly, you'll accommodate yourself to lacks but not without bewailing and/or resenting your fate. On the other hand, when you're positive in your outlook, your sense of gallows humor and black comedy comes to the fore and you meet adversity with a slice of wry wit or sardonic cleverness; the light touch for you relieves the heavy pressure of Saturn, your ruling planet.

With your adaptability in the pursuit of your goals, you're apt to go wherever opportunity beckons, indicating frequent changes of location. At your best, you're inclined to be friendlier and more sociable than is typical of Capricorn, which produces beneficial fringe benefits such as the support of others who speed up the achievement of your ambitions. You're likely to have a fortunate experience growing up that enables you to discover some important truths about life and, at the same time, discover your own identity, a turning point that could be the most important in your early development. Not partial to routine, the work you do should be versatile and interesting. You're a natural for a job or career in the entertainment realm or any business or profession that caters to public tastes or interests.

Edwin "Buzz" Aldrin (astronaut), 1930

Patricia Neal (actress), 1926

Federico Fellini (film director), 1920

January the 3rd (Saturn, Venus)
(and root digit for December 30 and January 12):

Initially more beguiled by the beauties that life offers than by visions of out-standing material or worldly success, you're less driven by unswerving ambition than the typical Capricorn. If you followed your Sun-Sign's more usual proclivities, you would head straight for the business world and start, if necessary, with an entry-level position, then begin your climb to the top and ultimately enjoy the benefits that accrue—even if you heart isn't in the work itself. Instead, with this birthday, you're apt to be attracted to a job or profession that you think will combine personal pleasure and creative expression with the effort necessary to achieve status and prosperity. On the way, there could be several twists and turns to negotiate before you arrive at the vocational challenge most likely to meet your preferred requirements. If for one practical reason or another you don't capitalize on a talent for the entertainment world or a career in the arts, your gift can instead become the pleasurable focus of your leisure-time pursuits. Meanwhile, despite an occasional glint of cynical charm, your abundant charisma attracts many admirers. Often very amusing, companionable and popular, you can be on choice if not numerous guest lists, thanks to your particularly wry, sardonic, sometimes self-deprecating brand of wit. If you don't circulate more often on the social or party circuit, it's probably because the demands of your work and the fact that you are frequently acquiring and/or improving your job skills have prior claim on your time.

You tend to have a steady emotional nature and to be rather self-suffi-cient. Unless a candidate for a relationship meets your sensible, dispassionate standards, you're not interested. Regardless of other compelling attractions, you're not the kind to marry a down-and-outer or a loser. In your view, what you see is what you get, and you like to see lots of future promise in a prospective partner before committing yourself to shared responsibilities. Love is all well and good, and you can be very loving, loyal and devoted, but you have to be sure that your mate, lover or other close associate shares your no-non-sense attitude about your version of the "three Rs": reliability . . . respect . . . and remuneration.

Mel Gibson (actor, director), 1956

Bobby Hull (hockey player), 1939

Victor Borge (pianist, comedian), 1909

Special to December 30 (Saturn, Venus):
You have excellent judgment and self-confidence and like to make the rules and set the standards that you and others are expected to conform to in the workplace. Very alert to openings that assure personal financial security and supervisory responsibilities, you are prone to making a career choice that includes the potential for the foregoing requirements. Relaxed camaraderie on the job is not your style; inclined to be pleasant and helpful but strictly business, your explicit dedication to your work takes precedence over any opportunities for familiarity or socializing with work colleagues, a diversion in which you may have little interest.

With your overall framework for success in life, you are happiest when all the pieces fit according to your formula. For example, you are most satisfied with a partner who exemplifies your ability to achieve your relationship goals and who reflects your no-nonsense outlook. You are capable of deep fidelity in a marriage or other enduring commitment, but being naturally reserved, you do not fall wildly in love after a five-minute acquaintance. It may take awhile for an admirer to woo and win you, but once one of Cupid's darts finds your heart and you declare your love, it is meant to be forever. Your emotions can be deep and intense, but unless you had lots of loving and touching in your family background, thereby establishing a pattern of openly expressing your affections, you tend to be rather undemonstrative.

Tiger Woods (pro golfer), 1975

Sandy Koufax (baseball player), 1935

Rudyard Kipling (author), 1865

Special to January 12 (Saturn, Venus [Sun/Moon]):
You are initially drawn during your formative years to the inviting attractions and pleasures that life offers; however, if interests of that nature don't turn into a meaningful career opportunity, you'll eventually compromise and pursue business, government or professional work that promises to pay practical dividends. It may not be as fulfilling or as much fun as the world of arts and letters, but your inborn pragmatism enables you to bite the bullet and endure the time-consuming effort needed to acquire a skill that guarantees good pay and future security. With your combination of ambition, imagination and brilliance, your innovative thinking can crystallize the diverse components of a business, research or creative technique into a uniquely cohesive, distinctively individualistic style or procedure.

You have your share of ups and downs, but like the Mountain Goat, impediments only intensify your determination to make your sure-footed way up the sloping terrain of obstacles to attain your goals. Less diffusive than other Sun-Signs with this birthday, you are willing to concentrate your efforts on one objective at a time until you win, and you don't spare yourself. At your best, you attain recognition and establish enduring standards in your field. Once your course is set, you're not likely to diverge much from it. You are also apt to be more sociable and versatile, on the job or off, than the typical Capricorn.

Kirstie Alley (actress), 1955

John Singer Sargent (artist), 1856

John Hancock (statesman), 1737

January the 4th (Saturn)
(and root digit for December 31 and January 13;
December 22 is a master number, see end of chapter):

Yours is the birthday of the patient builder, tireless and productive. You want safety and stability and recognition more than glamour or adventure. You know that the only place success comes before work is in the dictionary. With you, it's business before pleasure; you are willing to settle for deferred satisfactions. The statement, "When the going gets tough, the tough get going," could be your credo. You can take to the grind and pace of a demanding job or a business or professional career the way a duck takes to water. A patient, thorough student or researcher, you don't mind unexciting or even laborious routine; if necessary, you can exist on the minimum of amenities for however long it takes before your efforts and ironclad resolve pay off. When you're sufficiently motivated and determined, you are the victor in the battle to succeed; if at first you lose, you will try, try, again, having great endurance in the face of adversity. You'll probably have a hard struggle at some point, usually in youth, or may be slowed down by a physical indisposition. A memorable turning point in your life will occur around the age of 29.

Making headway won't be easy, but don't let it depress you; if you adopt a negative attitude, you can become discouraged by obstacles and conditions outside yourself over which you have little or no control. What you can control is your inner response to hampering circumstances. Avoid overdoing your sense of responsibility or finding an escape in drudgery, which will only further aggravate inner resentment. You may take on extra work or duties and then complain about them or be too tolerant of frustration. Then you're allowing Saturn, your ruler, to limit you, a plight that can worsen into a defeatist attitude that feeds on itself.

Let your willingness to work hard lead to something through the advantages of education and a trained mind or a very special gift. You profit from deliberately cultivating a more buoyant outlook and more self-esteem. Honest and dependable, you are well suited for a managerial or custodial position in business or government, or anywhere that your deep-seated sense of responsibility is an asset. Since home and family are important to you, marriage is likely to be for keeps. Just remember to balance your life with lighter interests, or your earnings can go for doctor bills.

Matt Frewer (actor), 1958

Dyan Cannon (actress), 1937

Sir Isaac Newton (scientist), 1642

Special to December 31 (Saturn [Venus/Sun]):
A challenging goal is to you the spur to increased initiative. You are very insightful and opportunistic, especially regarding the advantage of congenial networking to promote a meritorious crusade aimed at widespread public improvement and/or impact. Your charm and magnetism are potent assets; moreover, you know when and how to employ them to capitalize on your persistence and persuasive powers to wheedle support from people to achieve an objective. You're very adaptable to the career choice that seems to promise the most opportunity. Whether or not you come from advantageous beginnings, you hobnob easily with people from good financial or social backgrounds.

Well qualified for a responsible position in government, a profession or the world of commerce, the bright future you envision for yourself probably won't take long to arrive. Even if you have second-class talent, you have first-class ambition, which is all you need to get to the top. In your case, good educational preparation will equip you to rise swiftly through the entry-level ranks into the upper echelons of the career realm. If for some reason it takes longer to achieve liftoff on your career trajectory, your progress should be pretty well assured once you get airborne. You like to travel, yet do not like to live alone, a conflict that may be difficult to reconcile. It may take a try or two before you settle into a marriage or other enduring commitment.

Donna Summer (singer), 1948

Sir Anthony Hopkins (actor), 1937

Henri Matisse (artist), 1869

Special to January 13 (Saturn [Sun/Venus]):

Earthbound ambition more than a belief in luck urges you onward toward achieving your goals. The wry comment, "Success is simply a matter of luck . . . ask any failure," could be your credo. In your view, luck is opportunity and preparation coming together in propitious conjunction. If you respond with measured enthusiasm to events that send others into paroxysms of joy, it's because you know it's better to appear underwhelmed than foolish. You also know very well how the world turns: a peacock today, a feather duster tomorrow. Not that you're a cynic; you just don't have any fancy illusions.

In your efforts to succeed, don't be afraid to fail. If you don't fail, it means you haven't tried. If you encounter uphill struggles at the start of your career journey, don't despair; your talents are eminently marketable because you're willing to go an extra mile if a job or assignment calls for it. You are also adjustable and willing to make job or professional changes as time goes on if that is what it takes to keep your career viable, even in a somewhat different, less ego-satisfying direction. You have a feeling for the public pulse and know how to appeal to people en masse via the spoken or written word, music or some other milieu where your low-key charisma and leadership potential contribute to your success. Don't forget to make time for fun and relaxation, which provide a welcome respite from your admirable strivings to get to the top.

Julia Louis-Dreyfus (actress), 1961

Gwen Verdon (dancer, actress), 1925

Robert Stack (actor), 1919

January the 5th (Saturn, Mars)
(and root digit for December 23 and January 14):

Born to be restless and discontented in a subordinate position, you're out for the main chance. Impatient to get the ball rolling, you're apt early in life to begin your upward climb by seeking a job or position of responsibility. In that way, you quickly establish your personal credibility and willingness to work. You have a healthy appetite for power and independence. With your well-marinated mix of ambition, energy, drive and opportunity, topped off with a dash of street smarts, you're practically a shoo-in for worldly success whether in the creative realm, a business or a professional capacity. When you want something, you don't take kindly to the word no.

As life unfolds, you know how to capitalize on opportunities that stoke the fires of your ambition. Versatile and capable, you're usually fortunate in whatever you set out to do. Being achievement oriented, if a change looks as though it will advance your cause, you are willing to begin a fresh experience, even to the extent of learning a new skill. At the same time, at heart a cautious Capricorn, you don't rock the boat impulsively. You prefer well-planned transitions and always consider all the possible ramifications. In this vein, in fact, be wary of a possible hazard to be too obliging or accommodating, which can blunt or nullify your own ambitious forcefulness.

Getting involved in the power network and where the money is, lots of it, inspires you; you become very enthusiastic about affiliations that lead to bigger and better things. When you're on a roll, the pace of your activities could exhaust a less determined individual. In a contest for a prize you covet, you can become a relentless competitor—or an implacable enemy if sufficiently provoked, a defense mechanism of your aggressively ambitious spirit. You'll travel more than the typical Capricorn, but it will probably have a business purpose.

Diane Keaton (actress), 1946

Juan Carlos de borbon (king of Spain), 1938

Robert Duvall (actor, director), 1931

Special to December 23 (Saturn, Mars [Moon/Venus]):

Despite your charismatic persona that makes the task easier, the objectives you're destined to gain are likely to be forged out of hard work and persistence. Ambitious for recognition and/or leadership, you can be charming and diplomatic, impersonal and exacting, all at the same time, as you pursue a goal that enables you to commercialize your abilities. If your career propels you into the limelight, especially in the entertainment realm, you can be a captivating mixture of peasant passion and aristocratic restraint. In any case, you have a distinctive flair for tuning in to public tastes and trends and then capitalizing on this ability in a big way.

With your engaging, outgoing manner, you are excellent dealing with people in a social or official capacity, an attribute that helps you to advance more rapidly in a job, business or a profession. You can surprise people with your sly sense of humor, which can range from double-edged or mordant to the "down-home" variety. However, no matter how entertaining life's waifs, ne'er-do-wells or other inconsequential types may be at the moment, you won't be attracted to them socially (beyond being pleasant in impromptu encounters) and certainly won't consider them friends. You're drawn mainly to people who are responsible and dependable, perhaps other coworkers or professional colleagues who convey the impression that either they've arrived or are going somewhere in life. You don't mind talking shop with congenial companions. As noted, such types could also be a source of career advancement for you.

Susan Lucci (actress), 1948

J. Arthur Rank (film magnate), 1888

Jean Francois Champollion (Egyptologist), 1790

Special to January 14 (Saturn, Mars [Sun/Saturn]):
In your determination to make a name for yourself, your rise in life could be touched by occasional notoriety or controversy, as well as recognition or accolades, for your talent and/or accomplishments. The process of establishing your individuality could become a lifelong, consuming proclivity. You're not the type to back away from a rough- or raw-edged strategy that conflicts with establishment norms if that's what it takes to achieve an ego- or soul-satisfying goal. One thing is certain: Once you decide on a course of action that can turn you into a notable—and possibly colorful—public figure, wild horses would be unable to budge you from your intentions or self-assured attitude.

If there are challenging or discouraging setbacks during your early efforts to succeed, it would be to your advantage to overcome them so that you can eventually forge your way into the winner's circle. And unlike others who rise only to fall, whatever you achieve can be solid and dependable, worthy of enduring recognition or respect (even if it's grudging) and probably amply rewarded. All of which seems like a fair enough tradeoff in exchange for the seemingly fast and easy results that others sometimes enjoy. If it takes you awhile to learn from the school of experience, remember that it is more expensive in time, energy and results than other training opportunities. You have great inner power for constructive self-development if you concentrate and overcome your restlessness.

Faye Dunaway (actress), 1941

Andy Rooney (TV commentator), 1920

Albert Schweitzer (humanitarian), 1875

January the 6th (Saturn, Jupiter)
(and root digit for December 24 and January 15):
Although as a Capricorn you don't exactly throw caution to the winds, you're more apt than other members of your Sun-Sign to believe that the quickest way to succeed is to gamble on yourself—to decide what you want and then

go after it with everything you've got. In your haste, you could pay scant heed to what the consequences might be. It's not prudent to go out on a limb and worry about tomorrow tomorrow. If your childhood background was austere, your entrepreneurial instincts may have surfaced as a youngster by making money mowing neighbors' lawns or delivering newspapers and later on by working your way through college if that was the only way you could get an education. You were born with the Horatio Alger spirit and, with any luck at all, are destined to rise above the crowd.

You have powerful enthusiasms and equally strong aversions. For example, a Capricorn is typically willing to work hard to get ahead; when you are sufficiently motivated, you can put in eighty hours a week and insist that you relish it. On the other hand, you would rather take a chance and risk failure than waste time or an opportunity, and generally you wouldn't find it thrilling to settle for a pleasant job with minimum risks and a safe pension at the end of long years of labor.

Not noted for effusions of sentiment or romance, you are nevertheless attracted to marriage and family or some sort of comforting home life. However, if you go overboard with joy as you climb the success ladder, it could cause a conflict in that you might not have much time, thought or energy left over for love and/or domesticity. You can be very attuned to club or group membership and could become a guiding influence. However, when you become involved—whether it's a professional organization, a social or political club or a cultural association—you prefer it to be prestigious or in some way distinctive or exclusive. The friends you deem worthy of cultivating, in a sense prescreened, may also stem from such affiliations. The personification of middle- or upper-class virtues, you like to be a property owner. Very few things, in your view, take precedence over protecting, venerating and/or perpetuating the established order. Whatever your area of expertise or success, you'll be an expert at selling or popularizing it.

Loretta Young (actress), 1913

Danny Thomas (entertainer, TV producer), 1912

Carl Sandburg (poet, biographer), 1878

Special to December 24 (Saturn, Jupiter [Moon/Saturn]):
Determinedly ambitious and strongly independent, you have a powerful sense of your own dignity and/or self-importance. A paragon of self-reliance, partly owing to childhood conditions that prompted you to develop your core of inner strength, early experience would teach you not to expect anything on a

silver platter. Even when circumstances are one step above wretched, however, your belief in yourself doesn't falter; you manage to dig in and eventually come out ready for the next challenge. Once in a blue moon, you may experience a melancholy rather than a hopeful victory, but you're essentially a survivor and are likely to keep going well into your sunset years—or you should if you want your life to be a work-in-progress to the final curtain.

Since Saturn rules age, your rise or your maturity (or both) may be slow but sure, with your career promise or personal life beginning to show signs of fulfillment in your mid- to late twenties or early thirties. On the other hand, if your beginnings were truly humble, you might not bother with a lot of formal education and would get started earlier, probably in your teens, on your climb up the rungs of the success ladder. Thanks to your willingness to accept small beginnings in a job or career that promises big rewards, your achievement potential is exceptionally promising. Artistically talented, you are nevertheless more apt to be found in the business world or an administrative post.

Ava Gardner (actress), 1922

Cab Calloway (band leader), 1907

Howard Hughes (aviator, entrepreneur), 1905

Special to January 15 (Saturn, Jupiter [Sun/Mars]):
Your life can be an adventurous combination of pluck and luck. Your favorite speed is fast-forward, going full throttle. You have plenty of what used to be called gumption, the kind of drive, courage and initiative that can get you on the cover of *Time* or be worthy of a profile in *The New Yorker*. When your ambition isn't in overdrive, it's on autopilot. With opportunity usually hovering around you, you never have to worry too much about a job. You know how to make the most of your abilities and, somehow, something always comes through in time.

You are right at home with the movers and shakers of the world. The tempo of your job, business or professional activities is likely to be high voltage, with generously rewarding results. You know how and when to give your sagging career prospects a power boost. If your audacity and/or work thrusts you into the public domain, you can be credited with breakthroughs that shatter stale, hidebound tradition in order to make your job, business methods or a professional activity more relevant. On the other hand, detractors will consider you a maverick or a troublemaker. Whether for good or ill, you're out to shake up the status quo and leave your imprint on the changed conditions in the process. The risks you take as you go about achieving your goal could inspire wonder, admiration or trepidation. One thing you'll probably never be is dull or boring.

Martin Luther King, Jr. (civil rights leader), 1929

Lloyd Bridges (actor), 1913

Aristotle Onassis (shipping magnate), 1906

January the 7th (Saturn, Mercury)
(and root digit for December 25 and January 16):

Very observant about the practical value of anything that comes within the range of your experience, you tend to be utterly realistic in your appraisals—whether of people, a job opportunity, an item on sale or conditions in general. You are also very adaptable and have a talent for making the most of whatever you have to deal with in life. Your exceptional mental facility is the good news, and it is also the bad news if you think too much or too long about an important issue and then hesitate about making a crucial decision that can spell the difference between success and failure. You could also just coast along on your nimble wits and practical worldliness and realize only a small percentage of your estimable potential.

At your best, you're likely to have a superior intellect and can substitute clever resourcefulness for the traditional methods of making it into the big leagues of worldly accomplishment. For example, if you enter the fray of career competition with a good education, it will no doubt make it easier for you to get ahead of the crowd. If you are a school dropout, however, you will capitalize on your ambitious drive and inventive mind instead of a college degree and will start your climb to fame and fortune in your late teens or just out of them. It's wise to remember, though, that while many self-made millionaires don't have a high school diploma, it's not a recommended route to the top.

With your penetrating insight, you are a natural judge of character. You can be exacting and cool to those you consider beneath your intellectual level. Impatient with guessing games, you like people to be upfront and to stick to the basics. Not inclined to be loquacious, when you do talk, it's usually because you have something worthwhile to say. If you're not especially imaginative, you do have a rather dry, sardonic wit. Single-minded, realistic and consistent, you don't mind working alone. You're very conscientious but can be unemotional, unflappable and affectionately reserved . . . and, at the same time, popular. Much more serious than playful or lighthearted about romance or amusements, you can fall in love for keeps or, once discouraged, can decide that the whole business is not for you.

Nicolas Cage (actor), 1964

Katie Couric (TV talk show cohost), 1957

Millard Fillmore (13th U.S. president), 1800

Special to December 25 (Saturn, Mercury [Moon/Mars]):
With your tough-minded ambition, you're willing and able to fight your way up to a position of power, independence and authority. You won't be content for long on the lower rungs of the success ladder. A formidable combination of knowledge and mental vigor (hopefully in that order) is the keystone of the foundation upon which you build your success structure. The more you know, the more you are fortified with mind strength to compete in the rough-and-tumble workaday world. You're on the mental fast track and can commercialize any of your distinctive ideas and abilities. Beneath a charming facade, you can be as steely and determined as necessary to achieve your goals.

In the entertainment field, you're able to gauge and interpret public trends and tastes. If there's a problem to be resolved, you can get to the truth of the matter with blunt, unsentimental brilliance. Thanks to your keen observation, sharp insights and instantaneous mental agility, your entrepreneurial instincts are second to none. Your flair for leadership can find an impressive outlet in a key government post, the top echelons of the business world or a highly competitive profession. Your results-oriented thought processes may have benefited from constructive exposure to the requirements for success evident in your family background as you grew up. As for marriage and home life, you'll probably keep trying until you get it right.

Sissy Spacek (actress), 1949

Rod Serling (writer, TV series host), 1924

Clara Barton (founder of American Red Cross), 1821

Special to January 16 (Saturn, Mercury [Moon/Jupiter]):
You're dedicated when it comes to business, which you know how to mix with pleasure to turn your optimistic, enterprising spirit into a success-driven asset. You will benefit by keeping mentally stimulated with increasingly difficult tests of your skills, resilience and perseverance whether you pursue a career in the performing arts, the business world or a profession. If you typically relish any learning challenge that can carry you further along toward achievement of your worldly goals, you will go far beyond your beginnings whether they were poor or privileged; however, if you're not sufficiently motivated, you are

capable of coasting along on your inborn talents and enjoying life at whatever level you settle for . . . with no particular goal in mind.

As long as they are progressive, you will profit from maintaining and capitalizing on the courage of your convictions. It would take a lot of criticism and/or discouragement for you to lose heart. You think a lot, but even in your most solemn moods are not inclined to think failure. You have a lot of ambitious inner power and natural enthusiasm that enable you to stand up to a difficulty that would cause a less determined individual to wilt and/or throw in the towel. You're the type to enjoy your successes and to accept your delays or setbacks with dignity, letting them inspire and guide you on to fresh achievement. Your ample charisma can attract many admirers, but you may have to work at it to match your career success with an enduring marriage or other long-term commitment.

Marilyn Horne (mezzo soprano), 1934

Dizzy Dean (baseball player), 1928

Ethel Merman (singer, actress), 1909

January the 8th (Saturn, Uranus/Saturn)
(and root digit for December 26 and January 17):

You're destined to reach the pinnacle of success and to travel in style—but whether it's in a limousine rented for a spiffy occasion or your very own luxurious stretch model will depend on how you play your cards. To say that your talent, drive, energy and distinctive persona can make you rich and famous wouldn't be a tough call. Well . . . maybe rich . . . or maybe famous, if not both. But you would prefer the whole package and will aim for it, the higher the better. Regardless, you should be economically independent or on your way to financial security by middle age, if not sooner.

Anything that involves promotion, publicity, efficient administration—activities that can also turn magically into dollars—will attract your interest. Happiest in the corridors of power, you have zero enthusiasm for anything downscale; you'd rather mix with the upper masses. Whether in the creative realm (especially writing), the business world or a profession, you're willing to work hard to put over your original, farsighted objectives and, just as important, to make them pay. Although very practical and down to earth, you can harbor humanitarian feelings that prompt deeds you might keep hidden from view. Perhaps because you're so ambitious for prominence and success, you might think people will lose faith in your dynamic and hard-edged drawing power if they were aware of your more selfless proclivities.

Any field you engage in will, in a sense, be a business, because you will never stop short of success if you can help it or let anything interfere with your subliminal drive for material freedom and power. You not only can make plans like Aries, you can carry them out with the determination of Taurus and the vision of Aquarius. With your blend of ambition and broad-based accountability, a government post or prominence in a cultural or academic field is to you a public trust; great wealth and/or power entails great commensurate responsibilities. As a distaff Capricorn with this birthday, you prefer to marry a successful man (possibly the boss) or you yourself will aspire to an important job or career.

David Bowie (actor, musician), 1947

Stephen Hawking (author), 1942

Elvis Presley (singer, actor), 1935

Special to December 26 (Saturn, Uranus [Moon/Jupiter]):
An excellent organizer and an effective leader, you naturally gravitate to positions of authority and recognition. Unless you rise from the ranks of the aristocracy, there's a strong likelihood that you'll transcend your more ordinary beginnings to attain a higher level lifestyle and stay there. You have a special flair for big-time achievement, especially big business, are very aware of material advantages and can attain considerable security. You instinctively aim for a paycheck with a lot of zeros. Pricey four-star restaurants, posh hotels, an executive jet, Beluga caviar, a Fifth Avenue address—in short, the suite life, are in your future . . . or brighten your past if you're already the successful master of your fate.

If you're part of the workforce (and you assume that your job is unpromising), you could become a labor leader with a fat salary, an ample expense account and a generous pension. With your quick mind and sometimes quicker (and possibly sharper) tongue, you're not apt to lose many arguments. You call a spade a spade and can do it with plenty of enthusiasm and conviction. You can become a strong force in whatever context you choose to showcase your estimable—not to say formidable—abilities. With your incisive mind, intellectual courage and remarkable insights into the human condition, you know how to capitalize on your fondness for philosophizing to back up your job or career opinions. Despite occasional indications to the contrary, you're a survivor.

Carlton Fisk (baseball player), 1947

Steve Allen (TV talk show host), 1921

Mao Tse-tung (Chinese leader), 1893

Special to January 17 (Saturn, Uranus [Sun/Mercury]):
You take pride in mental accomplishment, your own as well as others', and in promoting the freedom to explore any idea or theory that advances academic knowledge and/or literate standards. Your interest in and respect for intellectual tradition and responsibility qualify you for a top job in the educational field, in any profession or in a government job or career where an inquiring mind, effective speaking style and a far-ranging outlook would be assets. Although your distinctive intelligence and remarkable versatility could find a successful outlet in the entertainment world or a business enterprise, you're probably better suited for the creative or scholarly realms, the medical industry or the ministry.

Whatever you accomplish can have significant appeal or impact, and you could achieve notable renown either in your particular field of endeavor or in terms of mass public recognition. Inclined to be articulate, opinionated and independent, you work better in an autonomous position as free as possible from supervision. You have considerable nervous energy stemming from a restless spirit, a puckish wit (when you're not being sardonic) and a fondness for amiable disputation. In that regard, however, the higher you rise, the more conspicuous a target you will be if differences escalate and you become involved in controversy; then you could be labeled a maverick by disgruntled colleagues (whose methods or ethics you might criticize) or other adversaries. You have better judgment regarding your career affairs than your emotional life.

Muhammad Ali (boxer), 1942

James Earl Jones (actor), 1931

Benjamin Franklin (statesman, scientist), 1706

January the 9th (Saturn, Pluto)
(and root digit for December 27 and January 18):
This birthday intensifies your ironclad resolve to rise above the ordinary aspirations of the general population. Whatever you do in life, the greatest obstacle to overcome may be your own bouts with suspicion about the real or imagined plots of rivals or opponents and/or discouragement. In a similar vein, not apt to forget an old grievance, you are good at spadework, such as digging up information that can undermine a competitor's strategy. Capricorn prefers cumulative progress, but your birthday mitigates against a steady, uneventful climb up the ladder of success. Your life can be disturbingly episodic—in any case unsettling to cautious Capricorn . . . the typical Gemini might love it.

At various disruptive junctures in your life, some serious soul searching and careful inward personal analysis may be necessary. You're programmed to win, but there will be times when you'll have your doubts as well as your share of frustration and the occasional defeat. You're inclined to be very personal and subjective, but if you encourage and can maintain an impersonal, universal outlook, you can avoid walking the high wire between success and failure. Skilled at using the power of suggestion to attain your goals, you can get associates or subordinates to do your bidding without actually requesting a favor in plain English. You're an expert in the twilight zone of schemes or opinions implied but not expressed.

Ambitious for power and prestige, government or public life is rewarding for you. You're very "establishment" but paradoxically could find yourself bucking the establishment over a controversial issue. You are capable of recycling your activist spirit by relegating a past failure to history and reinventing yourself to pursue a fresh or future goal. Your private life can be disorganized but not to the extent that you'll forego a try at family life and/or marriage, at which you can succeed—at least partially. Your ruler, Saturn, is the tester; your experiences enable you to eliminate character imperfections through successive and increasingly challenging trials and temptations.

Susannah York (actress), 1942
Joan Baez (singer), 1941
Richard Nixon (37th U.S. president), 1913

Special to December 27 (Saturn, Pluto [Moon/Mercury]):
Your vigorous mind and keen—not to say lacerating—wit are nicely balanced by your sociability and pleasure in diversions, but none of that will interfere with the business of getting ahead; with a Capricorn, hardly anything ever does. You're just as, if not more, determined to succeed than other members of your Sun-Sign. Level-headed, practical, and self-promotive, you do well in dealing with the public or in a profession, a business or the industrial realm. With your exceptional entrepreneurial instincts and buccaneer spirit, your dismayed or disgruntled competitors, critics or peers will find out soon enough that you're not only outspoken but wily and astute. Very little escapes your attention; you can seem to have eyes in the back of your head.

Rather loquacious, rarely at a loss for words, you might talk your way into gaining the support of a mentor or benefactor who admires your adroit mental facility, self-assured outlook, and enterprising spirit. You're very exacting and somewhat of a loner, at least in your thinking. But when teamwork is beneficial and/or essential, you know how to shrewdly estimate your leverage and when and how much to compromise in order to get what you want. You would not only be willing but would expect to make adjustments to get the best education or preparatory experience possible if it were a requirement for success. When iron discipline is necessary, you have it in plentiful supply, although you might camouflage it behind a veneer of engaging charisma.

> Gerard Depardieu (actor), 1948
>
> Marlene Dietrich (actress), 1901
>
> Louis Pasteur (chemist), 1822

Special to January 18 (Saturn, Pluto [Sun/Uranus/Saturn]):
No matter how discouraging things look, you're likely to keep trying and to become a long-term winner and not just a flash in the pan. You like to rub shoulders with upwardly mobile types or those who have already arrived or give promising evidence of the near-future possibility. Your intense ambition urges you on, perhaps more so than other members of your Sun-Sign, but you may also need to be more inventive and adaptable than other achievers before you reap the harvest of success. You're shrewdly aware of tastes, trends and the impression you make; when you discover what's hot with the public—whether an image, product, service or whatever—you'll try to find a way to keep it warm and to capitalize on its burgeoning (and hopefully enduring) popularity potential.

Your radar is sharply attuned to opportunities to get ahead in the world, one of which in your youth could tempt you to abandon standard schooling and to instead begin your early search for a suitable job or career opening. Willing to try anything once if it looks promising, you're ready to bend with shifting circumstances if that is what it takes to get your show on the road. You're attracted to money and security like filings to a magnet. If you have the kind of charisma that delights a substantial share of admirers, your abundant charm will pay handsome dividends in the entertainment or creative realm, the political arena or the business or professional world. Rather self-sufficient, an idealist in love and romance, disappointment in the realities of relationships could accentuate your independence and cause people to come and go in your life.

> Kevin Costner (actor), 1955
>
> Cary Grant (actor), 1904
>
> Daniel Webster (statesman), 1782

January the 11th (Saturn, Neptune [Moon/Sun])
(master number):

Yours may be the most challenging birthday number for your sign. It's admittedly quite a feat to combine the Capricorn requirement for concrete evidence and results with the need for practical idealism and a belief or confidence in intangibles. If you shy away from an understanding of metaphysics and spiritual illumination, the alternative paths that life leads you to may leave you confused and discouraged. Capable of inspired leadership, you're not likely to fulfill your maximum potential by settling for an ordinary concept of life or evading your obligation to pursue hidden or inner truth with conviction. If you do, and you stress commonplace goals and satisfactions, you may find that disappointment with life becomes more insistent with age, causing you to become disorganized, withdrawn and apathetic—which can have a detrimental effect on your relationship prospects.

Of course, as a Capricorn, you can't deny your intrinsic nature and completely avoid commonsense practicality. You can't drift into a comfortable fantasy world of make-believe that dodges life's cold realities. But the fact remains that you can't afford the narrow vision that emphasizes your creditable earthbound traits exclusively; in order for you to realize your remarkable potential, your attributes flourish best when they serve a larger vision. Meanwhile, any vaporous daydreams of success you might entertain aren't viable unless you're able to translate your visions into bricks and mortar or a reasonably accurate facsimile of fruitful usefulness. If you rise to the heights and fulfill your elevated spiritual or creative ideals, you're likely to enjoy considerable recognition and commensurate, if slow-but-sure, material rewards.

On the other hand, by developing inner strength and prudently following your imaginative inspirations, you won't be totally dependent on recognition, material success or the approval of others for your security; those rewards become auxiliary benefits to more meaningful personal fulfillment. And at your best as a unique member of your Sun-Sign, you won't dwell on past failure but will instead look ahead to the next opportunity to test your somewhat evanescent values and abilities. Shy and private in person, you could be a lot more forceful in public. Careerwise, you're well equipped for the arts (or businesses related to them), a profession (especially literary), a political career, or the world of finance (especially Wall Street, where your hunches could be very profitable).

Ben Crenshaw (pro golfer), 1952

Eva Le Gallienne (actress), 1899

Alexander Hamilton (statesman), 1755

(Note: This master number implies a variable alternative response influenced by the strength or passivity of the planet Neptune in your horoscope. If you don't feel that you are responding to the distinctive vibratory power of 11, you are instead expressing the more conventional qualities of 2, which you should read.)

December the 22 (Saturn, Uranus [Saturn/Moon])
(master number; this could be a Sagittarius Sun-Sign birthday,
due to the yearly variation in times when the Sun changes sign
[see Author's Note]. If you are a Capricorn, the following will apply;
if not, read the Sagittarius December 22 profile):

You'll probably be most successful implementing your intuitive promptings and visionary ideas within the framework of establishment acceptance, usefulness or necessity. A daring foray into a totally uncharted field can arouse too much uncertainty; you prefer at least a minimum feeling of familiarity or security in your pioneering activities. You may have a three-pronged need to find the central focus between (1) expressing your independence and originality, (2) gratifying your urge to experiment, build and expand in some new way in a previously unknown context, and (3) the pressure to keep the overall process within organizational and/or constructive guidelines. You're not likely to be impressed by trendy chic and hype; bare-bones facts will interest you more in your climb to success.

If you are too hidebound, however, it is possible for excessive caution to hamper your urge to express yourself independently, differently and/or progressively, but wariness and discipline provide your farsighted ideas the practicality and safety you are really most comfortable with. Nevertheless, authority, power and recognition won't flourish confined in a hothouse; you are happiest if they are productive in the broad-based world of affairs. Ever the practical optimist, you're more inspired if prestige and material gain accompany their fulfillment.

Your inventive proclivities—not to say genius—can find a rewarding outlet in the government realm, a profession or possibly a job or career in a creative or artistic field (if you can make it pay). You're remarkably capable and, when genuinely motivated, can turn virtually anything you touch into success. At the same time, it would very much depend on the nature of your work whether or not your achievement propels you into the limelight. In any case, you could be equally at home quietly pursuing an important goal or project without fanfare or garnering considerable public acclaim for your talents and accomplishments.

Diane Sawyer (broadcast journalist), 1945

Dame Peggy Ashcroft (actress), 1907

Giacomo Puccini (composer), 1858

(Note: This master number implies a variable alternative response influenced by the strength or passivity of the planet Uranus in your horoscope. If you don't think you are responding to the distinctive vibratory power of 22, you are instead expressing the more conventional qualities of 4, which you should read.)

CHAPTER 11

AQUARIUS

January 21–February 18

RULER: **URANUS** NUMBER: **22** ELEMENT: **AIR**

SYMBOL: **THE WATER BEARER** CO-RULER: **SATURN**

"I count myself in nothing else so happy,
as in a soul remembering my good friends."
—*Richard II,* Shakespeare

Chocolate-covered brussels sprouts, the Emperor Hadrian, space flights, the duck-billed platypus, Jack Benny, Frederick the Great, martinis with ice cream and the Statue of Liberty all have something in common with you: They all come under the sign Aquarius.

The pop image of the archetype Aquarian is the mad scientist—ominously poised between accidentally incinerating humanity or just as accidentally discovering the magic formula for all the world's ills—as he putters away, engrossed in his dials, electrodes and bubbly concoctions. He's perfectly at home in his white smock, thick glasses and hair like frayed nerve ends—studying the rest of us like so many white mice in a cage.

You're not exactly like that, because no Aquarian ever fits a prescribed mold, although you may be several notches beyond the collective mentality. You have a remarkably retentive memory but not for ordinary things: You can appear wearing one black sock and one brown sock or a tie on a T-shirt (which could someday become a fashion statement—you're usually ahead of the times). Aristotle may have had Aquarius in mind when he said: "There is no great genius without a mixture of madness." When you're part of the social aspic, you give it that unique flavor, or you'd just as soon not be an ingredient. You may not be fascinated by science beyond reading about Moon landings, but you're still an Aquarian and governed by the basic characteristics of your Sun-Sign.

You see life from the comprehensive, compositional point of view, a structure based on the dignity and integrity of the individual, even though some apparent freedoms may need to be sacrificed. Aquarius is the sign opposite Leo, the sign of monarchs. In your sign, however, every man is a king, not in theory but in practice—brotherhood not theorized but *lived*. Aquarian-born

Wendell L. Willkie, presidential candidate in 1940, proclaimed his "One World" concept, which is close to your ideals.

With the sign Aquarius ruling the zenith, or apex, of the United States chart, it is not surprising that Aquarian presidents like Abraham Lincoln and Franklin Delano Roosevelt have been at the helm during periods of significant social upheaval or reform. And being a native of the air-sign Aquarius, Roosevelt was the first candidate in history to fly to a convention to accept the presidential nomination. President Ronald Reagan, another Aquarian, appointed the first female justice to the Supreme Court.

The "anything" planet, Uranus, is one of your rulers—and the one usually identified with Aquarius. You're the one other sign, like Scorpio, however, to have two rulers: Your other ruler is Saturn. Fortunately for you, the more evolved side of Scorpio is more difficult to attain than the advanced levels of Aquarius because the former can involve intensely emotional choices. Pluto, the ruler of Scorpio, is the planet of the introverted power complex and the possibility for psychological or emotional implosions; Uranus is the planet of the extroverted will. The requirement in Aquarius is that cramped, narrow outlooks must give way to broader, objective concepts. The need is conceptual rather than primordial, mental rather than emotional, brain-teasing rather than soul-stirring.

Though you'd like to be free of *everything*, you're not quite free of Saturn. The planet of discipline leaves the measured pace of practical Capricorn behind and joins forces in Aquarius with the freewheeling spirit of Uranus. The catch is that you have to pass the tests of discipline (Saturn) before you can enjoy the liberty of Uranus. In the process, you can assume many unique identities.

The *one* way you are alike is in your determination to be *unlike* everyone else. The diversity of personalities in your sign ranges from flamboyant actress Tallulah Bankhead to headstrong General Douglas MacArthur of World War II fame. General MacArthur's willful independent streak clashed with President Harry S. Truman's Taurean determination to be the boss during the Korean War; when MacArthur balked, Truman fired him. An identifiable characteristic of your Sun-Sign is stubbornness, centered in your steadfast refusal to be bracketed by society. You create you own niche; if you get tired of that one, you move on to something else of your own invention. You feel that you're an original and would like to keep it that way.

It will help to understand the interrelationship of the Saturn and Uranus principles of your sign because they illuminate the differences between the two generally defined types of Aquarians—though the variety is endless and the boundaries are indefinite.

The Saturnian Aquarian is more restrained, similar to Capricorn, except that you're not as intensely practical. You are ambitious, not so much for self as for the betterment of conditions generally and the role you might play in a social breakthrough. You have quiet faith in the individual, in the underlying unity behind the diverse individualities of men and women—and in their right to be expressed. You have excellent concentration and are resistant to outside influences except as they are food for thought. You have good organizing ability and an objective attitude. You don't insist on total independence; you blend, however grudgingly, into the general social fabric. Having a measure of skeptical materialism, you believe in abstractions more willingly when they are one way or another supported by cold, solid facts.

Your orientation to life is mental, so you are typically interested in the humanities, science, mechanics and kindred pursuits, as well as a cerebral approach to the arts. You are apt to be an atheist or agnostic, with your own highly individualized concept of God or philosophy. You conclude that you can be decent without adhering to the clutter of formal, essentially manmade rules. Where you prefer to be free of the strictures of dogmas, creeds and outworn concepts, your Uranian counterpart will *refuse* to be bound by them. To the Uranian Aquarian, the differentiating significance of being Chinese or Israeli, black or white, simply doesn't exist. People are human beings first; it is not important where they come from but where they are going.

Unlike Capricorn, who isn't concerned with ideas unless they are practical, you are interested first in *ideas—often highly innovative ones*—even if they may have to wait for the realities to catch up to them or they may have little immediate practical value. Contemporaries can consider you arbitrary or label you a maverick, but then you're not as vulnerable to public opinion as the average person. You won't conform, like Libra, in order to bask in the warmth and security of "belonging." If a few noses get out of joint, so be it. You won't sacrifice ideals to expediency, nor will they fall prey to the establishment if its policies don't command your respect or fit in with your pet theories.

You don't thrive on respect or the visible accouterments accompanying success, like Capricorn. The utility and convenience of the amenities are more important to you for what they provide than as the symbols of status they might convey in the social hierarchy.

The Uranian sees *today* with the eyes of *tomorrow*, with no shying away from defying tradition and convention. The type of Aquarian you are is determined by the relative prominence of Saturn and Uranus in your horoscope. If Saturn, planet of the status quo, is angular, elevated or otherwise prominent, you are more the Saturnian Aquarian; if the planet of the future, Uranus, is powerfully placed, you will express the more unusual, avant-garde side of Aquarius.

Remember two things: First, divisions are seldom sharply defined, and interesting composites of people blending the two principles of Aquarius are common. Second, those born in a sign other than Aquarius who have Uranus strongly placed in their horoscopes will express the characteristics of the Uranian Aquarian, albeit with a *modified* emphasis. The difference is that the lifestyle of the Cancerian, Virgoan, or whatever will be the values through which the Uranian currents are expressed, such as (for Cancer) advanced notions of home life, parenting, environment or (for Virgo) innovative ideas concerning health, work, analytical procedures.

The Uranian Aquarians are the ones most apt to make headlines or change the course of history; they challenge the status quo. In the past, giants like Aquarius-born Francis Bacon and Galileo and Pisces-born Copernicus (Uranus angular in his horoscope) brought the mold-shattering shadow of the future into their particular age, with jarring results in their own lives.

Bacon's contribution to philosophy was to subject it to scientific (Aquarian) methods, with the burden of proof resting on acceptable data. Although criticized for being too mechanical, his striking observations about life made a lasting impact. A perverse Uranian development, due to a flaw in his character, led to banishment and enforced retirement at the close of his career.

Copernicus made a brilliant contribution through his treatise on the nature of the universe. His radical theory that the Sun was the center of a system around which the earth and the planets revolved forms the foundation of modern astronomy. In his time, his ideas were wildly unorthodox (Uranus), and he was forced by the church to recant.

Galileo, the inventor of the astronomical telescope, added significantly to our knowledge of the universe through his discoveries. His investigations confirming Copernican theories were too radical (Uranian-Aquarian) for the times, were subsequently denounced by the church and, along with Galileo's own teachings, were considered dangerous to the faith then current. He was tried in 1633 by the Inquisition, forced to recant his beliefs and spent his remaining years—after a short imprisonment—in seclusion. Since Uranus wasn't discovered until 1781, any radical departures from the norm—prior to that time—were subject to the limiting, crystallizing establishment influence of Saturn.

The Uranian Aquarian is the outstanding champion of liberty, though at times you can be a law unto yourself. Uranus is the planet of the unfettered ego. In pursuing the essence of this principle, you can assume that you are right and that the rest of the world is wrong. If you respond as a *negative* Uranian, you fight the battle of freedom selfishly for yourself. Your urge is similar to Sagittarius, only now, instead of the negative Archer's dilemma—a desire to be free of spiritual strictures—you want to be free of interacting social responsibilities, of having to conform in any way to the essential pattern of the sociological structure. A *perversion* of the Leo principle—your opposite polarity—feeds your craving to attract attention through whatever shallow means available. You can deliberately cultivate a capricious dissimilarity to everything and everybody in order to broadcast your "individuality." You become the insecure misfit—and you show it by wearing eccentric attire, displaying freaky behavior or expressing bizarre social concepts.

The Sun (love and pride) joined with Uranus (self-will) is a highly charged combination and can take many forms, some undesirable. At its worst, freedom becomes license; your life as such an Aquarian is one long adolescence. You become a noisome parasite at the kooky fringe of the social order, posturing as "idealistic," "original" or just "different" in order to excuse what is actually self-righteous monomania. Your concept of liberty is to do whatever *you* want to do, whenever *you* want to do it, regardless of others' rights. It doesn't occur to you that your behavior might be merely self-indulgent and childish. The negative Uranian Aquarian represents the *inversion* of genius, the power of Uranus unleashed irresponsibly through the "personality" to gain attention unobtainable otherwise—like funneling a hurricane through a keyhole. As astrologer Grant Lewi put it, "If you are an ordinary mortal, you have to look out for expressing the temperament of genius without getting its results or meriting its rewards." The inherent breadth of the Uranian principle can't be compressed into the empty vacuum of *self*-serving without evoking volatile results.

A negative facet of Uranus is a dislike of rigid schedules, drudgery, routine, anything humdrum. That's legitimate, but no Aquarian—or anyone else—will accomplish anything of importance without the *patience* of Saturn. You may have to tolerate your share of routine in order to express the essence of your birthright. Where Sagittarius focuses on "becoming" in terms of an ideal, the Uranian Aquarian is always "evolving" in terms of the future, and Saturn is the balance wheel of the process for the positive Aquarian.

You may be the professional controversialist, endearingly irascible or quietly dynamic; you're paradoxical. Aquarius can be inordinately generous, trustful of strangers out of all proportion to the logic of a situation—and then quixotically inconsiderate when cooperation and compromise would be to everyone's advantage.

You run the gamut from nonconformist egocentricity to profound humanitarianism. Your prejudices, if any, are against the forces that threaten to inhibit you. Be sure the reason that you think you're being inhibited is logical. Don't parade your eccentricities just because the authorities won't let you enshroud EPA headquarters in a plastic bag to keep out air pollution. You won't attract adherents to your cause; you'll just convince them that you're another misguided nut case.

Uranian antics might be excusable if the world were made the richer by some marvelous contribution resulting from them. Strangely enough, Uranians who do positively contribute—enrich life—by their genius are rarely the ones who proclaim their genius by personal eccentricities. Thomas Edison, Abraham Lincoln and Charles Lindbergh are outstanding Aquarians whose demeanor could be considered, if anything, straightforward or *understated*. Those of true greatness are generally modest about their achievements.

Whether you are the authentic pathfinder, ahead of the times, or merely abrupt and cantankerous, you are always magnetic—Uranus being the planet of electricity. It is also the planet of willpower; but when you're frustrated, nervous, erratic and self-willed, you become the paragon of *won't*-power. Then you are overly independent, rebellious and unpredictable. And you love to take the opposite side of an argument just to be different—exemplifying to perfection Sagittarian Winston Churchill's definition of a fanatic as "one who can't change his mind and won't change the subject."

Lacking true incentive, your independence may just be an inability to work with others. Are you independent or merely capricious and difficult? Reformative or merely irresponsible? Are you independent of the system just because you're lazy and don't like discipline? Or because you have something genuinely better to offer? Nearly 80 percent of the people in the Hall of Fame of great Americans are Aquarians.

The Age of Aquarius is the age of electricity—lights, telephones, television, space travel—and the age of immediacy—*shrunken* distances that force *expansion* of concepts, mind literally over matter. Reform movements, the increasing independence of the individual, the revolution in technology, the information superhighway and the global reach of the Internet are all part of the Aquarian phenomenon.

With your psychological compulsion to deviate from "whatever is," you can have unexpected insights into an as yet unborn future—the purpose being to disrupt life out of its cyclic rut. "If you always live with those who are lame, you yourself will learn to limp" could be your credo. Your alter-ego principle, the Uranian force, may refer to the pineal gland, a possible remnant of the "third eye" referred to by the ancients.

As a progressive Aquarian, you don't seek change because, like Aries, you are impatient with slow results; you are genuinely interested and curious about something *new*. And you don't seek something new just to flex the muscles of your individuality. You want to see what something new is like; you want to find out what makes it tick, see if you can make it tick any better or discover a better use for it while it ticks. You are interested in that thing for itself, not just because you want your ego to be identified with it.

Self-reliance and optimism are important to your progress. You need to focus your efforts, husband your forces—instead of resources, like Capricorn—because your Uranian restiveness can dissipate in discontinuity or aimless experimenting. Like Capricorn, you may be more successful later in life but for different reasons. Capricorn may spend years patiently rising through the ranks of an organization or a profession or establishing a business. You, on the other hand, may spend years casting around in various vocations until you finally discover the one unique thing that combines your various abilities usefully and profitably. Instead of eternally preparing for the future materially, as Capricorn does, you look ahead to it with an almost naive curiosity and enthusiasm; you're willing to take a chance on something new and untried, to experiment. If it doesn't have a built-in success potential, the Mountain Goat's interest—never mind enthusiasm—isn't aroused. Whatever is new and different always has a lurking fascination for you; instead of being thrown by surprising developments, you can relish them and capitalize on them—especially if they're in line with your objectives.

You have a flair for turning what is dull and familiar into something new and exciting, for making virtues out of necessities. For instance, modern methods of teaching foreign languages with visual aids speed up the learning process markedly by making it more interesting and painless. This is typically appropriate of the air-sign Aquarius, because verbal communications are an air function that helps to dissolve barriers between cultures and people.

You can profit from a good education, the usual accumulation of facts, which is how you are apt to assess it; to you it's only a springboard—not a guarantee, passport or high-class union card for fitting into the stereotype work or career image. Being mentally oriented, you are naturally able to articulate issues associated with broad human understanding and needs; when positively motivated, you respond to higher thought frequencies beyond the comprehension of ordinary individuals.

The most profound change that occurs about midway during the human life span has its origins in your sign. Both your rulers, plus the Moon, are the coordinates of a cycle that has an overwhelming effect on the ego and the psyche. The Moon rules the emotions, Saturn the self-preservative instinct, Uranus the higher frequencies of the neuromental system—characteristically more *unstable* during this popularly termed "midlife crisis" period. What happens is this: In any horoscope, the *progressing* Moon and the *transiting* Saturn move to a point exactly opposite their original birth positions in the Zodiac for the *second* time; concurrent with that, *transiting* Uranus moves to a position opposite its original place at birth for the *first* time. All these astrological patterns coincide at approximately the age of forty to forty-four. Having other purposes besides the reproduction of the species, an individual's physiological function is usually fulfilled by this time, and he or she is free to express it in other directions.

In most horoscopes, this development signifies a rechanneling of conceptual energies, a straining of the ego for release from the strictures of past patterns. A rebirth of varying degrees of intensity and effectiveness, its most commonly known result is to liberate women from the fear of pregnancy. Whether we believe in astrology or not, we function according to its timetables. For *all*, this juncture motivates a renewed urge to assert any latent individualism buried under the worldly necessities of the first forty to forty-four years of life. It can literally shake individuals out of themselves, with either gratifying or shattering results. Since *your* two ruling planets figure prominently in this process, it can have a pronounced effect on you or on any Uranian-type individuals born in other Sun-Signs. For nearly everyone, but you in particular, it's a chance to get out of a rut.

Uranian Aquarians with a positive orientation to life are always ready to break up the crystallization endemic to their other selves, but Saturn helps to maintain the balance, apply the brakes when inspirations threaten to get out of hand. Yours is the sign of quickened perceptions, intellect, intuitive flashes and inventive genius. If any sign could be said to have a computer for a brain, it's yours. You operate counter to the currents of tradition. Where Capricorn supports and preserves (and, if possible, capitalizes on) established order, you want to break new ground; in visualizing the future, you can differ radically from the established norm. The positive Aquarian is subliminally absorbed with the human equation, unconcerned with class distinctions. India, a Capricorn country with rigid class divisions, could motivate an Aquarian to institute reform. You have little patience with religious or secular differences; "religious" or "holy" wars, to you, are the height of human folly, the fictions of society compounded into idiocy.

You are creative, with remarkable insights into the human condition and the ability to articulate them; a career of broad public implication is especially favorable for you. Your amazing gifts can lead to a brave new world or, conversely, the Uranian nightmare of Aldous Huxley wherein everyone is a digit with computerized emotions. If you become too absorbed in the collective, you can become impervious to the emotional-psychical basis of humanity.

Those people of the future—with their large heads and small bodies like homo sapiens tadpoles—are probably Aquarians, the citizens of the Aquarian Age in full flower. When Bulwer-Lytton said, "Genius does what it must, talent does what it can," he separated the men from the boys—and the positively motivated Aquarians from the rest of mankind.

Franklin Roosevelt's Saturnian handicaps were the spur to his indomitable Aquarian spirit, through which his Uranian concepts were given their steel and might. In 1936, he said, "There is a mysterious cycle in human events . . . this generation of Americans has a rendezvous with destiny." World War II in his view was to "save a great and precious form of government for ourselves and for the world." Significantly, he didn't say "great and precious country" or "great and precious government." With his innate Aquarian sense of equality (and his meticulous Virgo ascendant), he differentiated between form and content, intention and actuality. And at the close of his life, he wrote, "Today, we are faced with the pre-eminent fact that, if civilization is to survive, we must cultivate the science of human relationships, the ability of peoples of all kinds to live together and work together, in the same world, at peace." How like an Aquarian to equate relationships with science. Now that the world has become a global village, FDR's words ring truer than ever.

Characteristically, your emotions are sifted through your intelligence; sophisticated, capable of lasting attachments, you nevertheless remain objective. You don't nurse memories of broken dreams or moon over shattered romances; you're the apostle of free love, believing that all should be free to do their own thing. Your moral code is your own; some notable Aquarians did their own thing long before it was fashionable—not that it's ever out of fashion with you.

The Roman Emperor Hadrian, an outstanding administrator and

campaigner, had his love for the beautiful Greek youth Antinous imperishably commemorated by the sculptors of his time. Frederick the Great, king of Prussia, a brilliant military tactician and an atheist, said, "Every man must get to Heaven his own way." Though married, his way, like Hadrian's, was to be more than friends with his male companions. Lord Byron had an Aquarian affair with his half-sister, but England didn't consider it just half as incestuous or immoral. Aquarians seem to sense that they exist "in all times, without boundaries" and don't subscribe to the social fictions, mores or hypocrisies of any particular time.

An Aquarian can be just as comfortable and find life just as enjoyable with groups of friends as with intimate, confining ties. Togetherness with a loved one isn't your great need once the initial raptures of romance are past; you'd just as soon spend time at the club, march in a protest or go fishing. With a positive Aquarian, an abstraction becomes a reality; a nonconformist Aquarian can turn a reality like marriage into an abstraction.

You're not in a hurry to settle down; when you are, you can marry a friend or childhood acquaintance. Where Capricorn isn't partial to divorce, you are. It's the Aquarian (especially the Uranian) viewpoint that it isn't realistic to think that people can learn about love and relationships from just one other person (or even one other sex). A little distant personally, you make up for it in your closeness to your fellow man. Of course, your mate didn't marry your fellow man, although it may seem like it at times.

After four days away on a fishing trip, for instance, an Aquarian male is as apt to come home with the crew as he is with the catch. His mate loves to suddenly fix dinner for ten, instead of for two—even after a hard day—especially if she's a distaff Aquarian. Speaking of her, she can pull the same caper: She can bring home the gang from the protest march for refreshments and to plan future strategies. You can imagine the "delicious" reaction of a Cancer husband—feet propped up—all settled in for an evening of his favorite television programs—having it all interrupted as the zealots troop in.

A distaff Aquarian is emancipated and uninhibited. She won't brook interference or supervision where her interests are concerned, and she'll grant you the same rights. Her principal requirement is to have a broad-minded mate. Expecting her to be glued to the hearth, ecstatic over all the homespun delights that would warm the heart of a Cancerian, for instance, is sheer folly. Forget it! Whether or not absorbed in a job or a career, she finds time to be off organizing block parties and tenant committees or aiding some candidate's bid for election. She's very diversified and loves to promote causes.

You may not have heard of Elizabeth Blackwell (although actress June Allyson or somebody played her in a film). She was the first woman licensed to be a doctor in America and, you guessed it, an Aquarian. And there's Gertrude Stein, the Aquarian genius who startled the literary world with her avant-garde poetry. In addition, she collected impressionist paintings decades before they became status symbols and extremely pricey. A champion of other creative innovators, her salon was the intellectual center of Paris in the early 20th century. It may be apocryphal, but the story goes that on her deathbed a friend asked her, "What is the answer . . .?," to which Gertrude replied "What was the question?" Now who else but an Aquarian, at life's most solemn moment, would answer a question with a question, would intellectualize ambiguously with a last breath?

You should be able to tell the Aquarian gal from the others at social events. The Lioness, for example, may sport some kitschy but feminine exaggeration of the current style to attract attention; the Virgoan will probably be understated in basic black and pearls, very "North Shore." The Aquarian will be the one to make the spectacular entrance: She might come in wearing just the pearls, with her head shaved, or topless, with a plastic microminiskirt, space helmet and boots. Uranus is far out in the Solar System, and the Aquarian's taste can travel the same orbit.

You are more apt to prefer chrome-and-leather furniture to antiques. If you do take a fancy to a relic of the past (because it reminds you of the future), it will be blended in with avant-garde things in a very eclectic way. Though you talk a good revolution, your dreams can be dissipated in the intoxicating vapors of a cocktail party. Or "talking" a mind-boggling invention will be your Uranian frequency of Aquarius at work—minus the force and application of Saturn necessary to give it form and usefulness in the world of reality. Do you remember Edison's words when he was queried about "genius"?: "One percent inspiration, 99 percent perspiration," answered the Aquarian responsible for the electric light, the phonograph, motion pictures and so on. These are all Uranian breakthroughs that changed the world—and were soon taken for granted by many with no comprehension of the dedication or effort involved.

Although your name doesn't appear on it, there is a tremendous monument to you standing in New York Harbor. Miss Liberty is the embodiment of Aquarian principles; she is telling us that whatever party is the party of the human race is the party of the future. Because such broad concepts impose a responsibility on each individual—to be worthy of mutual sharing by being willing to contribute unselfishly—we must patiently work to make the ideal a reality. The "work" is the Saturn part of the Uranian vision of the future, the role that all who participate in molding that future will utilize to advantage.

By applying the patience and application of Saturn to the common cause of a better life for all, the essential beauty of the Uranian dream, understanding and respect for all humanity by all humanity, through universal love and the intuitional mind, is fulfilled.

AQUARIUS BIRTHDAYS

Judgment of whether or not a birthday is propitious can be considered from two points of view: complementary or challenging. From the standpoint of personal progress and fulfillment, your destiny may flow more comfortably if your birthday is, or reduces to, an *inner* root number such as 1, 3, 5, 7 or 9. For career drive and achievement, your progress may be enhanced if your birthday is, or reduces to, an *outer* root number such as 2, 4, 6 or 8; the *outer* root numbers are less comfortable, more obstructive for you to contend with, but they are potentially very conducive to outstanding success. The 11 (master number) would be variable, but it generally would require more understanding and resourcefulness to integrate with the meaning of Aquarius. The 22 (master number), correlating to Uranus, ruler of Aquarius, is potentially very advantageous.

Remember, if your birthday is two digits (excepting master numbers 11 and 22), be sure to read the *root* digit or number first. For example, if your birthday is 29, read the 2 (2 + 9 = 11, 1 + 1 reduces to 2) birthday profile first and then read the special profile for 29. If your birthday is 14, read the 5 (1 + 4 = 5) birthday profile first and then read the special profile for 14, and so on. If a description in a "special" section contradicts information in the "root" digit (root number) analysis, the "special" interpretation applies more specifically to you. The first planet in parentheses following your birthday number is *your Sun-Sign ruler*; the second planet (or Uranus/Saturn for number 8) is *your birthday number planetary equivalent*. Subsidiary planetary influences (if any) are bracketed.

Each birthday profile includes celebrities who share the same birthday.

YOUR BIRTHDAY PROFILE

February the 1st (Uranus, Sun)

(and root digit for January 28 and February 10):

If you make a name for yourself, which is entirely possible in one context or another, it will be owing as much to the distinctive individuality of your work as to its quality. And if your achievement is extraordinary, it will probably represent a breakthrough or new departure of some sort in your chosen field of endeavor. Very inventive and adaptable in the workplace, you are able to originate new time- or energy-saving methods or techniques that are very advantageous financially or creatively to the success of a job, business venture or profession.

Although you are talented for the arts or the literary world, you are mainly creative in a different sense that could apply equally well to the world of commerce and especially to science. Thanks to your unique intuitive powers, you have the ability to deal with tasks or problems in a special way: You are able to discover a new principle or formula from familiar but heretofore unrelated phenomena and then unite them into a fresh, previously unknown synthesis. In the intellectual world, where you might be either for or against the current trend or fashion in thinking, you will speak (or write) your piece and stick to your guns regardless of the controversy your opinions generate. Your broad, perhaps unconventional viewpoints can imbue your personality with a colorful, provocative quality. To some, you'll be considered a pioneer, to others, an agitator when you assume or insist that your way is the only way.

Proud, independent and self-reliant, you have a fervor and/or confidence that you are able to communicate, particularly if your talents or activities bring you into the public domain. The opportunities you meet on the way to achieving your goals stimulate your urge for ego assertion. Perhaps rather detached, friendly but not by nature overly warm in manner, you work well with others if you keep mutual objectives in mind and remain aloof from ego clashes. In any event, you are ambitious and will be happiest in a position of authority or leadership. Marriage can be an important part of your life, particularly if your partner is a loyal helpmate and someone who can share or boost your pride in your accomplishments.

Boris Yeltsin (Russian leader), 1920

Clark Gable (actor), 1901

John Ford (film director), 1895

Special to January 28 (Uranus, Sun [Moon/Uranus/Saturn]):
You feel comfortable with people from all walks of life. With your finely tuned intuitive antenna, you respond readily and sympathetically to others, with the result that you can be unusually popular socially and romantically. You might not be so compatible, however, if anyone tries to pigeonhole you or interferes with or curtails your freedom to do things that interest you. A power struggle can ensue if people don't get the message about your ingrained—not to say determined—independence, a clue that you may not be well suited for the confines of a long-lasting relationship such as marriage.

You were probably out on your own at an early age, which could have made you somewhat sensitive and difficult. Feeling misunderstood, you may be talented but find instead that you have to work at some uncongenial job for a spell. Once you get your bearings, however, you have the power to rise steadily. Or you may be fortunate enough to begin your climb to success in a job or career that provides ample opportunity to dig in your heels and develop your capabilities. Either through your background or your own praiseworthy efforts to succeed (in more ways than one, you're frequently versatile), you have the potential to rise to a position of considerable leadership and influence in the arts, music, the law, the financial world or education.

Sarah McLachlan (singer), 1968

Alan Alda (actor), 1936

Jackson Pollock (artist), 1912

Special to February 10 (Uranus, Sun):
Your thoughtful strength, good sense and sound reasoning and judgment in coping with the complexities of large enterprises are your major assets. If you deal with the public in a job, profession or business, it can be a very satisfactory outlet for your abilities—which can include blazing a trendsetting new trail in work methods or goals. The responsibilities of group or public leadership rest comfortably on your shoulders. You are particularly talented for the entertainment world, government, philanthropy (fund-raising, dispensing grants) or a career that draws on your humanitarian and civic-minded spirit. If need be, you're capable of preparing for, or adapting to, practically any line of work in your quest for individualized expression until you find the career niche most suitable for your talents.

People are at the center of your interests; whether you're doing something for them or with them, mutually beneficial human relations are high on your list of values. Although you can be doubtful about the merits or aims of an undertaking, you're an expert at organization if the team spirit requires it—or at compromise in case a hitch develops. At your inventive best, your one-of-a-kind ideas are likely to be ahead of their time, which may be the reason you (or they) are sometimes misunderstood. Your lifestyle is apt to diverge from establishment expectations and might even raise a few eyebrows. When you go forth to conquer, it can be with considerable panache, enabling you to make a durable impression with your unique combination of personality and talent.

George Stephanopoulos (presidential aide, author), 1961

Roberta Flack (singer), 1940

Robert Wagner (actor), 1930

February the 2nd (Uranus, Moon)
(and root digit for January 29;
February 11 is a master number, see end of chapter):

Although not inclined to force your theories or idiosyncrasies on others, you'll certainly do all in your power to convince people that your way is the better way. Your pronounced independence and distinct individuality preclude much tolerance for compromise. You get along best with people who accept you the way you are; your engaging personality prompts people to assume that you mean well. The more diplomacy you can summon if tension develops, the more you will achieve gratifying results in relationships as well as the world of affairs, although the many (in your view) irksome adjustments necessary to your progress can make you nervous and touchy.

Your libertarian attitude, advocacy of unfettered freedom and interest in social reform and public enlightenment are some of the reasons for your personal popularity. Whether problems stem from conditions beyond your control or are of your own doing, they may demand a more emotional response from you than is natural or comfortable. You're typically rational and independent in your approach to life and would rather deal in abstractions, but sometimes conditions arise that must be dealt with emotionally. If you allow your feelings to become uncontrolled and swamped by circumstances, you can make decisions and act in ways you might later regret.

Strongly interested in people, with uncanny insights into human nature, the pulse of the public is as natural to you as breathing—and you know how to capitalize on it. Work that focuses on the needs of humanity will bring the chance for you to demonstrate your talents and to put your social theories and good intentions to the practical test. Well qualified for a job or career in government service, a business or profession keyed to public trends or fads would also be opportune for you. In the creative realm, you have a gift for the literary and musical fields.

Christie Brinkley (model), 1954

Farrah Fawcett (actress), 1947

James Joyce (writer), 1882

Special to January 29 (Uranus, Moon [Pluto]):

Born with remarkable insights into public taste and mass moods, your well-honed intuition is a key component of your flair for handling people. With these attributes added to your abundant talent, dynamic personal charisma and driving force to rise above the crowd, you practically have a guarantee to achieve whatever goal you aim for. You have definite likes and dislikes and can size up people pretty quickly; you're also shrewd enough to keep your conclusions to yourself if you think that by making waves at the wrong time you could get caught in a hazardous undertow.

With your mental orientation to life and psychological sagacity, you do well in service organizations, scientific or other research, writing, government, the healing arts and any work done with or for the public, such as social work or the entertainment world. When you decide on or pursue an objective that requires the cooperation or approval of other people, few can resist your grasp of a situation or your ingratiating appeal. You like a feeling of power and control and don't accept supervision or rejection easily, so it is best to avoid a job that is too hidebound or circumscribed. You need to be able to express your versatility, vitality, ideas for improvement and leadership qualities in whatever work, profession or business that enables you to maximize your distinctive abilities. With any luck at all, your love and marriage prospects benefit from the same qualities of judgment and understanding that contribute to the success of your career and other encounters.

Oprah Winfrey (TV talk show host), 1954

Tom Selleck (actor), 1945

William McKinley (25th U.S. president), 1843

February the 3rd (Uranus, Venus)
(and root digit for January 21, January 30, and February 12):

Your unusual flair for creative expression enables you to capitalize in a big way on your keen sense of the public pulse. Your intuitive feeling for beauty and pleasure tells you what people like and are eager to respond to, and you are only too happy to deliver it in full measure. With your distinctive personality either the route you travel to satisfy your worldly ambitions or your unmistakable individuality will set you apart from the competition. In fact, if you fulfill your extraordinarily unique potential in the business, professional or entertainment world, you may not really have any competition. Although as a student you might endure your share of instructional drudgery to develop your technical skills, it could very well be a brief interlude, thanks to your impatience to venture forth early in life and instead rely on learning while doing as you climb the success ladder.

You are likely to have unusual social affinities and to gravitate toward people who are apt to be offbeat in some way. You tend to march to a different drummer than the general population or the conformists of the mainstream establishment. An uncompromising idealist in terms of your love life, your independence can result in a sort of ambivalent intensity. You might stray from your ideal and be swept away from sensible emotional moorings by an exciting love-at-first-sight romantic fling—but eventually you'll have to face the disparities in values and tastes between you and your new attraction when the initial thrill wears off. Such a relationship, fueled by an overload of excitement, exists on rather fragile foundations and can be threatened by sudden fits of rivalry, jealousy or other whims of the moment.

In the social or creative realm, you are likely to go your own way and veer from popular public taste or fads. You like and enjoy people for what they are and not for what they have. You could express a dismissive attitude toward well-known cultural icons and instead beat the drum for your own lesser-known or less-appreciated favorites in the same field who don't quite make the grade as superstars in the mass popularity domain. In other words, among singers, you could prefer Mabel Mercer to Barbra Streisand. Although your convincing sincerity and persuasiveness find a congenial outlet in the business world, your best opportunities lie in the artistic or professional milieu; there, your idealism and gift for expression can achieve notable results. Whatever you do, success will be in direct proportion to the broad appeal of your conceptions.

Blythe Danner (actress), 1943

James Michener (author), 1907

Norman Rockwell (illustrator), 1894

Special to January 21 (Uranus, Venus [Moon/Sun]):

You're likely to be more ambitious for community recognition, career status and security than the typical Aquarian; with your feet solidly planted on terra firma, you're also apt to be more practical and self-determinative, if not as independent. If your family beginnings are less than privileged, you'll accept whatever job or menial task is available in order to acquire an education or training that provides a better opportunity to get somewhere in the world and enjoy prosperity. Once you're on the right track, you can be a tireless, highly motivated worker, eager to triumph in your skills and stamina, a shining example of expertise and success for coworkers or others in your field.

Once you're established and busy in a job, a profession or the world of commerce, you're not the type to wallow in worry if life becomes difficult; more likely to be devil-may-care in the face of your own problems, you can also be an inspiration to people around you who could use moral support. Friendly, charming, sincere and a smooth talker, you're not usually a loner; you thrive on family life, group ties and social activity. If necessary, you could even make a contribution toward social betterment that requires a very selfless attitude or personal sacrifice. The artistic, creative or scientific field is a more congenial area in which to express your talents than the competitive business world unless it includes a socially elevating purpose.

Geena Davis (actress), 1957

Placido Domingo (tenor), 1941

Christian Dior (fashion designer), 1905

Special to January 30 (Uranus, Venus):

With your dynamic personality, self-assured appearance and persuasive manner of speaking, you give the impression of authority. Whether or not you back it up with commensurate ability, determination and accomplishment is up to you; given your innate abilities and a reasonable amount of opportunity, the prospect for fulfilling your potential is exceptionally promising. Your occasionally caustic wit finds expression in twitting authority figures, especially the preening variety. Well qualified for a theatrical or other public career, your sense of drama and ability to articulate a subject, news, information, knowledge or wisdom can be influential and a source of inspiration on either side of the footlights. Your charm could be masked somewhat by your generally serious mien that gives way, at appropriate times, to a dazzling smile.

Your social theories stem from the idea that good and bad always coexist and we might as well get used to them inextricably mixed together in periods of history as in people. Although your ideas and visions can originate as lofty concepts, you're able to implement them at a down-to-earth level that can enlighten or benefit people and enable you to leave your mark in your chosen field of achievement. An efficiency expert, you know how to get things done better and more simply as well as more economically. A student of history, with a keen political sense, your talents can find a gratifying outlet in social service, education, government or the law, any of which could be combined with a business career. Success in marriage may be more elusive than success in your other areas of endeavor or accomplishment.

> **Vanessa Redgrave (actress), 1937**
>
> **Harold Prince (director), 1928**
>
> **Franklin D. Roosevelt (32nd U.S. president), 1882**

Special to February 12 (Uranus, Venus [Sun/Moon]):
If you're among the more irreverent, free-spirited Aquarians, your off-the-wall charm and derring-do exuberance are big assets for social and/or romantic popularity. You can be one of the most constantly fascinating personalities in your circle or in public life, known for your sharp wit, happy iconoclasm and gift for broad-based networking. With your friendly, candid, entertaining approach to life, you have no difficulty in attracting people of brains and influence who contribute so much to your progress. You're inclined to be very opinionated, especially about politics and culture, and voluble and articulate in your comments about them and other controversial topics; if you rise to a position of prominence, your likes and dislikes can have considerable influence.

Likely to be very expressive and talented, even multitalented, you're particularly qualified for a career in the arts, music, the entertainment world—or the business side of any of these fields, such as an agent or publicist. With your persuasive sincerity, you're gratified when your efforts to spread the word about quality in the arts or government have the intended effect on people eager for history, information or enlightenment. Your eclectic taste runs the gamut from traditional, plain-spoken ruggedness to the most futuristic avant-garde style. If you are a Saturnian Aquarian with this birthday, you tend to be more intellectual, humanitarian or scientific; you also have a deep sense of mission. Whether you're self-taught or classically trained, you may have to tolerate your share of fill-in jobs before you find the work or career that leads onward and upward to success.

Judy Blume (author), 1938

Abraham Lincoln (16th U.S. president), 1809

Charles Darwin (naturalist), 1809

February the 4th (Uranus, Saturn)
(and root digit for January 31 and February 13;
January 22 is a master number, see end of chapter):

Skeptical and hard to convince, your outlook is colored by your awareness of life's realities and inequities and the need to right the wrongs of past generations that perpetuated ideas of inferior social stereotypes. Not apt to make excuses for society's shortcomings, you may wonder why it took until 1919 for American women to obtain the right to vote or until the 1960s for civil rights to become a national issue. Equipped by talent and adaptability for almost any calling, you are capable of auspicious achievement. When you get going with your job or career endeavors, your many innovative ideas will open the door to far-sighted opportunities that promote achievement of your goals through patience, perseverance and iron-willed discipline.

Efficient and cautious, you may experience disappointment or dissatisfaction in your emotional life through your quiet austerity and reliance on mental rather than emotional resilience. Projecting a steely magnetism if a man or a sort of detached warmth if a woman, you can be difficult to understand when provoked. Beguiled by your friendly manner, those in your circle discover your no-nonsense core when an issue reaches a critical stage. You can surprise those who assume you are vulnerable to sentimental entreaties or that you can be manipulated by an appeal to your emotions. You feel most honest with yourself when choices are based on your version of the bedrock principles of humanitarian ideals; the common denominator of reason will be your deciding frame of reference in any important situation.

If you encounter restrictive conditions when you begin to make your way in the world, you can become extremely wary and subtle as you weigh the consequences of commitment against your treasured independence. You have to be thoroughly convinced of the ultimate value of a choice before sacrificing the latter for the former. If you opt for a public career, the unquestioned integrity you project even when you are controversial wins grudging respect from people who disagree with you. Your surface pride in conflict with a subliminal lack of confidence helps to keep your ego balanced and under control. You see the repressiveness of living in terms of its effect on great masses of people rather than as a personal grievance. Your ideas are likely to be original and advanced and perhaps startling or arbitrary to those less visionary or opinionated.

Betty Friedan (feminist, activist), 1921

Ida Lupino (actress), 1918

Charles A. Lindbergh (aviator), 1902

Special to January 31 (Uranus, Saturn [Venus/Sun]):

Your possibilities run the gamut from being a strong advocate of the status quo to being openly rebellious toward tradition and the establishment. You can assume that either you owe a debt to society or that it owes you a living. Your open-minded attitude about people in general is likely to stem from influences surrounding you during your growing-up period, during which your experiences may have been counter to what might have been expected from your family beginnings. If you come from a privileged background, for instance, your parents or elders may have seen to it that you mixed and mingled with people from all walks of life and became acquainted with their typical lifestyles in order to instill in you a well-rounded viewpoint about life's realities. If you come from a disadvantaged start in life, you're all too familiar with life's grittier aspects.

You can be both aberrant and charming, enabling you to get by with strategies, projects or activities that could lead to rejection or failure in less sophisticated hands. Thanks to your affable personality, people tend to believe in your sincerity whether or not they're sold on your expertise, which, in any case, is likely to be top-notch. Once your reputation is established, you can become a popular favorite at work, in business or in a profession. Particularly talented for the creative realm, you can strike a chord of heartfelt responsiveness and win recognition for your exceptional musical or literary abilities.

Suzanne Pleshette (actress), 1937

Norman Mailer (novelist), 1923

Franz Schubert (composer), 1797

Special to February 13 (Uranus, Saturn [Sun/Venus]):

When you finally arrive at your destination on the road to success, you may have the feeling that you were preparing for it all your life. Whether it's the job in the arts you always wanted or a coveted position in the business world or a profession, your duties are likely to fit you like a second skin. You don't have to cultivate a reputation for getting along with people; you come by it naturally. You're able not only to carry out the preestablished procedures and responsibilities of an enterprise but also to add some brilliant strokes of your own.

Whether it's your compulsion to work or your pride in the result, you can be very fluent and productive in the creative world or government. When functioning at your optimum level, your abilities and personal appeal transcend ethnic differences, language barriers and national boundaries. At their most innovative and inspired, your ideas and words, whether spoken or written, tap into the odd psychological twists as well as the shards of universal spirit inherent in the fears and joys of ordinary people—insights that make you articulate, sympathetic and possibly very popular in the public domain both locally and/or the world over. Your observations or opinions may tend more to the Delphic than the controversial. Your versatility can pay off in a number of ways; no matter what you do in your rather adventurous life, you're likely to prosper.

Peter Gabriel (singer), 1950

Stockard Channing (actress), 1944

Kim Novak (actress), 1933

February the 5th (Uranus, Mars)
(and root digit for January 23 and February 14):

If you are able to control your restless independence, you will probably accomplish more in life through teamwork than by going it alone, but it may not be easy if you allow your potentially irascible disposition to gain the upper hand. Your social or working relationships are enlivened by abundant energy and vitality. A tough negotiator, you bring plenty of intellectual vigor to support your views when others clash with your opinions. If that fails, you might just bulldoze your way through to victory. In a position of authority (and you generally prefer that to a back seat), you can be an outspoken maverick as far as conservative establishment ideology is concerned.

The ambivalence demonstrated by some of you about right and wrong is an example of your innovative, not to say highly unorthodox, thinking. You prefer a cerebral, open-ended approach to beliefs; the absolutes or dictums uttered by people claiming divine intervention or citing some nebulous source will trouble or irritate you. You're not impressed by the pronouncements of (to you, so-called) authority figures unless you already share their ideals or values. In your mind, a papal decree may not be worth the paper it's written on. Your rather enigmatic philosophy can be summarized in a Chinese proverb that says, "Life is a search for the truth, and there is no truth."

Very sensitive to the way the world is treating you, you might not be as cognizant of your impact on others' sensibilities. If you're slow to anger, you can be quick getting over it. Interested in causes and pursuits that have broad social, cultural or educational ramifications, you excel at creating or publicizing enterprises that promote your enthusiasms. Drawn to challenging career situations that can benefit from your fast-paced working or entrepreneurial style, the course of your life is likely to be episodic with various peaks, valleys, endings and new beginnings as exciting new ventures stir up your progressive spirit. You'll cover a lot of ground, both literally and figuratively, as your life unfolds.

Jennifer Jason Leigh (actress), 1962

Roger Staubach (football player), 1942

Adlai Stevenson (1952 presidential candidate), 1900

Special to January 23 (Uranus, Mars [Moon/Venus]):

Your strong, perhaps gritty temperament is camouflaged by your sociable demeanor and genuine interest in and concern for people. In your quietly dignified, unpretentious way, you like things to go smoothly and constructively, with as little fuss and bother as possible. You know people and their foibles and how to successfully plan activities with them. Although you might be highly educated, you find out more about life and gain more knowledge from experience than from books or formal study. Your ingratiating manner attracts opportunity; you can be brilliant and unconventional in your approach to your work when you discover new avenues of inspiration, methodology or expression to explore. Practically any job, business or profession commensurate with your abilities is likely to benefit from your inquisitiveness, self-assurance and perceptive insights.

People with whom you work and who make a modest contribution to the success of a venture can be surprised at your generosity in sharing credit when, truthfully, you may either have been the source of most of the inventive ideas or done the lion's share of the work. To say that you are well liked by coworkers, employees or your boss would be an understatement. You not only can receive impressive recognition and respect for a job well done, but also garner considerable affection as well. Though you don't appear to be holding anything back from friends, lovers, or group members, they're left with the impression that there'll be something new and exciting about you when next you meet. If your career brings you before the public, you attract abundant popularity for your distinctive persona as much as for your memorable capabilities.

Caroline (princess of Monaco), 1957

Humphrey Bogart (actor), 1900

Edouard Manet (artist), 1832

Special to February 14 (Uranus, Mars [Sun/Saturn]):

Typically Aquarian, you're apt to go your own way as far as beliefs, tastes and personal behavior are concerned; what's more, you could do it with a vengeance. If you come from a traditional background with an establishment cultural heritage, you can break away from early influences as your noncon-formist views emerge and become the guiding principles of your life. You can be intensely humanitarian and intolerant of what is, to you, hypocritical dogma that perpetuates medieval thinking and teaching. A loyal champion of the underdog, you'll fight the good fight against bluenose censorship of all kinds. Your fierce independence can delay or block easy achievement of your worldly ambitions, your determined pursuit of which can entail much action and many changes as your destiny unfolds.

Your potent magnetism attracts admirers, but you can be tempted to overcompensate for a lurking inferiority complex with an excess of social or romantic bravado. Beware of allowing quantity instead of quality in relation-ships to become your motivation to achieve ego-gratifying popularity. While you're busy climbing the success ladder, don't forget to express your attributes of sympathy, humility and patience that serve to draw others to you affec-tionately. If you become too distant, self-absorbed or confident (which can be a pseudo self-confidence), others will assume that you manage quite well alone and might feel obliged to accommodate the preference you project, when what you really want is congenial teamwork, companionship and respect, not necessarily in that order.

Drew Bledsoe (football player), 1972
Hugh Downs (broadcast journalist), 1921
Jack Benny (comedian), 1894

February the 6th (Uranus, Jupiter)
(and root digit for January 24 and February 15):

Independent, optimistic and progressive are among the estimable attributes that give you a head start in the success sweepstakes. You cherish respectabil-ity and can be a leader in your community or in the world at large if that is where your job, business or profession leads you. By capitalizing on your tal-ents and charismatic personality, you have the potential to build a life of distinctive achievement for yourself. If your work takes you into the public domain, you can set the kind of example that inspires others to reach their own goals. In any case, thanks to your engaging personality, you're likely to enjoy considerable social as well as romantic popularity.

Along with your highly developed intuition, you are inspirational and inventive and may feel that you have a mission in life. With your civic-minded, group interest outlook, the realm of politics and government could all be improved in your view, and you'd like to be instrumental in the process. If you become a valued member of the workforce or an activist for a cause or carve a career in a profession or the competitive world of commerce, you always seem able to tap resources of power and know instinctively how to make your efforts pay in either prestige or prosperity—or, with your luck, both.

Your interests bridge the gap between the very old and the very new. Antique oddities could fascinate you as much as the first commercial flight to Mars (for which you might be first in line to buy a ticket). Who knows? To your way of thinking, you could as easily meet Mr. or Ms. Right on Mars as anywhere else. You're big on "firsts" and might be the one to pull off the first interplanetary marriage. In any case, you are apt to sample several (or more) relationships of varying description before you settle into a pattern of marital or domestic contentment. You are born with the urge to merge and to experience the blissful delights of love and joyful togetherness; of all Aquarians, you're most apt to be affectionate and sentimental—the hands-holding lover. Whether or not you marry and have a family, however, you're sure to have a family of friends. Enthusiastic about all life, you believe that *all* of us should somehow share in the world's bounty and happiness.

Tom Brokaw (TV journalist), 1940

Ronald Reagan (40th U.S. President), 1911

"Babe" Ruth (baseball legend), 1895

Special to January 24 (Uranus, Jupiter [Moon/Saturn]):
Because of your sober, serious-minded outlook on life, your typical Aquarian traits can go into reverse. You could as easily be a counterrevolutionary as a revolutionary. You are just as likely to prefer the status quo and to protect the established order rather than join forces with radical activists whose principal aim is to abolish it; your sympathies depend on their motives. Revolutionaries who lack objective vision or a feasible plan to improve conditions and who are mainly motivated by a power grab are in your view nothing more than egocentric, monomaniacal destroyers. If you are accused of being too ideological or contentious, it's because you are willing to defend your own controversial ideas or opinions as forcefully as necessary.

You may be more effective pulling strings behind the scenes than in an upfront position. If you begin your working life with the right job or get started early enough in a promising career, your success and popularity can be broad-based and long-lasting. Whether you're restless and uncertain or stubbornly self-assured, your originality and dependability can win you high marks in any field you choose to express your talents. As adept at looking back and drawing inspiration from the past as you are at setting your sights on the future, your theories and creative imagination can attract considerable public notice or popularity for bridging the gap between folklore traditions and contemporary or farsighted innovations.

Neil Diamond (singer), 1941

Ernest Borgnine (actor), 1917

Louis De Wohl (author, astrologer), 1903

Special to February 15 (Uranus, Jupiter [Sun/Mars]):

Independent, logical, tolerant, sociable, idealistic and generous, you are frequently a step or two ahead of the crowd. Your success potential increases when you associate or work with people who appreciate your broad vision, responsible attitude and organizing abilities; a circumscribed job with limited horizons or scant public impact or exposure would be a dead end and a waste of your time and tireless energy. You are attracted to large-scale enterprises and like to be involved with influential, cultivated or creative people who value your expertise and cooperative spirit. If you are the very personable kind of worker or executive this birthday indicates, you inspire confidence, friendly rapport or affection in the people you deal with.

Whether in a responsible job or in the business or professional milieu, you have a quick intuitive grasp of a situation's requirements. You're not partial to a long, drawn-out learning process in order to tackle a project with which you have little or no prior experience; an extended apprenticeship (at low pay) is not your style. You're more apt to leap right into an unfamiliar venture and quickly learn the ropes as fast as you can while pursuing it. Fortunately, you have plenty of ambition and vitality to keep you moving ahead vigorously and progressively into more complicated duties and/or advanced levels of accomplishment and prosperity; the sky's the limit when you get going and apply yourself. Although it may not head the list, marriage is among your life's priorities and provides an anchor of security if and when you make the right choice, preferably someone who matches your own enterprising spirit.

Claire Bloom (actress), 1931

Susan B. Anthony (social activist), 1820

Cyrus McCormick (inventor), 1809

February the 7th (Uranus, Mercury)
(and root digit for January 25 and February 16):

Your combination of intelligence and intuition is your greatest asset. Whether your words are spoken or written, you have a talent for communication, particularly in connection with social issues. Your success potential stems from your rare ability to articulate your thought-provoking insights with depth, precision and convincing integrity. You have a deep and complex mind; if you focus on insightful, offbeat creative accomplishment, you can make a notable contribution in the field of arts and letters, science, the humanities, the law or government.

With your trenchant perception of life's inequalities and your own independent spirit, you're not partial to rigid schedules or other restrictive circumstances; you may have to develop a taste for the disciplined concentration and work habits that are necessary if you are to resolve life's challenges with mental depth and cultivation. Your flair for original and progressive thinking makes you a good organizer for projects intended to modernize or otherwise improve conditions in a job, business or profession. Your intuitive grasp of a situation enables you to envision possibilities that others miss and to unify the disparate parts of a concept into a well-rounded, workable whole that will show promising prospects for success.

You relate better to numerous and various types of people according to how you think about them rather than how you feel about them. An emotional response to someone who interests you socially or romantically is not your style; you're more likely to express your affection for people through congenial or exhilarating mental rapport. When adjustments are necessary in your life, you are capable of managing a detached viewpoint that can see you through most difficulties; you are not apt to wallow in a miasma of emotional hangups. Be cautious of giving the impression of too much self-sufficiency, however; others may take what you project at face value and leave you high and dry in the love or marriage department.

Garth Brooks (singer), 1962

Sinclair Lewis (novelist), 1885

Charles Dickens (novelist), 1812

Special to January 25 (Uranus, Mercury [Moon/Mars]):
Fired by a healthy spark of ambition and the competitive spirit, the more you gain in your initial efforts to get ahead, the more intrepid you become to advance further and achieve extraordinary success. If conflicts occur in your job or the pursuit of a career, you aren't shy about expressing your opinions, especially if you disagree with establishment rules, regulations and the narrow vision of "authorities"; to you they can be exasperating impediments standing in the way of reform and progress. Instead, you're more in tune with workers' rights, their day-to-day hard labor and dependability, their overall contribution to the success of a business or professional enterprise.

With a mind like a computer and nerves of steel, you function best on the mental fast track; when faced with a complex, daunting challenge, your can-do spirit swings into action and enables you to come through with flying colors. When combined with your unique gift of intuition, there's no stopping you. Versatile and adaptable, you can tolerate the episodic, erratic opportunities typical of the entertainment world or in any occupation, business or profession that flourishes in the public domain or requires quick thinking. Likely to leave your birthplace early for a locale that offers better outlets for your talents, you could also settle into a lasting marriage or comparable relationship.

> Dean Jones (actor), 1935
>
> Corazon Aquino (Philippine president), 1933
>
> Somerset Maugham (writer), 1874

Special to February 16 (Uranus, Mercury [Sun/Jupiter]):
You may be either a beguiling contradiction or a delightful revelation to people you work with. Despite your ebullient, extroverted nonchalance, you're inclined to take your job more seriously and yourself less seriously than expected by coworkers or those whose spirits are lifted when dealing with you in a business or professional capacity. You don't shy away from major responsibilities; they benefit from your earnest thoughtfulness if not from your occasional temperamental exasperation. Travel may loom large in your career pattern, along with your share of material luck; thanks to your zestful vitality, plucky attitude, generous spirit and crowd-pleasing magnetism, your endeavors to get ahead in the world are apt to be ringed with dollar signs.

You prefer to move right along in life; there may be interruptions or changes in direction but probably few major delays or setbacks. Quick to respond enthusiastically when prospects for a new adventure appear on the horizon, you can make up your mind pretty fast if you feel qualified to say "yes," especially to a career proposal or a promising turning point in your fortunes. Naturally articulate, you can think on your feet and say the right (and frequently clever) thing when a spur-of-the-moment development requires it. If your early life is hampered in some manner that stalls your forward momentum, that experience could be the prod driving you more optimistically toward success.

John McEnroe (tennis player), 1959

Ice-T (rapper), 1958

Sonny Bono (entertainer, politician), 1935

February the 8th (Uranus [Saturn/Uranus]),
(and root digit for January 26 and February 17):
Your urge to express your individuality and innovative concepts in a big way must first submit to the necessity for patience and discipline in order to be effective. You are fortunate that your quickness of mind and speech and pace-setting creative vigor are durable assets that can serve you well and into your sunset years. Not inclined to think small, the promotion and publicizing of humanitarian causes, fund-raising, dispensing grants, organizing large-scale enterprises and so forth are natural assignments for your special gifts. Whatever you engage in, you like to see the possibilities of expansion that will enable you to reach even greater numbers of people when you proselytize for your ideals. Your blend of intuition, originality and inspiration can land you a listing in *Who's Who in the World* or a similar roster of notable achievers.

The spirit of the rebel lurking within you comes to life when you defy establishment conventions and tackle projects that authorities or colleagues feel have little or no success potential. If you choose the most promising field for the development and expression of your talents, you'll prove them wrong. Even if you don't become widely known, it's possible for you to enjoy popularity and respect in your particular sphere of activity and/or influence. Multitalented, you have a flair for the entertainment world, literary field or artistic realm. You're also qualified for research, politics or the business or financial milieu, particularly an enterprise that depends for success on fulfilling broad public expectations.

You could be an expert, either in writing or some related creative realm or in evoking the beauty and significance of the natural world with elegance and precision. Not likely to be impressed by the latest trends (you're more apt to originate one), the changing fashions in art or literature would have little effect on the control, clarity and estimable standards that set your work apart from the crowd; you're inclined to go your own way with your distinctive style, which stems from a mix of exceptional skill, sympathetic humor, sharply individual vision and fervent independence. A possible hazard is for you to give too much importance to the spotlight, the glitter side of popularity and acclaim. With your aversion to anything phony, it is always to your advantage to look beyond appearances for life's most rewarding values.

Ted Koppel (TV newscaster), 1940

Jack Lemmon (actor), 1925

Lana Turner (actress), 1920

Special to January 26 (Uranus, Saturn [Moon/Jupiter]):
Politics, education, government, creative expression, humanitarian causes, anything else of wide public interest are grist for your mill—which can grind away nonstop when you're sufficiently motivated. Whatever you do, your work has to interest you, or you soon become bored and indifferent. It's even better if your job pays off either in recognition or prosperity, preferably both if you have your way. Where recognition is concerned, you may not care whether it's notoriety for an escapade or publicity for an achievement, just so they spell your name right. Your familiarity with the history of class struggles and/or your sympathy for the underdog can be the springboard for your broad understanding and charitable outlook on humanity's problems.

You know how to turn on the charm when you want something. You also know how to turn it off when you insist on something—all within a short space of time—like in the same conversation. Nevertheless, you are usually cheerful and optimistic, certainly no handicap in regard to social and/or romantic popularity. Likely to have a wide circle of friends among achievers in your own or a related career realm, you could fall in love and exchange wedding vows with someone who shares your career interests. Your family background was probably favorable in one way or another, which helped you to get off to a good start in life. If it wasn't all to your liking, you'll soon enough assert your individuality. You'll have a contented home life if you can possibly manage it.

Wayne Gretzky (hockey player), 1961

Paul Newman (actor), 1925

Douglas MacArthur (U.S. general), 1880

Special to February 17 (Uranus, Saturn [Sun/Mercury]):
A loquacious conversationalist, you love to talk. With your Aquarian instincts, you enjoy talking with just about anybody on a wide range of subjects, but particularly those of social significance. You also don't shy away from controversy; you revel in a good-natured debate. You see latent possibilities in familiar enterprises that others miss; with your inventive turn of mind, you can bring pioneering insights to your chosen field of work by giving standard artistic, professional or business methods an unusual twist. Especially equipped for an administrative, statistical or research post in a large venture, you should avoid any career direction that doesn't offer sturdy growth potential and/or a chance to express your vision and versatility.

Your humanitarian sympathies can surface if you express yourself in some creative form; in the process, you're likely to dignify individuals, especially life's unfortunates, in a way that transcends generations and national boundaries. With your broad-ranging talent for assessing the big picture and its ramifications, you are not easily discouraged or thrown off course by unexpected events. You know how to act most effectively during a crisis that could threaten the stability or ongoing momentum of an enterprise; you merely exert your ability to work with people of disparate views and provide a central focus when issues accelerate. Unusual intellectual diversions could be your means of relaxation from career pressures.

> Michael Jordan (basketball player), 1963
> Rene Russo (actress), 1954
> Hal Holbrook (actor), 1925

February the 9th (Uranus, Pluto)
(and root digit for January 27 and February 18):
Your life could exemplify the idea that nothing is permanent except change. Your effort to find a unifying focus for the unusual combination of liberal, democratic, mystical and metaphysical forces that motivate you could be responsible for your episodic life pattern. If you allow your intense feelings to rule, your fortunes can resemble a roller coaster, way up sometimes and way down at other times. If your mind rules, you have a better grip on the way things turn out. You may not be thrilled by the requirement for intelligent, disciplined mental effort to ensure successful outcomes for life's major issues, but the increased stability that results will make your existence more pleasant—not to mention more productive—as it unfolds.

Whether you advocate establishment mores or are inclined toward selective indignation for transgressors, you are apt to live chiefly according to your own moral code. You aren't necessarily averse to emotional or career variety, especially if a new lover or a new job, business or professional direction is more exciting or includes the potential for it, but you would no doubt rather choose the time or the reason to make changes. As either an admired colleague or a feared enemy, depending on the particular circumstances, you're apt to be a personality to be reckoned with, especially if you rise to a prominent position in your circle or in the public domain.

You are a fascinating example of contradictions. On the one hand, you can be overly generous in one context or another and endanger your own security; on the other, you can be just as tight with the purse strings if you feel taken advantage of and/or feel you have a score to settle. Any key decision you make or action you take can be based on very personal reactions to a situation, especially a difficult one. This birthday intensifies your Aquarius independent streak (read stubborn); it could be impossible (barring divine intervention) to change your mind or your take-it-or-leave-it attitude. If you feel offended, you can be arbitrary and stick to your guns to right a real or imagined wrong if for no other reason than to mollify your resentment. Not overly practical, you're more suited for a profession than for the competitive business world.

Mia Farrow (actress), 1946

Joe Pesci (actor), 1943

William Henry Harrison (9th U.S. president), 1773

Special to January 27 (Uranus, Pluto [Moon/Mercury]): Your creative originality can be the mainspring of the unique way you present your highly successful ideas. During your periods of intense mental activity, your motivation is likely to be your evaluation of the world we live in and the effort of individuals to come to terms with both the rewards and the trials and tribulations of life on this planet. Your goal for yourself or others is a journey toward self-discovery and positive self-esteem, which can be a major step to understand—if not completely to resolve—life's problems. In any case, you'll sift through subtle clues others miss as you try to get to the bottom of every question or issue with as much penetrating insight as possible. You enjoy and can profit from articulating your findings.

Your persuasive, low-key, confidence-inspiring speaking style, admirable calm demeanor under pressure and quick (occasionally caustic) wit are formidable assets if your job includes firsthand contact with the public. You know how to get down to basics and to decisively eliminate anything superfluous in your

346 **YOUR STARS ARE NUMBERED**

dealings with people. With a special talent for writing or music, you'll probably do better in the entertainment milieu or a profession than in the business world. You also have a flair for politics, the law and the communications industry (TV, radio, etc.). You do well financially, mostly by using your brains. You are interested in all progressive ideals and can be the champion of anything new.

Bridget Fonda (actress), 1964

Mikhail Baryshnikov (ballet dancer), 1948

Donna Reed (actress), 1921

Special to February 18 (Uranus, Pluto [Sun/Uranus/Saturn]):
A master of insurgent strategies, you're able to juggle several opposing creeds and alliances in your efforts to advance in life, and through subtle politicking, you can manage (most of the time) to come out ahead of the game. You have a flair for diplomacy and are able to reach out to everyone in a conflict. To describe you as subtle and clever would be an understatement. You seem instinctively to know people and their likes and dislikes, strengths and foibles, and how they will react to a particular situation, especially if you have a role in it. You can give the impression of belonging to a group and, at the same time, walk a thin line and maintain your cherished independence.

If you become involved in politics, you're likely to do it under the banner of reform. With your highly individualistic personal style, if you rise to the top in a profession or the business world, you'll stand apart from the crowd in one way or another. Any attempt to pigeonhole you into a predetermined mold would be an exercise in futility. Your comments or opinions (such as your aversion to phonies) can be an intriguing mix of candor, humor and boldness, which can arouse admiration and confidence in your integrity and capabilities from associates or the public. You expect to be rewarded for your talents with recognition, responsibility and money—and as generously as possible.

John Travolta (actor), 1954

Helen Gurley Brown (magazine editor), 1922

Jack Palance (actor), 1920

February the 11th (Uranus, Neptune [Moon/Sun])
(master number):
You can run the gamut from brilliant inventiveness all the way to maddeningly (or dangerously) irrational thinking or feelings, with fetchingly odd or distinctively original inspirations surfacing somewhere in between. Your ideas and outlook are likely to veer considerably from mainstream thinking and

conventional establishment lifestyles. In the fashion world, you might startle your peers and/or the public with your avant-garde (if not outlandish) designs. Or in the film, theatrical or publishing milieu, you could be equally provocative with your sophisticated insights into the human comedy, with the accent on wit, suggestive images and an exceptional understanding of people and their hopes, fears and assorted idiosyncrasies.

In another context, such as today's unnerving world of explosive events and terrorists (or freedom fighters, depending on your sympathies), you could be an actual revolutionary battling a political system or government you disagree with or hate. With your susceptibility to delusional influences, misguided political activities are an insidious hazard to avoid. As time goes on, you could have a change of heart about your beliefs and begin a new life. Your highly individualistic proclivities, radical sympathies or covert activities are likely to be masked by your quirky, misleading Aquarian persona; people you deal with or the public probably find you charming, considerate and a perfect lady or gentleman, traits that can deflect awareness of your true intentions.

At your pioneering best, supported by a firm practical base and strict discipline, you can tune in to the collective psyche to market your talent or product. Whether or not you deliberately cultivate it, your sense of realism can be so penetrating that you rarely, if ever, let your flights of inspiration or odd notions cause irreparable damage. You aren't partial to conventional or orthodox thinking, preferring "new thought" ideas. You function well in the research, scientific, technological or inspirational fields and could become a spokesperson of prominence. Gifted with an inventive mind, if your creations are promoted with force and application, you could make an outstanding contribution and gain fame and fortune in the process.

Sheryl Crow (singer), 1963

Burt Reynolds (actor), 1936

Thomas Alva Edison (inventor), 1847

(Note: This master number implies a variable alternative response influenced by the strength or passivity of the planet Neptune in your horoscope. If you don't feel you are responding to the distinctive vibratory power of 11, you are instead expressing the more conventional qualities of 2, which you should read.)

January the 22nd (Uranus [Saturn/Moon])
(master number):

"Anything Goes" could be your theme song. Unconventional, shrewd, free-

348 **YOUR STARS ARE NUMBERED**

thinking, ambitious and farsighted, you can be light-years ahead of the crowd when it comes to visionary ideas, trendsetting social concepts, scientific break-throughs, creative innovation or lifestyles in general. You're not partial to cookie-cutter outlooks and are instead very much in favor of doing your own thing and letting others do theirs. If you indulge the maverick tendencies of your birthday, however, you can rank near the top of the major leagues when your penchant for total freedom and/or experimentation gets out of hand. Then you jump in and break the rules or make up new ones that are more accommodating to your offbeat whims. You're the type to run for public office on some obscure, far-out ticket with scant prospect of winning. In this quirky one-of-a-kind mode, you might even startle your dinner guests with an exotic concoction like squid and rattlesnake soufflé.

The brightest possibility for you is the genius potential of 22. Your birth-day is the dynamic combination of the electrical power of 22 operating in its own trail-blazing field of Aquarius. Your ideas can be astonishingly inventive and constructive, with broad humanitarian implications and/or mass public appeal. As an effective political activist, you may have deep psychic roots in the historic tradition of protest against tyranny or oppression. You don't take orders if there's any reason to question their validity and are always ready to challenge the status quo when a wrong needs to be righted—such as when a callous official selects a mostly poor neighborhood for a toxic waste dump.

You are a willing worker but not partial to routine. Your great gifts are your remarkable intuitive promptings and distinctive style; if other testimonies con-cur, you can make a notable contribution, achieving fame along with other rewards. At your best, you're the trendsetter par excellence, intrigued by future frontiers as well as new thresholds of knowledge and experience that make life more exhilarating, convenient, comfortable and fulfilling. Some people's eccen-tric behavior or life's oddities that are eyebrow-raising to others can seem perfectly natural to you. Those you love share the excitement when they open their eyes, like you, to seeing things in unusual new ways.

George Balanchine (choreographer), 1904

D. W. Griffith (pioneering film director), 1875

Andre Marie Ampere (physicist, inventor), 1775

(Note: This master number implies a variable alternative response influenced by the strength or passivity of the planet Uranus in your horoscope. If you don't think you are responding to the distinctive vibratory power of 22, you are instead expressing the more conventional qualities of 4, which you should read.)

CHAPTER 12

PISCES
February 19–March 20

RULER: **NEPTUNE** NUMBER: **1** ELEMENT: **WATER** SYMBOL: **THE FISHES**

"God shall be my hope, my stay, my guide, and lantern to my feet."
—*Henry VI*, Part II, Shakespeare

From the Sistine ceiling to the dream dump, from sublime creativity to the murky depths of disillusion, Pisces runs the gamut. Your Sun-Sign is the most idealistic, imaginative, impressionable, empathetic sign in the zodiac; it has contributed to the world numerous geniuses in the fields of music, art, painting, poetry and science. Pisces is also the sign of extremes, not of elemental intensity like Scorpio but of nebulous apprehensions troubling to the soul.

Your symbol is the Fishes. Your ruler is Neptune, the god of the sea in Roman mythology and known as Poseidon in Greece. The Fishes represent the two halves of experience: the half that your physical self (limitation and mortality) encounters is separate but linked to your other half (the astral realm), which is your unconscious, emotional response to experience. The Fishes swim in opposite directions, symbolizing your need for an anchor of stability somewhere in between as one part of you goes upstream against the current while the other part flows out with the tide.

You yearn for some unattainable utopia in the depths of your being, a place where no one ever goes hungry, where fluffy white clouds drift across a sunshine-filled sky, where children laugh and play and grow up unfettered by worries, where there is no meanness or cruelty and where everyone lives happily ever after, joyously contributing to, and sharing in, the common good.

Unlike Virgo, which would be happiest if it was a perfect world, Pisces would be happiest if it was a compassionate, caring world. Of course, the blend of your water-sign sensitivity, expansive feelings and vivid imagination can prompt you to be a daydreamer who hasn't much taste for the rough-and-tumble world of everyday realities. Typically empathetic, your heart goes out to those less fortunate, the waifs and strays you encounter as you make your way through life.

The mystic of the zodiac, you can have dreams about past or current events or experience remarkable future impressions or forebodings before they happen. You are less likely to doubt life after death or prior to birth. You generally see nothing implausible in reincarnation, the Law of Karma or the Akashic records. You can be like a telepathic short-wave receiver; messages from the beyond or events in vivid detail can be transmitted through you from the astral realms of the universal unconscious. As a psychic sponge, you can actually tune into another person's feelings, especially someone in distress.

Being on intimate terms with nature, feeling your roots linked with the all-in-oneness of the cosmos, things like encouraging plants to grow by talking to them seem as natural to you as watering them. Since the thought can give rise to the act, your instinctive curiosity about the unknown may nurture your affinity with it. When you function as a channel for the cosmic intelligence, your consciousness penetrates the veil of ordinary everyday affairs. You then become a conduit for the great unseen; information originating spontaneously in your psyche is transmitted into your consciousness for whatever use you choose to make of it. However, just as water flowing through a rusty pipe is questionable or tainted, messages or insights coming through you will only be as pure and rational as you are. This is the reason that trance mediums or clairvoyants can lose their power, or their gift comes and goes; the impurities of a flawed personality can clog the channel of cosmic consciousness. The divine intelligence isn't going to select a faulty instrument for such wondrous revelations.

Through the successive initiations of the Zodiac, each Sun-Sign becomes increasingly challenging in its implications. In Pisces, we arrive at the summit of cosmic expectations: *compassion.* Your ruling planet, Neptune, has no roots materially. Your element is water, restless and agitated, possibly because you're an emotional reservoir of arcane, discursive information; your hidden agenda, the distillation of fresh initiatives from past experience, marks the threshold of a new cycle in life—the impending Aries outrush into experience. Pisces is the proving or seeding ground preparing the fulcrum for the next wave of incarnations.

Whereas Virgo, your opposite Sun-Sign, classifies and purifies matter for ultimate usefulness, you classify and purify feelings—relinquishing those unworthy of humankind's instincts. That's why your sign is called the universal solvent: All choices are broken down to their essence to facilitate formation of the purest amalgam from the finely grained particles remaining in your consciousness from past or current experience.

How, you may ask, can a Sun-Sign capable of such glorious achievement as the ceiling of the Sistine Chapel in the Vatican be called the dream dump, the dustbin of the Zodiac, the repository of psychic garbage? It's because Pisces can be more preoccupied with fantasy and how beautiful life *can be* than with the unromanticized necessities that turn dreams into concrete realities. The measure of your fulfillment and happiness is how willing you are to come to terms with cold, practical facts and weave them into the tapestry of your dreams. Since many of you may find that any dream is better than none, it's advantageous for you to concentrate on one that has a chance of working, of making it come true in the world as it is.

Ideals aren't of much value without the willpower and purpose to give them communicable, workable form. In your insistence on the efficacy of your dream, remember that you can't build a house from the top down. It must rest securely on an earthbound foundation of blocks carefully put into place, one at a time; that is the crux of your challenge. Your approach can be ill-formed and tenuous. You can float haphazardly in the ethereal realms, be too self-absorbed and then, if you fail, become disturbingly withdrawn. A Pisces in despair is as cryptic as Egyptian hieroglyphics; in the subterranean depths of your soul you are talking another language, mostly indecipherable to you or anyone who tries to dredge it out of you when you are in one of your dolorous, agonizing moods; that's why you at times can seem so vague or remote to companions. When you're unusually quiet, of course, people may mistakenly assume that you are depressed, when actually you're just in one of your placid, faraway moods. You don't see the necessity for bubbling constantly or for being "on" all the time. People who are can be tiresome to you.

As the last sign of the twelve, the treasure as well as the trash of the entire Zodiac is at your disposal. The most ephemeral and receptive of the Sun-Signs, Pisces is susceptible to the positive and negative features of all twelve of them; you thus have, altogether, twenty-four basic choices. Will you stress the spiritual, transformative side or the erotic abandon or vindictive side of Scorpio? The glib, diffusive side or the usefully informative and learned side of Gemini? The puffy, preening pride or the loving generosity of Leo? The carping criticism or the constructive discrimination of Virgo? And so on.

The reason for your sign's possible difficulties becomes more evident as the principles and pitfalls of each Sun-Sign culminate in Pisces. No wonder you can feel a heavy burden. This is why some of you just drift along with the currents and vent your random feelings: Perpetually poised between psychic acceptance and rejection, day-to-day grappling with life's realities can become wearying. The restless receptivity of your psychic antennae can make you nervous unless you're anchored to your spiritual center. When you are, however, you gain serenity from your basic framework of sterling values accumulated along the path of the evolutionary spiral. When your most commendable inner instincts coincide with the requirements of the material world as it is, you won't be as thrown by seemingly harsh events, some of which stem from the interpretation *you* put on them.

The planet of love, Venus, is exalted when found in your sign, a combination that denotes love and compassion tempered by divine justice. You can go overboard, however, and be too tolerant of others' shortcomings. When your sympathy is selectively misdirected, you're just being indulgent, giving your emotions a self-gratifying workout for their own sake. Your compassion ceases to be a virtue when you don't heed moral principles that serve objective needs for the broadest common good. Your ruler, Neptune, is the planet of obligation; there are times when you must value justice more than your sympathies, must go against the grain of your feelings—symbolized by the fish swimming upstream. As a negative Piscean, you will espouse lopsided standards. For example, if those you admire break a law for a cause they believe in, you will condone it because you believe in them or the same cause. If those you don't like break the same law, for whatever reason, you would judge it differently. The criminal act, the clearly broken law that can be harmful to blameless people, would not be the central factor in your judgment. You must have a clear picture of right and wrong, good and evil, and must not judge subjectively or mystically but impartially.

If charisma is not one of your conspicuous attributes, don't let it trouble you; although there are notable exceptions, you're not meant primarily for the limelight. The source of your satisfactions usually stems from the work you perform or the benefactions you bestow. In case you achieve prominence, it will either be through an important contribution to humanity, possibly involving personal sacrifice, or from factors in your horoscope that add drive, ambition or an outstanding talent that produces more personal glory in the public realm than is typical of Pisces.

Your soul can become the refuge for a lot of agonizing. Your energies are directly linked to your psychic responses. You're so subjective that, when depressed, your energies give out; you don't wilt, you collapse. Then you don't retreat from reality, like a Cancerian would, you *disappear*. You may sleep a lot because you find more solace in the arms of Morpheus than in the cold embrace of the realities of day-to-day survival.

Self-deprecation and self-belittlement can be your greatest shortcomings. Since you are typically reticent, people who come on strong may impress you. However, you can be too ready to believe boastful types or to read more value or excitement into surface trappings than the truth of a situation warrants. You might admire (and perhaps envy) those who are flashy "swingers" and to whom you bestow more social or romantic desirability than you do on yourself. It might not occur to you that such types are merely loud and showy. You may just be unknowingly shortchanging yourself by your self-abnegating attitude.

As a consequence, being dishonest mostly with yourself, you can assume that your qualities are of minor import. Don't forget that others are apt to put the same valuations on things that you do. If you inwardly feel that you're an undeserving nonentity, others will only be too happy to oblige and conclude the same thing. Whatever you project will rebound like a boomerang. But if you are true to yourself, you won't be deceived by others' flamboyance. You will know how to evaluate pretense, flashy display, phony facades. If you don't come by it naturally, you should train yourself to distinguish between true worth and empty bombast.

Just what is your dream? Do you want to be "happy"? With your vivid imagination, that could be a large order to fill and could take some doing, like completely restructuring your concept of reality. Are you willing to pay the price? Or are your dreams beyond price, beyond realization? When you fantasize dreams beyond any hope of realization, then you're vulnerable to delusions. That's where the dream dump and the psychic garbage come in. You then find solace through escapes that temporarily soften or dissolve the hard edges of reality. Unfortunately, this doesn't really solve anything on the inner level, where it matters. Resorting to pseudo-solutions that yield instant nirvana becomes the only way you can sustain longed-for euphoric satisfactions. Willpower fades into amorphous desire gratifications; in order to maintain these feelings, you can become caught in the undertow of drugs or alcohol.

You might forget that the world isn't really any more harsh on you than it is on others who never need to resort to escapes, although it may seem so. Your timeworn defense about others' lack of feelings is not convincing; excusing your wayward judgment that way is simply the interpretation that you are putting on what reality requires of you, but you don't want to face that fact. Wishing that things weren't the way they are won't solve anything nor will indulging in artificial means to justify your wish. Doing something about it through positive thinking is the only way out for you.

The public in general can mask a bushel of smug self-righteousness and parade all kinds of half-truths behind an ideological facade, such as a religious or cult doctrine; as long as it is labeled "idealistic," you can be impressed. Because of your sensitivity, you might think you have an exclusive on feelings about ideals. However, those who don't necessarily agree with you have ideals and feelings, too. Natives of the other eleven Sun-Signs are also against war and suffering and for motherhood and the flag. It's easy to be for virtues, but you may not like the personal responsibility behind the agonizing facts some-times necessary to provide virtues a safe place in which to flourish.

You're only too aware that the world, by and large, snickers at those who sacrifice their lives to doing good and labels the hard, blustery "go-getters" the admired, shining heroes of the mass public. They're at the head of life's parade, all aglow with their jutting chins, toothpaste-ad teeth and pushy smiles fixed in concrete. If one is toppled, however, in an accident or whatever, who's at his or her side, ministering to their pain? *You are*—or someone else who exemplifies your good Samaritan Pisces virtues. The world and its heroes need you; in fact, they couldn't survive without you. If at times you've been the mushy, bleeding heart do-gooder, we've had more than our share of flashy cardboard heroes, too.

If you tend to be on the negative side, you should refrain from accepting the popular appraisal that you are a patsy or a loser just because you espouse sympathetic virtues. That is only another opinion, offered mostly as self-defense from people who wouldn't have the courage to *feel* as honestly as you do. Unlike many others, you aren't afraid to empathize emotionally; even when your judgment is askew, it's an honest, heartfelt mistake. By overcom-ing your aversion to cold facts, you can take pride in your convictions and be confident that your principles are the ones that have provided continuity to life through quiet strength.

Whereas Scorpio has an introverted power complex, your introversion is masochistic. Some of you find self-justification, salvation, only in giving something up. As a negative Piscean, you will deliberately choose a situation where you are sure of being a loser—like falling in love with a hopeless neu-rotic whom you want to help or reform. That way, you share his/her suffering, which is what you want to do in the first place. It would be sheer folly to offer you a good, healthy relationship based on normal give and take, for you would consider it "unfeeling" for the one in need. Your emotions can become spongy, drenched in treacly sentiment, like going down in a vat of maple syrup for the third time.

Borrow a page from Leo's book: Be a little (or a lot) more proud. Although Leo does not require a reason for pride (the Lion can always invent one), you may have one (or more) that you're not even aware of. Glow more confidently about your accomplishments. Don't be so supplicating. Borrow an impulse from Aries: Be more assertive. You probably don't have any more reason than the next person to feel inadequate, but, of course, with a little effort and your masochistic streak, you can always drum up something.

You're either drawn to others' suffering or register it within yourself. You're not likely to be an advocate of vivisection; you can even have ambivalent feelings over dispatching a roach or a mouse. One Piscean of record had occasion, while performing her morning ablutions, to witness a maternity event in her bathroom: a pregnant roach in the full throes of an obstetrical crisis. She watched the events in wonderment, until common sense overcame compassion, whereupon mother and brood were flushed into eternity—but not without ambivalent pangs of regret at the necessity for such a clinical denouement. Since Mehitabel isn't likely to be squashed underfoot or so summarily dispatched, you may feel that Archie is not really deserving of such an ignominious fate either. Needless to add, the death of a pet, sad for anyone, is traumatic for Pisces.

You're so emotional that you can become unstable; you can be victimized by your weepy sentiments. Being the apotheosis of sentimental romanticism, you can cherish pressed violets in a book of poetry, lace valentines or initialed hearts carved on a tree trunk or a park bench. As a distaff Piscean, you are especially vulnerable to building fantasies of a dream lover. You can meet someone who gives you a little attention and scant encouragement and immediately imbue the situation with an aura of romantic fantasy all out of proportion to the reality. You could indulge in little delusions like "He doesn't call me more often because I'm a threat to his bachelorhood" or "He's so much in love with me that he's afraid to see me." You can be too willing to put your lover, whether deserving or undeserving, on a pedestal. Instead of facing the facts (your euphemisms for which are "cold," "cynical" or "unfeeling"), you, as a gushy enchantress, can talk yourself into being content with a bone. You should learn to pick one—you would make more progress in the love stakes. Then you won't accept tenuous threads in lieu of a full-blooded commitment. You can become a winner instead of just placing, showing or finishing last in the love and romance sweepstakes. Since you can cry three times a day, you figure that you might as well get some mileage out of it. Then you can use tears as a weapon—the same way that Scorpio uses sex.

The signs ruled by Venus, the lower octave of your ruler, Neptune, give some keys to your nature. You can be as stubborn as Taurus (the earth Venus) and as indecisive as Libra (the air Venus). Since stubbornness is the negative form of determination, how you apply that trait will determine the benefits or the liabilities. Combined with a positive spirit, you are faithful and home-loving, an ideal mate or parent. Your home, if somewhat untidy, always looks delightfully lived in.

With the wrong partner, you can mutually encourage each other's weaknesses. The film *The Days of Wine and Roses* illustrated how devastating this can be. Avoiding deep involvements with others until you know all about them and their histories should be your first step in relationships; you're inclined to expect the best from unfamiliar or possibly dubious situations. Seeing everything except yourself through rose-colored glasses, you are susceptible to an active and difficult relationship history with numerous love affairs. Because of your escapist tendencies, you can have uncontrolled appetites, a confused morality; much of your emotional activity can be *entre nous*, with consolations outside an unhappy marriage frequent occurrences.

An unusually loyal friend, once affections are given, those who would consort with you should allow for your moods; your expression can change when company changes, and you're very sensitive to the atmosphere around you. You tend to pick up the moods or characteristics of people you're in contact with. Considering your empathy for life's unfortunates, you're oddly contradictory in your choice of friends, gravitating more toward pillars of the community than hapless dropouts for friendship or socializing. You hobnob easily among upwardly mobile types, perhaps because they set a no-nonsense example that inspires you to persevere in the attainment of your own admirable, if sometimes difficult to achieve, objectives.

Since yours is the sign of the Fishes, it's prudent to remember that sharks are fishes, too; a vindictive Piscean can be treacherous and invent all kinds of frothy justifications for it. A really vengeful Piscean can be a sneaky menace. When people voice suspicions about something being "fishy," well . . . now you know whose traits they're talking about. When your feelings are muddled or you're in a retaliatory mood, you should talk things over with an impartial friend who sticks to the facts and can offer objective suggestions.

Careerwise, you may have difficulties if you try to carve out a future based on egocentric ambition or where willpower or force is essential to getting ahead and staying there. Not usually competitive or the type to storm the battlements, you prefer to gain things *without* fuss. Yours can be the eager spirit, but your physical energy and drive may be spasmodic since they depend on your emotional status. You can often be found in a job or career that requires a nighttime, weekend or other non-traditional schedule. This means that your personal wants and desires are apt to play second fiddle to the main theme—your life's work or related efforts to achieve success and security.

You're not happiest working alone, although you may work in secluded surroundings. This is one of the reasons you are frequently found in the health care field, although that has its hazards: You are susceptible to picking up the symptoms or ailments of others. Paradoxically, you're a specialist in understanding psychosomatic illness. There's a healing quality about your Piscean sympathy. Fittingly enough, hypnotism and anesthesia coincided with the discovery in 1846 of Neptune, your ruling planet.

Although you can adapt to almost any occupation, you're best suited for a profession. You usually have no great craving for public acclaim or attention, yet you can possess great abilities for a glamorous occupation in the arts or entertainment field or where the unreal is a factor, such as in acting (especially film), photography, magic and so forth. Since Pisces rules the feet, it's no coincidence that ballet superstar Rudolph Nureyev was a Pisces, as was his legendary predecessor, Vaslav Nijinsky.

Your Sun-Sign has contributed its share of legends to the entertainment world. Among the memorably distinctive film stars are Jean Harlow, Elizabeth Taylor, John Garfield, Anna Magnani, Cyd Charisse and Jerry Lewis. In various related fields are found such notables as Enrico Caruso, Marian Anderson, Johnny Cash, Jackie Gleason, Nat King Cole, George Harrison, Liza Minnelli, Harry Belafonte, Edward Albee, Glenn Miller and Harry James.

With energizing aspects and a special talent, you can have an extraordinary career, especially in an artistic or unusual pursuit, your greatest success lying in the development of a gift or a skill. You're even good at public relations—sensing what will have the best effect, not necessarily what is the exact truth. You know how to embellish facts for a public impressed and/or manipulated by hyperbole. In any case, your dependability assures you a certain amount of security; unless you're extremely foolish, you never lose the ground you've gained and usually manage to have the material things necessary for comfort. A pitfall can lie in being overly devoted to "service" as an abstraction, feeling too conscientious or "duty bound," resigned to your "lot." Then you can get trapped on the self-abnegating treadmill, from which you have difficulty extricating yourself.

Great figures born in your Sun-Sign are among humanity's immortals, each one a magnificent contributor in his particular sphere. Inspirations you've plenty of, and the following Pisces examples had the grit and energy necessary to bring them into powerful realization. Michaelangelo had an abundance of all three traits. He painted the sublime Sistine ceiling, one of the world's greatest masterpieces, which necessitated lying on his back for four years, perched on rickety scaffolding a dizzying height up from the floor of a cavernous Renaissance chapel. He complained continually, and sometimes bitterly, about his physical discomfort (back pain, paint dripping into his eyes, etc.), but he stayed the course the whole miserable time until his great work of art was finished. He was also the principle architect of St. Peter's Cathedral in Rome. His numerous creations express a universality and force that transcend limitations of style and primitive technology. The title of a book about this extraordinary genius, appropriately titled *The Agony and the Ecstasy,* describes the dilemma, dedication and greatness inherent in Pisces to perfection.

Albert Einstein, one of the outstanding physicists of all time, is famous for his theory of relativity, but he is not as famous for his interest in astrology. Scientists would rather you didn't know about that. Although his discoveries contributed to the development of the atom bomb, he was a typical Piscean: a staunch pacifist, active in the cause of world peace.

Frederic Chopin, an original genius in music, one of the ten or twelve greatest composers of all time, has sent the spirits of millions of listeners soaring through his inspired masterpieces. Creating new forms, or imbuing old ones with fresh insights, he suffered personally and triumphed creatively. Typical of Pisces, he had visions and hallucinations that became the inspirations for some of his best-known compositions.

A true romantic, Chopin was not without wit and a surgical insight into the sentimentalized foibles of his day. As a teacher, his remark on the way "English lady pianists watch their hands play the wrong notes with such feeling" is loaded with meaning for you. Unlike many Pisceans, he was intensely disciplined, the precise perfectionist. More typically Piscean, however, he lacked healthy stamina and continuously struggled against one physical indisposition or another. Two notable aspects of his music are its chromaticism, tones seemingly without an anchor of resolution, and agitated rhythms, both immediately traceable to the depths of Piscean characteristics.

Music based on chromatic themes and harmonies has a rootless quality—seems poised in thin air or in a state of suspension. This, coupled with Chopin's agitated rhythms (the two fishes at cross-purposes), gives the effect of a stream's restless fluidity, now flowing swiftly, then troubled, perhaps momentarily diverted, then surging onward again. Someone has said, "Great music—where theories and thought are lost—is a psychical storm, agitating to unfathomable depths the mystery of the past within us. It stirs psychic memories, perished passions, and expired exultations." How beautifully Chopin fulfilled that description of the art he practiced with such dedication and personal sacrifice.

The plight of Shakespeare's Hamlet, expressed in the famous soliloquy, sums up the Piscean's challenge: "To be, or not to be" is your soul-stirring question, too. To be what? Practical? Resolute? Confident? Sensible? Sympathetic? Responsible? Determined? Creative? You have so many choices, but the master key to the right ones for you is enlightened compassion tempered by disciplined feelings, a realistic ideology and a productive agenda.

PISCES BIRTHDAYS

Judgment of whether or not a birthday is propitious can be considered from two points of view: complementary or challenging. From the standpoint of personal progress and fulfillment, your destiny may flow more comfortably if your birthday is, or reduces to, an *outer* root number such as 2, 4, 6 or 8. For career drive and achievement, your progress may be enhanced if your birthday is, or reduces to, an *inner* root number such as 1, 3, 5, 7 or 9; the *inner* root numbers are less comfortable, more obstructive for you to contend with, but they are potentially very conducive to outstanding success. The 11 (master number), correlating to the planet Neptune, ruler of Pisces, would be advantageous. The 22 (master number) would be variable but generally would require more understanding and resourcefulness to integrate with the meaning of Pisces.

Remember, if your birthday is two digits (excepting master numbers 11 and 22), be sure to read the root digit or number first. For example, if your birthday is 29, read the 2 (2 + 9 = 11, 1 + 1 reduces to 2) birthday profile first and then read the special profile for 29. If your birthday is 14, read the 5 (1 + 4 = 5) birthday profile first and then read the special profile for 14, and so on. If a description in a "special" section contradicts information in the "root" digit (root number) analysis, the "special" interpretation applies more specifically to you.

The first planet in parentheses following your birthday number is *your Sun-Sign ruler*; the second planet (or Uranus/Saturn for number 8) is *your birthday number planetary equivalent*. Subsidiary planetary influences (if any) are bracketed.

Each birthday profile includes celebrities who share the same birthday.

YOUR BIRTHDAY PROFILE

March the 1st (Neptune, Sun)

(and root digit for February 19 and 28, March 10 and 19):

Inspirational, versatile and ambitious, your potential runs the gamut between a modest ripple at low tide in the world of achievement to a surging wave at high tide in the entertainment realm or in some other creative, business or professional capacity. Whether your impact is great or moderate, however, you are likely to be uncompromising in your integrity and dedication to maintaining the highest standards in your work. While you might be ambivalent about a struggle to reach the top and prefer to be an escapee from the competition wars, your desire for recognition or to play a leadership role in one way or another can thrust you—whether you like it or not—into the unsettling fray that's part of getting ahead.

If you are more imaginative than practical and disciplined, you can dream up all kinds of wonderful plans to accomplish a goal and then procrastinate and fail to bring them to realistic fruition. In life in general, but particularly in the workplace or your career strivings, always keep your feet securely planted on terra firma; if you don't, a misguided delusion could exaggerate your prospects for success and undermine your best intentions to showcase your talents and to better yourself.

When your self-propelling mode quietly shifts into high gear, your calming influence and willingness to carefully listen to everyone will enhance your stature as an administrator and/or for doing a standout job in your field of endeavor. Your broad sympathies and deep understanding enable you to get along with a wide spectrum of people, whether the high and mighty or the general public, or even with people who aren't on your particular wavelength. At the helm of an enterprise or in your personal life, you are usually ready with a helping hand or a bit of comforting or encouraging advice. Reserve some of your sense of humor, the kind that can give other people a lift, for yourself. It will come in handy when, even with a generally satisfactory existence, you might have inner longings from time to time that are hard to express or are unattainable, which can result in nerves and tension. Of all your abilities, music, writing, acting or any related inspirational field may be the most promising outlet for your distinctive expressive style.

Ron Howard (director, actor), 1954

Harry Belafonte (singer), 1927

Glenn Miller (bandleader), 1909

Special to February 19 (Neptune, Uranus, Sun [Sun/Pluto]):
Although you might originally train for a profession, you could become dis-satisfied with your prospects and eventually shift into the manufacturing or business world because that's where the money is, at least in the amounts you can dream about. However, with your keen awareness of public tastes and markets for products or services, plus your foresight and entrepreneurial instincts, the odds favor a successful outcome to any of your ventures. Your adaptability and flair for sensing opportunities enable you to turn more than one job or career into an income-producing activity. You could be a whiz at any work or skill that requires specialization or technical wizardry.

You're not the type to settle for surface or ordinary satisfactions; whether or not you're subconsciously motivated, your quest for a fresh challenge serves your need to plumb the depths within yourself. With your combination of independent spirit and emotional insight, you perceive reality in terms of uni-versal truths, which you might express in writing or the scientific field. When problems occur, you're able to see both sides, enabling you to be both objective and sympathetic in your conclusions and/or able to dredge up a solution that promotes a consensus or a workable compromise and all-around satisfaction. If you're from a working-class background and respond positively to your ambi-tious spirit, you'll probably begin your efforts early to rise above your origins. Marriage and family life could be among your rewarding accomplishments.

Jeff Daniels (actor), 1955

Lee Marvin (actor), 1924

Nicholas Copernicus (astronomer), 1473

Special to February 28 (Neptune, Sun [Moon/Uranus/Saturn]):
Capable of decisive as well as inspired leadership, particularly in a crisis, there would be little doubt about who is boss if you rise to a position of authority in a job, profession or business. When a bold move is necessary that includes an element of cutting questionable corners, you're able to make one well within the boundaries of ethics and responsibility. With your sensitivity to mass tastes and trends, your marketing skills would be an asset to any enterprise that depends on consumer popularity for success. In the creative realm, your specialty could be to make use of dreams and of dreamlike, ethe-real atmospheres that are remote in space or time, suspended as it were in a magical realm of your own imagination.

You might not possess what are considered the standard attributes for reaching the top, such as forceful aggressiveness backed up by boundless energy and drive, but your ambition is nevertheless effective when you decide to pursue a goal. Possibly very gifted, the main hazard to fulfilling your estimable potential, whether in the competitive business milieu or a creative field, could be your tendency to become moody and to withdraw, when trouble strikes, into your private little world—where you are safe from a challenge or a confrontation. One way to bolster your self-confidence and initiative is to get as good an education as possible or to acquire the skills necessary to succeed in a special line of work. Otherwise, it may be difficult to tap or to find a satisfactory outlet to express your deep wells of creativity.

Tommy Tune (dancer, choreographer), 1939

Linas Pauling (chemist), 1901

Michel de Montaigne (essayist, critic), 1533

Special to March 10 (Neptune, Sun):

You prefer work or activities that bring you to the forefront; you are not likely to become enthused about tasks or interests for which you'll gain little or no praise or recognition. Very imaginative and idealistic, your dream of success, if it includes personal popularity or credibility, is most apt to become a rewarding reality when it is firmly based on practical possibilities. Your high-strung emotional drive can deplete your vitality, so it's a good idea to pace yourself sensibly. Your ambitious spirit could combine your determination to make a name for yourself with the gentle sensibilities of a dedicated artist or visionary.

In the creative vein, you could become a leader credited with breakthroughs that change forever the way things are perceived or accomplished in your field of endeavor—which could easily be life changing for people in one way or another. Particularly suited to the entertainment milieu, you are also well qualified for a profession, especially in the health care industry where you could make a significant contribution. With your special flair for color, you could be effective in the arts, whether in the fine arts, commercial design or in some autonomous promotional or administrative capacity. If you make time for a variety of interests (especially a hobby or pleasurable pastime), it will help to keep you healthy and prosperous.

Sharon Stome (actress), 1958

Chuck Norris (actor), 1940

A. Honegger (composer), 1892

Special to March 19 (Neptune, Mars, Sun [Sun/Pluto]):

You may not depend as much as the typical Piscean on reassuring emotional feedback to sustain you as you make your way through life. You're more apt to rely on your psychic antennae, shrewd insights and/or a vigorous defense to meet a challenge than to retreat into a protective refuge when threatened by a testy issue or a showdown. Not as much of a daydreamer as other members of your Sun-Sign, you're likely instead to become bored, restless and inattentive unless you keep busy. You also have a knack for clandestine activities, such as keeping your plans and ventures to yourself until they are well developed and you're ready to spring them without fear of a competitor beating you to the draw.

Whether or not you get an early start on your job or career ambitions, you're rather anxious and would like to see fast-paced results from your initial efforts to get ahead. As a Pisces, you could have strong feelings about labor conditions, animal shelters, subsidized housing, the Environmental Protection Agency, affordable health care and so on, with the difference that you are willing to swing into action against anything that oppresses or otherwise adversely affects people and life in general. Whatever goal you decide on, you're capable of plucky determination and focusing all your energies to achieve it. Particularly talented in the creative realm, there can be an element of colorful adventure in your life, unusual for Pisces.

Bruce Willis (actor), 1955

Philip Roth (novelist), 1933

Irving Wallace (novelist), 1916

March the 2nd (Neptune, Moon)
(and root digit for February 20 and 29, March 20;
March 11 is a master number, see end of chapter):

Your exceptional versatility and receptivity to people and situations around you are among your most valuable assets. Sensitive and alert to popular tastes and trends, you know how to provide in advance a product, skill or an idea for public betterment before the rest of the population is aware of the need. Although qualified by your adaptable abilities for almost any job, you are likely to feel more at home in a profession such as writing, publishing, the academic realm or the political domain. You aren't as well suited for the rough-and-tumble commerciality of the business or industrial world, but you would nevertheless have a feeling for inspiring productive teamwork in your coworkers.

Normally reticent and agreeable, it might require some rigid self-discipline for you to express yourself forcefully when assertive tactics are necessary in the face of mounting difficulties. Your ability to tune in to others' feelings is a substantial asset when dealing with issues that require emotional empathy.

However, when you're responding negatively to situations that arouse strong feelings, pettiness and touchiness can overcome your more typical desire to employ solicitous means to resolve a distressful situation.

On the other hand, you may need to keep your own emotional empathy in check. For example, the discouraging conditions you are sometimes exposed to in the world of affairs can arouse your sympathies to such an extent that you can become too passive, too yielding or too forgiving, when taking a firm stand would be more advantageous. Compassion is a noble virtue, but nothing is gained by letting it become indulgent timidity. You can feel wounded in the depths of your soul if someone you admire and believe in falls from grace, causing a profound disillusionment that could take a long time to get over but that you'll never forget. Many changes early in your life may have left you feeling emotionally insecure as you reached the threshold of your climb to success, but as you gain in self-confidence, your rise is steadier and more assured.

> Mikhail Gorbachev (former Soviet leader), 1931
>
> Tom Wolfe (writer), 1931
>
> Desi Arnaz (actor, bandleader), 1917

Special to February 20 (Neptune, Moon):

Versatile, friendly and outgoing, you're likely to express your ideals in any one of several career paths you could follow. Whether you express yourself in music, acting, writing or one of the other creative realms, you are particularly adept in dealing with the public, with whom your work can be very popular. At the same time, you could also receive official critical acclaim for your efforts, which, in one way or another, are set apart by your distinctive imprint for style and quality. If you attain the heights of success, you could also establish new techniques and standards in your field and gain additional renown as a critic, publisher or teacher. Or you could discover a new direction in arts and letters.

You might sometimes get the impression, when your feelings are misunderstood, that you are living in the outback of the emotional world. If so, it might be owing to bestowing your affections on undeserving people in situations that don't fulfill your ideals and your intensely romantic nature. If you make the mistake of falling in love with love itself or you otherwise stray from the path of sensible emotional gratification, you will sooner or later have to face the cold realities. With your ability to move easily among the rich and famous, you could use your talent and shrewd instincts about people to prosper and eventually join their upscale ranks.

Cindy Crawford (model), 1966
Sidney Poitier (actor), 1924
Ansel Adams (photographer), 1902

Special to February 29 (leap year only, Neptune, Moon [Pluto]): Although you may not appear to try to impose your will on others or to seem forceful in achieving your ambitions, you nevertheless have a reservoir of subtle power that can be just as effective as others' more overt aggressiveness; you could be the master manipulator of understatement or for recycling material that has served you well in a previous endeavor or another context. And in a show of boldness, confident that most people won't know what you're up to, you may not feel that your ploy needs to be even thinly disguised. Your initiatives or projects may seem conventionally typical, but there can be a lot more to them than meets the eye once your inspiration takes flight.Easily bored, inquisitive and probably restless as you grew up, you could drift quite a lot in search of a vocation that can hold your attention. Luckily, you're able to deal with the changes (or upsets) that life brings you way and to somehow capitalize on them. When you discover your true abilities, you are capable of settling in and becoming very determined and successful in your chosen field. In a situation that is confusing to others, you know how to get down to the nitty-gritty and to separate the wheat from the chaff—not necessarily taking a lot of time for diplomacy. You can do very well in the arts, but you also have an aptitude for leadership in the business world or politics. Through controlling your temperament and harnessing your energies, you'll give practical expression to talents that can be exceptional.

Michele Morgan (actress), 1920
Jimmy Dorsey (bandleader), 1904
Gioacchino Rossini (composer), 1792

Special to March 20 (Neptune, Moon):
Your knowledge of people and studies are your passport to success as you wend your way through life's competitive challenges. With your understanding and sympathy for life's outsiders, you thrive on the daily hustle and bustle as you go about putting your ideas across, most likely in work to improve the lot of the disadvantaged or to apply your expertise to any area of public assistance such as social welfare. In the health care field, you are well qualified for a career as a doctor or nurse, a physical therapist, a pharmacist, a medical supply and manufacturing representative and so on. An opening in the rapidly burgeoning

biotechnology field could be an exciting, progressive, lucrative choice. Or you could prosper in a business or profession related to any of these activities.

You might need to be careful of becoming too adjustable and accommodating in your devotion to your work, but the kind of work that attracts you frequently requires nighttime, weekend or some other odd schedule. Needless to add, this implies that your personal life is likely to play second fiddle to your job, which presupposes a very understanding mate if you expect a marriage or serious commitment to last. One solution would be to work together. In the artistic or entertainment realm, a creative process that uses film or some form of illusion could provide inspiration for your special talents. With your vivid imagination and psychic receptivity, the worst that you can visualize probably never happens to you, but your apprehensions, if uncontrolled, can affect your nervous system and slow you down.

> Holly Hunter (actress), 1958
> Spike Lee (director), 1957
> Carl Reiner (actor), 1922

March the 3rd (Neptune, Venus)
(and root digit for February 21 and March 12):

Whatever you do is more likely to have emotional rather than intellectual appeal, but this does not mean that you don't have a fine mind. It's just that your feelings and psychic input will probably influence the outcome of your ventures more than complex mental analysis, too much of which can impede the free flow of your inspirations. Strongly drawn to the world of culture, you have a highly developed aesthetic sense and are attracted to people of creative power. Friendly and good-natured socially, with a whimsical sense of humor, you'll tolerate worthy but tiresome people singly or in groups out of sympathy if nothing else. Supportive and idealistic, you're always there if someone needs a shoulder to cry on.

At heart a confirmed romantic, your important alliances, when they are deep and lasting, are built more on respect and admiration. However, some of you could be known in your circle (or by the public if you're famous) as much for your fascinating amours, bohemian lifestyle or irreverent quips as for your distinctive creative abilities and abundant charm. Ultraromantic and impressionable, whether or not you enjoy that ultimate touch of magic in your love life will depend on how far your emotions stray from reality. Distaff Pisceans are especially prone to romantic fantasy. For example, a youthful unfulfilled crush on someone, possibly a teacher, could become a secret lifelong obsession, continuing even after a happy marriage to a wonderful partner. If this self-deluded Piscean happens to bump into her irresistible dream lover many years later, he probably won't even remember her.

If you become an artist, you're likely to paint more dreamscapes than landscapes. In the advertising world or in connection with other commercial ventures, your work could be particularly imaginative. You could turn the functional study of economics into an esoteric science and might receive considerable recognition for your experiments and discoveries. The less inclined you are to emotional scattering, the easier it will be to bring your gifts into practical focus, or at least sooner rather than later in life. In any case, you're apt to believe strongly in anything you're doing; otherwise, you wouldn't be doing it.

> Diana Barrymore (actress), 1921
>
> Jean Harlow (actress), 1911
>
> Alexander Graham Bell (inventor), 1847

Special to February 21 (Neptune, Venus [Moon/Sun]):

Because you are able to tune in to forces and vibrations that others are only dimly aware of, you are frequently creative, mystical and/or artistic. As an advocate of equality and broad intercultural understanding, it would be easy for you to believe that, beginning in childhood, the focus of education and social change should accentuate democratic living and the colorful ethnic mix. Your motto could be "diversity within unity." However, as a typically reticent Piscean, more gently persuasive than assertive, you're too civilized to force your views on anyone. In any case, your work is likely to speak for itself; if you fulfill your potential, you won't have to push for recognition. Very adroit and expressive, your psychic radar can go to work to master the technical aspect of creative discipline. When you have an inspiration, the subject or theme will seek the form or the form of your idea will seek the theme; when they converge, you're able to compose, paint or write and enhance the final result with your own distinctive imprint. If you're lucky enough to be exposed to an emancipating influence, which might prompt a career change, your work can be suffused with the brilliant imagery of your experience and observations. This talent and your hunches, of course, can be equally useful in more mundane pursuits, such as figuring out a puzzling bottleneck in a routine business or professional venture. On the way to finding your true niche in life, you might be a political activist or lead a more adventurous existence than your poised demeanor would suggest.

Kelsey Grammer (actor), 1955

Nina Simone (singer, pianist), 1933

Ann Sheridan (actress), 1915

Special to March 12 (Neptune, Venus [Sun/Moon]):
Multitalented, with a flair for the commercial or promotional side of the arts, you know the value of publicity and how to advance yourself and/or a business or professional project that prompts your unflagging enthusiasm and devotion. Some may consider you to be too self-absorbed, but, to you, an individual with something to offer is a legitimate instrument of awareness, a fine-tuned center of consciousness and experience, a mirror of life from which springs creative inspiration. When your gifts are properly employed and focused, you have the power to transcend the personal and to benefit a situation, whether it be a job assignment or a creative project, with your unique vision.

With your strong interest in yourself and in your own destiny as a well-spring of worthwhile ideas, you should have little trouble in convincing others to believe in you and the values you represent and espouse. Your influence could be the spearhead of fresh directions in music, literature, philosophy, the theater or education, the kind that can leave a permanent imprint on suc-ceeding generations. There are hazards, however, to harboring or nurturing extreme depths of feeling; avoid a tendency to be too introspective, or you can withdraw into a personal twilight zone and resort to artificial means to bolster your disappearing self-confidence. Your abundant imagination and psychic receptivity need to be counterbalanced with a firm grip on reality and a will-ingness to deal with the world as it is rather than as some magical never-never land you can imagine and yearn for it to be.

Liza Minelli (actress), 1946

Edward Albee (playwright), 1928

Jack Kerouac (writer), 1922

March the 4th (Neptune, Saturn)
(and root digit for March 13;
February 22 is a master number, see end of chapter):
If you approach life with a sort of cautious optimism, you're on the right track. When you fulfill your potential and rise to the top, it means you have overcome a lingering uncertainty in your abilities or your doubts about what life has to offer. It also denotes that you· were born with or have acquired wisdom, which, instead of speed, is required if you are to reach the upper

echelons of success. Work habits that may function productively on the lower rungs of the workforce or in a career endeavor may be a handicap higher up where calm, considered decision making is more important than haste, especially in your case. Although versatile, equipped with diverse talents to succeed in more than one field, you tend to have a bottom-line mentality; whatever seems to promise the biggest payoff, perhaps to support your other interests or a serious avocation, will become your principal career focus.

Along the way, there can be a pitfall or two (or more), probably attributable in some measure to your sensitive, not to say vulnerable, nature. You tend to expect decency and fair play in the world of affairs and can be sorely disappointed by the reality. Whereas a Leo in a confident mood can feel larger than life, you, when down in the dumps, depressed, despondent, can feel *smaller* than life. You don't have to be physically attacked to feel wounded; your bleeding can be inner and psychic. Since you can be overly subjective when conditions in your life become difficult, be wary of devotion to service as an abstraction or to feel too duty-bound. In your negative mode, your typical response to trouble is to retreat deeply within yourself instead of figuring things out in a coldly rational way.

The solution is to resist becoming immobilized, to refocus your attitude and energies progressively, to rediscover your worth and abilities and then accomplish something that reinvigorates your self-confidence. At such times, you will profit by not allowing your submissive or sacrificial feelings to take over; never sell yourself short. If it seems that you endure more challenges or discipline to gain the same ground that others seem to manage with less effort, perhaps your rewards are more soul-satisfying. Capitalize on your muted magnetism and potential for material good fortune.

Paula Prentiss (actress), 1939

John Garfield (actor), 1913

Knute Rockne (football coach), 1888

Special to March 13 (Neptune, Saturn [Sun/Venus]):
Although you might have ample reason from time to time to turn a doleful countenance on the world, your generally sunny disposition masks the strong undercurrent of duty and muffled anxiety in your nature. With your magnetism and popularity, you should choose your companions carefully, especially in an amorous encounter that can provide you with a month's worth of romantic daydreams; you could be easily hurt if you make an ill-advised choice and the individual is oblivious to your possibly exaggerated sense of devotion

and emotional sensitivity. Avoid drifting into a sacrificial attitude about love. Maintain a healthy outlook that you deserve your share of happiness.

If you're in the creative realm as an artist, actor, writer or musician, you are deeply aware of all the time and effort that are involved in the creative process but that once in a while the rewards justify the agony and deliver the ecstasy. You can soak up experience like a sponge, mull it over in your psychic reservoir and then squeeze it out in whatever form your expertise finds a productive outlet for it. Whether it's in your private life or at work, and depending on your realistic attitude, the resourceful insights thus gained enable you to steer a constructive course through life. With your keen eye for significant developments in your line of work, or in politics, art, the theater or changing conditions in general, your observations, conclusions and skills can be influential in your sphere of activity and lead to success.

Dana Delaney (actress), 1956

Jersey Joe Walcott (boxer), 1914

Percival Lowell (astronomer), 1855

March the 5th (Neptune, Mars)
(and root digit for February 23, March 14):

You can seem more confident, self-insistent or even aggressive to others than you really are. Underneath, you may be uncertain about many things, as though you are peering into a clouded crystal ball. The tidal direction of your vitality, which waxes and wanes, determines the amount of energy you have at any given time for a task. It may be best to avoid any job or career activity that requires a constant flow of physical activity. It's very important for you to pace yourself sensibly by catching the ebb and flow of your mental, and especially your psychic, strength; otherwise, you may have trouble maintaining power and a steady pace when you shift into high gear.

On the other hand, if it's necessary to be forceful about an important issue, you may have to summon as much energy, not to say derring-do, as you can muster in order to deal with the problem as successfully as possible. At such a time, the impact you make could be a deciding factor; you can't afford to be a sheep in wolf's clothing.

When life is rough, you might feel as though you were born with more than your share of cosmic-issue scar tissue on your soul. One result, however, is that what you lack in bounce and bluster, you make up for in deeper sensitivity and emotional power, which can be very appealing to the people you deal with or an audience if your work brings you before the public.

You can be very conscientious, an activist swept up in a cause, which is somehow connected to, and reflects your attitude toward, everything you do in life; it is an outer expression of your secret feelings. With your restless disposition, it can be easy for you to use up your recommended daily allowance of energy in exertions that aren't necessarily productive. You aren't always certain as to where your energies can be most profitably deployed, but they are probably better suited to some sort of autonomous, cyclic job or in a profession than in the demanding, competitive business world. With your mesmerizing gifts, you're as likely to be a winner whether you earn a Ph.D. or you're a high school dropout who learns through experience to achieve your dream.

Samantha Eggar (actress), 1939

Jack Cassidy (actor), 1927

Rex Harrison (actor), 1908

Special to February 23 (Neptune, Mars [Moon/Venus]):
Your outgoing sociable personality masks your more naturally reserved disposition. You probably lead a private life of your own within the framework of your apparently expansive outlook. Owing to your inner core of nervous tension, you may occasionally overreact when someone rubs you the wrong way, but you prefer to get along with people, for mutual benefit, if you have a choice or any control over an edgy situation. It's a good idea to avoid doting on the trivial errors of others; it could be a problem, however, trying to determine which ones are trivial. What you mainly want is for people to leave you alone to do your own thing, an attitude that you will manage to, or prefer to, convey in as nice a way as possible, thus assuring your popularity.

In your view, education or any effort toward upliftment of the masses is for the purpose of teaching people how to think, not what to think, and to tune them into the beauty and enchantment to be found in music, art, literature and the spiritual force, the cosmic glue that binds things together. You have considerable power to overcome obstacles. Your formidable stride in the success milieu can be attributed to a combination of receptivity, subtle charm and winsome determination. You grew up with a respect for the advantages of material good fortune; if you're willing to meet your obligations in life, you can tap into that vein of prosperity, status and personal fulfillment.

Peter Fonda (actor), 1939

William L. Shirer (journalist), 1904

George Frederick Handel (composer), 1685

Special to March 14 (Neptune, Mars [Sun/Saturn]):
Deeply ambitious, you'll probably encounter a lot to overcome on the way to personal fulfillment, but you're not the type to do it with seize-the-moment aggressiveness. You're the utterly realistic, practical idealist with deep convictions about making your mark in the world of affairs. Your unique combination of persistence, psychic receptivity and patience spares you the futility of chasing rainbows or tilting at windmills. Although you will venture into the thick of things to achieve a goal, you dislike competition and would rather keep the worldly hubbub at arm's length. To some, you will be seen as talented, efficient, solicitous, honest, good-natured, compassionate, even a genius, while others will see you as flamboyant, selfish, intimidating, cynical, humorless and injudicious—in other words, an enigma. Barring concrete evidence one way or the other, only you know the truth.

Be careful of confronting life with too much philosophical calm and emotional resignation or you can drift into a rut from which it would be difficult to extricate yourself. While it's admirable to keep busy and do your job as well as possible, you can be too conscientious and settle for less than your optimum potential; it is more important to work smart and to make all your efforts count for something than to become a drudge while others forge ahead to receive recognition in the world of achievement. You are aware of the value of a good education and will prefer excellent schooling and/or some sort of vocational training to a hit-or-miss preparation when you reach the threshold of your job or career aspirations. You have the innate power to succeed and can make a notable contribution in your field of endeavor.

Billy Crystal (actor, comedian), 1947

Michael Caine (actor), 1933

Albert Einstein (physicist, mathematician), 1879

March the 6th (Neptune, Jupiter)
(and root digit for February 24 and March 15):
At your captivating best, you are able to rise to great heights in any field of endeavor for which you're qualified, with an ability to turn dreams into realities and make them the cornerstone of your estimable accomplishments. On the other hand, when you have gone astray and need to mend your ways or sacrifices are necessary, you feel hemmed in, stifled or put upon; then your woes prompt the morbid side of your imagination to go into overdrive, and you show the moody, anxious and apprehensive part of your nature. You can become tight-lipped, curt and evasive and will shut yourself off from people.

Unless events are beyond your control, your proclivity toward inflated expectations, overconfidence or the gambling instinct is usually at the root of your troubles. Be wary of playing hunches that can be costly.

A willing, enthusiastic worker (perhaps to a fault), you are discreet and can be trusted with activities that are best conducted behind closed doors. More optimistic and adventurous than the typical Piscean, you prefer a job that promises responsibility, recognition or advancement far beyond the entry level, or a professional or business career that includes lots of upward mobility potential. And should the going get tough and bring some lean times, you're more apt to grit your teeth and stay the course than admit failure, and you will continue on the lookout for the next chance to forge ahead and/or take on the next expansive challenge.

Your love of nature is very sympathetic, which endears you to your mate or significant other, and it can make you a treasured member of your family or social circle. You often keep your innermost thoughts and feelings to yourself but not, like Scorpio, out of a need for secrecy; you may assume that they'll sound like troubles, feeling instead that you should be listening while others unburden themselves to you. You can run the gamut where money and security are concerned; you can get your own financial affairs into a mess through carelessness and ill-advised generosity, or you can be thrifty to the point of miserliness, but your potential for attracting a handsome income or wealth is excellent. The trick is to not let it slip through your fingers.

Shaquille O'Neal (basketball player), 1972

Ed McMahon (TV personality), 1923

Michelangelo (sculptor, painter, architect), 1475

Special to February 24 (Neptune, Jupiter [Moon/Saturn]):
You're not likely to resist a hard luck story aimed right at your tear ducts. If you think divine intervention is going to right the world's wrongs, don't bet on it. Lots of good goes unrewarded and plenty of people get by with murder—figuratively and sometimes literally.

But that knowledge wouldn't deter you from your course. You could have an invincible moral sense and become very active in the cause of justice and peace, especially the shameful use of government power or some other misguided authority to harm innocent people. To say that you are very versatile and could succeed as a writer, actor or in some other job in the entertainment realm would be an understatement.

With your willingness to serve and your management skills, you will do well in an occupation that provides basic needs for the general public. A field of endeavor that promotes the human spirit, dignity and responsibility is very congenial for you. In this vein, a career in the law, the arts, ministry, social work or a similar field would make excellent use of your talents, as would a job in the maritime world, such as shipping, cruise director and so forth. With your strong sense of duty and obligation, you may often be found early on the job, leaving late, working through lunch or on weekends or filling in for an absent colleague or coworker. When storm clouds gather and threaten difficulties, you're more apt to batten the hatches than abandon ship. You could find personal independence and travel important factors in achieving your career goals. Married life and domesticity would be very agreeable with your nature, including plenty of tolerance for the burdens that might go with it.

Edward James Olmos (actor), 1947

James Farentino (actor), 1938

Winslow Homer (artist), 1836

Special to March 15 (Neptune, Jupiter [Sun/Mars]):

You are less apt to be a shrinking violet and more apt to speak your mind than other members of your sign when confronted by difficult issues or a business or professional challenge. Even if uncertainty lurks beneath the surface of your personality, you're likely to give the impression of self-confidence, and, in the competitive world, that can be a notable asset, almost as good as the real article. You have plenty of energy and probably more stamina than the typical Piscean, which you know how to, but may not always, put to productive use. The success of your ventures will depend on how objective you can be and your ability to play down your inclination to be very self-absorbed.

Whether you are a hopeful romantic or a hopeless romantic, you are likely to experience emotional burnout somewhere among your amorous escapades. Love could be an elusive goal, probably because your dream is more of a mirage than an attainable reality as far as your chances of fulfilling it are concerned. Multiple marriages or commitments are a likely outcome of your uncertain—not to say adventurous—feelings.

Nevertheless, in other contexts, you're able to maintain your sense of humor and equilibrium. In the career realm, you have the ability to touch the emotions of people you deal with and/or attain notable public popularity if you are in the entertainment world, which would be very congenial for your sensitivity and talent.

Harry James (trumpeter), 1916

MacDonald Carey (actor), 1913

Andrew Jackson (7th U.S. president), 1767

March the 7th (Neptune, Mercury)
(and root digit for February 25 and March 16):

Although your ideas can drift submerged in the waters that have no shore, when your mind is sharply focused, you are able to imbue and/or articulate your psychic impressions with a remarkable degree of intelligence. When what you feel and what you know converge, it is an exceptional combination for dealing with life's day-to-day realities or the more complex issues that crop up from time to time. That is the good news. The downside is to beware of making a critical decision when your feelings are turbulent and you have trouble sorting out your thoughts when they are at odds with or clash with your feelings. At such times, when conditions are murky, you will be easily distracted and will have difficulty concentrating, especially if you have a Vesuvian temperament and it spins out of control.

You are especially creative, and whether your desire to articulate beauty finds an outlet in writing (especially poetry), art, music, the theater or in some related field, such as costume, fashion or scenic design, directing or architecture, you can draw on an abundant inventory of introspective ideas from which can spring imaginative flights of fancy. On the other hand, if you don't keep your thinking cap on straight, you can go to extremes; you could sour on life and champion the cause of the downtrodden with questionable or fruitless tactics. Your convincing way with words can turn you into a spellbinding speaker who is able to stir up the destructive passions of an extremist group.

Whether or not you bother to complete a formal education, you can show an early interest in the career realm in which you eventually flourish. Once you get going, your rise will be a work-in-progress, with typical stops, starts and changes, until you receive recognition and assume the important responsibilities that go with your level of skill or, in some cases, your exceptional expertise. Outside of the arts, you would have a talent for a business or profession that depends more on your instinct for public tastes and trends than nuts-and-bolts practicality for success. In the health care field, working as a specialist in alternative or holistic medicine, or as a therapist, would be your forte. Relationships can be disappointing if you evaluate realities too subjectively.

Willard Scott (TV weatherman), 1934

Thomas G. Masaryk (Czech patriot), 1850

Luther Burbank (botanist), 1849

Special to February 25 (Neptune, Mercury [Moon/Mars]):
You don't mince words, but when you have something pungent to say, you can sharpen your barbs with a sly sense of humor that could further exasperate—if not infuriate—a listener already in a surly mood. Whether it's a collision or a meeting of minds, you don't shy away from controversy. With your exceptional psychic perceptivity flowing through your sharp intelligence, you have a rare flair for turning an artistic triumph into a commercial success, a combination not always easy to accomplish. Whether in the arts, a profession or the business world, your keen insight reveals what the public wants and is willing to pay for, which you are only too willing to deliver. You are stimulated by the idea of success and enjoy the excitement of winning and outsmarting your competitors, who may respond with grudging admiration.

Matching wits with you could be a real challenge to those in your social circle or in your closest relationships. Where the latter are concerned, you like sparkling conversation and repartee with sophisticated types and would never settle for a dull-witted companion or marriage partner if you can help it. Despite your mental sagacity in other contexts, however, you could be like a rudderless ship emotionally, at sea where your instinct for love and romance are concerned. Perhaps you need to dig deeper in your relationships for the values that keep two hearts beating more permanently as one. When you do, you discover happiness. Meanwhile, you're not likely to find life boring.

George Harrison (singer, guitarist), 1943

Jim Backus (comedian), 1913

Enrico Caruso (tenor), 1873

Special to March 16 (Neptune, Mercury [Sun/Jupiter]):
You are very persuasive, especially about a project you believe in. When you have a worthy or poignant cause to promote, a sad story to relate, you can coax tears from a stone or cash from a contributor if you're involved in fund-raising for a deserving enterprise. The arts or a profession may be more congenial for your abilities than the rough and tumble of the business world, although even there your self-assured intelligence could give competitors a run for their money. When functioning at your optimum capability, practically any assignment, job or career can benefit from your expertise

and/or managerial skills. You have a way of connecting or cooperating with others that is deep and efficient, buoyant and balanced. Any productive relationship that you become involved in, even if it seems light and breezy on the surface, is likely to be intellectually rooted. You're not the type to forego academic credentials and will probably have an extensive educational background or training in a specialty or skill by the time you reach the threshold of your ascent into the career realm. You have a keen appreciation and prodigious talent for networking and know how to attract influential people to help promote your ambitions. With any luck at all, in fact, you yourself will become influential in whatever sphere you strive to achieve your goals. Your thinking is very flexible and enthusiastic, especially regarding life's upside potential. Marriage is important to you and is apt to be for keeps.

Erik Estrada (actor), 1949

Jerry Lewis (comedian), 1926

James Madison (4th U.S. President), 1751

March the 8th (Neptune, Uranus, Saturn)
(and root digit for February 26 and March 17):

Your generally affable personality can mask the steely determination that underlies your endeavors to get to the top of whatever line of work you decide to excel in and/or concentrate on. Although your eye is on the main chance and the big picture of success, somewhere in the depths of your being you are emotionally ardent and sincere, with plenty of sympathy for those who have been victims of society's indifference or mistakes. Not only do you have strong feelings about injustice, you're not an armchair do-gooder; you'll go to bat and expend considerable time and energy to right the wrongs that come to your attention. The spoken or written word can be one of your most effective weapons, which you don't hesitate to use.

Independent in thought, feelings and actions, you have a farsighted outlook that arouses your curiosity about life outside the mainstream or along the less-traveled byways. Whatever you do personally or career-wise is not apt to be a repeat of the same old formulas that tend to govern the general population. Your way, your style, is likely to be uniquely different and individualistic, yet within the framework of success according to establishment standards and deserving of the conventional rewards such as fame and monetary riches. And thanks to your distinctive imprint in your chosen field, you'll probably enjoy long-lasting popularity simply because you could be irreplaceable.

The downside of your commendable pioneering spirit is a tendency to be excessively independent, which could result in hazardous self-absorption and eccentricity. If you slip into a negative Piscean mode, you might forget your manners in your effort to get your way and may give diplomacy short shrift, thus alienating people who can help you on your way up the success ladder. Just remember that when you want something, honey goes further than vinegar. When you're on the right track, however, you are the epitome of the practical idealist with a wide-ranging vision that can enhance any large-scale enterprise.

Your gift for the arts can flourish as actual creativity, or your insights may be valuable in promoting the artistic creations of others.

Kathy Ireland (model), 1963

Lynn Redgrave (actress), 1943

Cyd Charisse (dancer, actress), 1923

Special to February 26 (Neptune, Uranus, Saturn [Moon/Jupiter]): You have a lot of faith in yourself and your beliefs, including your ingrained optimism and visionary outlook on the future. You seem to know the magic formula for a special appeal to people; whether in the public or the social milieu (or both), you have appeal in abundance. Your potential for high-profile public notice or popularity is well above average, not to say exceptional. You generally give the impression of always looking forward to tomorrow, intensified by your expansive expectations of what the new day will bring. If it brings disappointment, you can always find a way to rationalize it, tap your wellspring of enthusiasm and move on to the next challenge, ready to reap a future reward you are sure is within your grasp.

Although you can be affable and conciliatory on the surface, you have plenty of backbone and can be a tough customer protecting your interests when push comes to shove and you are threatened by divisive issues or the bum's rush. You are able to maintain an icy calm in the midst of turmoil. Whether your skills derive from a good education, specialized training or the raw-edged school of experience, you are fully capable of rising far above your origins, especially if you were born into humble circumstances—which may be your prod to achievement.

Michael Bolton (singer), 1953

Johnny Cash (country singer), 1932

Jackie Gleason (actor, comedian), 1916

Special to March 17 (Neptune, Uranus, Saturn [Sun/Mercury]): Whether you are quiet or loquacious, you have plenty of talent and, even better, know how to talk shop to make it pay. At your most efficient and creative, your mind and feelings combine so effectively that you can churn out mountains of work without ever looking ruffled, frantic or hurried. Although generally soft-spoken, it doesn't mean that you can't be emphatic and stand your ground when a situation calls for it. Especially in the arts, you are a stickler for quality and will accept nothing less than the best if you have any choice in the matter. If asked to explain your gifts, you might be the first to admit that your abilities stem from the subconscious, instinctive or prophetic realm and that words cannot reach the depths of human dreams.

Humanitarian and psychic, your talents might work best in some custodial capacity, such as maintaining and/or building on previously established standards in a business, profession or in the realm of writing, publishing or some centuries-old art form. Or you might be instrumental in protecting the rights or the interests of others. In the entertainment field, you could achieve considerable popularity and become a public favorite. Thanks to your combination of enterprise and intellectual courage, you have plenty of staying power, which bodes well for a long career if and when you make it to the top.

Kurt Russell (actor), 1951

Rudolph Nureyev (dancer), 1938

Nat King Cole (singer), 1919

March the 9th (Neptune, Pluto)
(and root digit for February 27 and March 18):

Along with your pleasant—not to say charismatic—personality, you can seem calm, cool and collected on initial contact. Your winsome, sympathetic, even humorous facade, however, can be deceptive; your feelings run deeper, and you can be much more forceful than your amiable demeanor would suggest. Your iron-willed ego strength, self-assertiveness and reserves of emotional power can surprise those who have an ax to grind and assume that you will smile sweetly and be a pushover. It might be easier to get blood from a turnip than to get you to capitulate and change your mind once it's made up, especially if you have strong feelings about a particular issue. Meanwhile, your own potential for stirring up others' emotions, whether for good or ill, is great.

You can be shrewd and enterprising about money; your hunches are usually profitable, qualifying you for work in the banking industry, a Wall Street brokerage, an investment fund or the business world in general. With your affinity for the realm of make-believe, a job as an agent, publicist, stage hand or cameraman in the entertainment world could be a productive outlet for you, especially in connection with film. Or you could excel in a career in that medium as an actor, dancer, singer, director or writer. Your gift could run the gamut of versatility, with an equal flair for comedy as well as drama or even the classics. You would resist typecasting.

With your pronounced determination to make your mark one way or another, setbacks or obstacles that would discourage others aren't likely to deter you. You probably knew what you wanted to do in life early enough to get a head start on the competition. Not easily intimidated, you tend to overcome Piscean uncertainty while pursuing your ambitions. You're capable of the disciplined training, self-promotion, and the do-or-die spirit required for achievement in the world of music, academia, architecture, theater, or related pursuits. When you're not busy getting ahead in the world, beating the drum for a political or social cause could be an ideal outlet for your compassion. Workplace and other demands may make it difficult to focus on your personal life and/or marriage. Avoid suspicion, jealousy or possessiveness, or happiness will be elusive.

Bobby Fisher (chess player), 1943

Raul Julia (actor), 1940

Leland Stanford (philanthropist), 1924

Special to February 27 (Neptune, Pluto [Moon/Mercury]):
You know how to arouse emotions and to lift others' spirits through your ability to communicate the deepest feelings, especially when they stem from star-crossed misadventure or tragedy. In the world of arts and letters, you probably feel that someone who has not experienced great emotion is unable to convey the real thing and is only capable of a clever imitation. With your insistence on authenticity, you may prefer to soar between heaven and hell, between great exaltations and deep disappointments—extreme passions that alone make life vital, exciting and truly meaningful. In this context, what you will avoid at all costs is giving the impression of deadly uniformity. The contentment of the unambitious is not for you. With any luck at all, you can make a memorably distinctive contribution in your field of endeavor and achieve worldwide recognition.

Whether in public or private life, you are capable of reinventing yourself if you find the early part of your career aimed in a fruitless direction. Once transformed with a new image or a more arresting persona (or both, with your talent a given), success comes more easily within your reach, enabling you to capitalize on intelligent, thoughtful changes. With your notable combination of mind and emotional power, you are versatile and adaptable; if opportunities dry up in one area of your field of endeavor, you'll find a different but equally effective outlet for your skills. Although you might not be as scrupulous or successful in your personal life, few would doubt your devotion to your job or your professionalism. With your restless nature, you'll thrive better on variety than routine.

Ralph Nader (consumer advocate), 1934

Elizabeth Taylor (actress), 1932

John Steinbeck (novelist), 1902

Special to March 18 (Neptune, Pluto [Sun/Uranus/Saturn]):

The sense of power that you can derive from overcoming obstacles helps to cultivate your belief in the divine plan and your rightful place in it as it pertains to your ambition. Whether you find release for your emotional energies through willing service in some universal calling or in the business or professional realm, your specialty is an aptitude for large ventures. For example, if you become involved in fund-raising for a worthy cause, it's not apt to be a nickel-and-dime operation. Your hunches and insights keep you at the ready for a dynamic new trend that challenges your management or marketing skills, especially if it's liberally ringed with dollar signs.

You might envision yourself as a servant to all in a humanitarian role, but you're not apt to donate your services unless you're in the ministry. You function better in an authoritative or leadership position than as an underling; in the latter capacity, there may be occasions when you have to follow orders that conflict with your conscience or your grasp of realistic considerations. You're the practical idealist who thinks big, especially if your job brings you before the public—in which case, the bigger the better. You could be known for your self-discipline, precision and punctuality. When uncertainties surface in your life, your farsighted outlook and determination enable you to get on with your dream.

Peter Graves (actor, TV host), 1926

Nikolai Rimsky-Korsakov (composer), 1844

Grover Cleveland (22nd and 24th U.S. president), 1837

March the 11th (Neptune [Moon/Sun])
(master number):

At your most creative, your imagination soars upward on gossamer wings of inspiration, sometimes into a realm of fragile uncertainty. The thought of war or violence could make a pacifist's hair curl, but yours would stand on end. In the arts or the entertainment field, you're able to tap the universal reservoir of psychic receptivity and express the heights of joy and beauty as well as the depths and despair of shattered dreams. In the business or professional realm, your insightful hunches enable you to be decisive, coolly analytical and tuned in to public tastes and trends. Just as many Pisceans with this birthday are well qualified for the health care industry, you could be an expert who can save an ailing company or a department of one that needs revitalizing. You can be very concerned about the plight of the downtrodden and feel that it's your mission to give the huddled masses something to dream about. If you're not prepared to act in some practical way, however, your dream may be on a collision course with discipline and responsibility. You're likely to espouse standards according to your own feelings and subjective taste rather than establishment values and to make choices that incur adverse comment. For example, your critics might accuse you of pandering to the lowest common denominator of public taste. However, when a job you do or an enterprise you manage or take over not only survives but also prospers, even your critics have to grant grudging credit for your abilities.

Your vocational opportunities can lead you into out-of-the-way situations and/or unusual occupations. If the work you do includes the potential for being influential in one way or another, you'll like the profession or business even better. Whether you come from a privileged or a blue-collar background, you might fear poverty. If you achieve wide popularity that is possible with your birthday, though, your financial prospects are equally promising; you can accumulate a bigger nest egg for a rainy day than most of the population. A contented marriage and/or family life, if you can manage it, will be a supportive asset as you wend your way through the thickets of your career endeavors.

Sam Donaldson (TV news reporter), 1934

Harold Wilson (British prime minister), 1916

Lawrence Welk (bandleader), 1903

(Note: This master number implies a variable alternative response influenced by the strength or passivity of the planet Neptune in your horoscope. If you don't feel you are responding to the distinctive vibratory power of 11, you are instead expressing the more conventional qualities of 2, which you should read.)

February the 22nd (Neptune, Uranus [Saturn/Moon]) (master number):

Whether you're trying to turn your vision of utopian idealism into a working reality or are swamped in an ocean of emotion, it wouldn't be unlike you to strain compassion or credulity to its outer limits. Your unique combination of psychic receptivity and intuition can provide you with a grasp of complexities far beyond ordinary comprehension. When you're in tune with the infinite, you can see the solution to a challenging project or to the bottom of troubling issues as clearly as if you were peering through pristine waters to the floor of the Caribbean.

Very humanitarian, you can be the martyr to a cause either in your personal life or in some larger context. You might put up with inconveniences or burdens or rationalize a sacrifice that an Aries wouldn't give a minute of his or her time or energy. Made nervous or depressed by opposition, you don't understand why, since your motives are so worthy (to you, anyway), you should have to deal with strife. Be careful of perverse independence not backed up by sensible motives. The abstract recesses of your psyche can be filled with doubt or fear; not knowing what you're afraid of can make you anxious and edgy. You're not likely to give up or shirk your responsibilities, however, feeling that it's your duty to face whatever difficulties come your way.

You may as well accustom yourself to the fact that the rest of the world is not on your wavelength of empathy and heartfelt identification with lost causes, such as the poor and the homeless. Well suited for public life, if other testimonies agree, you can become as well known for your wayward behavior as for your outstanding talent. You have pronounced abilities in the arts, government or an inspirational field, wherever sensitive leadership and broad as well as deep understanding are an asset. Avoid worry; it will only weaken your vitality. You are more sensitive to psychosomatic illness than most, and you should remember that, in your case, recuperation from a physical indisposition may be slow.

Drew Barrymore (actress), 1975

Frederic Chopin (composer), 1810

George Washington (1st U.S. president), 1732

(Note: This master number implies a variable alternative response influenced by the strength or passivity of the planet Uranus in your horoscope. If you don't think you are responding to the distinctive vibratory power of 22, you are instead expressing the more conventional qualities of 4, which you should read.)

YOUR BIRTHSTONE
AND COLORS

ARIES (March 21–April 20)

Your birthstone, the diamond, has been one of the most sought-after possessions in history. This glittering precious gem par excellence has adorned the crowns of kings and queens for centuries, typified by the dazzling beauty and inestimable value of the crown jewels of England. In modern times and in a more conventional context, the diamond is today a symbol of love and betrothal. You can see why the diamond is your birthstone when you consider the many magical powers attributed to it. As an emblem of fearlessness and invincibility, it was believed that owning a diamond would convey superior strength, action and courage, all qualities that should ring a few bells where you are concerned.

Chemically, a diamond is plain crystallized carbon, the hardest natural substance. Only a diamond can cut another diamond. The most desirable color for a diamond is clear white, or colorless, but your birthstone is available in various colors—known as a fancy diamond in the trade—and is more valuable if the color is natural instead of artificially induced. For example, a natural "canary" diamond is much more valuable than one that has been turned yellow by radiation and/or a heat process. When acquiring your birthstone, keep the "four C's" (color, clarity, cut, and carat weight) in mind, for they are your guidelines to quality, value and price. If and when you decide to purchase a diamond, the more expertise you can bring to the transaction, the better—and insist on the right of independent appraisal by another gemologist before making a final commitment.

The color that best exemplifies your spirited, restless nature is red. Its variations, such as red-orange or deep hot pink, are also affiliated with your Sun-Sign. If you wear these colors, or enliven your outfits with them as accents, you will be in tune with your stars. These colors in your home or office, as the main scheme or as bright touches, will give it the feeling of a place where things happen. In any case, you're happiest with bright, cheerful colors in a comfortable environment designed for useful activity as well as a haven of warmth and relaxation away from the hectic pace of your everyday activities.

TAURUS (April 21–May 21)

The emerald, said to have ancient links with the planet Venus, your Sun-Sign ruler, is your birthstone. Well known in ancient civilizations, and one of the most highly prized of all gems, it is the green variety of the mineral beryl. Although emeralds are found in Brazil, India and Siberia, those from Colombia are considered to be of the finest quality. In Roman times, emeralds were obtained from the famous mines in Egypt. One notable identification advantage of emeralds is that they are rarely flawless, so a stone that is absolutely clear is either exceptionally rare and pricey—or a fake. The most desirable color for this gem is vivid green, the color of fresh, young, green grass, perhaps with a very faint tinge of blue. The emerald is a hard stone, but it is brittle and can easily chip, so great care should be taken when wearing it. It's probably best protected as earrings or a pendant worn around the neck rather than as an everyday ring.

Because of the great popularity of your birthstone, it is prudent to have some knowledge and expertise regarding it before you purchase one. Imitations are abundant, and fine synthetic emeralds are now common; although less costly than the real thing, they are not inexpensive. Of all the precious gems, emeralds seem to be more prone to a variety of ingenious techniques and subterfuges that can falsify or artificially inflate their value. Instead of going home with a genuine emerald, you might be the unwary new owner of a cleverly disguised bonding of glass (manufactured complete with "flaws"), imperceptibly glued on top of quartz, the resulting ersatz "emerald" then cut to look authentic. And that's only one trick! Another one is a treatment involving cedar oil and polymers, used to minimize imperfections in an emerald. Unless you're willing to invest some time in the study of emeralds before investing in one, let the buyer beware!

Green, the dominant background color in nature, is the most compatible color for you. Since most of you have a "green thumb," you're apt to be wonderful with plants and flowers, both indoors and outdoors. To add a further soothing, relaxing, "woodsy" touch, warm browns, russets, soft blues, aqua, pinks, warm beige, pumpkin and pastel shades generally would be compatible for your Sun-Sign.

GEMINI (May 22–June 21)

The pearl, alexandrine and moonstone are associated with your Sun-Sign. As with any investment, it will repay you to know something about your birthstones before spending your money. Pearls have been treasured since medieval times; even earlier, they were recognized as a symbol of modesty, chastity and purity. A fine genuine pearl, meaning natural or Oriental, is a precious gem, relatively rare in nice sizes—and very pricey. Today, however, the pearl market is almost entirely dominated by the "cultured" variety, which, in the finest grades, is also not inexpensive. These are artificially produced by inserting a mother-of-pearl bead into a live oyster, which then secretes a pearl coating over the irritant. Pearls come in gray, black, pink, white or cream and in various shapes and sizes, any combination of which determines the value.

Alexandrines are extremely rare and very expensive. Russian in origin, the possibility of finding one in any but the finest jewelry stores is very unlikely. Their distinguishing feature is that they change color from green in daylight to raspberry red in artificial light. If you see an alexandrite that measures more than 1/2 inch in width, you can be sure it is a fake—which is fairly common. With alexandrines and pearls, it's essential to verify the authenticity of your gem.

The moonstone, considered to be a good luck stone (especially for lovers), is the most familiar variety of the feldspar minerals. As a more moderately priced semiprecious gem, it is colorless, with a silvery or bluish sheen, but it may also be orange, pink, yellow, steely gray or pale green. The gray stone may show a good cat's eye. Inferior imitations, hardly worth bothering with, are simple to spot compared to the real thing.

It's easy to see how yellow is the color associated with Gemini. You need only think of things like "yellow" journalism (Mercury, your Sun-Sign ruler), exemplified by sensationalism in the news media, and other literary examples to get the idea. Historically, yellow has been associated with spirituality and the mind. In any case, yellow is identified with one form of communication or another. Cool blues and greens also complement your mercurial temperament.

CANCER (June 22–July 22)

Your birthstone, the ruby, has been prized throughout the ages, particularly by royalty. It is the red variety of the mineral corundum—which also includes sapphires, which come in several colors, including yellow, but the most popular and best known is the blue sapphire. Burmese rubies are considered the finest, especially for their vivid red color, known as "pigeon blood" red or "Oriental," with a faint undertone of blue. The ruby is hard and brilliant, with a hardness of 9 (on a scale of 1 to 10), thus, it is very durable and wearable in a variety of styles and settings.

When flawless and of the most desirable color, a ruby, along with a similar quality emerald, can be pricier than a diamond. A ruby is generally smaller in size than other precious gemstones. Because it is of greater density, a two-carat (carat is a weight measure) ruby will appear smaller than a two-carat diamond. The reverse is true for emeralds, which weigh less than diamonds; thus, a two-carat emerald will appear larger than a two-carat diamond. When cut as a cabochon, one variety of ruby exhibits a six-ray star effect and is called, appropriately enough, a star ruby. In this form, the power of the ruby, a sensitive and vital stone, is said to be enhanced.

In the East, your birthstone for centuries has been reputed to attract friends and good fortune and bring cheerfulness to its wearer. Other early beliefs gave it credit for driving out evil thoughts, reconciling quarrels, controlling passions, promoting tranquillity and preserving health. The ruby is also believed to protect against poisons and fevers and to repel evil spirits and bad dreams. These attributes spread with the popularity of the gem and are widely found in the writings of medieval Europe.

Today, with all the advances in modern technology, particularly in precious stone simulations and substitutes, the purchase of a ruby in the larger, more expensive size requires knowledge and caution. The latest synthetic rubies are the Chatham and Kashan types, so close to the real thing that even some expert gemologists have been fooled. Let the buyer beware, and be especially cautious if you are offered a bargain.

In colors, iridescent hues can be very appealing in your surroundings or apparel and will complement your retiring temperament. You're also at home with softly patterned fabrics with silvery glints and a glow of richness and depth, particularly in muted tones of sea green, soft blue, blue violet, magenta, soft beige, taupe and sand—all of which can help to blunt the effects of life's sometimes grating tempo.

LEO (July 23–August 23)

The carnelian, sardonyx, peridot and chrysoprase are all gemstones for your Sun-Sign, and gold jewelry enhances your regal aura. Carnelian, sard and sardonyx are reddish, orange, apricot and brown members of the quartz family, more particularly the chalcedony branch. Carnelian is moderately hard, translucent to opaque, and its warm uniform color, durability and wearability have contributed to its popularity. The chrysoprase is a green chalcedony, often dyed green, and is usually cut in cabochon style. According to legend, since the carnelian enhances the ability to speak out both boldly and well, it is recommended for anyone who has a weak voice or is timid in speech. It is frequently a component of antique as well as contemporary jewelry and is suitable for engraving or carving, particularly in cameos. Still relatively inexpensive, its great warmth and beauty offer an eye-catching complement to your fashion colors.

These gemstones were highly valued by ancient civilizations. The Romans often wore the sardonyx carved with a likeness of Hercules or Mars as a talisman, rendering its wearer brave and daring. Alexander the Great is said to have worn a chrysoprase in his girdle during battle in order to ensure victory. The sardonyx and chrysoprase were thought to protect the owner from venomous reptiles and insects and from infections. As neck pendants, they were believed to attract friends, encourage marital happiness, induce self-control and alleviate pain.

The peridot, also a favorite of the ancients, is another gemstone acceptable for Leo. This transparent, yellowish green to deep chartreuse gemstone was considered to be quite powerful as an aid to promoting friendship, curing or preventing diseases of the liver and alleviating dropsy. As the peridot is a comparatively soft stone (6.5 on the scale of 1 to 10), it is easily scratched or damaged and should be worn with great care. Most of your birthstones are relatively affordable, the most expensive being the peridot in the finest examples.

Since the Sun, your ruler, is exalted in Aries, the diamond is also regarded as being compatible with your personality, perhaps due to its invariable resplendent presence in most royal collections. The colors most suitable for your vivacious Leo personality are bright shades of orange, red and yellow, which burst forth with brilliance and chase away the dark. They not only make you feel better and lift your spirits but also enable you to look your best. Gold and royal shades of blue and purple should also be included in your color schemes.

VIRGO (August 24—September 23)

Your birthstone is the sapphire, a member of the corundum family of minerals, like the ruby, which is the red version. Blue sapphires are the most common and popular, and they come in such variations as Burmese, Ceylon, Australian, Kashmir, Montana, Thai and Oriental, the latter simply an older term meaning "genuine." Of these, the Burmese, Ceylon and Kashmir have the most desirable color and are the most expensive. The Australian sapphires are very dark, practically indigo in color, and are more common and affordable. Many of the darker sapphires contain some degree of green—and the more green, the less valuable. The lighter blue stones are usually from Ceylon (Sri Lanka), and the richest blue sapphires are Burmese and the most expensive.

The sapphires from Kashmir are also a beautiful shade of blue and also quite expensive. Although pricey in the finest examples, sapphires, in general, are the most expensive precious gems after diamonds, emeralds and rubies—in that order for stones of comparable size and quality. Remember, too, that a two-carat sapphire or ruby will look smaller than the same carat weight of a diamond or emerald, both of which are lighter in density. Luckily for you, sapphires come in a variety of colors. A pink, green, yellow, amber or white (colorless) one, known as a fancy, is more affordable than the highest-quality blue variety.

Since very ancient times, the sapphire has been considered to be the most spiritual of stones and to have deep religious significance. The old Hebrews revered it, and the ring of King Solomon is said to have been set with a sapphire. It has also been used for generations in the bishop's ring as an emblem of pontifical rank. It is the gem most often dedicated to Oriental deities. Among the very special properties attributed to it, the sapphire is considered to be a potent love talisman, arousing deep, loyal and constant affection in marriage. The cabochon star sapphire is said to bring good fortune and protection. Six, the number of rays in its star, is the number identified with Jupiter; hence, it is said to have potent powers and brings luck to the wearer. As with all expensive gems, however, the sapphire has its synthetic and cleverly fabricated imitation. There are various techniques to remove flaws from natural sapphires and to change or improve their color. There are "Ceylon" sapphires that never came from Ceylon (Sri Lanka).

You like sensible colors and would never choose anything too bright, garish or nerve-jangling. For your attire or in your home surroundings or place of business, light blue and pastel shades of gray and green and blue-green, with a discreet bright accent here and there, would be compatible with your reserved personality and conservative lifestyle. White-on-white designs, for example, could appeal to you because they offer subdued vitality through pattern without creating color problems.

LIBRA (September 24–October 23)

Your gemstone is the opal, divided into two types: The opal with a background color of gray, blue or black is called black; the others are called white. Despite its foreboding reputation, the opal is not unlucky, and its association with misfortune has never been merited. It is one of the few noncrystalline gems, and it is a hydrated type of silica, brittle and not particularly durable for everyday wear. The cabochon cut is the best for bringing out the exciting flashes of color shown in precious opals, of which black opals with an abundance of red are the most expensive. The Mexican fire opal, which ranges from nearly transparent to shades of yellow to orange and red, is more frequently cut as a brilliant. Opals are mined mainly in Australia, Mexico and South America. Less expensive varieties of opal are known as rose (or potch), hyalite and hydrophane, which do not show the play of color of precious opal.

In ages past, the opal was venerated as a stone containing the spirit of truth. It became a symbol of fidelity and assurance and, later on, of the efficacy of religious feelings and prayer. The ancient Greeks believed it to bestow the power of foresight; they thought, if not used selfishly, it enabled its owner to make prophecies. During the Middle Ages, it was thought to have powers connected with the eyesight and was believed to sharpen the vision of its wearer. It is also said to enhance the ability to settle disputes. The opal is affected by the weather, changing its brilliance with variations in temperature and humidity. When gleaming brightly, it portends good fortune; when relatively dull, it warns of disappointment.

With opals, as with other desirable and costly gems, there are many opportunities for misrepresentation, so care must be taken when purchasing one. The most common technique of deception is known as the doublet or triplet—an enhanced gem made from a translucent top affixed by black cement to a bottom part of a cheaper opal or other material that forms the base. Of course, there's nothing wrong in selling the synthetic type as long as it is identified as such. In fact, it is an affordable alternative for someone on a budget. As for colors in your environment or attire most compatible with your personality, you will find that soft shades of robin's-egg blue, rose, mauve, lilac, pink, lavender, taupe, celadon green and pale or sand beige bring out your best.

SCORPIO (October 24–November 22)

Your birthstone is the topaz, an aluminum silicate crystal that is found in Mexico, the United States, Sri Lanka, Japan, Russia, Nigeria and Zaire. The most famous source, however, is Brazil, and the finest golden topaz crystal comes from the Ouro Preto region. The golden-brown shades have more water than fluorine and are more costly than those with more fluorine than water, which are blue or colorless. Gemstones containing a hint of pink are often called imperial topaz. Although the buyer should be aware of fakes and imitations, true topaz also occurs in very light green, light greenish yellow and violet shades.

Very frequently, citrine is mistaken (or sold) as topaz, and while citrines can be beautiful and are authentic gemstones in their own right, they are not as valuable as topaz. Citrines palmed off as topaz have names such as "Rio Topaz," "Madeira topaz" and "Spanish Topaz." The topaz is a symbol of love and affection, and it is said to improve the disposition as well as to assure faithfulness in love and marriage.

As for colors, rich textures, deep wood tones and large-scale patterns would appeal to you. You are at home with large, subtle designs and such colors as deep reds, russet, browns, cognac, magenta, maroon, bronze tones, nutmeg, olive green and murky indeterminate hues. You would find these colors a restful and inspiring background for the more colorful but carefully modulated accents in your attire and surroundings.

SAGITTARIUS (November 23–December 22)

The turquoise, your gemstone, is a microcrystalline mineral highly prized throughout Asia and Africa. The ancient Egyptians, Chinese and Sumerians used this beautiful opaque stone in jewelry for its attractiveness as well as its therapeutic qualities. In Egypt, in particular, the turquoise identifies with both feminine and masculine spirits, such as Isis and Osiris, whose legend is the symbol of resurrection and eternal life. The best color for the turquoise is light to dark blue or blue-green. The finest examples come from Iran; the Persian turquoise, an intense and pleasing blue, is considered a very rare and valuable gem.

Since ancient times, the turquoise has been a symbol of courage, love and success. It has long been associated with native American jewelry and art. Beware, however; fakes are easily manufactured and are numerous. You should obtain a certificate stating that your purchase is a "genuine, natural turquoise." Also, great care should be taken to protect the turquoise from abuse, such as contact with grease or soap, which can discolor it, or from scratches or nicks, since it is easily damaged.

In tune with your questing spirit and shifting moods, colors suitable for your environment and attire could be more diverse and venturesome than for other Sun-Signs. For instance, sky blue to wedgewood and deep blue, warm shades of gray, purplish hues, russets and golden tones would be compatible with your preference for surroundings that incorporate subtle contrasts of style, color and pattern. These choices would complement your unsuspected need to occasionally withdraw into a peaceful haven in order to recharge the restless energies that are the wellsprings of your exuberant nature.

CAPRICORN (December 22–January 20)

The garnet, a silicate mineral, is your gemstone. Garnets are most commonly wine-red or have a brownish cast, but they also come in other colors, such as green, yellow and orange—but not blue. Sources of gem-quality stones include the Czech Republic, Slovakia, South Africa, the United States, Australia, Brazil and Sri Lanka. The emerald-green demantoid is the most prized of all garnets, and the finest fiery specimens come from the Ural mountains in Russia. According to legend, the garnet denotes loyalty, energy, devotion and sincerity. It's supposed to stop hemorrhaging or other blood loss, cure inflammatory diseases and dispel anger and discord.

Garnets can be relatively inexpensive, under $20 per carat, or very pricey, more than $3,000 per carat. The tsavorite (green garnet), one of the most beautiful, is somewhat less expensive than the demantoid, and it can be mistaken for an emerald of the finest quality; it is, in fact, clearer, more brilliant and more durable. A garnet in certain shades of red can be mistaken for the ruby; in yellow, it has been confused with the precious topaz.

In colors, you find understated tones compatible and achieve elegance through a choice of rich fabrics. You are likely to favor such dark tones as deep brown, burgundy, dark olive, hunter green, cobalt and indigo or navy blue and indeterminate hues such as puce, taupe, beige, gray and even black in order to satisfy your conservative nature. Touches of contrasting colors or accents of gilt or silver brighten and enrich what might otherwise be monochromatic and dull. You are partial to colors in furnishings and attire that suggest security and that set you and your home apart from anything run-of-the-mill.

AQUARIUS (January 21–February 18)

The beautiful amethyst, your birthstone, is a form of quartz crystal. In legend, the amethyst has strong connections with spirituality, altruistic motives, peace of mind and self-discipline. Available in shades from light to dark purple, the finest, most brilliant and expensive examples come from Siberia.

More generally, the amethyst is moderate in price, relatively hard and in good supply. It is a most versatile and wearable stone. However, be careful when shopping for one because "fine" amethyst is being produced synthetically.

Since the unusual is normal for you, your choice of colors in home decorating and attire can run the gamut from the bizarre to the unexpectedly conventional. Most of you, however, are not apt to be happy with the cookie-cutter look in your surroundings. In any case, whatever your choices, they are also likely as not to be tasteful and, at the very least, interesting, if not eye-catching. Colors compatible with your sign include purple, magenta, violet, mauve, plum, sand beige, ivory and maroon—and such off-shades as ice blue, mustard, olive or puce. Oddities can interest you, too, such as mixing colors or fabrics and patterns in ways that could be unusually inventive.

PISCES (February 19–March 20)

Translated literally, the aquamarine, your birthstone, means "sea water." Ever the visionary, when you dream about your birthstone, it signifies that you will meet worthwhile new friends. The aquamarine is a crystal, a member of the beryl family. The name can be traced to Greek and Roman times, and it is probable that beryl and variations of it (heliodor and morganite) were known in the prehistoric era. The beryl includes the emerald, but your birthstone, if less expensive, is more apt to be free of flaws and less brittle and more durable than the emerald.

Color-wise, the aquamarine runs the gamut from greenish white, light blue and pale sea-green to deep blue, which is the most valuable and desirable color. Long considered a semiprecious gem, it has lately graduated into the more precious, pricey category in the larger sizes and deep blue color. Down through the ages, aquamarine was thought to be an emblem of purity, which probably originated in the East.

The colors most harmonious with your generally quiet nature and sometimes moody and retiring disposition include blue-green, pastel shades of pink, yellow and blue, and purple hues, such as mauve, violet and orchid. If you wear these colors, you'll find that they are in tune with, as well as complementary to, your sense of refinement and taste. Combinations of them would also be appropriate color schemes for your home surroundings, either as accents or the dominant palette for your overall decor to create a soothing, restful ambiance.

ABOUT THE AUTHOR

As a writer, researcher, teacher and counselor, Lloyd Cope is a veritable astrological power-house. In each sphere, his originality and vision have always set him apart from—and ahead of—the crowd. And, during his more than 35-year career, Lloyd Cope has never been afraid to go out on an astrological limb; in fact, he thrives on bringing the future in a little ahead of schedule.

Cope's unique, broad-based talents are most evident from his pioneering work in the dynamic field of astronumerology. In 1971, with the publication of his best-selling *Your Stars Are Numbered*, he was the first author who explicitly combined the wisdom and power of both ancient arts to develop his remarkable collection of individual birth date profiles. The first book of its kind, *Your Stars Are Numbered* was the trailblazer for subsequent books on the same theme by other writers. Then, with the publication of his prize-winning *The Astrologer's Forecasting Workbook* in 1982, astrological predictive technique took a quantum leap forward with Cope's mastery of astrology and numerology.

Cope's impressive forecasting track record provides ample testimony to his innovative techniques. His predictions, regularly published well in advance of events, have earned for him an international reputation for accuracy in forecasting political outcomes, global affairs, economic swings and stock prices. As the stock market columnist for *Horoscope Magazine* for sixteen years, Cope's financial acumen has been widely praised and cited in *The New York Times, New York Daily News, Wall Street Letter* and the prestigious *Portfolio Letter*, published by Institutional Investor. In the rarified world of astro-economics, Cope is a "blue chip" writer and lecturer of international renown.

Lloyd Cope was a contributing author for more than fifteen years to Dell's Horoscope Purse Books and Yearbooks, best-sellers on four continents, which are published in numer-ous languages. Corporate giants such as Proctor & Gamble and AT&T have sought his services. He numbers among his clients Hollywood and Broadway celebrities, Wall Street professionals, private investors and members of the international diplomatic corps.

As one of the most compelling voices of the New Age, Lloyd Cope has been covered and quoted in *Cosmopolitan, Life, Look, The New York Post, Harper's Bazaar, Il Messagero* (Rome), *The Daily Yomiuri* (Tokyo) and many other international, national and regional publications since 1964. He has lectured extensively from coast to coast and has appeared on numerous radio and television programs.

Lloyd Cope, PMAFA, has been a Professional Member of the American Federation of Astrologers since 1966, and a member of the National Council of Geocosmic Research since 1984. He is listed in the *Dictionary of International Biography*, and is a member of the American Society of Journalists and Authors, Inc. Lloyd enjoys art, antiques, music, vin-tage trolleys and automobiles—and living in New York City.